MW01174773

TRUTH. FICTION.LIES

Confessions of an Italian, Irish-Catholic, American Immigrant to Canada

Patrick X Walsh

To Rod
in gratitude for an
enlightening friendship,
Pat
[Have fun peeking at the lies!]

Suite 300 - 990 Fort St
Victoria, BC, V8V 3K2
Canada

www.friesenpress.com

First Edition – 2019

ISBN
978-1-5255-4366-1 (Hardcover)
978-1-5255-4367-8 (Paperback)
978-1-5255-4368-5 (eBook)

Biography & Autobiography, Educators

Distributed to the trade by The Ingram Book Company

TABLE OF CONTENTS

for Jacqueline
and all the people who enriched my life

"For a writer, all things must be turned into art, especially those that affect him most deeply."
R. J. MacSween

"Pilate asked him, 'What is truth?'"
John 18:38

"'There is no better hiding place,' for deception, a man says, 'than somewhere as close as possible to the truth, something all good liars know.'"
Rachel Cusk in *Kudos*

"Memory, in short, is engraved not merely from the life we have led but by the life of the mind, by all the lives we so nearly led but missed by an inch, and–if we grant enough leeway to the imagination–by the lives of others, which can cut into ours every bit as sharply as our own experience."
A Guide for Writing a Memoir by W. G. Sebald

"The world I live in, the objects I manipulate, are in a great part my constructions . . . The worlds the writer creates are only imaginatively possible ones; they need not be at all like any real one."
Philosophy and the Form of Fiction by William Gass

"When I was young I could remember anything, whether it had happened or not."
Memories of a Southern Farm by Mark Twain

"I should like to die in knowledge
That at least I have called out."
Jerome by R. J. MacSween

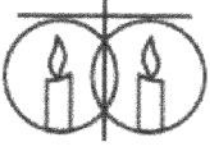

Foreword

Among the most famous closing lines in books of literature in the English language is this passage from George Eliot's *Middlemarch:*

But the effect of her being on those around her was incalculably diffusive: for the growing good of the world is partly dependent on unhistoric acts; and that things are not so ill with you and me as they might have been is half owing to the number who lived faithfully a hidden life, and rest in unvisited tombs.

It is, as many have pointed out since Mary Ann Evans wrote it in 1871, a perfect summation of the life of the novel's heroine, but it is also so much more. And now that it is known over generations and centuries, now that it is "famous," its meaning and purpose doubles back upon itself with even more force. It is, of course, a slightly muted critique of fame, but more importantly, it is a celebration of the collective social and political humanity of ordinary people–those hidden lives who make our lives better or, at the very least, not so ill.

Engaging and celebrating the lives of ordinary folk for the growing good of the world has been a major part of the life work of my mentor and close personal friend, Patrick Walsh, for at least 60 of his 81 years. Yes, I am biased as my opinions and comments reflect a professional and personal relationship as student and sometime colleague of almost 45 years. Trained originally as an English professor, Dr. Walsh would never play the flat academic scale, nor could he comfortably wear the cliché of teachers teach; though, to be brutally honest, his presence in the undergraduate classroom was the most compelling, intimidating, and dramatic I have ever witnessed. His natural flair for drama (theatre his mission) coupled with the 6 foot 2 frame of a linebacker and a voice Orson Welles could have dubbed as a double . . . well, you get the picture.

But the classroom, for all its pleasures, challenges, and security was never going to be enough. Though it could be argued that in the history of education the towers of Catholic colleges and universities were never as ivory as they should be, they were comfortable enough, especially as time went on. The quiet life of the scholar teacher has its attractions, but for Patrick it would never be enough, he had to engage the world directly: whether that involved fund raising for his university, serving on the local town council, helping to establish and run a senior care home, supporting and volunteering for his local church and diocese, promoting local and regional theatre . . . And while doing all this, writing hundreds and hundreds of pages of prose, poetry, fiction, drama, polemics, journalism, reporting, sports writing, and letters that include among them: a full-length history of the town he spent the majority of his life in; a full-length drama on Canada's greatest sacrifice during the Second World War; film commentary and participation on Bruce Beresford's *Black Robe*; a novel, The Cave, about Ireland's New Grange megalithic site; Mad Shelley, an award-winning play for the Dominion Drama festival; a book about hockey; and many, many elegies and eulogies for friends, colleagues, and loved ones. While doing all this, he painted dozens of paintings (another gift) both abstract and realistic, designed a chess set from Connemara marble (there is one still on display at the St. Francis Xavier University library), and illustrated and wrote for *The Antigonish Review* (in the early stages, he also did the publishing, layout, covers, and design).

Recently, some journalists and critics have observed and questioned both Terry Eagleton and Slavoj Zizek about the nature of their religious beliefs. Two of the most famous and celebrated philosopher-theorists of our time, Zizek, though a professed atheist, will not condemn the history or ideology of Christianity outright as so many of his fellow travelers of the left have done and insist that he do as well. Interestingly, he also does not condemn the ideology or complete history of communism. Eagleton, also a figure of the left and a lapsed Catholic of British-Irish heritage, has written many critical and sympathetic apologies of both Christianity and the faith of his fathers and childhood. He will not commit, though, when pressed, as to whether or not he has returned to the fold.

For my old friend and mentor, this has never been a problem. Though he is undoubtedly a post-Vatican II Catholic who embraces the social justice platform of his Church first and foremost, he is, and remains, a practicing, regular, Mass-going Catholic. In this of course he reminds me of another mentor of mine (and his): Roderick Joseph MacSween. A priest and a professor at StFX, for many decades, MacSween had an enormous influence on both of our lives and the nature of the Catholicism and Christianity that he practiced is easily recognizable in the life and work of his protégé, Patrick Walsh. The Catholicism that Pat espouses (and I don't see him as a cafeteria Catholic or as an Orthodox one) reminds me of the critical political theologian Dr. Rudolf Siebert of the Frankfurt School. Pat once hosted Dr. Seibert at StFX in the early 1990s, and he would have heard him speak about the nature of both twentieth-century theology and the present state of the church. When pressed on the crisis in modern faith and, in particular, the scandals roiling constantly out from Rome, Seibert always argued for staying the course with the Church, hoping to change it from the inside in order to keep what is sacred from being lost. It is a view very similar to Reverend Rod MacSween's, and to one expressed by one of MacSween's favorite writers, Evelyn Waugh. Once, when corresponding with his life-long friend, Diana Cooper, Waugh insisted that "One cannot embrace something as serious as the church, for a whim, a love for another–(not God) or as an experimental medicine." For Patrick Walsh, his religion has never been an experimental medicine or a whim, though it has always involved the love for another and not just his life-long travelling partner Jacqueline, but certainly her above all others.

Dr. Stewart Donovan, Professor of Irish Studies
St. Thomas University, Fredericton, New Brunswick

Preface

7 a.m. MT June 23, 2018. I awake from a dream at the Summer Solstice.

In my conscious mind is an image from that dream that sums up the essence of my life. I understand now why this Confession is being constructed in my 82nd year of existence. It's a complicated story and yet simple at its core: I am a storyteller.

A common platitude is that every person has a story to tell. This Confession is an attempt to tell my story. Gentle reader, my story and your story are alike, for we all share an inevitable end. This story will be about what my life experience has led me to believe.

All literary works of substance are attempts by the storyteller/artist to explain what it means to be "human." And the great mystery of being human involves our relationship with the infinite. How and why can we, as finite beings exist, and what is our relationship to Existence itself? In other words, after all the millennia of human history, we still cannot answer definitively the basic question of philosophy: How can "existence" be ONE (infinite) and MANY (individual) at the same time?

This may seem heavy sledding for high school or university literature classes, but all the great works of literature, as opposed to the trivial, have a moral dimension. All the great works deal with the great unanswered questions of human existence. Who am I? Why am I here? What is my destiny? Why do I suffer? Why do I have to die? Where does happiness lie? Try untangling those questions in the current state of the world and the technological challenges of our time. No wonder we turn to the great works of literature and art and religion to find out what the great minds of the past have discovered, and how their life experiences might help us to understand the mysteries of life.

Time to return to my dream. I believe in the biological theory of dreams: that all dreams are attempts to solve problems of our conscious state. But the language of dreams is not words which are abstractions representing our perceptions in sound, but the more primitive language of pictures which preceded sound. When we slip into unconsciousness each night, the more primitive parts of the brain keep working to enable us to breathe to dream in picture language. An example of primitive logic is that things that happen at the same time have a causal relationship. Witness the belief of primitive people that if an earthquake occurred at the time of an eclipse, the eclipse must have caused the earthquake. Here is my dream, and what it means to me:

> *In a classroom at St. Francis Xavier University [StFX] in Antigonish, Nova Scotia, which I attended and later taught in for 37 years, I am on the second floor of the Old Building, the first part of Xavier Hall. I took classes in that room as an undergraduate and then often taught in that room. The view out the window overlooks Confusion Square where the students crisscross between classes.*
>
> *The people in the room are unknown to me, except for Sister Maria from Goa, who recently was assigned to our parish in Calgary, Alberta. A discussion is taking place, but without words. On the old blackboard, I see first of all writing I cannot read, but I know it deals with the eternal questions mentioned above.*
>
> *We are seated casually around the room, some in student chairs of the old days with one-arm writing panel. Some are seated on the floor, around the blackboard as around a campfire. I am pacing about walking around the room seeking answers to the questions being discussed.*
>
> *Suddenly, as the angle of the light changes as I walk about, I see the entire blackboard is subtly shaded with a giant face covering the whole board. The face reminds me of Dr. Moses Coady, the great dynamic leader of the Antigonish Movement in the 1920s and 30s, which preached lifelong continuing education to advance the cause*

of the poor and needy of society. But I sense that the face is the face of God, not the familiar face of a bearded Jesus, but a fatherly face of a wise man of strength and compassion, like Coady, who I met in his final years in 1954.

As I move towards the blackboard excitedly, I see not just the writing, and not just the face of God absorbing the writing, but that there are deeper and deeper layers of human faces that make up the face of God. I am awestruck by the multilayered blackboard picture, which unites my lifelong philosophy of teaching, my understanding of God, and the relationship of humanity to God, in one beautiful complex image.

I think, Sister Maria, did you do this? *But she demurs, and a young man with a clean, narrow face and glasses, seated beneath the window looking out on Confusion Square, says, "I did it." I exclaim excitedly, "It's brilliant. Brilliant. It's the ONE and the MANY!" And I awake with the thought that I have had a glimpse into Teilhard de Chardin's spiritual and scientific speculation that everything in the universe is fated to spiral towards a final point of divine unification: the Omega Point.*

Of course, the images and pictures and incidents of whatever writers compose must come from their life experience, whether they are actions they experienced themselves or acquired from reading or viewing. All the images in my dream are from my life and education. What is my problem to solve in the dream? Here I am intensely involved in the compilation of a Confession in the form of a miscellany, a book containing various literary compositions. These compositions are documents from my life of some 82 years. These bits and pieces are memories of my past, are consuming my present, and are pointing to my future, which is the future of us all. Having lived longer than I ever conceived because of my family history, I am facing my demise sooner rather than later. What has it all meant? My dream has certified that my life to this point has been enriched by my experience and dreams and aspirations by an intense involvement with the people of my forbears, my family, my friends, and colleagues. Through this myriad mass of people I have struggled to know myself, the meaning of my life, and that mysterious force of creation itself, which I have come to believe is Love incarnate and living: my God.

In this Confession, I hope you will see "One Man's View" of a life filled with all "my prayers, works, joys and sufferings" of each day. It has been a most happy life, primarily through a blessed family and a woman of grace beyond understanding. Through all the joy, and the inevitable suffering, *Amor vincit omnia*, love has conquered all.

* * *

Teilhard de Chardin (1 May 1881–10 April 1955) was a French idealist philosopher and Jesuit priest who trained as a paleontologist and geologist. He conceived the vitalist idea of the Omega Point (a maximum level of complexity and consciousness towards which he believed the universe was evolving):

You are not a human being in search of a spiritual experience. You are a spiritual being immersed in a human experience.

We are one, after all, you and I. Together we suffer, together exist, and forever will recreate each other.

It is our duty as men and women to proceed as though the limits of our abilities do not exist.

The Documentary Nature of this Confession

If I were writing an ordinary autobiography, I would look back over my 82 years of life experience and filter my life through my current state of sensibility. However, you will find herein all documents as originally presented. No document has been altered in its language, other than type face and layout or omission of a redundant item. [One exception to this declaration to be TRUTHful is the omission of a spiritual notebook of my youth with intimate prayers that are egregiously emotional, which prudence and pride demand that I keep between me and my Maker.]

Normally looking back, I would have the tendency to edit some of the youthful and other less graceful documents–in light of my hopefully more mature state of mind. But I feel that by letting these documents stand in their original state, readers will have a more accurate and, I hope, more truthful and interesting time, seeing the interaction of TRUTH, FICTION & LIES developing. I have opted to use American spelling rather than English spelling, for the primary audience is in North America.

When I was in high school I came across Klara Roman's book on handwriting analysis. I could see in my own handwriting my ego, flamboyance, and curiosity. Further, my writing revealed that everything that happens to me sinks into my memory and becomes a permanent part of my personality. Witness that one of the closing documents of this book relates an incident that happened to me some 79 years ago! The journey though these miscellaneous documents will reveal the intersecting of TRUTH, FICTION & LIES in one life.

Acknowledgements

The idea for this autobiographical project came to me when I registered for the 60th Annual Homecoming of the Class of 1958 of St. Francis Xavier University. I had spent fully half of my life of 80 years at the university. The memories were extremely powerful. Life in Antigonish had been rich and fulfilling and leaving had been occasioned only by practical circumstances of family and future care.

Yet many close family and friends now live half a continent away. I had a garage full of boxes of documents spanning now nearly a century of relationships and activities. And the thought flowered to form those happy memories, and the challenges and triumphs of those years, into some form that could be shared. Why not create an autobiography by selecting documents, arranging them chronologically [loosely] and according to the peripatetic geographical phases of our great life journey?

The project seemed simple and straightforward–so why not give it a go? Well, in the proof, after getting started it was obviously a more imposing challenge than I first realized. Librarians and archivists are great friends of authors delving into history; among those coming to my aid were those of my two universities: Archivist Kathleen MacKenzie and Mary Rose Laureys of St. Francis University, and Catherine Carlyle and Cindy Weibe, Library Services Specialists, of St. Mary's University, Calgary; also from StFX, Joe MacDonald, Executive director of Government Relations and Krista McKenna, Varsity Athletics & Communications Manager. Friends and family had to be enlisted to make the dream a reality. Among many supporters, I thank some superb typists, Menchie Sabater and Heather Schilling; a proofreading wife [a life-long editor of my writing], Jacqueline; a well-read proofreader extraordinaire, John Lynch; an intrepid son-in-law, Dr. Neil White, who was on call for computer glitches and problems around the clock because we live together; Brenna Murray, whose computer skills saved the day in the homestretch; grandsons, Brian and Peter

White and Conor and Duncan MacDonald; and JC Schmidt, "Pioneer" student at St. Mary's University, who started as a willing indentured slave to the project and ended up a principal assistant to his friend, the author; son Greg, my personal computer guru who serves from a distance of 4,853 km away in any and all computer emergencies. Gracious thanks to my colleagues and friends Sheldon Currie, James Taylor and Phil Milner for carte blanche use of their materials to spice things up, as well as James William Johnson for excerpts about *The Antigonish Review* from his Master's dissertation. Finally, my appreciation to my student, colleague and friend, Stewart Donovan for his gracious Foreword and editorial advice. These friends and family members made this project a reality, but any miscues or mistakes remain the sole responsibility of the author.

Chapter 1
Italian, Irish-Catholic Heritage

My earliest memories begin before Pearl Harbor and World War II (1941 USA entry, not Canadian). Grandma Walsh is my very oldest memory. I read somewhere that your earliest memory is a key to your life, which seems true to me. Being the first grandson, I was being rocked in my grandmother's arms, the coziest, warmest, and most comfortable spot in my little universe–the fair-haired boy, obviously special and much loved.

Grandma Cicchetti, "Mamelle," was a tiny dark Italian woman–very, very dark. Her maiden name was Maria DelNegro. She was the most gentle, loving woman. We had breakfasts together: she would take a large round soda cracker with a cow imprinted on it and crumble it into a cup of coffee with sugar. What a treat.

I think both those Grandmas were so special because my mother had a heart attack at the time of my birth, and in the ensuing years I spent an inordinate amount of time with these grand ladies.

By far the most traumatic incident of my first five years in North Adams happened in the winter of my fourth year. Down the back hill from our house was the Bus Pond, so named because off-duty school buses were parked nearby. Becoming adventurous one fine winter's day, I wandered out on the ice of the pond. The slipperiness of the ice was fun, until the ice shattered under me. Plunged under the ice, I panicked for breath with icy water going up my nose and into my ears. I remember clawing at the ice above me and thrashing wildly, for I did not know how to swim.

I was not aware that a passing high school boy saw me go under the ice. He was big enough to wade into the pond, breaking the ice before him. He grabbed me and dragged me to shore. I could only shudder and blubber, and when he wanted to take me home, I resisted. I knew my mother would be angry. So I just pointed up the hill to the other side of the apartment where we lived, and I headed for refuge with "Auntie" Mill–not my real aunt, but a childless neighbor who treated me like the child she did not have. Mill[ie] and her husband, Walt Brackley, were quintessential fictional Aunt and Uncle, but in reality they spoiled me. Aunt Mill immediately wanted to take me to my mother next door, and no matter how I resisted, for the first time she exhibited sternness quite surprising. I was shocked when she delivered me to my angry mother, who behaved exactly as expected: she peeled off my wet boots and clothes and then spanked me. It was the quickest way to warm me up, I realize now, and when she stopped spanking me, she hugged me, and apologized as best she could, sobbing over and over, "O, Patty, O Patty!"

As the years passed, I never learned how to swim. I developed a story that because of this incident, I just couldn't stand water going over my head, I would panic. However, this cover story was to hide the fact that I was embarrassed by my fatness, which made me different from the other kids. For the first years of my conscious life I was tormented as "Pat! Pat! The big fat rat!" and often beat up by little 'gunslingers' who themselves were beaten up by bigger kids. By about the sixth grade my high grades enabled me to create a new persona and maneuver my way out of trouble. So I was forever avoiding any situations in which I would be naked with others. As I became more knowledgeable about sexual relations, I became worried that I would not be able to ever be married. But after the death of my parents and the fading call to the priesthood, when I knew I wanted to get married, I went to Dr. Bianco, our family doctor, who assured me that I was capable. So the quest for the fair maiden of my dreams was eventually fulfilled and resulted in five children and ten grandchildren. Through many years of unreasonable fears, the story of Bus Pond ruled, and I never learned to swim. But I did overcome my shame and was able to play basketball and handball, and be comfortable in locker rooms because I could hold my own on the courts.

I remember starting school in Grade 1, no kindergarten, at Brayton School in North Adams, Massachusetts, at age five. Two things stand out about school: before the school opened in the morning the students played a game. One student, a boy, would spin another, a girl, around and around by the arm, faster and faster, finally flinging her loose. The girl would spin and stumble across the school yard, and when momentum allowed, she would freeze into a statuesque position. The beauty and creativeness of the frozen poses captivated me.

The second (and traumatic) incident began in the classroom. Every student needed a school box containing a pencil, a pen and nib, an eraser, and a protractor. Your family had to provide the school box. Special grandson that I obviously was, I had a magnificent blue school box–immediately the envy of my classmates, who had the drabbest school boxes in America [*my opinion*]. Being a chubby lad with slicked-down hair and gold-rimmed round eyeglasses (courtesy of my Uncle Tony, whom you will meet later), I was properly bullied–AND the teacher took my school box away. [*Today I suspect the teacher was trying to protect me, but back then, the teacher's next move struck me as monumentally unfair and undemocratic, even though I didn't know the meaning of the word!*] The teacher said, "All students should have a similar, equal school box." Not realizing at the time this act was as unfair as the seizure of Alsace Lorraine by Hitler, I damn well knew it was not grandmotherly. It was wrong.

A bit later, I had worked out my plan. I raised my hand and asked to go to the lavatory. Once in the hallway, I made my move. Seeing a janitor coming, I hid behind a propped-open door. When the coast was clear, I popped out the door and headed home.

On the State Road, which turned into West Main Street where I lived, I realized it was too early to go home, so I dawdled. But state police cars were coming and going. If they looked at me, I scuffed the dirt, pretending to look for a lost dime if they stopped to arrest me. My fear was TRUTH, the dime FICTION, tending to LIE if leaving school were a crime!

Unapprehended by the law, I headed home–too early–to be met by my frantic, but relieved mother. The school had called her. I felt safe, until she said, "Your father will take care of this when he gets home from work." Under my parent's big double bed was the only spot where I could scramble for safety. They would both have trouble trying to ferret me out.

Father arrived.

"Well, Mother, I think we shall have to call the warrant officer."

"Oh, no, Duke, not the warrant officer." Mother seemed properly concerned for my fate.

"It's his job to catch bad boys who skip school."

"He didn't really skip school, he just left early."

They didn't know about or realize the painful, unfair loss of my beautiful blue school box.

"Skipping or leaving early, the warrant officer will have to find him and lock him up."

"Will they allow us to visit him?'

"Maybe at Christmas."

Doom loomed. But I was saved by World War II, even though it hadn't started: the next morning we found out that my father had a new job and we were moving to a little town of 3,000 named Sidney, New York, down along the Susquehanna River near Pennsylvania.

Saved! But, then I realized we would be leaving my two grandmas. I was beginning to catch on that life could be fickle, very fickle.

In the second grade in Sidney I learned a valuable lesson: One of my classmates was a little fellow who played the role of a bumble bee in a play put on by the High School. But that's not what made him the most important and impressive student in my class; his uncle was General Jimmy Doolittle, who led the first U.S.A. bombing attack on Japan on April 18, 1942.

We had a test. The multiple choice question was:

If the sun rises in the east and sets in the west, a shadow would move from

a) east to west, b) north to south, c) west to east, d) south to north?

That was easy: I circled *c) west to east.* Then I saw that Warren Doolittle had circled *a) east to west.* Oh, God, I must be wrong. Warren Doolittle must be right. I erased my answer and circled Warren's answer. There was a reason I was so intimidated. I was having trouble reading, and just beginning to succeed in school–but I wouldn't find out why until 55 years later. But I did learn then that cheating is a bad policy. We won the war, and in 1955 I would find out my father played a role in our Allied victory. Much more important than the lost school box was being taken away from my mother's Italian neighborhood and my father's Irish family. You'll be meeting them in the documents coming up. They become more and more influential in my life after we return from the war, by moving from Sydney, to Auburn, New York, for one year and back to North Adams, from 1947 on.

From the notebook of Carmen Cicchetti 1932 [age 22]

To My Wedding Day

Brimful of desire, unreaped ripe
Overflowing, burstful, all unrequited
O Cathedral hearted spouse to be
Hope of all art thou to me.
To me a toxin urgently dear
Not to be tasted full yet a year
Nightly thy casement begs, beseeches
But conscience bars my frantic reaches.
Thy door a thing that thwarts me sore:
And yet my heart says, "Not before!"
Must I comply with man-made tape
Forged by God to keep lovers chaste
When may I vaunt to friends of mine,
"This is my love, and for all time."

F. J. Walsh
(Written July 1932 to Carmen from "Duke")

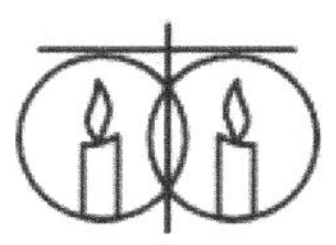

Carmen Cicchetti 1932 Francis "Duke" Walsh

Francis "Duke" Walsh, my father-to-be, sent this sonnet, "To My Wedding Day," to my mother-to-be, in 1932. I consider these thoughts to be the beginning forces of Pat Walsh's existence. They were anxious to be married, but the Italian custom was for the youngest child to care for the parents in their old age. Joe Cicchetti was the youngest child, but when he eloped with a non-Catholic girl, he was estranged from the family for a while, and it fell to my mother, next youngest, to care for her parents. It took some four years more of engagement before Uncle Joe was reconciled with the family, and my parents were married August 22, 1936. Conscience was important to both my parents.

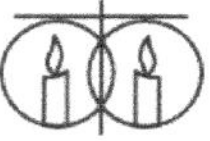

The Italian influence in my childhood and youth was stronger than the Irish, so I thought. The Italians were the primary mine of material for my early writing. In the summer of 1957, while home from college, Monsignor Donahue, the pastor and overseer of the school, hired me to paint classrooms in St. Joe's High School. The school had just acquired a new-fangled tape-recording machine. The Monsignor allowed me to take it home and see how it worked. I was testing it out in the living room just outside the kitchen where the real Cicchetti siblings were gathered. It sounded interesting, so I let the tape run and recorded them without their knowing it. That recording was basically what is in the first play I ever wrote. I had to reorganize it and figure out connections and make slight revisions, but it was the essential spine of dialogue and situation.

That autumn back at St. Francis Xavier University in Fr. Rod MacSween's Creative Writing Course, Father asked us to write two pages of dialogue, to get the feeling of spoken language. The taped conversation popped into my head. As I was writing, Tom Concannon, an excellent actor and director, dropped in and asked about the dialogue I was writing. He took a gander, and asked me to write it up into a one-act play for the Interclass Play Festival. He was directing the Senior Class entry. As they say, the rest is history.

As far as we knew, ours was the first creative writing class at a Canadian university. We had begged Fr. MacSween to teach it, but the Academic Dean, Monsignor Cyril Bauer, could not allow credit for the course. However, when the adjudicator Claude Bede, a StFX graduate and noted Canadian actor, praised the play and awarded us prizes, Monsignor Bauer walked down the aisle to where Fr. MacSween was sitting and said, "Everyone in the class will get credit for taking the writing class."

I had an inkling of Academy Award Night, and it was the hook that reeled me into a life of playwriting.

Every character in the little drama was based upon a real person in my mother's family. The events in the drama, based upon the real-life recorded incident, are in one sense, the TRUTH. But, after all, the characters in my mind were FICTION–words upon a page who were figments of my imagination. In another sense, the characters become LIES betraying my living memories, for in this, my very first play, I discovered a phenomenon known to many playwrights: characters assume an identity of their own, and often contradict the purposes of the writer, or the circumstances being created. I had intended that my mother, Carmen Cicchetti, would be the heroine of the tale, but my aunt Bessie Cicchetti Pessalano, eluding my control of the story line, became the heroine. It was a deep insight into the reality that characters are never the living person. Yet Bessie's takeover in no way detracts from the TRUTH of the characterizations I intended, allowing not only the TRUTH of the story to emerge, but revealing the weakness of the author to control his materials or his characters. The play was called *The Flowers*, and in it, all the vital and demonstrative strong-willed members of my mother's immediate family turned a simple event into a major family battle. From the oldest, Aunt Annie; to Uncle Tony, and his wife, Mary; to Aunt Bessie, and her vociferous husband, Pete Pessalano; to my mother, Carmen; to the baby in the family, Uncle Joe; they ended up fighting over who put the flowers on their mother's grave. By the time the play is over the raw emotions of everyone on stage have been strewn about like Christmas wrappings. I had more control over the characters in my writing than I did in my own life, yet I would find that in the world of words, characters would be as disruptive of my FICTIONal worlds, as my thoughts and actions were disruptive of my TRUE world.

The Flowers became my first performed and published work, featured in the student magazine, *X-Writes*, which my printing background allowed me to make for our class. Yet, before I ever published anything, I began to record my impressions of my family in stories. I had an urge to write–to share the aches and pains and joys of my life, but vicariously conceived in my mind–freeing me through FICTION from criticism in the TRUTH of my real life. I now realize how much these early stories revealed about the forces at work in my youthful formation. Enter my uncle, Tony Cicchetti, who was so much a part of my early life, and the life of my whole family, that I took the name "Anthony" for my confirmation name, in the hopes to bring my wayward uncle back into the bosom of the Church.

My Uncle Tony

"That's our cousin," said my Uncle Tony as we watched the Cleveland half-back plunge over for a touchdown. Of course, I didn't believe him, but I had to listen; it was 1949, and he had the only television in our neighborhood–a 36-inch set like they have in barrooms. Listening to Uncle Tony wasn't ever boring, and as long as you could see Steve van Buren pounding into the line, who minded?

"Aw, go on, that's not our cousin."

"Sure it is. What's the matter, you don't believe your uncle? No respect today. No respect at all."

"Prove it."

He smiled as he jiggled the ice cubes in his drink.

"His name is Chick Cicchetti. He's a cousin of ours."

Jiggle, jiggle, and the clinking of ice.

"How come they don't pronounce it right? The announcers are saying Jah-gay-dee, not Ch-ket-ee."

Jiggle, jiggle, and the clinking of ice.

"You know Jack Brickhouse doesn't know how to pronounce anybody's name, right? Besides, this cousin is from Chicago. The family just gets tired of correcting people when they say it wrong."

Jiggle, jiggle of ice.

I thought, then, that he might be telling the truth. My mother *had* been born in Chicago just after my grandparents arrived from Italy, and just before they moved to my hometown of North Adams, Massachusetts.

I spent the next few weeks–really, the next ten years–bragging about my cousin from Chicago who played for the Cleveland Browns with Otto Graham and all those guys.

It wasn't until I was in college that I read in the Sporting News that Chick Jagedi had retired from the Cleveland Browns. There it was–J-A-G-E-D-I, not C-I-C-C-H-E-T-T-I! I always forgot to bring that lie up whenever I visited Uncle Tony, and when my sister called last week and said he was dead, I remembered I had never confronted him with Chick Jagedi. I hope I forgot on purpose.

* * *

Uncle Tony was the best man at my parent's wedding. He had met my dad at the local ball park. Dad was a pitcher and Tony was a right fielder–good hit–no field. To catch a fly ball or throw the ball was something only to put up with so you could get up to bat and smash the ball. A catch was a catch was a catch–but a double with a hook slide into second base was a work of art that brought every young lady in the stands to her feet with a perfect oval on her lips.

Tony the sharp and immaculate dresser–my mother told me once when she was mad at him, how he used to throw shirts back into the bluing tub and make her start all over again if they weren't absolutely perfectly presentable–took a liking to my dad. Dad had a wicked spit ball–it was legal back then. In one game, my father had 17 assists–only one ball was hit out of the infield. That meant Tony could rest in right field and save his energy for an attempt to stretch a double into a triple. Also, my father was a sharp dresser, known as "Duke." I'll tell you how he got his nickname.

Tony took Frank Walsh home to supper and grandma Cicchetti fell in love with him. "He's a reall-a Duka!" she beamed–because Dad ate everything she put in front of him–and that clinched it–an Irish boy who eats Italian cooking must be a "Duke!"

So when Dad fell in love with Tony's youngest sister, Grandpa–an old fascist bully–never had a chance to chase him off–he was already a member of the family.

Tony was handsome in my parents' wedding picture: a thin mustache, no sign of a pot yet, and an air of being someone of value and importance. If North Adams were Chicago, he would have been a mafia boss.

But before the wedding, before my father met my mother, he used to hang around with Uncle Tony and his girlfriend, Mary Gilliotti.

After college, my father was selling insurance, and one day he came home from work and there was a moving van outside the house. My father asked his mother what was going on.

"We're moving to Boston."

"Who?"

"Me and Lucy and Mary, and Alice and Louis. And you, if you want to."

"No."

"Okay."

"Goodbye."

"Goodbye."

So dad moved in with Tony and Mary who had been married a short time. They used to drive around the Berkshire Hills, playing ball on the weekends in the old Tri-State League.

Then my father threw his arm out–and they used to just watch the games. They took off every once in a while and took the train to New York to see the Yankees play. Dad had pitched for Columbia University when a young guy named Lou Gehrig was playing first base–so tickets were no trouble.

But most of the time the three of them traveled around Western Mass. Tony had a little coupe with a rumble seat. When Tony and my Dad had too much to drink, they'd get into the rumble seat and sing their way home while Mary drove.

It became a legend in the family that all three could eat a full quart of ice cream anytime they stopped for a snack.

* * *

My folks' wedding was the last time Tony was in church until his daughter Carolyn got married. And even then he didn't make it past the vestibule.

My grandfather Cicchetti wouldn't go to church because it was too hot, and he always felt dizzy, and God didn't expect people to go to church and be sick and faint, did He?

I never worried too much about Grandpa not going to church because he was a nice little old white-haired man. Almost an image of a merciful God.

I had on occasion experienced the *justice* of God from Grandpa. He had a wide straight-razor strop which he administered to my backside whenever I acted up during a visit with the grandparents on summer vacations during World War II. Grandpa told me that strop had raised his boys to be good and a little taste of it wouldn't hurt me. I just couldn't picture Grandpa whacking Uncle Tony. But when my drawers got dropped the puzzle of the past faded rapidly and the present was all that mattered.

Grandpa never ate meat on Wednesday. That's right–*Wednesday*. When Grandpa was 18-years-old and a shepherd in Italy on a hillside in Santa Lucia about 20 miles north of Venice, he fell off a cliff and went into a coma for days and days. He woke up on a Wednesday, and in his gratefulness to God's mercy, never ate meat again on Wednesday. My mother told me, so it must be true, that one Wednesday, Grandma put meat in front of Grandpa and he slapped her and hurled the dish against the wall. My mother never forgot that. However–on Fridays, Grandpa ate meat!

Whatever Grandpa had in his blood that made him dizzy in church, I guess his oldest son, Tony, had it, too.

When I went through my religious phase, about the time I made my confirmation and became a soldier-for-Christ, I worried about my Uncle Tony. He had avoided the religio-military draft, and the firstborn's destiny of the priesthood. I used to talk religion *at* him. The one theme of all his replies was, "I'm not going to go to church and see those goddam hypocrite-bastards going to communion and looking holy. They all owe me money and I see them sinning all over the goddam place. Well, I'm no hypocrite." End of discussion.

I tried to pull off a minor miracle by taking the name of Anthony for my confirmation name–but it didn't work.

Uncle Tony, who belonged to the Italian parish and my father who belonged to the Irish parish, both went out and collected money for the new Italian church. Father Russo, who coached the Saint Anthony Crusader's football team, got all the athletes in town to collect for the fund and my father dragged Tony along.

My father was pretty friendly with Fr. Russo from that time on. In fact, I was baptized in the old Italian church. Well, we moved away to New York State during the war and when we came back to town after the war my father decided to send us kids to the parochial high school, St. Joseph's High, which belonged to the Irish Parish, St. Francis, where he had gone to school. So my father went to see the old Irish pastor to register me at the only Catholic High School in town.

Monsignor Dunphy plopped at his desk, listened to my father's request, and then threw him out, saying, "Remember when you collected money for the Italian church? Well, go back there." That meant we had to pay full tuition–so my father had to write to the bishop to get back into his Irish parish, and bring his Italian-church baptized son with him.

Uncle Tony laughed and laughed about that. He told everybody he could about how the goddam church was so goddam concerned about money. Ha, ha!

My father took me aside and explained that Monsignor Dunphy was just getting old and that people do things like kids sometimes. It's called second childhood. They don't like growing old.

Uncle Tony overheard Dad telling me this and laughed harder than ever, until tears were running down his cheeks.

So, although, he never set foot in the new church, which didn't get built for twenty years, Tony ploughed through the snow and rain for quite a few years collecting money for the church.

Well, twenty years later, his daughter had to get married in the old church. "Had to get" refers to the old church, not the getting married. She married a Baptist convert, who is a daily communicant and a member of the Third Order of Our Lady of Mount Carmel–and if anybody is a saint, he is. He's one of only two people I know who actually has an aura I can perceive.

Well, there was a hurricane the day of the wedding and the bride had to be helped into church under a big piece of plastic–and I was one of the young cousins who tried to prevent hurricane Hazel from tearing the bride up before the marriage. I was supposed to be an altar boy that day, but I grabbed the chance to hold the plastic because I was having my own personal little religious crisis and making bad confessions during those years, so I just stood in the vestibule with Uncle Tony.

He looked just like he did in my folks' wedding picture—the flower in the lapel, a streak of gray in the sideburns, a little bit of a pot now, but a prosperous pouch of a pot, not a beer belly. One of our cousins, who once won the Metropolitan Auditions of the Air and sang sometimes in the Metropolitan Opera, sang the *Ave Maria.* It was so humid, and everybody was wringing wet, with either sweat, tears, or nervousness. At the back entrance, we could hear the bridal couple exchange vows, and when his daughter said, "I will" good and loud, I heard Uncle Tony suck in air and begin to sob. He turned away when I looked at him and leaned his head on the book rack, dropping real tears on "The Sacred Heart Messenger" and "The Liguorian." I know I wasn't old enough to do it, but I did anyway. I put my hand on his shoulder. The fact I could feel bone surprised me.

* * *

Uncle Tony was a superb chef. He was better than Aunt Annie, his older sister—everything she cooked was flat. Better than Aunt Bessie—she overcooked everything. Better than—God forgive me—my mother Carmen—she used only hamburger and cheap ingredients. At least this is what Tony told his sisters, and his brothers, and a select group of neighbors, that is, those with first-rate gardens.

According to Aunt Annie, Tony killed everything by spicing it to death. It was like World War II. By the time he had put in a pinch of this from Spain, a dash of that from France, a nip of this from Ireland, a bunch of that from Poland, a slice of this from Germany, and just a wee sprig of this rare leaf from Portugal, whatever was in the pot had surrendered.

According to Aunt Bessie, Tony thought he was a great cook because he had been Grandma's favorite, spoiled rotten and now too busy cooking for the Elks and Eagles and Lions—beasts who ate everything raw, anyway.

According to my mother, Tony *was* a good cook, but not really a master because everything he cooked was too rich for him to eat himself. What was the sense of cooking for others and wasting all that money on overpriced fancy wines and rare spices?

So they all fought over who made the best sausage. Each claimed the prize—on the basis that her sausage was closest to the kind Grandma used to make.

One day Uncle Tony confided to me that to tell the truth, Romeo Gallese, the corner butcher, made the sausage most like his mother's, but he would, and never could, admit this to his sisters.

* * *

Uncle Tony used to live next door to us until the flood of 1948. The neighborhood was tree-lined and spacious. We owned a duplex that was occupied on the other side by my father's boss. That used to frighten me, and the day I hit Melissa Jones, the boss's daughter, in the eye with a snowball, I thought my father would be fired. Uncle Tony laughed when I told him my fear. He said if Eddie Jones fired your father he'd be out of a job in six months.

Uncle Tony's house was always dark. It was the kind of big old house that would show too many cracks if somebody put light bulbs in the lamps. We had to be quiet whenever we went into that house because Uncle Tony, who had spent the afternoon listening to the Yankee ballgame and cooking supper, always went to bed around six o'clock.

He got up at 5:30 or 6 a.m. and went to work. He was an optician, and I've never been to an eye doctor in my life. Uncle Tony would have me read the dates on the calendar in his office, and then give me glasses. The letters were still blurred, and I went for years thinking he was a quack. One day, when I was in high school and only a couple of years from knowing it all, I spoke up:

"How come the numbers are still blurry?"

He'd put a new lens in front of my eye.

"How's that?"

"Better, but the numbers are still blurred."

"These are just right for you."

"Uncle Tony, I want to see the numbers perfectly, no blur, sharp, distinct."

"How old are you?"

"Sixteen–almost."

"You still stink of milk."

"Why don't you give me better lenses?"

"Here, goddammit. How's this?"

Tony stepped behind me and held two fat lenses in front of my eyes. The numbers were clearer than ever before–brilliant–they leaped off the calendar and pierced my pupils.

"Perfect. That's perfect, Uncle Tony. Perfect. That's what I want. Grind those up. Okay? Please?"

"Sure." He didn't move.

"They're okay, Uncle Tony." I tried to move my head away, but he vised my head on both sides with his forearms and kept the lenses in front of my eyes, and directed at the calendar.

"It's okay. Let go!"

"Shut up, you smart-ass."

I stared at the calendar, and the numbers stared back. I began to blink. Water welled up and dribbled down my cheeks. I noticed then that while the numbers on the calendar were crisp and clear, the desk just in front of me was melting. Real tears began to flow. Uncle Tony sensed my shame, and released me.

His voice was softer now. "If I put those lenses on you, you'll be blind in three months. It takes time to strengthen your eyes."

I never questioned him again when it was time to change lenses.

* * *

Uncle Tony never opened his shop until around 7:30 or 8 o'clock. When he got to town around 6 or 6:30, he went to Molly's bakery across the street. He'd talk with the bakers and order coffee for everyone, saying, "I'm buying," and nobody ever argued, especially the little man who ran Pizzi's Dress Shop. Then Uncle Tony would go to the shop and begin to grind lenses. When someone came in, he'd come out of the back room where he ground lenses, wiping his hands on his white apron which was spattered with smooth grinding mud.

Little old ladies who just wanted their glasses straightened out used to drive him berserk. When they walked out, he'd begin to curse and swear, and complain how they came to him to get the glasses straightened and fitted, but let Dr. Flaherty send their prescriptions to Pittsfield to be made, and of course Dr. Flaherty would have time to straighten and fit their glasses only if they made an appointment with the no-good Irish bastard. Apparently, my father was the only good Irishman Uncle Tony ever knew. I guess that's because he ate Italian food without complaining, even the next morning.

The policeman on Eagle Street always had a cup of coffee in the shop, the postman stopped by even if there was no mail, and the two Gazaniga brothers from the furniture store next to Molly's Bakery were always running in and out.

The Yankees dominated conversation for years. If the Vatican had struck a medal for St. Joseph DiMaggio–of course, this was before he married Marilyn Monroe–my uncle would have just about trampled the Good Shepherd to get back with the other 99. The only good player the Red Sox had, of course, was Joe's little brother, Dominic DiMaggio.

I couldn't understand how Uncle Tony would root for a New York team when he lived in Massachusetts and should have been rooting for the Boston Red Sox. Had he no sense of loyalty? At first I thought it was because of Joe DiMaggio, a truly great Italian. Then I found out about my dad playing with Lou Gehrig, and being partial to the Yankees. So, Uncle Tony's choice to back the Yankees became understandable. But finally, I found out the truth. While the first reasons might have bent the twig toward the Yankees–Uncle Tony's faith was in winning. He made lots of money betting on the Yankees. I overheard my dad and mom talking about it quietly one night. Mom was almost crying, and my father kept saying he didn't know how to do anything about it. He had spoken to Tony, but it was no use. He owed money to everyone, but kept on betting. He always managed to squeeze out of trouble some way or other, usually through some miracle triumph of the Yanks over the Sox.

During the McCarthy era, Senator Joe, not Charlie, the commie-pinko bastards came in for a lot of verbal abuse. Just about everything that came up got cursed–including Aunt Mary. You see, Uncle Tony went to bed by six o'clock every evening. Uncle Tony drove home from work at one o'clock in the afternoon in his pink Cadillac to his new ranch-style home–to which he had moved after the flood humiliated him because he had to leave his house in a row-boat, in the posh colonial New England village of Williamstown, where Cole Porter had a summer home, and Sinclair Lewis had an estate, now a Carmelite monastery, and the latest notable to move in is novelist James Gould Cozzens, next to the Rockefeller family farm–Aunt Mary, who was also a dispensing optician, but never ground lenses, would go to work. She worked at the shop dispensing the lenses Tony had ground, and then around 5:30 she would leave to go home. Meanwhile, Tony, in the house he had built and never paid for, cooked and never tasted a supper while listening to the Yankee game on the radio, and then went to bed with his bottle. Mary would arrive just after Tony went to bed. She would throw out the supper and have a sandwich and read 'til the wee hours of the morning. Aunt Mary and Uncle Tony used to pass one another on the highway somewhere between Notch Road and the Four Acres Restaurant. Battleships passing in the night.

So Aunt Mary never heard the cursing. She would go to work in the afternoon and straighten out the mess on the work bench and the mess on the desk and the mess in the cabinets of glass frames and lenses. The next morning Tony couldn't find anything, and the cursing would begin.

The choicest cursing was reserved for the relatives. Uncle Tony would give the family eyeglasses for cost—well, that's the way it would start out. But we had an army of cousins, Cicchettis, Delnegros, Cardillos, Gillottis, Pessalanos, even by marriage, some Ozlislos. And their glasses were tricky to grind. For instance, my glasses are thick at the edges but very thin in the middle. Uncle Tony would get them ground just about right, start to polish them, and *crick!* Start over. He'd get through the polishing on the second set and put them on the glass trimmer to cut them to the shape of the frame, and—*crick!* Start over. By then, any old ladies wandering into the front shop would turn around and waddle out as quickly as possible.

Uncle Tony lost a lot of money on me over the years. Now my kids are just getting their first pairs of glasses. I'm glad for Uncle Tony's sake that he died before he had to start on the next generation.

* * *

In Williamstown, the Taconic Country Club is *the* in thing. Naturally, Uncle Tony joined. They have carpet in the locker room, electric ice-water coolers every three holes, and when they held the United States College Championships there, Jack Nicklaus, then an undergraduate, made a hole-in-one on the fourteenth hole. A plaque commemorates the feat.

During that tournament one member of the club was assigned to keep Uncle Tony at the bar and away from the tees. Guests who were playing on the course for the first time knew when Uncle Tony was three holes away even though they had never seen him. He is remembered today for his cursing and for wrapping so many clubs around trees, water-coolers, golf carts, and ball-cleaners, that no one will ever beat his record. He hated to lose.

* * *

One day Uncle Tony grew old. When my father died at age 51, Tony came to the house with a big bowl of meatballs, put them on the kitchen table, and just stood there, as my mother sobbed. "Oh Tony, oh, Tony." He never said one word. He cried.

My mother said, "You never visited Pa when he was in the nursing home." My grandfather had died three years before. Tony turned around and walked out.

When my mother died at age 47 two years later, Tony didn't come to the church, but when we came out the front door in the procession after the funeral, I could see him across the street near Hirsh's Drug Store. He turned away when I looked at him.

* * *

The son-in-law with the aura came to train with his father-in-law as an optician. Several of the gang of nephews had trained as opticians under Uncle Tony, but had left for one good reason or another. I didn't think the son-in-law had a chance. He got up as early as Tony, but went to daily Mass and communion. He never said a word about Tony's cursing, never raised his voice, never talked back. And he was a crackerjack optician. He gave Uncle Tony beautiful red-headed grandchildren, started a hearing aid business to complement the optical business and started going to college on the side.

This arrangement and the daily crisscross with Aunt Mary went on for a number of years until Uncle Tony got sick. He needed an operation because he was losing the use of his right hand and arm. The operation would open a gash from the base of his neck to the top of his skull. There was no way anyone was going to get him under the knife. The family thought of getting him drunk–or of overpowering him. They called in his favorite nephew, who plays the clarinet for the Boston Symphony Orchestra, and this nephew, who himself has a mortal fear of flying and has to get bombed out of his mind every time the Orchestra flies anywhere, convinced Uncle Tony to get the operation.

Tony insisted upon going to the Bennington, Vermont, hospital, where he would be close to Dr. Ram, the only goddam eye surgeon in the country, who goddam well wouldn't let the butchers hack him up.

Everybody was very hopeful. A nurse came in to prep Tony for the operation and began to shave the back of his head. She scraped him with the straight razor. He probably had her frightened purple with his cursing. One little nick and that was it. He fought his way out of the bed, knocked down the nurse, put on only his pants and took off in his car. The Vermont State Police caught him near the Green Mountain Park Racetrack heading for Williamstown.

He had the operation and went back to work–and the only thing I could notice was a tiny white line on the back of his neck. Also, every once in a while he would stretch his right arm out with his hand over his head and flex his fingers.

The son-in-law took over more and more of the business and Uncle Tony had to give up golf.

Father Pagano, who had converted the son-in-law, dropped into the shop every day. If he hoped to bring Uncle Tony back to the fold, he never really had a chance, because Father Pagano was always serious and never joked. He could reach a Baptist, or any other serious person, but with postmen, cops, bakers, or ballplayers he never had a chance.

The son-in-law and Father Pagano had all kinds of literature lying around the office: *Catholic Digest*, *The Messenger*, *Our Sunday Visitor*, and the like. Aunt Mary always straightened them out and neatly arranged each morning for Uncle Tony's arrival.

I knew the end was near when one day I went into the shop and Uncle Tony had taped on the wall a picture of Satan as a bare-ass satyr peering lewdly over his shoulder. I never mentioned it. Neither did the son-in-law, nor Father Pagano, nor Aunt Mary.

* * *

I had moved away from the hometown after college and I was back visiting the son-in-law when Uncle Tony's daughter mentioned his girlfriend: Uncle Tony's eighteen-year-old girlfriend. A real teasy bitch. She had cracked up his pink Cadillac and had even stopped Aunt Mary on the street and insulted her.

I got a phone call here in Canada from my sister last week. Uncle Tony had dropped dead opening the door to his pink Cadillac. His funeral was held last Thursday in the spanking new St. Anthony's church he helped to build. It was the first time he had been to church since the wedding in the hurricane. I suddenly realized that when he used to reach up with that right arm and flex his fingers, he was making a last desperate grasp at the life that was ebbing away.

And I know one thing. When the devil reaches for my Uncle, Tony will try to kick him with a $55 pair of unpaid-for-wing-tip-Florsheim shoes–and he'll try to kick him where it will do the most good.

And I hope Uncle Tony doesn't miss.

*

This is FICTION, a story, but it is pretty close to the TRUTH as I perceived it–at least the spirit of the TRUTH dwells therein.

Here follows my first published short story: a dive into the subconscious world of my dreams–actual childhood dreams, seared forever into my conscious memories.

Finally, I Admit I Have a Knob on My Nose

- from *The Antigonish Review* Vol.1, Number 2 1970

MY DREAM

March 8, 1952

Last night I had a bad dream.

I was in a black box lying on my back and I couldn't see anything because it was dark in there.

My stomach felt funny. It felt funny peculiar.

I could hear my Daddy shouting at me. From outside the box, he has a big voice. Then I heard a noise. Click, Click.

The box began to shake.

The top of the box went up and the light hurt my eyes. So, I shut them, but they began to water anyway. So, I began to cry.

I could hear someone breathing funny.

When I opened my eyes, I saw a man staring at me. A strange man.

I didn't know him, and his eyes were empty. I mean they were all white and didn't have any brown or blue, or any color in them.

When I looked again he was gone and my mother was mad about what I had done in the bed. My Daddy told me to stop sniffling, but I couldn't.

This is the picture of the man I saw.

All dreams are significant. They indicate something important. They are either dreams of desire or anxiety. Most of my dreams are anxiety. Atomic war or I'm being chased. Things like that.

Of course I know that the images in our dreams come from our ordinary experiences which we translate into a hidden language, so we don't have to face our real self.

In one dream that I had a lot, I used to run a few steps and get up in the air about two or three feet and then float along for about ten yards before landing. Dreams about flying are supposed to be about sex, so I guess the fact that I only got a little way off the ground isn't too bad.

The dream that really bothered me from the time I was a little kid, was of this eyeless hairless man.

I would be in a box, and it would be dark, and the box would begin to quiver and shake and then float down a black passage. Then the box, which I realized was an open casket with me in it sweating and breathing hard, would go down a long slide and crash through a swinging door. A blaze of light hit my eyes. And the eyeless hairless man is standing there with a huge axe in his hands. He begins to raise the axe and I knew he was going to chop my head off–and then my father jumped him from behind and grabbed his arm and I woke up.

That dream used to come back again and again.

But today I found out why I had those dreams. In *Scientific American* there was an article about how when someone is sleeping the pulse beat gets very regular and begins to set up vibrations in the bed and the bed will sway to the rhythm of the sleeper's pulse. All that foolishness about gliding and sliding was just an attempt by my unconscious to explain the movement of the bed.

When I was an ignorant ten-year-old I was scared, I admit. But my father never saved me. It was my own unconscious.

June 8, 1958

My father acted like a sap today.

I was getting ready to go to a dance and I had a nice long hot bath. Then I was taking it easy just sitting there in the bathroom. I have to admit that it was taking me quite a while but not that long.

Anyway, he knocked at the door a couple of times and I said, "In a minute."

Then he banged on the door and I had to bend over and reach to unlock it and SPLASH, he threw a big glass of cold water all over me.

I'll never forget the look in his eye.

October 15, 1958

I never saw my father cry before. I was beginning to think maybe he never had.

They shipped his father's body home from California. Grandpa had gone out there when I was just four and I can't remember much about him, except that he used to sit in a rocking chair near the front window, making clouds of pipe-smoke. My mother used to race back and forth trying to keep the ashtrays clean. It was a losing battle.

The old man was tough. He had a stroke out there and to prove he was able to get up and around, he sent pictures of himself standing up with two canes. But my father looked real close at the pictures and in one of them he saw someone sticking out from behind Grandpa. "The grand old fool. That's Louie crouched behind him to prop him up."

Well, today, they had the funeral. The wake had been postponed for four days because the body got lost somewhere at the Chicago airport. My father was cursing for the full four days. Anyway, they only had the wake for one day, and the people marveled at how my father didn't cry at all. I looked at my grandfather, and even forgot to pray, when I knelt down at the casket. The old man was thin, and his lips were wrinkled. I remembered the man in the rocking chair as fat. His eyes were closed, but somehow, he didn't look peaceful at all. I could imagine him glaring at my father. I could even imagine him glaring at me, right through his lids.

My father was the last one to say a prayer before they closed the casket and started for the Church. When Mr. MacIsaac started to close the casket, my father stopped him, and hugged his father and sobbed and sobbed. My mother finally got a couple of my cousins to help him away from the casket. They took him out to the car.

Mr. MacIsaac said something to my mother and she said, "Yes, there's no sense in that," and she accepted grandfather's watch from the undertaker.

By the time we got out to the car to ride to the cemetery, my father's eyes were dry, but red, at least.

April 7, 1959

I got that ugly feeling again today.

My father laughed at me again. Every time he does, I get sick.

The first time I had that feeling that I can remember was the day he called me an "oaf"–I was so dumb I thought it was something great. When I asked him what it meant he laughed and told me to look it up. I got sick. When I looked at him again I noticed the dark pores on his nose. And his eyes looked dull.

When I was small and had fevers and chills and upset stomach, he used to calm me down and get me to sleep by holding my hand. Now he laughs at me and I get chills and fevers and upset stomach.

George and I were playing catch in the yard and I was giving a real baseball holler to him, just like the guys on the town's semi-pro team.

"Chuck-it-in-there-kid, fire-it-in-there, baby. Atta-boy. Nice-fire. Nice-fire. The-way-you-fire-it-in-there-kid."

I missed the ball and it hit me right in the nose. From a catcher's squat, I landed on my butt.

My eyes cried.

I looked up, and my father was on the porch, laughing.

I didn't even feel my nose, just the pit of my stomach. It's a good thing I didn't have the ball in my hand or I would have thrown it all my might right in his face. Right on his nose.

March 8, 1962

Ten years!

Each year is like the whorl on a newly cut tree. I can track back to sometimes the 3rd or 4th ring.

The earliest memory of my father is early in the morning, when he would get up to go to work. He put the smallest sauce-pan on the gas stove and boiled enough water to shave with. He would pull and stretch his face into weird shapes to get into every little crevice. He looked funny and I used to laugh, but he never said anything.

My mother showed me grandfather's gold watch. It had an enamel Sacred Heart painted on it. Someday it would be my watch. From grandfather, to father, to me, to my son, to my great grandson, to . . . I used to sneak into the bedroom when my mother was busy in the kitchen and wind it up and hear it tick. I would stare at the minute hand until I could see it moving. When I wound it up the button made a smooth clicking sound that I really liked. One day I wound it too tight and I heard a snap.

One look and my mother knew I had done something wrong. She kept pressing until between sobs I blurted out my fatal mistake.

"Your father will take care of you, Mister, when he gets home."

"Ma, please, don't tell him. Please, Ma."

She told him.

He looked at me for a minute, never saying a word, then crooked his finger and pulled me on an invisible rope to between his legs where he sat on a kitchen chair. I was ducking and flinching and inching my way to the spot, never close enough, until he squeezed me between his knees. The dam burst.

Usually in these situations he gave me a backhander, but it never arrived. I gradually dried up and puffed to a stop while he sat looking at me. His hands rested on his kneecaps like a priest waiting patiently for a visiting priest to finish a sermon. I gulped my final wordless plea and looked at his face. I was surprised by how close his nose was. I could see the hairs in it. And his face had black smudges on it from his fingers, which had become covered with ink from the newspaper he always read on the bus home.

I thought how tired his eyes looked. His face was sad, and I remember wondering if I was as sad as he was.

Without saying a word, he took my hand in his and opened his knees. I backed up and he rose and took me by the hand like we used to go for an ice-cream cone and led me into the bedroom where he picked up the gold watch.

"You can't wait to have this, can you?"

I was trapped. I knew a yes was as deadly as a no, so I remained speechless, hoping my mother would come to the rescue, but she stood in the doorway and watched. This was one of the times she knew enough to keep quiet.

The time was silent. The gold watch was in front of my face lost in my father's giant hand. I asked God to please let it tick, and I'd never touch it again. Silence.

Still holding the watch in front of my eyes, my father led me through the living room, dining room, kitchen, into the back hall and down the cellar stairs into the darkness.

"Jim, don't. Jim. Jim?"

My mother was too late. The only thing she could do was click on the cellar light, but that wasn't going to help much I knew.

We stopped in front of the furnace. That was a magic place. I used to crouch on the stairs and watch my father start a fire by throwing a jar of kerosene into the furnace. The way the flames used to try to reach out and grab him made me think of a dragon. But that day, there was a good coal fire going.

"Jim? Jim?"

No answer from him, so she tried me.

"Michael? Michael?"

My father let go of my hand, and I noticed how white my fingers were where he had been holding them. With the gold watch still in front of my eyes, he reached across with his other hand, opened the door of the furnace, and as I stood numb, he gently dished the gold watch into the gaping mouth of the dragon. Yellow flames licked the watch, and it began to slide into the glowing red coals.

I looked at his face, and it seemed as if all the faces he used to make while shaving came to his face, except they weren't funny because there were no globs of shaving cream, and the only noise I could hear was my father's heavy breathing, and the red glow flickered on his face, which was sweating and the hairs in his nose were moving.

My mother sifted the lump out of the ashes about three days later. I kept it in a box in the bottom of my bureau, and when my father died I rode back on my bicycle to the cemetery after the funeral and filled the box with dirt from his grave. The men working in the cemetery thought it was funny, but kind of a great thing for a kid to do, but I couldn't help smiling at them.

Now I shave every morning. I very carefully trim the hairs that protrude from my nose with a fingernail clipper.

And I am aware that if one whorl of a tree's life begins to distort in one direction, all the whorls after that are affected by it.

Good Friday, 1963

My pea-brain rattles around in a tin box.

Tonight, I understand.

In a deep-freeze melancholy, I wandered into St. Francis Church for the Holy Thursday Vigil.

My father used to wake me up and we'd go to keep watch from 3 to 4 a.m. on Holy Thursday night. He chose that hour because the fewest people would be there. There were never more than ten. We never spoke much on the way to church, but I used to enjoy the walk. The night was so quiet, the clicks and clacks of our shoes echoed down the streets where such sounds were swallowed by traffic during the day. The large circular window over the main altar I used to think of as the eye of God. During Sunday morning Mass, the sunlight would beam through the colored glass, but during the vigil at night it was a dark eye. Dark, but nevertheless, always watching.

I was thankful my father used to rest his rear on the seat because if I had to kneel up straight all the time I would have minded terribly.

It was during the vigil, I don't remember which one, that I noticed now my hands were exactly like my fathers. The same kind of hair on them, in the same places. Even the fingernails were the same. That was noticeable, because that was the time I stopped biting them after I tore one thumbnail half off and it bled.

The reason I think back to those vigils is that that was the first time I noticed the little tiny knob on the side of my father's nose.

This morning I saw the beginning of a similar little knob on the side of my own nose. It's been there for some time, but I kept dismissing it as a pimple. But I can't claim that anymore. I think that might be why I went to the Vigil tonight for the first time since my father died.

The eye of God was there, still watching. And the structure of the eye became clear to me.

Intricate and unique. Each little twist and turn of cell or molecule in the structure of that eye was the same for my father as for me, except for a slightly different angle of view.

How could he help it? What chance did he have?

What chance do I have?

A.M.R

Chapter 2
Happy Days 1950–54

The days of high school and adolescence were happy. We were a group of 40 young Catholics from different ethnic parishes from all over the city: St. Francis, Irish parish; St. Anthony's, Italian parish; Notre Dame, French parish; and surrounding communities, two Polish parishes and one Irish parish in nearby Adams, Mass.; and some lovely intrepid hearts who were bussed in 24 miles one way from Readsboro, Vermont. Forty of us. The public high school had twenty times as many students. We had a hard time winning anything–baseball, basketball (not enough students or money for a football team), but at Debating we were champs even against the biggest Catholic High School, Cathedral, 3,000 students, in the diocesan city of Springfield, Mass.

We were blessed by being too young for WWII and Korea, and too old and gone away for Viet Nam. Our class was amazingly cohesive, most of us too poor to drive 10 miles to New York State to drink. Mainly, like dry sponges, we just sucked up our teens by learning about life in a benign little commune.

For me, being back in the Italian milieu again after the War was a five-ring circus–except Grandma Cicchetti had passed away, and Grandma Walsh, who used to visit from Boston, had moved with three aunts out to California. So the Irish influence seemed to have disappeared, until years later, when I found out I had been formed, not so much by a middle-class white American society, but more deeply by a very conservative Irish-Catholic society.

Friendships were deep and lasting. The four males left alive of the class are all still in contact, except, to my great sorrow, my closest friend for over 60 years. Trump was the straw that broke the back of our friendship. But I'm getting a bit ahead.

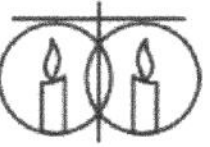

Here is another unpublished short story about *death*: first, involving a stranger, then someone as close to me as humanly possible, and finally as I enter my own psyche. In the Baltimore Catechism of my youth, we young Catholics were introduced to what was termed the Four Last Things: that is, Death, Judgment, Heaven, and Hell. Note that 75% of the Last Things are pretty damn scary. And the first frightening step into the unknown is Death, which consumed me for quite a while. Eventually, I would see myself sinking into Hell, which being eternal, gradually edged out Death in my fears. But first, here's Death.

THE TRAIN

The four o'clock train had been sitting for over 20 minutes on the siding outside the mill. As I walked along the road toward the bridge, I noticed a small clump of people up near the railway trestle.

I padded toward the group, cutting through soot-covered scrub grasses.

Then I saw the arm. It was lying a few feet away from the tracks. It seemed to be perched precariously on the gray rocks of the rail bed. It had been sliced neatly across the forearm. The bone, surrounded by a ring of liver, surrounded by a ring of orange fat, formed a small target that seemed only two-dimensional. The sun was making it greasy. It could have been a melting wax arm. The glitter of a ring reflected the afternoon sun.

I stared. Why wasn't the arm bleeding? As I tried to focus my eyes to see more clearly, I became aware of ragged chunks of bloody flesh, speckled among the rocks, and grass, and on the railway ties, where dark rings indicated the forming of grease spots.

I looked at my feet. I had stepped on a chunk of the flesh. My stomach clutched.

A cop turned from the clump at the trestle and began to run toward me. "Get the hell away from there," he shouted. He waved his hand like an awkward woman.

"I'm sorry," I mumbled. "I didn't know. What happened?"

"Some batty old lady got run over by the train. The engineer thought she was a sack of clothes. The poor guy is all shook up. It wasn't his fault. He couldn't have stopped anyway. Look buddy, you've got to leave. Move it. Move it."

He stared at me until I got down to the road. When I snuck a look the second time, he was walking back towards the trestle. The members of the clump were walking through the grass near the edge of the trestle. I could hear them shouting, "Here's some more over here."

"Yeah, over here, too."

"What a mess."

A blue panel truck from Ferris' Garage bounced across the bridge toward me. The two Ferris brothers jumped out. Louie, the butcher, still had his dirty white apron on. Jimmy, the mechanic, had on a pair of greasy coveralls.

Louie grabbed me by the arm. "What happened? What happened?"

"Some lady just got run over up on the trestle."

Jimmy was running by me up towards the tracks. I saw him running, and then I heard screams. I didn't realize at first that it was the same man screaming, "Oh sweet Jesus." The scream ended in a choking sob. Louie dropped my arm and ran toward the tracks. The searchers were frozen among the grass, staring toward the brothers.

A cop grabbed Louie just as he reached the spot where Jimmy was hunched on the ground rocking back and forth. Louie busted the cop in the mouth with an elbow. But as the first cop reeled back, two others grappled him back and held him against a train switch. Louie struggled and pulled as Jimmy keened on in long sharp wails.

"Let me go, you bastards. That's my mother. That's my mother's ring. Oh, momma, momma."

The cops and trainmen swarmed over the brothers. Jimmy was supported by three men and came away from the tracks quietly and haltingly. Four cops dragged and pulled Louie down from the tracks to the panel truck. One young cop was trying to soothe him. But two of the others beat him against the door of the truck, slapping him in the face.

"I thought I told you to get the hell out of here." I began to walk toward the bridge in agonizingly slow motion. My eyes seemed to be seeing too much. Things far and near merged into a mass of crystal-like images.

*

I had walked through the back door into the kitchen every day. Mother was always over the stove cooking. Today I opened the door and did not see my mother. I saw a fat brown woman, with wispy gray hairs falling on a wrinkled neck. Her big drooping body hung limply. The colors of her clothes blurred. How fat those two arms were. And even though I looked at the back of her head, I could see the Rice Krispies around her eyes. I wanted to hug and kiss and squeeze her.

To hug and kiss and squeeze her harder and harder and harder.

I backed out the door, and it clicked shut as loudly as a casket cover.

II

The train pulled through northern Maine, swirls of December snow flowing from the sides of the cars like foam from the prow of a boat.

The telegram had been brief. COME HOME IMMEDIATELY STOP DADDY HEART ATTACK STOP IN HOSPITAL STOP MOTHER

The Registrar, Fr. Edwards, propped on two crutches in the Registrar's wicket had been adamant about my missing Christmas quizzes. It couldn't be permitted. I had become brave at 18 and told him, "My father is dying and I'm going home, and I don't care what you do about it." He blinked at me.

My mother was not crying. She said, "He's stayed alive to see you." As the elevator door sliced her from my view and caused my ascension, I knew that tears would be popping from her eyes.

The oxygen tent made it seem as if I were peering at him through a mist. He hadn't been shaved, and a towel was draped over his head. He smiled.

"Get my horse and spear, son, and we'll tilt some windmills." He did look like a knight with that towel draped over his head.

For the first time since I got the telegram I had hope, but that night the doctor told me there was no hope, no hope at all. This was the second attack in less than five years.

They wouldn't let my mother go to the hospital anymore after that. Her own heart was too weak.

The next morning, he couldn't talk. I stayed alone with him in the room from 8 a.m. to midnight.

The next day was the last. The watch started early in the morning. He was breathing in chain respiration. Short rattles of gasping, long moments of silence, then short rattling gasps. The pauses became longer and longer. I recited the Penitential psalms from the college prayer-book, over and over and over again.

My hand was on his knee. I could feel his knee growing harder and stiffer and colder. My fingers ached but I refused to let go.

About midnight, my cousin Angie, a nurse, came and said, "There's nothing you can do here. You have to go home and put your mother to bed." I didn't want to leave. I knew what would happen once I left the room.

I went.

As I walked in the front door of the house the phone rang, and I was glad I had left the hospital to be home for my mother to hold on to. She heaved with heavy sighs.

It was 20 degrees below zero the day of the funeral. Flowers and some kind of fake grass hid the frozen clods of earth. Wind whipped the tent flaps so loudly I couldn't hear the murmur of the priest.

Momma was strong–my brother and sister were quiet.

I rode home in the front seat of the limousine and looked back at the long train of cars puffing gray exhaust.

That afternoon, after all the aunts and uncles left after the big meal was finished, I went into Momma's bedroom where she sat on the edge of the big double bed. I put my head in her lap and said, "Momma, I haven't cried because . . ." and she stopped me.

"I know," she said, "thank you. You can cry now."

I cried myself to sleep.

III

Last November, I jumped out of bed on a Sunday morning with a terrible charley horse in my left leg. I felt faint–and as I bent to put my head between my legs to get blood to my brain, I knew I was going to fall.

I tried to call to my wife.

I couldn't grab anything to hold on the wall. My head exploded in a blast of lightning. The pain. The pain.

It was probably my heart. I was sure it was my heart. It must be my heart.

My wife bent over me. "What's the matter, honey?"

"I don't know. I can't feel the left side of my head. My left side is numb."

She threw a blanket over me and went to the phone. I could hear her saying ". . . some kind of attack . . ."

In the doorway, my youngest daughter called to the others, "Come see funny Daddy, falling on the floor."

I looked up and smiled at them, thinking how good it was to see them all together before I left.

I didn't leave.

The doctor got me into the bed, took my blood pressure, explored my chest and back with his stethoscope, and informed me that I was as strong as a horse. A mere fainting spell. Too bad about hitting my head on the tile-covered cement floor.

IV

Tonight, I finished reading *The Algiers Motel Incident*, which is about the three negro boys murdered by the Detroit police during the Detroit riots. The truth about that situation will never be fully known. The brutality of the murders is hard to imagine.

Death.

But I can imagine what it must be like. It must be like getting hit by a train. A blinding burst of lightning and pain. Lightning and pain. White flashing lightning. White.

[You will note that certain memes (and people) are appearing in succeeding works, with noticeable variations of tone, texture or particulars. This pattern of repetitious variation will be with me to the end. The complexity of their meanings

will reflect the changes in my life and my understanding of challenging life experiences and relationships.]

The high school years created rich memories for me. I evaluated those memories in my speech as class president four decades after we all scattered to the four winds.

On Returning Home Forty Years after High School Graduation

"You're a grand old school, with your purple and gold,
Which will always uphold our faith;
With your emblem too, and courage true,
Victoriously we shall rise!" were stolen lyrics from a Broadway musical.

We were good at that.

"It's a grand night for singing, the moon is bright above."

Every kid was in the musical, and every living relative was in the audience.

How else could hissing clarinets seduce the crowd to ecstasy in "My Blue Heaven"?

How else could "The Little Dutch Mill" earn an encore, with Carol Adams singing alto as I sang soprano wearing Mary Agnes Gould's blue snow pants and the sequined blouse of the girl I would marry? The school musical was a symbol of the way we would face the world–everybody in it, no optioning out, everybody's spark of talent tapped to the root. Such triumphs were necessary in a school winless for four years in basketball and baseball.

The class of '54 was a winner for all four years–at selling Christmas cards so we could get a party at the Old St. Joes School Hall. Winning that party would prove as important to me as winning the Korean War. (The object of my desire and dreams would come out for the class parties, which meant four opportunities to spend time with her–a prime tactic in my strategy of seeking her affection!)

The cataclysmic moment of my destiny would strike like lightning at our Freshman reception. *She* was sitting there, composed and serene, eyes cast down, untouchable, saintly, and otherworldly. I turned to Mel and said, "There's the girl I'm going to marry!"

And the next four years turned into a strategic campaign worthy of a Byzantine Emperor aided by so many of you, my classmates. Years later, my children would ask their valedictorian mother, "If you were so smart, Mum, how come you married Dad?"

Answer: "I just got tired." A war of attrition that outlasted the Trojan War by a full year. Forty years later, a rare triumph for continuing peaceful relations between complete opposites.

Our keepers for the four years at St. Joe's were as different as the seasons of the year. The Winter of the cool, imperious Sister Loretta Joseph, who insisted that the covering over a building was not the bark of an ignorant dog–"ruff, ruff"–but the carefully enunciated and civilized "rooof."

The Spring of the tender, loving care of Sister Agnes Clare, who could nurture and bring to life the germ of goodness in the heart of any one she came in contact with.

The Summer of the arbitrary yet enthusiastic Sister Helen Theresa, who shone on all her charges with a hot staring critical eye.

Last, and in no way least, the fruitful Autumn of Sister Eleanor Maria who brought all to ripeness and triumphal graduation: the goddess of fulfilment who sought to hook our wagons to the stars. She was our only winning coach and the debating stage her arena of encounter with the future. An irresistible force meeting an immovable object, she was a rare amalgam of substance and style, reason and emotion, soldier and actor, servant and master, nun and bishop. If the age had permitted tournament jousting, she might singlehandedly have conquered the Russians! With astute political skill, she manipulated the Affirmative and Negative Debating teams: she never put Jackie and me on the same side.

Sister Eleanor Maria's willing champion and prime press agent Monsignor John P. Donahue–Remember another stolen tune?

"Hail, Monsignor Donahue,
Shout till the rafters ri-inng"?

Front row, l-r: Mary Ellen Spencer, Monsignor John P. Donahue, Fr. Leonard Burke, Jacqueline Duguay, Back row, l-r: John Koonz, Mary Derengowski, Jane Burke, Patrick Walsh, Francis Peter Millette, and William Sullivan.

Given half a chance, he would have nuked the commies into oblivion. Yet he gave his anxious heart and soul and mind and body totally to the kids of St. Joseph's School and the Sisters of St. Joseph. Espousing so zealously his church's knightly code he alienated many, yet the earthly hell that collapsed around his withering white head was a road he paved with good intentions–he wanted the best, as he understood it, for those in his sacred charge.

After all, the Monsignor brought us the enigmatic Frank Matrango who would rock our boat near to swamping until we caught on that he was really a gruff old teddy bear.

He was flummoxed by Mary Ellen's photographic memory and Donnie Filiault's statistical recall. Donnie almost singlehandedly drove Bucky Bullet's sports quiz off the air.

Free on weekends, we could take off for the hot spots–like Pedrin's Miniature Golf, where Mel and I were left behind one night when Mary Ellen and Jackie drove off and left us. [Of course, they did come back to drive us home, which gave us both hope!]

Or how about all the way into the Dalton intersection for the new 19 cent hamburger and 15 cent frappe–the burger so small with an obscene little dropping of mustard and relish, for cryin' out loud, and the frappe so thick to suck you wouldn't have enough energy left for a hickey–and with a stupid name like that old farmer, McDonald, how could such an outfit ever succeed?

The *St. Joseph's Scribe* school newspaper logged our triumphs, and our defeats, our joys, and our sorrows, the May celebrations processing to the shrine of the Blessed Virgin Mary, the Passion play each Lent, the Senior Class play, in which Sr. Eleanor Maria took advantage of the actual chemistry of our furtive love lives.

I hung around the paper, becoming the Scribe artist, not out of any inspired artistic intent, but just to hang around the editor. The campaign continued. Frank Matrango, to help me out, got in trouble for asking on her exam paper if Jackie had a date for the Christmas Ball.

Remember those annual excursions into the outside world at Look Park? The opportunities for otherworldly social experiences in an exotic setting–a veritable Club Med of the fifties? I can remember to this day what *she* was wearing: black toreadors and a red sweater! A true age of innocence!

MISTER Matrango cemented his memory in our hearts by blasting a home run in the softball game to beat the Junior Class–a true All-American!

The Class Trip to Washington DC is etched in our collective memories like a Currier and Ives calendar: The infamous Lincoln Hotel where Clare Nary made her Paul Revere bounce from room to room and bed to bed announcing the bedbugs were coming!

The dreamlike flight through the night to Annapolis on the bus with *her* in my arms, transformed into a nightmare when Father Burke scolded, "Enough of that, enough of that."

We stood proudly in front of the Capitol for the long wide camera shot.

We prayed silently in the sacred presence of the Lincoln Memorial.

We rode the rollercoaster at Palisades Park, even if we really didn't want to.

On the return to the hotel, we were higher than kites on the Empire State Building and lower than whale droppings because of a candied apple. [*2019 comment: The other couples were smooching, but 'you know who' whiled away her time eating the candied apple I had been foolish enough to buy her!*]

The parties we had were notable for what is now called on TV "slow dancing."

Was there anything to do more sensuous and delectable and subversive? You bet your life. And we did, after graduating, of course.

Graduation was a blur, and after a long lingering evening in "The Mill on the Floss," it was over–we slid each to a new life, some to remain in North Adams and Adams and Readsboro, and some to Morocco and Canada and Ireland and Puerto Rico and Iowa and California.

And miracle of miracles, the class president would marry the valedictorian and they would live happily ever after—well, not quite so easily as it is done in the movies—for we all left the warm and nourishing womb of St. Joe's and entered the buzzing, whirling, flashing, universe known as "the real world!"

What a helluva surprise, eh?

Here we are together again forty years later, battered and bruised and assaulted by the harsh realities of life. Have we changed? You bet your life—literally. Willie is gone to rest, and the rest of us are exercising the only alternative: existing, surviving, enduring—going fiercely and defiantly into that dark night.

We are older, if not wiser, because we have been challenged in both mind and body.

We have witnessed and experienced pains and heartaches we were too innocent to anticipate. We have worked out a method of coping with change—some in tune with our inherited traditions, some driven to new awareness of foreign and exotic philosophies—but all of us formed and imprinted in mind and soul by our common experience at St. Joseph's High School.

In the secret recesses of our own hearts, we have managed to survive the assault of the world on our souls working out as best we could our relationships with our Creator or whatever Force or Mind rules the universe of things and ideas.

We have not been alone in that journey to the present here—Sister Eleanor Maria, who came to visit us in Canada, I didn't recognize at the airport, because from the woman who towered over us, she has shrunk at least three feet, slowed by heart attacks and age. Surprise—she wasn't much older than we were—St. Joe's was her first assignment!

Tonight she retires as President of Our Lady of the Elms College to be replaced by Sister Maura James. Eleanor Maria is now Mary Dooley, Maura James is now Kathleen Sullivan, and Loretta Joseph is now a French Countess, having abandoned the congregation and her doctoral studies in Paris to get married and live in a chateau with a probably splendid rooof! (Remember how she criticized our hick pronunciation of "ruff" as undignified?)

A couple of years ago, Jackie and I found Frank Matrango on Cape Cod lucky to be alive after serious heart struggles. He bubbled with stories of his "wunder" years at St. Joe's. He admitted he misses the Berkshires terribly–and he was scared to death of us when he came to teach in '53. His cocky swagger and self-assurance hid a trembling psyche–he was petrified. Perhaps after the fact we can better appreciate how he must have felt–we were as strange to him, as he was to us.

The last time I saw a frail Monsignor Donahue shortly before he died, he had 37 cents in his pocket. Whatever faults he may have had were certainly outweighed by his generous and loving care of those in need.

The Church we lived in during our four years in Paradise has changed too. Vatican Council II broke the back of a repressive institution, and it has been chaos ever since.

The golden age has become tarnished. Priests and sisters have disappeared. St. Joseph's is now an empty shell devoid of the laughter and raucous noise of children, hallowed halls echoing instead with the wheezing of the aged–an old folks home.

Adam and Eve were driven from the Garden, Cain slew Abel, America scrambled from Korea to Viet Nam to Beirut and the Gulf to Haiti. We have scrambled for our lives too–married, divorced, borne children, and lost family–we have prayed, despaired, fallen and risen again–but we have endured and come face to face with the essence of human experience–our destiny is to suffer and die.

St. Joe's told us that but we didn't really know what it meant until we left the cocoon. We have had moments of joy and exaltation and achievement as well, for to appreciate the pain we must experience the joy–thus we come to know the true price we are paying for life.

Not despite, but because of, the assault of the world on us, we each recognize there are no definitive answers to the essential problems of human existence in reasonable and human terms. The only answers to life's mysteries are beyond the grave in the realm of the spirit, in the realm of faith. We find such answers in the depths of our hearts, in the peace surpassing understanding.

The bonds we were privileged to share in our years at St. Joe's are beyond understanding. They are whispers and murmurings in our memories. The childlike gladness, the innocent desires, the adolescent secrets, the dreams and aspirations, the help and kindnesses, the darts and arrows of teenage angst, the discoveries of learning, the thrill and agonies of first love, the victories and defeats of dreams and nightmares, the sharing and the comforting, have been part of our ability to survive the greater challenges that were lying in wait for us.

I have stood on windswept beaches in Ireland, mountain tops in the Canadian Rockies, rocky coves in Nova Scotia, forests in Austria, at the Colosseum in Rome, joyful with a child in my arms, helpless with a child-created broken heart, peaceful hand in hand with Jacqueline—each of these moments was endured with a knowledge of a common bond with the Class of '54.

My encounters with the matter and energy and spirit of the universe have given me a realization of the unity of all life. Our four years together were a foreshadowing and prologue to the four decades to come.

Whatever has been of worth in life was experienced in miniature in our four years—the patterns are as universal as the myth of Adam and Eve and the Garden, as Jesus and his passion, as the generating of new life, as the following of parents and the leaving of children, as the laying down of our lives in the service of others, as the witnessing that, yes, Love IS possible.

For both these sufferings and blessings we have shared I give deep thanks to you all, and to the Power that made such deep human experiences possible.

God bless you all, Class of '54.

I have tried to give you a taste of my Italian background, and a wee bit of my Irish background, which will be fleshed out soon. But underlying all my life experiences has been my Roman Catholic background. Of all the experiences of my life, my Catholic background has been the most tumultuous.

Remember my Uncle Tony's son-in-law, Bob Moulton, a convert who became an ordained Deacon in the Catholic Church? He and I were very close, and much of our closeness was the Catholicity I was born into, and which he bought in to. A simple phone call from Bob triggered a retrospective of my ever-evolving Catholicity.

Patrick X Walsh

A Thanksgiving Phone Call

When I hung up the phone, memories of my Catholic childhood and youth flooded my mind. But, gentle reader, as my wife reminds me, my memory is often faulty, which may be an occupational hazard for a professor and playwright. But, as I am driven to write by some inner force beyond my control, I shall proceed in the light of the following wisdom:

> *Whoever thinks that in this mortal life one may so disperse the mists of the imagination as to possess the unclouded light of unchangeable truth, understands neither: neither what he seeks nor who he is that seeks it.*
>
> –Augustine

Here's what washed up on the shore after my tsunami of memories.

Imprinting the Tabula Rasa

The first poem I learned at my mother's knee was:

"Lovely Lady, dressed in blue,
Teach me how to pray.
God was just your little boy,
Tell me what to say.
Did you lift him up sometimes,
Gently on your knee?
Did you read to Him
The way Mother reads to me?
Lovely Lady, dressed in blue,
Teach me how to pray.
God was just your little boy,
Tell me what to say."
Another early prayer was:
"Angel of God, my guardian dear,

To whom God's love commits me here:
Ever this day be at my side,
To light and guard, to rule and guide.

Amen."

I remember once, when my mother was in the hospital, even before I made my first communion, staying with my Uncle John and Aunt Agnes out on State Highway, where they lived near a turkey farm with a constant babble and gobble in the air. They used to get up early on Sunday and take me to the 6 a.m. Mass at St. Francis Church, the Irish church. We always sat in the back row of the packed, darkened church, and I could never see what was going on. I did want to see what was going on up front.

The Mass

When our family went to the Italian church, St. Anthony of Padua, and I finally saw the ceremony of the Mass, I was enthralled. I loved the candles, the flowers, the statues, the colorful vestments and robes, the mesmerizing stately movement of altar boys and priests, and enveloping all, the songs and the rumbling of the organ, and the soaring sound of the choir. A mysterious world unfolded before me, drawing me to explore its uncharted realm. Whatever was going on must certainly be very important, for my parents and everyone else were deeply entranced. The hum of the Latin puzzled and intrigued us at the same time. What secrets lay behind these magical goings on? How quiet everyone could suddenly become; bells would ring, sweet-smelling smoke would rise heavenward!

Later, at home, over my ordinary clothes, I cinched up one of my mother's black dresses and said Mass on a card table with candles, a wine goblet of juice, and a Ritz cracker of a host, with my little sister serving as altar-boy/girl. The Mass was a mysterious and powerful ritual which obviously made me, mother's first, a very special child. She used to whisper to her friends about my little liturgical dramas and mention how thrilled she would be if I became a priest.

I did not know then what I found out much later: that she had suffered a heart attack while carrying me; that the non-Catholic lady doctor had presented my father with the classic choice of "saving your child or saving your wife?" Being a college educated Catholic [Niagara College with the Vincentians] father gave the right answer: "Do your best to save them both."

Mama's Promise

The doctor did. And in gratitude, my mother promised the Blessed Virgin Mary to do all in her power to encourage me to become a priest. So very early on, I absorbed the encouragement and believed I would become a priest–which seemed to me a very fine lot in life. We always had priests at the house. One day, my father told me, "Pat, priests are very lonely men, they need friends." So I was used to seeing priests at the house for Mother's fine Italian cooking, followed by card-playing with Father, with the men stripped to their undershirts on hot summer nights, enjoying a cold beer. Mother was always adopting priests: especially Italian priests, or one crippled priest from the Irish parish who played the violin while she sang. Mother was in demand as a singer in Church for both weddings and funerals.

The Sacrilegious Altar Boy

I became an altar-boy about age five before making my first communion–which was unusual. Our small parish in Sidney, New York, was in dire need of altar servers, and the priest, during a card game, asked my father why I couldn't be an altar boy; after all, I was pretty big for my age. Not having made my first communion was no obstacle to the priest–the Sisters would teach me the prayers, in Latin in those days, and my first communion could be accelerated.

So I made my first confession without really grasping the finer points of the sacrament. My mother had always proclaimed that I was a good boy, a fine boy, and that I was destined for the priesthood. I got in the confessional box, and in the dark panicked. I had no sins! I made up some sins, which seemed to do the job, and the priest knew who I was, and gave me a couple prayers to say, and I was at the church that Sunday with the rest of the kids who were older.

When the priest came down from the altar to give us communion, we filed up and knelt down at the altar rail and received the host, and then we went back to our front-row seat. To this day, I don't understand what happened next. The priest went back up the steps of the altar, fussed a bit, and then came back down to the altar rail to give communion again–I suppose to the rest of the congregation. Some of my fellow first communicants–all girls, as I recall–went up to the altar-rail again. Not wanting to be wrong, I started up again, and the next thing I know my father grabbed me by the shoulder and ushered me back to my seat. I was mortified. Not a good beginning for a future priest.

My problems were only beginning. The next Sunday I was on the altar serving Mass–but really did not know the Latin responses–which were incomprehensible mumbo jumbo. So I mumbled and stumbled and tumbled through a response, which the priest charitably ignored. He went up the three steps and then went to the right to read the Epistle. I DID know that when the time came for me to move the book to the other side of the altar, the priest, with his back to the people, would reach out with his left hand and touch the altar. He did, and I genuflected, circled to the right, went up and got the book, carried it down the steps, genuflected again and took it up the steps to the other side of the altar for the reading of the Gospel. Survival.

At a subsequent Sunday, a visiting priest said Mass, and while reading the Epistle, I noticed he had a really twitchy little finger on his left hand–it kept wiggling up and down, up and down. I thought he must have some kind of disease to cause such an ever more violent twitching–until he finally just lifted the book and carried it to the other side of the altar for the Gospel. I felt sick–another gaffe–he didn't touch the altar–he just twitched his finger–THAT was the signal. My future ordination began to grow into a mountainous challenge instead of a forgone coronation.

Every Saturday afternoon, my father and I walked to church for confession. I merrily made up and recounted sins to our friend, the card-playing priest, received a gentle absolution and went to communion–once–at each Mass. Then some beastly little friend informed me in a casual conversation that "If you tell a lie in confession, you commit a *sacrilege*." I knew about lying, but not knowing what a sacrilege was, I asked, much to my regret for the next decade. Answer: "A sacrilege is a sin against something sacred–and it is so bad it can't be forgiven and the sinner is doomed to hell!"

Thus began my life as a double agent, a schizophrenic sinner-saint: a good Catholic boy destined for the priesthood, and a secret committer of sacrilege week after week–a monster of unforgivable depravity. The standard symbolism of light and darkness, happiness and sadness, truth and falsehood, heaven and hell, good and evil, was in the very marrow of my rotten little bones. With no way out, I played the role of a Catholic Gemini for the next nine years.

Good Days and Bad Days

Fortunately, the bifurcation of my life was balanced. I was a good boy in a loving and close-knit family, with a mother who was a great cook, and a father who was smart and kind. When I was sick, my father could sit beside the bed, lay his cool hand on my fevered brow, and I would become peaceful and calm. My mother always made me feel like a prince–so much so, that I conned my little sister, Mary Ann, into playing the Little Maid to my Little Prince. When my little brother (seven years younger) arrived, I could see in him the goodness, warmth, and athletic excellence missing in my own life hidden behind my façade of piety: Fran really *was* a good boy.

We had family get-togethers with my mother's family, a mélange of wild and crazy, hugging, kissing Italians who were forever singing, laughing and arguing about anything and everything. Most of my father's family had gone to Boston long ago, except for Uncle John. Weekends occasioned rotating Italian family feasts, especially after the War, the Big One–WWII–at Aunt Bessie and Uncle Pete Pessalano's, Aunt Annie and Uncle Tony Cardillo's, Aunt Mary and Uncle Tony Cicchetti's, Aunt Arolyn and Uncle Joe Cicchetti's, and Aunt Angie and Uncle Leo Mullen's. [Angie was daughter of Aunt Annie, so really Mother's niece and my first cousin, but being nearly as old as my mother, she became her best friend.] Uncle Leo, like my father, Francis "Duke" Walsh, was another quiet, wise, and kind Irishman who ended up in this mad Italian vortex!

We had good days, when I was in my good-boy mode: birthdays, VE Day [end of the War in Europe]. VJ Day, end of WWII, when our prayers for victory after Mass at the foot of the altar were finally answered. And we had bad days, when I was in my sacrilegious mode: Mother nearly died after Fran was born on leap year day 1944–which couldn't possibly be because of my badness? Cousin Gerald Pessalano, who used to babysit me, was killed in Luzon in the Philippines on the last day of the war. [I was the altar boy for his funeral in 1947 with the incense censer at the front of the parade down the Main Street of North Adams, when he was brought home for burial.]

The Baltimore Catechism: The Rules of Morality

The Baltimore catechism became the source of my middle-class, white New England, American, Catholic upbringing; I would realize, years later, while pursuing a PhD at the National University of Ireland, that it had been really a very conservative Irish-Catholic upbringing:

Here are the first questions in the Baltimore Catechism:

Who made the world? God made the world. Who is God? God is the Creator of Heaven and earth and of all things? What is man? Man is a creature composed of body and soul, and made to the likeness of God. Why did God make you? God made me to know Him, to love Him, and to serve him in this world, and to be happy with him forever in the next.

Obviously an impossible fate for the likes of me–hopelessly trapped into living a happy Catholic boyhood on the outside, and being the most miserable of sinners on the inside: openly loved by family, secretly despised by myself and, without doubt, by God, who, one dreaded day, I would stand before to hear my inevitable personal judgment: "Depart ye cursed into the everlasting hellfire!"

I could recite the Ten Commandments, the gifts of the Holy Ghost [not a Spirit yet!], the difference between a Mortal and a Venial sin, the seven Sacraments, and on and on. I had to pass through several stages of life before realizing that morality is not primarily about rules and commandments, but about making a journey towards God and happiness, about becoming a moral agent who knows how to struggle with hard decisions and decide what is right as we shape our lives and choose paths to take. [Fr. Timothy Radcliffe OP]

Yet in my young yearning heart of hearts, I believed this Roman Catholic Church was a good and beautiful institution. It embraced my parents and family. The Pope, Pius XII, was a saintly man, because my mother loved him and my father admired him. The Church and my parents were good and true, the trouble was me. I did so much want to be like them.

St. Anthony of Padua – The Italian Parish

The Italian church had a thriving congregation, with a Pastor, Fr. Mangiello, popular and beloved, who was succeeded by Fr. Roccopriore, a kindly, rotund little man with a thick Italian accent, whose sternest words were to the women of the parish: "Please, please, ladies, do notta kiss the feet of the new statues. You lipasticka makea the statues looks like a piecea raw meat!"; and a young, handsome, athletic, modern American-Italian priest, Fr. Russo, and a Fr. Posco. The Venerini Sisters, who were all tiny and would have fit in well with a bunch of hobbits, had a little school. I remember staying there sometimes in the summer when my mother was in the hospital. We always took afternoon naps, with the window shades drawn and a soft glow of yellow sunlight bathing the room. The Sons of Italy fraternal society was active, and the parish sponsored sports teams, including the St. Anthony Crusaders Football Team. My Cardillo cousins, Pete and Fran were stars, until Pete went off to the Aleutians to navigate a PB24Y in WWII. At meals at Aunt Annie's, I sat on the bench between Pete and Fran, who were Goliaths in my eyes, and who taught me not to smack my food or chew loudly, because every time I did they elbowed me unmercifully. My arms were black and blue and sore until I was thirteen–in my memory, at least.

St. Anthony's was a going concern, with three priests and the nuns. The Parish was fundraising to build a new church, because St. Anthony's was a little church, pretty non-descript, off Holden Street, up an alley across from the Sprague Electric Company–North Adams' principal employer. Most of the Italian immigrants arriving in North Adams in the early twentieth century found work in the textile mills and shoe factories clustered along the Hoosac and Hoosick rivers. The Parish and their priests were the Italians' protection against the dominant Protestant class in the city of some 20,000 souls.

St. Francis of Assisi – The Irish Parish

In the 1940s and 50s, the Irish parish of St. Francis Church in the center of town was a larger church, with a Monsignor Dunphy and Fathers Scanlon, noble and stately; Murphy, a giant of a man with an ever-present five-o'clock shadow, and Burke, a roly-poly glad-hander. Others who came and went earlier included

Fr. Tom Sampson, a big man appropriately named, and Fr. Nicholson, who played basketball with us and whose brother would end up being my roommate at college in Canada. At St. Francis the Knights of Columbus were the Catholic counterpart to the ruling forces of the Fraternal Order of the Masons.

The parish had a school, the original my father attended, and which was the brick Old School hall when I attended the big, new stone St. Joseph's High School across the street. The original rectory was torn down and a huge new rectory built beside the church, where the old convent for the Sisters of St. Joseph, before they moved into a new convent built for them in the 1960s by Monsignor John P. Donahue.

When he built the new convent, nearly bankrupting the parish, he knew that the rickety old convent's plaster ceilings were falling down on the sisters as they slept. He loved those sisters. The last time I saw him on a visit from Canada shortly before he died, he revealed to me that he had 37 cents in his pocket, and he couldn't understand why the people's weekly contributions were fading away. I understood that many parishioners were turned off: his fiery sermons against the "communists" and the "garbage pails of secular colleges" were driving people out of the pews. He was a terror in the pulpit, but a saint to so many people down and out and in need–a throwback to an earlier age.

Monsignor Donahue encouraged my vocation to the diocesan priesthood and encouraged my father to send me to St. Francis Xavier University in Nova Scotia, renowned for producing many priests.

"Duke" Walsh and Carmen Cicchetti

In the 1930s, when my father's family moved to Boston, he stayed in North Adams to work and to court my mother. My father had admired her for several years from a distance, and never made a move, until one day while he was having a meal at his best friend's house, Tony Cicchetti's house, in walked Tony's youngest sister, Carmen–the young woman my father had cherished in mind only. In 1936, they married [the consecration of their family to the Sacred Heart of Jesus on the day of their wedding hangs today in my home in pride of place], and the next year I was baptized at St. Anthony's parish. This was not according to rules and regulations: for my father had been raised a member of St.

Francis Parish, had attended St. Joseph's School, grammar and high, and while married in his wife's parish, should have been attending St. Francis Parish, like his brother John. But father was an athlete and ball player, and his friends and new extended family were all at St. Anthony's, so that's where we went for Mass. Father even helped Uncle Tony going door to door soliciting funds to build the new St. Anthony's Church.

My father was daily communicant and loyal Catholic all his short life. He read the *Tablet* newspaper, a Catholic paper from Brooklyn, which was sold outside the church on Sundays, along with the *New York Times*. The *Times* was our entertainment, spread out all over the living room Sunday afternoons before the arrival of television in our lives.

Father was friends with priests, but he didn't take any guff from them. We never had a car, so he used to walk to Mass at six in the morning, then walk down the Main Street to Brackley's News and Tobacco shop for a paper, and then wait for a ride to work. One morning in Brackley's, a Catholic man he knew from the Irish church had a heart attack and was dying. My father went the phone and called the rectory for a priest. The priest [not anyone named earlier–a young fellow who was around very briefly] answered the call and asked, "What parish does he belong to?" My father never told me exactly what he said–I never heard my father swear ever, and he rarely got angry–but the priest got the message loud and clear that if he wasn't at Brackley's posthaste, he would never answer a telephone call again. A dying man–from any parish at any time–with his immortal life at stake–must be attended to! He was.

"Duke" Walsh vs. Monsignor Dunphy

During WWII, our family moved out of town where my father worked for a magneto factory. When we moved back to North Adams after the war, we started to go to St. Anthony's again. We were living next to a public school where I went because it was easier for my mother. When I finished grade 8 at public school, there was no question but that I would attend St. Joseph's High School. Students from other schools had to pay tuition, so father decided it was time for the family to go back to St. Francis Parish, a fiscally and politically prudent move. When father went to the Irish rectory to register, Father Scanlon told him that he could not do so. "Why not?" says father.

"I don't know," says Fr. Scanlon, "but it's orders from Monsignor Dunphy. You'll have to see him."

"Get him," says Father.

Monsignor Dunphy is wheeled into the office. The question is put.

Says Monsignor Dunphy, "Do you remember you were raising money to build that Eye-talian church? Well, that's where you can stay."

Says Father, "I'm going to the Bishop."

"So go," says Dunphy. Father did.

That fall I entered St. Joseph's High School, *sans* tuition, to the great benefit of my sacrilegious self. The very first day I espy and admire from afar, in father's manner, a *tres jolie* French girl from Notre Dame Church, a block up the street from St. Francis Parish.

Notre Dame – The French Parish

Notre Dame Parish of that day was another going concern with a pastor and two priests serving parishioners of Quebec origin making a livelihood in the textile mills and shoe factories with the other poor Catholics. The church was reminiscent of French architectural flourishes, but not quite as large as the Irish church. The organist was there for the magnificent organ, but not necessarily for the liturgy. He delighted in thrashing out tunes employing every pipe and pedal. He was good, and he knew it.

The Sisters of St. Anne had a convent set back beside the church, and they ran a grammar school with a playground divided by a mesh wire fence to keep the boys and girls at play separated from any occasion of sin! The vestments at Notre Dame were very French with fleurs-de-lis galore, and albs of intricate lace. The priests vestments were laid out in precise patterns: cincture looped in patterns, chasuble and alb draped precisely over the cabinet counter. The masses were mostly in French, but a later one in English. Certain elegance permeated the ceremonies. Whenever our family caught a more convenient Mass there, because the church was near Aunt Annie's on Liberty Street, the sermons seemed terribly long because I didn't understand the words. In my college years, a truly saintly, wise, and effervescent French priest, Fr. John P. Richard, would become my spiritual director and encourage my vocation. He was conveniently the spiritual director of the French girl and encouraged her vocation, too.

In addition to these solidly established parishes, later there was a satellite church called Holy Family out on the road to Williamstown in the shadow of Mount Greylock.

Catholics in Their Place

In the social strata of North Adams, I came to understand that Catholics were not in the upper echelons. We were the laboring classes. Aunt Annie worked part-time in the Jarish Box Factory and cleaned for the Flood family on posh Church Street. Her husband, Uncle Tony Cardillo, worked on the road crew for the city. I loved to go on the truck with him to repair the asphalt roads. Uncle Pete worked on the railroad. Uncle Joe drove a bus. Uncle Tony Cicchetti was highest up the scale, an optician, who every year traded in for a pink Cadillac, to demonstrate to all and sundry his heightened standing. My mother and father were the first children in their families to go to college, father in business, and mother at the local Normal School for teachers.

NO DOGS

My father didn't talk much about his family, and years later while in Ireland I discovered that most likely my great-grandfather, Sean Walsh, had come over to North America during the Irish troubles in the late 1800s. He had been quarantined on an island off Montreal in the St. Lawrence because of plague on the boat. He met a Miss Norah Barnes on the boat, and the two of them escaped and entered the United States illegally, going down the freedom road via Lake Champlain, to settle in Dorset, Vermont.

Even my father remembered seeing signs in shops and businesses reading "NO DOGS, NO IRISH." The Irish were not welcomed in many places, and it wasn't really until John F. Kennedy was elected president of the US in 1960 that the Irish arrived in the upper classes. Even in 1960 there were some non-Catholics in North Adams who spread rumors–how seriously I can't imagine–that there were guns in the cellar of the old St. Joe's school and the Catholic churches that would arm the Catholics for takeover of the USA if Kennedy got elected. There was another joke going about that the final message of Our Lady of Fatima would be opened in 1960 and that it would say "Vote Kennedy." Others maintained that it would be the bill for the Last Supper.

My paternal grandfather, Patrick, for whom I was named, was born in Dorset, Vermont, becoming a stone cutter in the granite quarries until silicosis of the lungs drove him to North Adams, where he became a policeman and met Helen Lanoue, of French descent. The earliest memory I can recall is being rocked in my Grandma Walsh's arms in our house on West Main Street–comfortable, safe, and loved and petted. Grandma had been born in Westfield, Massachusetts, and as I liked to think years later while living in Nova Scotia, had been descended from French prisoners deported from Louisbourg by the English and New Englanders after the fall of that French Fortress in 1758 and dispersed to the western hinterlands of the Massachusetts Commonwealth. Years later, I wrote a play performed at Fortress Louisbourg and named the heroine Helene Lanoue.

Dandelions

The Italian immigrants, including my forefathers, were not allowed to live in the city of North Adams, but were consigned to the hillside dumps across the railway tracks to the west of the Hoosac River in the shadow of the Coca-Cola ledge. In the 1920s, a young woman, for probably a hefty fee, had painted the Coca-Cola script logo on the sheer face of the ledge, visible from anywhere in the valley. The Italians, including Grandpa Pietro Cicchetti, who could neither read nor write, were however, great gardeners: every little plot had tomatoes and pole beans, and Grandma Maria Cicchetti's *pastafazoola* (a homemade soup with small pasta rings and pole beans) kept everyone alive. The Italians thrived on the hillside.

During the War, while living with Grandma Cicchetti because my mother was sick again, I remember how breakfast was a big Cow Cracker broken into a cup of coffee with a very slight pinch of sugar, because everything was rationed. Every morning, Grandma and I would go out and wind our way up Walnut

Street picking dandelions along the road. Grandma would wash the dandelions and throw them in a pot of water with a chicken in it. This pot was always stewing on the stove and was called "*mineste*," which sounded to me like some kind of "mess." To this day, the smell of a boiled dinner of greens makes me slightly queasy.

Grandpa Cicchetti, urged by the Church, took the wedding ring off Grandma's finger to send to the new leader who would make Italy as powerful as the Roman Empire once again. The leader was Benito Mussolini, and that dream was quickly buried when WWII broke out. Here in Canada, I found out later, the fathers of some of my classmates and one of my professors at St. Francis Xavier had been incarcerated in camps for the duration of the War.

Holy Mother Church

The Catholic Church in North Adams, through its individual ethnic parishes, was the cocoon protecting the lower-class papists from their Protestant masters. I absorbed the implicit attitude that the non-Catholics might have wealth, fine homes, positions as bosses, and cars–and bigger cars, and belong to the golf club–but we Catholics had the one, true religion. We would be saved and those "others" were destined for exterior darkness and the gnashing of their finely polished dental work. We Catholics banded together socially, politically, and theologically. Our Church was truly a Holy Mother Church, caring, nursing, teaching, protecting us in this "valley of tears," our "one, holy, Catholic, and apostolic" rock of faith to cling to.

Post-War Paradise

After the Big One–WW2–life was good. We got new houses in other parts of town. We ate like kings and queens. Payday father would bring home a strudel, pile fruit cocktail and ice cream on it, and we would end up in a sugar stupor. Little did we realize that the pastas, the desserts, and the "longer, finer Pall Malls" filtering their cigarette smoke would kill my father at 51, and my mother, even though she didn't smoke, two years later at 47.

The second generation Catholics stepped up the scale:

Angela Cardillo Mullen became an OR nurse.

Pasquale Cardillo became first clarinet with the Boston Pops, and E-flat clarinet with the Boston Symphony.

Pete Cardillo became a High School Principal.

Francis Cardillo became a school teacher and leader of the Williams College Marching Band.

Christina Cardillo sang in the Met and la Scala.

I got a PhD and became a university professor.

The French girl got a math degree, and after raising a family of five children, became editor of the oldest continuing weekly newspaper in Canada.

"Happy Days" at St. Joe's High School

At St. Joe's High, with religion being the first class of each school day, my knowledge of my faith grew from practice and ritual to a rudimentary understanding of the history of the Church. The Sisters of St. Joseph of the Springfield Diocese of Western Massachusetts taught and administered the school, under the pastor, represented by Fr. Scanlon for the first three years, and then Monsignor John P. Donahue in my Senior year.

Good things happened to me at St. Joe's. Fr. Scanlon approached my father and suggested I should develop my artistic skills–I could draw a line or two–with private lessons. My father had no money for private lessons, but Fr. Scanlon, who was privately well-off, quickly explained that he would pay for my private lessons. So for two years I studied with Leo Blake, the highest paid commercial artist in the US during the Depression [he was in charge of the Simpson-Sears catalogue]. Leo Blake–then retired to Stockbridge, Massachusetts, next to the studio of Norman Rockwell–would drive up to North Adams once a week, and with a group of adults, we would work at the home of Marty Melcher, and occasionally say hello to the lady of the house, his wife, Doris Day. They were not there often, but visiting Marty's mom. Later, when traveling, they would sublet their Hollywood home to Roman Polanski and Sharon Tate. Enter Charles Manson and his posse.

Sister Eleanor Maria SSJ [Mary Dooley]

The most influential Sister at St. Joe's was Sister Eleanor Maria SSJ, who if the Church had been enlightened could have been, in our opinion, Pope, or at least a Bishop. She was a dynamic and indefatigable teacher and inspiration and mentor for many of us. She set out to get as many of us as possible into college–with scholarships. Our life at St. Joe's was a buzzing, whirling universe–and we were challenged on every front. Our sports teams then were quite pitiful–we had two hundred students and the public high school had 2000. We never won a game of baseball or basketball in my four years there–and we didn't have a football team. But boy did we have a debating team. In the four years I was there, we won the Western Massachusetts debating championship three times and retired the first cup in 44 years.

I hung around the school newspaper because that French girl wrote for it, and she soon became editor. I eventually became the cartoonist. I also hung around the debating team my first couple years because that French girl was on the team–she was a brilliant writer of arguments who supplied the three speakers on her team with rebuttals. I grew six inches in the summer between my sophomore and junior years. My first day back at school, Sister Eleanor Maria grabbed me by the lapels, pinned me to the wall, and told me I was going out for the debating team. "Why?" I asked, thinking it was my deeper voice and my brains. Her answer: "Because I need someone tall on the team." I sure didn't feel very tall after that. But that speech training, with a final championship debate one year in front of 3000 people at Cathedral High School in Springfield, set me up for a life of lecturing and teaching in secondary school and then university. When I made the team my father took me down to the finest men's shop and bought me my first suit—for $20.

We prayed before class in school for all kinds of good causes. We had our catechism recitations. We had retreats, extended seminars of prayer, discussion, sermons, and exposition of the Blessed Sacrament, with visiting priests encouraging us to consider vocations to the priesthood and sisterhood. My father had made it very clear that it was the duty of every young Catholic man to consider a call to the priesthood. We had May processions to the grotto of the Blessed Virgin Mary behind the convent, with the girls in angelic white dresses and boys in white shirts with ties. I became a reader of the dialogue Mass, reading the English text of scriptures in the Mass, while the priests read *sotto voce*. I now knew the altar boy prayers, especially because we studied Latin for two years—a good preparation for the seminary. We sold Christmas cards to raise money for the school; I was a whiz at that, often selling for classmates of a more retiring nature so they could make their quota. We put on a school musical every year, directed by St. Eleanor Maria, and every student in both the grammar school and high school was in it—which, of course, ensured that every parent and aunt and uncle and cousin would have to attend. We made good money every year.

The Very Best Day of My Life to Date [1951]

One of the very best days of my life dawned during my sophomore year at St. Joe's. That French girl had been in my sights for some time. She was so perfect, so beautiful and so good. If I didn't make it to the seminary, maybe she would be perfect for me. But, of course, I was not worthy of her. She was thinking of becoming a nun. And I was as phony as a corked bat, a whited sepulcher, a Judas betraying with a kiss. It became clear that my double life would have to come to an end. And I had found the way. I discovered the concept of a "general confession"—not just the past week's sins, but the past life's sins—and if all that mountain of sacrileges I had built up could be forgiven in a "general confession"—I would be free, free at last, Lord God Almighty, free at last!

However, I was still afraid to go to the priests who knew me. I remembered one day confessing a "real" sin, a new sin of impurity I had accidentally stumbled upon, disguising my voice in a high pitch, only after absolution, having Fr.

Murphy ask me, "Pat, would you mail this letter for me?" I nearly passed out in mortification. To avoid such a disclosure of my Sin of Sins, I decided that the safest priest in town was kindly old Fr. Roccopriore at St. Anthony's.

Every moment of the fateful day is burned into my memory like an un-erasable computer disk. I sat for most of the afternoon on the metal pipe fence at the foot of the driveway up to St. Anthony's, waiting for all the common sinners to go to confession. When they walked by me, they didn't hear the pounding of my heart, the blood pumping in my veins, the throbbing in my head. I looked as ordinary and as good as they looked.

Across Holden Street on the side of a brick building, a sign painter was painting a sign of Elsie, the Borden Cow–the advertising for dairy products and ice cream. "I'm Elsie, the Cow, my milk is so sweet" is all I remember of the jingle. I admired his skill and the speed of his work. As he neared the end, the line of newly cleansed parishioners leaving the church began to dwindle, and I knew my Agony in the Garden was at hand.

I waited until the last person came out and then entered the confessional, making sure the heavy velvet curtain was completely closed, and knelt down. The little door slid open. I began.

"Bless me, Father, for I have sinned. Father, I want to make a general confession."

"Oh, my boy! How old are you?"

"I'm fourteen, Father."

"Oh, you are so young. You don't have to make a general confession."

"Yes, I do Father. Please."

"Okay."

And out it poured from me, surely like a flow of molten lava from Kilauea. The fires of hell would dim in comparison. And when I was gutted, I waited for the peal of the Doomsday bells.

"You are a gooda boy, Jesus loves you. You are a gooda boy. You are now safe in the arms of Jesus, and you must never, NEVER tell these sins again–they are forgiven. Jesus loves you. He will always love you. You be a gooda boy, and doan worry, never again."

I had been expecting a frightful penance, something not quite medieval, like sackcloth and ashes and standing in front of the church and proclaiming to all my sinfulness. Thank God such penances were no longer given. But I certainly expected to say rosaries for many months to come–surely great sins deserve great penances. I was so happy I was ready for retributive justice.

"For your penance, say one Our Father, one Hail Mary, and one Glory Be."

I could not believe my good fortune. As I bounded down the steps of St. Anthony's, the sky looked a deeper blue, and the world was bright and gay again. Elsie the Cow was worthy of the Sistine Chapel. I'm sure I ran home, but in my mind my strides were several inches off the ground. I entered the back door of the house and there was my mother stirring a big pan of spaghetti sauce for the Sunday feast. I tiptoed in and hugged her from behind, and kissed her and hugged her and dropped tears of joy on her surprised face. She dropped her wooden spoon. "Now look what you've made me do. What has gotten into you?"

"Ma, I am the happiest I have ever been in my life. I'm so happy, Ma, I'm going to explode. I'm just happy." Of course, I couldn't tell her why–I had to let her keep her dream of a priest son alive.

Man Proposes; God Disposes

All the days of my life since then have been a mixture of great joys and happiness–leavened with the inevitable pains and sorrows of loss and sufferings, but borne in the flowing waters of the life of my Church. After high school, the French girl joined the Sisters of St. Anne. Fr. Richard wanted me to go to the seminary in Montreal. Monsignor Donahue wanted me to get a University degree before going to the diocesan seminary. Rank hath its privileges, so I went off to Canada and StFX.

My father died before Christmas of my sophomore year, and my mother a year and a half later on her wedding anniversary. My sister, who nobly turned down a full scholarship to Manhattan College in New York, stayed home and enabled us to keep the Walsh family trio together. That changed my plans for the seminary.

I graduated from StFX. The French girl left the convent and studied at Anna Maria College in Worcester, Massachusetts. I taught at St. Joe's, and then Catholic prep schools in Connecticut and Boston, and then at St. Francis Xavier University for 37 years. In 1960, I married that French girl from Notre Dame, and we volunteered for the first group of Papal Volunteers for Latin America

[PAVLA], but before we could go our first child was on the way and they didn't have means to care for pregnant women or little babies, so our life eventually turned to Canada and my beloved StFX. We have five children and grandchildren in the double figures.

I have been active in the Church all these years, training lectors, forming parish councils, doing bible studies, working for bishops and dioceses, designing and publishing a prayer book, serving on task forces in the health care field, writing some prizewinning plays on biblical themes, and spending a lifetime collaborating in numerous projects with the Sisters of St. Martha of Antigonish, Nova Scotia. My wife and I worked our way through the implications and changes of Vatican II, and are daily communicants, blessed with numerous parishes and clergy surrounding our lives. As we enter our golden years fighting off blood clots, sleep apnea, multiple heart stents, and colon cancer, we find an ever deepening understanding of our faith and the vicissitudes of our Church. We share with each other the *gift* of our faith and we are entering ever more profound depths of love and devotion in old friends and new friends, including Jews and Muslims and people of no professed faith.

North Adams Catholics Today

With Deacon Bob Moulton on Mount Greylock

The phone call that triggered this outburst of memories was a conversation with Bob Moulton, a cousin by marriage to Uncle Tony Cicchetti's daughter Carolyn. Bob, a convert [my mother was his godmother], is a married deacon in North Adams. He called to wish me a happy American Thanksgiving. And he updated me with the news of the Catholic Church in North Adams:

I already knew that the Bishop of the Springfield Diocese was the first bishop in the United States to be indicted for abuse.

Notre Dame Parish is no more. The church, the school and the convent are no more, and the Sisters of St. Anne are gone.

St. Joseph's High School is now a publicly-owned old folks' home. The convent is closed, and the Sisters of St. Joseph are gone. [Sr. Mary Dooley/ Eleanor Maria is retired at Our Lady of the Elms College in Chicopee, Massachusetts, where she was a distinguished President. She was also President of the Women Religious of North America. She suffers from Alzheimer's.]

St. Francis Parish is closed for the winter, and the rectory is permanently closed.

Holy Family Parish is no more.

St. Anthony's Church, the ONLY Catholic Church in North Adams, remains, but the Venerini Sisters are gone. [The only priest of our years still alive is the retired saintly Fr. Peter Pagano, beloved by my mother, spiritual director and source of great grace to Deacon Bob, and friend of Padre Pio.]

The nine to ten thousand Catholics of North Adams are now served by ONE priest.

The Catholic Church of North Adams is now the Church of the Diaspora.

Where Is the Spirit?

The Spirit will always be with us, and I know and believe that the Spirit is in every human being by virtue of our individual humanness. But what does the Spirit have to work with? That dear hearts depends on us.

In the introduction to the Bible class my wife and I are taking three days a week at St. Mary's University College in Calgary, Alberta, we are studying the Gospel of Mark this week. The deep awareness is that Jesus is not only the glorified, glowing, kingly Messiah of otherworldly aspect, but he is also the most marginalized of human beings, a laborer, rejected by the authorities, his friends, his family, and casting his lot with the downtrodden, the poor, the diseased, the widows, and outcasts. He suffers the most degrading and ignominious death devised by humans. To follow this Messiah is to reject wealth, the world, power, and glory, and to embrace the agony in the garden and the pain and suffering and loneliness of inevitable death–and thus encounter the fullness of the mystery that is God.

Mark 8: 22-26

They came to Bethsaida. Some people brought a blind man to him and begged him to touch him. He took the blind man by the hand and led him out of the village; and when he had put saliva on his eyes and laid his hands on him, he asked him, "Can you see anything?" And the man looked up and said, "I can see people, but they look like trees walking." Then Jesus laid his hands on his eyes again, and he looked intently and his sight was restored, and he saw everything clearly. Then he sent him away to his home, saying, "Do not even go into the village."

Once healed, the formerly blind man doesn't fit into the village, the civilization. The process of healing takes two stages: first seeing dimly, then seeing clearly. This two-stage process happens even with Peter when he acknowledges [sees] and declares that Jesus is the Messiah–even though Peter doesn't really understand yet what being the Messiah really means. Jesus turns the meaning of "Messiah" upside down from what people expect. All of us must understand that we need to be transformed in our minds and hearts when we experience life and a relationship with Jesus.

The Phone Call

Bob's phone call brought me the realization that in the days of my Catholic childhood and youth, I saw only dimly what Jesus called me to be. The glory days of the institution I grew up in are revealed at last as counter to the message of the suffering servant as opposed to a triumphant political Messiah. All those years, was I seeing as dimly as Peter the true nature of the community of "the way" that Jesus was calling us to embrace? Peter took what was coming to him and finally saw clearly, becoming a Saint. Will the Church of my youth in North Adams eventually see clearly? Will the Church of my old age in Calgary, headed in the same direction, eventually see clearly? Will I ever see clearly?

I hope and pray so.

Patrick F. Walsh Calgary, Alberta

November 25, 2006

Frank Matrango: All American

Frank Matrango

Born in Springfield, Massachusetts in 1926, Matrango went to the Cathedral High School and served in the United States Navy during World War II. He then received his bachelor's degree in education from the College of the Holy Cross in 1952 and his master's degree in education from North Adams State College. Matrango was a teacher and counselor at St. Joseph's High School, in North Adams, Massachusetts. Matrango, a Democrat, served in the Massachusetts House of Representatives from 1969 to 1983. In 1984, Matrango moved to Hyannis on Cape Cod, where he died in 1996 after a brief illness.

Dear Terry and children,

My brother Fran has just notified me of Frank's passing. I sit down to write this little note for you about our dear friend.

Monsignor John P. Donahue, the new pastor at St. Francis Parish in North Adams, had a keen interest in education. He had arrived in the diocese of Springfield, his hometown, from the eastern end of the state, when Worcester was split into a separate diocese and he was forever marooned in the Berkshires.

Monsignor Donahue arrived in North Adams from Pittsfield in 1953. He didn't like *his* high school, St. Joe's, being a doormat for the public schools in the area. St. Joe's, enrolment not quite 200, had no football team, and a basketball team that hadn't won a single game from sometime after Noah's flood up to and after the Monsignor's arrival. In baseball, St. Joe's had not beaten Drury High in North Adams since my father did back about 1927.

But we were great debaters under the tutelage of Sister Eleanor Maria, Sister of St. Joseph, who was the Monsignor's right hand man–uh, woman–and who would have been Bishop if such a feat were possible. As a championship debater and soon-to-be Senior class president, life at St. Joe's was proceeding according to God's infinite wisdom in a plan of divine equanimity–until Sr. Eleanor Maria called me into her classroom before the first day of school and announced that the Monsignor had hired a new teacher, and that she expected me to provide leadership in making this new teacher feel at home. This was a strange request, because we sincerely liked the Sisters of St. Joseph. But when we found out the new teacher was not a sister–and, in fact, not even a woman–panic spread like a forest fire.

The Monsignor had hired a Holy Cross graduate, Captain of the All-America Baseball team, a third baseman used to eating line drives like popcorn, and an *older* man who had been in the armed forces, and probably knew how to actually kill people, to be our history teacher and coach! Jack the Ripper might have been easier to swallow. Sight unseen, the man was in trouble. He wasn't a nun, and he was very much a man–and the even tenor of our ways was doomed.

Frank Matrango arrived. He wasn't *that* big, we noted with approval. He had obviously caught a line drive or two on the nose, but that gave his dark and rugged Italian good looks an aura of mystery and intrigue. The girls twittered and gushed. He was kinda cute. And that accent–was it New York? It didn't matter–it was *different.*

The problem was, he *was* different. He talked different, he taught different, he even *thought* different. [I know that the word should be "differently," but that's the way we thought and talked then!] The man came on very aggressively.

He asked questions, put people on the spot. He explained things different. He sure as hell wasn't a nun. And he was tough. Big-city tough. Jesuit tough. He was more smart-alecky and quicker with a retort than anyone we had ever come up against. He could squash anybody who tried any scam or evasion. He had our number–and we didn't like it one bit.

As Senior Class President, I was deputed to approach Sr. Eleanor Maria and tell her that this guy had to go. He didn't know anything about teaching and, well, he just didn't fit into the scheme of things at St. Joe's. Sr. Eleanor Maria entertained my presentation for about as long as George Steinbrenner listens to a manager. I was out on my very red ears in a matter of seconds with a very clear message that Mr. Frank Matrango was here to stay and that we'd better learn to like it.

Faced with no alternative–we liked it! And gradually, as we discovered Frank was really interested in us, that he really wanted to help us do well, that he was always interesting and lively, that he talked tough and inside was a pussycat, we actually liked *him*. He was intense when he talked, yet utterly devoted to the Sisters and the Monsignor. We noted that his marks were fair and his standards were high.

One big tall guy–and we had only one big tall guy–who was the big deal on the basketball team before Frank arrived, showed up at practice late, as was his custom as the only 6 footer on a desperate team. He thought Frank couldn't get along without him. Surprise! Frank wanted guys who wanted to play for a *team*, guys who would show up on time and do their part in making a team successful. So the big guy was gone, and we were all in amazement at Frank's gall. He would rather lose with five small guys than win with a big sookey showboat. And lose we did; we didn't win a game Frank's first year, but he built a team, and the next year in the first game of the year those five little guys beat the State Champs, Pittsfield High, 31–30! [Up at college in Canada, my roommate and I, both from St. Joe's, danced on the dining room table when we got word of the victory! Even a thousand miles away we could feel the rightness of Frank's thinking.]

Pretty soon, the members of the class of '54 were so chummy with Frank that he became our confidant and Dutch uncle. It was great to have a *man* to go to with our problems. I soon had him advising and consoling me about my love life and the difficulty I was having in getting my one true love–the valedictorian and class genius–to go out with me. Frank was very sympathetic. So sympathetic that when he corrected one of Jacqueline's papers, he wrote a note on it: "Are you going to the Christmas Ball?" One of the girls saw Jackie's paper, jumped to Bob Beamon-ish conclusions, and went running around telling everybody, "Mr. Matrango asked Jackie to the Christmas Ball!" All hell broke loose, but Sr. Eleanor Maria calmed us down, and poor Frank learned the hard way that you have to keep the students at a bit of a distance. [By the way, she didn't ask me to the ball.] By risking such scandal, Frank proved his concern for us and our troubles, be they academic or amorous.

His first year ended triumphantly at the annual school picnic at Look Park in Northampton: an annual school celebration that was as thrilling to us as a trip to Disneyland for today's kids. Our Senior class played the Junior class in a softball game, and Frank played third base for us. We could see his competitive spirit put to work on our behalf; he played third base, not bad for an old guy, and batted in a gentlemanly way until the game was on the line in the last inning when he swatted a mighty home run and we rode triumphantly home on the bus, enjoying the sweet savor of a life about to be dispersed forever.

Frank settled in and became part of St. Joe's and North Adams forever. I went away to school in Canada and picked up my relationship with Frank when I returned to teach at St. Joe's in the fall of 1958, fresh with a BA and fortunate to have a male friend on staff who had become my Dutch uncle and advisor. I was still chasing Jackie, and Frank had to live through two more years of Dear Abby advice-giving.

I began to travel with the teams, keeping score and watching Frank in action. I can remember watching him put the little basketball players through their practice before a small school tournament: he would walk every player through the plan, giving them instructions about each opponent and how to move and play as a team. "If you follow the plan and do what I have showed you to do, you can win." Both his knowledge and his confidence were deeply impressive and obviously inspirational. And we did win!

Even when we didn't win, the lessons he taught his players about how to lose were as impressive as how he taught them to win. I remember one baseball game at Noel Field. St. Joe's was losing by a large score and we were having our last bats. One player, who shall mercifully remain unnamed, being way down in the batting order, took off his cleats before the game was over. When Frank spied the empty shoes, he made Vince Lombardi look like a Welcome Wagon lady–"quit" was not in his vocabulary nor in his work ethic. No one ever made that mistake again.

I remember one night in Pittsfield, when my brother Fran was pitching a night game before a huge crowd, and everybody was uptight. Frank handed him the ball, and my brother, who was very, very, dark and suntanned, started to the mound. Frank shouted for him to come back and everybody tensed up. They wondered what the urgent matter was, the profound advice to be bestowed in this fateful moment. Frank said to my brother, "When you get to the mound, Fran, I want you to turn around, face the crowd in the stands, and smile a big wide smile. Got that?"

"Sure coach, but why?"

"So the crowd will know you're there!"

Hey, I'd like to tell you we won, but we lost 1-0, when Mark Belanger got the only hit and scored a runner who had reached on an error. But my brother did beat Drury for the first time since my father did 32 years earlier.

I shared my work and my pains with Frank. He informed me when I revealed my qualms about teaching, that he had been absolutely petrified when he first walked into our class at St. Joe's. He had come on so strong because he had found the classroom a new and deep challenge–he was not at all certain he was in the right job and the right place. As a student I had not recognized his fears, but as a new teacher, I now realized what he had gone through. Like Frank, I would have to suck it up, and apply myself to my work. I began to understand how much he had gotten a kick out of us, how much he had understood our fears and our aspirations, our foibles and our raw emotions. His genuine love of young people and his commitment to take risks for them was a sign of his deep commitment and his manly values of fair play, decency, and honor. These qualities would enable him to leave the west some day and create a greater good for a greater number in the state capital. But the people he touched at St. Joe's and in North Adams would become a part of him that he would always hold dear.

Jeannette Tash (a French lay-teacher) and I had a neat little trick we would play to get our paychecks on time. The tight budget and hard times at St. Joe's often made it difficult for the Monsignor to pay us on the due date. Jeannette and I would take turns going to Sr. Eleanor Maria or the Monsignor and telling them, "Mr. Matrango is wondering if he can get his check this week." I needed the money to make trips to Worcester to see Jackie on the weekends–she was a student at Anna Maria College. Frank found out about our scam one day, but he never ratted on us. I think maybe it was as useful for him as it was for us!

I was finally successful in getting Jackie to a dance, and then we were engaged, and when I left St. Joe's in 1960 to teach in Worcester after getting married, I took credit at my farewell dinner to give a little speech about how I had landed Jackie, and that having set an example for Frank I was now able to give him advice on success with women. I now expected he would follow my lead and land Terry! And he did. And Jackie and I enjoyed the wedding. I never let Frank forget he had gotten married *after* me.

We moved to Canada and had to follow Frank's career through the relatives and the Sisters. Several years ago Jackie and I had the great good fortune to mount an expedition to Cape Cod, and we found Frank at home and spent a wonderful afternoon reminiscing about our days together at St. Joe's. We were impressed by the deep affection and sincere devotion he expressed about the people and the places he had grown to love in the Berkshires. The man had entered into the fullness of life with people who had needed him and who had loved him and who had appreciated his goodness and decency. They were part of him, and he was part of them. And the best thing was, Jackie and I were pleased to see that he held us in affection and esteem as much as we held him so. We enjoyed reliving with him the piece of life we had shared in those younger and vibrant days.

We want to tell you, Terry, and your children we never met, that Frank was our teacher and our friend, and in both instances he gave of himself with decency, honor, genuineness, and deep affection. We send you our deepest sympathy and our prayers. We are grateful for having known Frank, and we trust your memories of him will sustain you in the life he gave you.

Most sincerely,

Pat and Jackie Walsh, St. Joe's Class of '54

P.S. Please, if you ever come this way to see Nova Scotia, do let us know and let us host you for a visit in honor of a true friend.

I was becoming aware that the important things in my life were, and are, not so much events as people. The most important single aspect of our human values is our relationships with other people–and through our relationships with others, our relationship with our God (however we may define, or not define, that mystery of creative love!).

The Circle Psalm

I

our minds o lord cannot measure your greatness
the best we can envision is a circle
the most simple and most perfect of symbols
with no beginning and no end
but what does your circle enclose
and what does your circle exclude
to see you do we start in the center
or do we start at the edge

II

at the edge of your universe
Hubble shows us stars that can swallow
not merely our solar system
but the galaxy we cling to the edge of
and the galaxies outnumber the sands
of Abraham's promise
and are expanding at the speed of light
into the darkness beyond our imagination
and you o lord created this marvel
of an expanding sphere ever reaching

and if we start at the center of matter
in the tiniest bit of energy
within the charges of spinning atoms
of particles as minute as the spinning galaxies are huge
we cannot come to an end
of the depth of your being
we cannot conceive of the marvel
of how matter and energy can be alive
in the circular womb of your love

in the face of the unfathomable
we look about us every day
and feed on the circles you send us
the circle of night and day
the evident nocturnal and sunlit hidden journey of our moon
the spring and summer, autumn and winter seasons
echoing the birth and youth, maturity and age of our lives
our blue globe's trip of each year around the sun
the rise and fall of dynasties and nations
the ebb and flow of our continental plates
echoing our daily tides
over millions of years

too overwhelming o lord
we struggle with the circle of our little lives

our particle of time
our nanosecond of three score years and ten
we all begin in the circle of a single cell
impregnated with another cell
taught and empowered by your love
and the cells multiply
and form our bodies
and our brains
with a circle of nerve synapses
with more connections
than particles of matter in the universe
and we are an ever-living pattern of your circle
we are minds and souls

VI

being thus empowered
each self reaches out for the other
and in the encircling arms of love
we share the power of your creation
and when we come together in your name
to reach out with our minds and souls
in sorrow and in joy
in pain and celebration
in confusion and trust
in giving and receiving
in fear and in sharing
in praying and giving witness
we find o lord the farthest reaches of your circle
and the inmost mysteries of your love
we come together in this psalm
to sing with joy
because in this circle here today

we are one with you and within you
to the farthest star in the universe
and the deepest particle of energy
for the center and the edge are the infinite ONE

for the St. Joseph's High School class of 1954
September 4, 2004

Chapter 3
The Great Adventure 1954–58

To tell the TRUTH, I was petrified about going to college. I was afraid I would not pass the language requirements. I packed a 400-pound foot-locker with everything I owned. When I graduated, I went home with everything I owned in one suitcase.

I pictured deep snow banks year round, with sandaled monks, trudging to class. I'd have nothing else to do but study. And pray in my cell. Typical Yank.

I knew nothing of Canada, except that we had whacked their ass in the War of 1812. Then, curious about this strange new land, I took a course in Canadian history and got a snoot full of facts that challenged my American version of history.

I met and made friends with incredible people who would shake me to my Yankee roots and break me out of the Hoosac Valley to a citizenship of the world.

On the very first evening on the campus, I encountered a man who would make me an offer I could not refuse: a vision of life-long education in the service of our fellow human beings and God. One day on the StFX campus would change my life forever.

Patrick X Walsh

Day of Entry – A Recollection

From The Alumni News 1963

The train slowly rumbled and clacked over rain-swollen soil. Stolid files of spruces swayed in the drizzle. Endless telegraph poles were strung to the edge of the world. I was travelling to St. Francis Xavier University.

In September of 1954, in the twentieth century, a train couldn't drop off the edge of the earth—or could it? An-tig-onish, or was it An-tee-gon-ish, might be as mythical as Xanadu, or Coronado, or Lilliput.

I remember the numbing hours. Scenes of farewell kept flooding my mind. A sobbing mother, reluctantly allowing her firstborn to go forth to the unknown wilderness that the Micmac (Today: *Mi'kmaq*) Indians claimed was a place-where-the-bears-knock-the-leaves-off-the-trees-while-looking-for-beechnuts. A wordless crushing handshake from a suddenly older and grayer father. Tears tumbling freely from a little sister who would be a woman by the time of my return. Toothy grins from a kid brother who would at last be freed from hand-me-downs of both clothing and platitudes.

I could picture the family clearly; all comfortably situated in familiar bedrooms falling asleep, enclosed by friendly walls, unsuccessfully attempting to imagine my fate. Their faces melted slowly into the darkness twisting endlessly behind the reflections in the train window.

As hundreds before had been, so was I throttled awake by a red-eyed conductor, 3:30 a.m., Atlantic Standard Time. A shuffle down a lurching aisle; three metallic clicks until pulled off the last jolting step by a suitcase containing at least twenty-five items of clothing I would never need; a bleary glimpse of a railway station as menacing, musty, and forlorn as countless others living in any train-traveler's memory; a speedy taxi ride down a deserted small-town Main Street, often to be meandered in the future at similar times of murky doubt; Jack the Cop, with bobbing flashlight, will-o-wisping me to an empty bed in a strangely monastic cell; finally, the prayers muttered in time with throbbing veins while staring at shadows on the ceiling. I fell asleep.

"This is the day the Lord hath made!"

How comfortably the sun swathes the first morning, complementing the exhilaration of the birth of an adventure. A brisk shower, a crisp knot in the tie, a tang in the autumn air; wide smiles, clutching handshakes, fresh faces; a chattery, clattering breakfast line, a jumble of names to be sorted later, a discovery of a mutual bond through geography, heritage, or blood–and already the yesterdays fade as the aerie of StFX's atmosphere begins to envelop youthful spirits. The lucidity, the warmth, the camaraderie of a new world quickly bury a former life, which will be resurrected only when the new life begins to grind and reshape the past.

Morrison Hall on the right, looking toward Aquinas House and Xavier Hall.

Quite rapidly, a young mind can be plucked from the womb or the arcane past and hurled into the buzzing, whirring, flashing universe of the future. As my life at "X" began, I filed with my new companions into the University Auditorium. In a carefree mood, we accepted the strictures of an imposing dean of men as well as the precise tabulations of a sharp-eyed bursar.

Then to the podium hobbled a man with a face hewn from the Nova Scotia coastline and a voice raspy enough to scale fish. By what means could such a crude relic of the past capture such a frisky audience? Grating out rough words, the old man tottered to the sides of the podium as floppy as an old hat. I recall distinctly hoping the old gentleman wouldn't make a fool of himself. At first it was like watching a juggler who keeps dropping the third ball.

As his voice ground on haltingly, the crowd became muted. Twisting and twitching ceased. I found myself afraid to move my head; I was convinced that he was forging answers to the problems of the world–not an idealist's wild fantasies, but a wise old man's practical steps to a better world.

An electric charge poised over the audience. The old man hammered on spraying sparks. He flung his arms out from sea to sea. He thundered to a close. As a bolt of lightning clears the air, so his words left our minds fresh and glad.

Dr. Coady walked offstage.

Monsignor Moses Coady in his prime.

In 1963, when I returned to StFX, I found numerous changes: new buildings, new faces, new ideas. The Dr. Coadys, the Father Tompkins, the Doc Dans are all gone now.

Across the campus, yellow construction helmets bob about the site of the new library, and its glowing copper roof points to a scalloped sky sliced by fading jet trails.

* * *

[Monsignor Moses Coady was the first director of the extension department, St. Francis Xavier University. He developed a program of Adult Education, continuing life-long learning, involving economic self-help for the economically depressed. In 1959, the Coady International Institute was opened to continue his work in emerging nations to this day.]

[Here is the note from the Alumni News introducing me to the campus at the end of my bit of memoir above: *Patrick F. Walsh is a native of North Adams, Massachusetts, who was educated at St. Francis Xavier University and returned to that institution last year as a member of its faculty. Following graduation from StFX, he studied journalism at Boston University under the sponsorship of the Wall Street Journal. Since 1958, he has taught at some of the outstanding schools in New England, and is currently combining his teaching at StFX with studies for his Master's Degree at Boston College.*]

My college years were times of great happiness and great suffering and pressure: so much challenging experience, such personal loss, such struggling in love, all making the discovery of my true vocation in life an agonizing decision. The next piece some consider choppy and confusing–but if McLuhan was right, the medium is the message; the style reflects the pattern of my undergraduate life.

The Miracle of 1950 That Ended at Christmas time 1955

Duke has been dead now for 54 years. The gateman came to his funeral, but who remembers now?

Carmen died two years later, just before their wedding anniversary. There was an article in *TIME* a couple of months ago explaining that people die when they want to die. Who knows?

*

The middle finger of his right hand, his pitching hand, was shorter than his fourth finger and therefore only his second longest finger. His spitball [a legal pitch in his time] did eccentric things. He had 17 assists in one game–off little dribblers in front of home plate.

*

His wife had a bad heart. She had her first attack when their first son was born.

"No more children," the doctor said. "I'm sorry."

*

Duke had been a student waiter at Columbia University in New York City, where he was a scholarship pitcher on the baseball team. His first baseman was a big kid named Lou Gehrig. But Duke wanted a Catholic education, so he transferred to the Vincentians' Niagara College near the Falls. They pitched him every game and he threw his arm out.

*

Good-bye, Lou. Good-bye, Babe. Good-bye, Joltin' Joe DiMaggio. Good-bye, good-bye, Mr. Huggins.

*

"You were the beginning of all my troubles, and you'll be the end," she used to shout at the boy. She was right.

*

They had two more children. Those were the days. Pat the oldest. Four years later, Mary Ann. Four years later, Francis Joseph, Junior. Never to be called Junior.

"I hate that damn name, 'Junior,'" Duke said. So Francis Junior became "Black Diamond." The Italian of his mother's side overwhelmed the fair Irish of his father's side.

*

"Hey, Pat! There's an ambulance at your house." Pat thought immediately it was his mother. After Fran had been born, she had had seven heart attacks in one afternoon. She lost twenty pounds just lying there sweating. And Pat was the beginning of all that trouble. They had rushed her to the big hospital in Cooperstown, New York. Yeah, Cooperstown, home of baseball's Hall of Fame. Ha-ha, chuck-it-in-there-kid. Fire-it-in-there–atta baby. Chuck-it-in-there-kid."

*

After Duke graduated from Niagara University—1930, BA in Commerce—he got a job sweeping floors in the Arnold Print Works in North Adams, Massachusetts, for $14.00 a week. He came home from work one noon and found a moving van in front of the house his father had built before he died.

"What's this all about?"

"We're moving to Boston," his mother said.

"Who?"

"All of us. Me, Lucy, Alice, Mae, Louie, Anna."

"Good-bye, Ma."

"Good-bye."

He moved in with his flamboyant Italian friend, Tony, and Tony's new wife, Mary. They had a great time. Driving around the countryside during New England Indian Summers, drinking and eating meals of ice cream—only ice cream, quarts of ice cream. Who knew then?

*

It wasn't his mother. She met him in the front hallway. She was being tough, he could tell. But she was mush inside.

"Mama?"

"It's Daddy. He has a bad stomach ache."

Pat was twelve, but he tasted wishful thinking in his mother's voice—and knew it was heart trouble.

His father was a big man, an athlete. On the cot near the dining room table—he hadn't been able to make it upstairs to the bedroom—he looked like a little boy. Pat remembered a picture of Tom Sawyer going fishing: curly hair, head tilted to one side.

"Hi, Dad."

"I'm okay, son. Just a little indigestion."

The ambulance attendants lifted Duke onto their rolling cot. Pat reached out to hold his father's hand—it was cold—and it struck him that his father's hand had always felt warm before.

*

Duke had been going to Tony's mother's house for over a year. Mrs. Cicchetti loved him. He ate everything. All the spices and sauces.

"He's a nice-a boy. So handsome. He's a Duke-a, that-a boy. He's a reall-a Duke." That's how he got his name.

*

Pat's classmates at St. Joseph's High School–his father's school years ago–prayed for his father. That was standard procedure. Mostly they prayed for grandfathers and grandmothers. Last year it had been his grandmother, his father's mother.

She had died–not in Boston, but out west. They had shipped her body home from California by airplane and the casket got lost somewhere in Chicago. That had been exciting. Pat had been able to hold off for six days from accepting Clare Nary's bid to the Children of Mary's Ball. After all, he couldn't go if his grandmother's body wasn't found, could he?

He wasn't really that impressed by his grandmother's death. And the girl asking him was the wrong girl. He faintly remembered his grandmother from visits to Boston during World War Two–more vividly he remembered the air-raids and blackouts. But, none of his classmates had ever lost their grandmother's body.

They found her.

The wake was a hum and buzz and slow procession of gray people in gray suits.

Pat started to cry, though, when Mr. Flynn began to close the casket and his father rushed to throw himself on the casket and kiss his mother goodbye. The first time Pat had ever seen his father cry was a shock. And his father's back was hunched and quivering and suddenly looked thin.

*

Tony's youngest sister, Carmen, was a dark Italian beauty. She sang the lead in all the Gilbert and Sullivan operettas at the Normal School–the local teacher's college. She was a good girl. She didn't have to beat off the boyfriends; her father scared the shit out of them.

Carmen often passed Duke on the street and paid no attention to him at all–he was so much older. But he paid attention to her. He quietly loved her in his own mind as he watched her walking back and forth to Normal School–not knowing she was Tony's sister. Silently watching for over two years. Then one night he met her at supper at the Cicchetti home.

Tony was their best man.

*

Duke never owned a car. Too expensive. He would walk. Or get a bus. Or ride to work with someone.

He walked to early morning Mass every day before work.

He always said "hello" to the gateman at the plant.

*

Duke and Carmen dated.

"Would you like to go to a movie?"

"Yes, let's go to that movie at the Paramount. It's been playing for over a month."

"Which movie is that?"

"Refrigerated."

So Duke took Carmen to her first movie in an air-conditioned theatre.

*

"I'm sorry, Carmen, there's nothing we can do for Duke," Dr. Wright said. "It's only a matter of time. You must take care of yourself. Think of the children."

She thought: *It's all wrong. I should be the one to go. I've had it for years, and he has been so strong. But, why, doctor, why? Duke is so quiet. And I'm always screaming and having heart attacks. Why?*

*

Pat remembered the lickings he got from his Dad. They were few–and therefore individually memorable–and justly deserved.

The Sunday morning he was supposed to be watching Francis. Pat was sitting on the stoop across the street playing cards with Billy Lilly.

A screech of brakes screamed at the neighborhood.

Pat looked up and saw Francis in diapers squatting in front of a car in the middle of the street and his father coming out of the house in his undershirt, one-half of his face smooth shaven, the other half lathered with shaving cream.

His father scooped up Francis with one hand almost as an afterthought as he headed for Pat like a runaway train. Pat didn't move–of his own volition–but was plucked from the doorstep and held at arm's length during the march home. [A feat of strength he realized only years later.]

When his father bounced him onto the bed, it had been a fun feeling that somehow caught in the pit of his stomach when he stopped bouncing.

The belt buckle left welts.

*

Carmen and Duke had been engaged for six years. The snag was that Carmen's younger brother, who as youngest was supposed to take care of their parents, eloped–with a Protestant girl, no less–and it became necessary for Carmen to help at home.

Duke was working out of town in Greenfield, 45 miles over the Mohawk Trail, so the pressure was off–at least during the week. Of course, it depends how you look at it.

Duke wrote poems for her.

*

Duke was a great walker. He enjoyed walking–and would have walked even if he did have a car.

Family spats were rare, but when they came, he always won. Carmen would initiate warfare with a raging Italian salvo. She would diversify her attack with wild waving of her arms like some mad semaphore sailor in battle.

Duke remained cool under fire. He retreated. He went for a walk, leaving her cannons with no target in range, thus losing the battles and always winning the war without firing an answering shot.

But silence is a heavy burden.

*

For the first time, Pat took the prayers of his classmates seriously. They invoked St. Jude, Patron of Hopeless Causes.

*

"Duke, your wife's in trouble. Her heart is under an incredible strain. We are going to have to terminate the pregnancy."

"No, doctor. You will not. You will do your best to save them both."

On May 26, 1937, at 4:30 p.m. on a Wednesday afternoon, Patrick Francis Walsh was born and Carmen Cicchetti Walsh had a heart attack.

*

During the War years, they lived in Sidney, New York, a little town of 3,000 on the banks of the beautiful Susquehanna River, where the English poets Robert Southey and Samuel Taylor Coleridge had wanted to establish a pantisocracy at the beginning of the nineteenth century. Duke did time studies to speed up the manufacturing process for the Scintilla Manufacturing Company–the only producer of magnetos for aircraft engines in the United States at the beginning of WWII. Everybody in Sidney felt pretty good about the article in "The Saturday Evening Post," calling it "the little town we couldn't do without."

*

Andy Durocher, one of Pat's classmates, a sleepy, almost classic phlegmatic, walked across town during an electrical storm and gave Carmen a small vial of St. Jude's Holy Oil, guaranteed to do the impossible. Carmen, as usual in an electrical storm, was blessing the house with holy water. She accepted the vial with no questions and sincere gratitude.

*

Six years later, going through his father's papers, Pat found a citation from the Secretary of the Army, James Forestall, commending Duke for his service to his country. At the beginning of WWII, when airplane manufacturers needed magnetos desperately, the process took nine months from order to delivery.

After Duke time-studied the process, Scintilla was delivering magnetos in three weeks. His father had never spoken about the letter or his role in the War.

The plant closed in February of 1946. The War was over.

*

"May I, doctor?"

"It can't do any harm, Carmen, and it's beyond our power."

Carmen, helped by cousin Angela, a nurse, serving a twelve-hour shift for no money, anointed Duke's chest with St. Jude Holy Oil. Then they rolled him over and anointed his back. On the left side of his back was a long, deep scar from an operation he'd had when he was five years old. His father, an Irish cop, wouldn't let the doctor take him to the hospital, so they operated on the dining room table.

The two women covered him up and Carmen read the petition to St. Jude, and then went home to put the kids to bed.

*

1947 was a year of great promise.

Duke was Treasurer and kept the books for the Barr Manufacturing Association in Auburn, New York. BMA made clocks with no faces–only numbers, like a speedometer. It was fascinating to watch the numbers tumble into place. Great post-war seller.

Carmen and Duke bought a huge home from a very old couple who had been servants of the owner of a large estate in Auburn, where the Count de Lafayette had visited during the Revolutionary War. It was a dream house–for only $9,000!

At church, Carmen met the Rossis, *paisans* of Purina and Rossi, spaghetti makers. The Walshes used to visit the Rossis, and Carmen would sing in the grand room that had a harp in it, and the children would run through the gardens of the Rossi estate playing cowboys and Indians with the Rossi kids. Pat loved visiting the Rossis, because at Easter time their sideboard was populated by a vast menagerie of not only Easter bunnies, but more exotic giraffes, elephants, tigers, and beasts of every type–all solid chocolate. The War was definitely over.

*

Carmen's heart was balky.

The officers of the BMA called Duke in after nearly a year of service.

"Duke, we like your work."

"Thank you."

"You have a promising future with us."

"I hope so."

"Now, we know you have some new obligations: your home, some doctor's bills, and some new acquaintances to–well–to keep up with."

Duke waited.

The owner had to continue. "Well, you know the company is doing quite well."

"Yes."

"But, we could be doing even better."

"How can I help?"

"Well, Duke, you know the government takes quite a bite out of us in taxes. We know you can handle the figures–and if you do–we are willing to pay you in the five-figure bracket. You see, we can all benefit."

"We're doing everything possible now."

Silence from the bosses.

"Are you asking me to. . . ?"

"You're good with the figures. It won't be any trouble. What do you say, Duke?"

Silence.

"Well?"

Duke took a pen from his pocket, reached across the desk, and began to write on the office pad.

"What's that?'

"My resignation. Effective immediately."

Two weeks later, the Walshes were back in North Adams where Duke was walking to work and saying "hello" to the gateman at the Arnold Print Works.

Good-bye big house, good-bye Rossis, good-bye Lafayette, good-bye five-figure salary. Good-bye, good-bye.

*

Duke did the dishes–and washed the floors–and did the laundry–whenever Carmen needed a hand.

When the children got old enough to help, Duke became the Inspector General of the Dishes. Inspection was toughest after spaghetti and meatballs. He would take a supposedly clean plate from the drainer and, looking up at the ceiling, rub his fingers over the eating surface. Then he would take Pat or Mary Ann's hand and gently guide it over the path his hand had just examined.

"Feel that?"

"Yes."

"What is it?"

"Cheese."

"Is the plate clean?"

"No."

He would slide the dish into the hot, soapy suds for another scrubbing.

*

Duke recovered.

Doctor Wright, who was associated with the doctor taking care of President Eisenhower, couldn't explain how Duke had recovered.

But Carmen knew–and Angie–and Andy Durocher–and Pat–and the whole Grade 9 of St. Joseph's High School.

Duke went back to work for another five years.

*

In 1955, just before Christmas Exams at St. Francis Xavier University in Antigonish, Nova Scotia, Pat, now a sophomore, got a phone call from his mother. "Daddy's had another heart attack, come home immediately."

Pat went to the office of the Registrar, Fr. W. X. Edwards, who was crippled and walked with two canes. Pat explained that he had to go home because his father was dying.

"You can't go home–you have to write your exams."

It cannot be recorded here what Pat said in reply–but he was on the train going home that night. Fr. Edward's never mentioned the incident, even when

Pat took an English course from him his Senior year, and even after he came back to teach English at the college. Pat never mentioned it either.

*

In the North Adams General Hospital, Duke looked like a medieval knight in a movie. He had always been clean shaven. Pat remembered how his father would sharpen the razor blades by rubbing them in a glass–they would last twice as long that way. Duke could not lift his hand. His eyes teared up. Pat took his hand. It was cold, again.

"You look like a knight, Dad, with that towel draped over your head."

Duke smiled.

Pat had a pulse of hope.

When he was going home from the hospital that night, cousin Angie, on duty yet again, told him, "He stayed alive until you came home from college."

*

Pat knew then that the end was near.

The next day they sent his mother home, telling her there was nothing she could do, and she would need her strength to care for the children.

The StFX Student Prayer book had the penitential psalms in it. Pat recited them over and over again. His father drifted in and out of sleep. Pat recited the rosary over and over, all three mysteries. He said the beads to the Holy Ghost. He said the Seven Dolor beads.

He moved his chair closer to the bed and put his hand on his father's knee. As the hours passed he could feel the knee stiffening and growing cold. His father began Cheyne-stokes breathing: falling silent for longer and longer spells, then gasping for air, snorting and hissing. Then silence–and then paroxysm again.

Cousin Angie appeared at his side.

"You have been here for 27 hours. You have to go home now and take care of your mother. That's what your father would want."

Pat knew Angie was right. But he didn't want to leave. He believed that as long as he could recite the psalms and pray, his father would hang on. As long as he could feel his son touching his knee, he would know that his son was with him.

Pat remembered that once when he had been sick, with uncontrollable spasms of shaking and trembling, his father had come into the room and laid his hand on his forehead–and immediately peace and quiet and calm had descended on Pat. It was some kind of holy, mysterious flow of energy between a father and son, some grace floating from a realm beyond measure by merely human means. It was here in this hospital and Pat didn't want to let it go. But he knew he had to be with his mother. He waited for the next long pause between gasps and left the room.

When he went in the door, his mother met him and he knew that within minutes of his leaving the room his father had been transformed to eternity. Pat never cried for five days until they returned to the house after the burial. Then he collapsed in his mother's arms. She understood that he had to be strong for her and Mary Ann and Francis. She understood.

*

His Aunt Bessie and Aunt Annie were all aflutter. They were begging Carmen not to let Dr. Wright perform an autopsy on Duke–don't let them cut him up.

But Carmen prevailed. Dr. Wright had been giving Duke an experimental drug and an autopsy would perhaps reveal how it had influenced his heart. This would be very useful for heart sufferers in the future. Carmen consented.

*

Dr. Wright ushered Carmen and Pat into his office in Williamstown. He looked at them for a moment, and then shook his head.

"We can't understand it."

"Didn't the drug work?" Carmen asked.

"Yes, yes, the drug behaved the way we expected, it was just not enough and not in time. Yes, thank you. The drug will be useful if used earlier."

"What don't you understand, then?"

"Well, when we examined Duke's heart, we found the scar tissue from his first heart attack five years ago. The scar tissue showed that the entire back of his heart had been blown open. There is no way his heart could have functioned with such massive damage. We can't understand or explain how a man could live on after such an attack. We have no idea how he carried on for another five years."

*

Was it a miracle? Dr. Wright was not a Catholic. He might even have been a nothing. But C.S. Lewis told us we cannot prove the efficacy of prayer, for any worldly methods or scientific methods for doing so do not exist.

Was his father's survival of the first heart attack a miracle?

Pat can't say that this was a miracle.

But he can believe that it was a miracle.

And anyone who says it is not cannot know the blessings of the relationship of a man to his human creator and to his divine creator. Every day that passes, Duke Walsh's son feels closer and closer to his father–to both his fathers.

Patrick Walsh Antigonish 1969

The Last Christmas

my fat Italian mamma made *crispadella*
sprinkled with powdered sugar like Bethlehem's hillsides
my father sat in *his* chair reading the *Transcript*
inky black blotches of news print on his nose
from pushing up his glasses

the bob-tailed tiger tom cat crapped in the corner
under the Christmas tree
and I was nominated with no choice
to go nose first to clean it up
while my sister trembled in fear
of my unspoken desire of revenge on that ancestor of Garfield
while "black diamond" brother watched
with big wide dark brown eyes

after clutching my father's arm
when being put into the cellar
the cat went out the front door into a snowbank
I was glad to see him go
but little did I realize that was to be our last Christmas
because sooner or later everyone goes
out into the snowbank
like tiger cat flung unceremoniously
out the front door into the cold exterior darkness

my Daddy went first
towel over his head unshaven
like a Knight on a lost crusade
perishing on a distant shore
choking out his last breaths
knee growing stiff and cold
under my own fevered fingers

Mamma too tried to carry on following him
into the endless desert less than two years later
on her wedding anniversary
seeking her knight in shining armor across the final bar
she left in a hurry no bags packed no fond farewells
just leaving the spaghetti sauce on the stove
a taste of the final harvest bubbling away
before the moon rose silent and silver
over Forbidden Mountain brooding
as it still does over the Hoosac Valley

little sister fusses over her brood of bristle boys
and single blushing rose of Carmel
little brother "black diamond" like coal
crushed by weight of unbearable pressure
still sparkles with life against the odds
having bypassed his last Christmas twice

So here I am at my 50th Christmas repeating patterns
looking for a fat tree so you can't see the central stem
getting ready for an orgy of turkey with meat dressing
trifling with desert a new tradition picked up in Ireland
children scattering
into distant mountains turbulent cities
because their noise is drumming elsewhere
I can hear the house I built for them whisper in the night
before I slide into buried memories of my own childhood
in living dreams technicolor and stereo

I never hear my wife approaching anymore
silent ever present to soothe the unsteady moment
with a soft eye and a hand touching me

Spiritual Notebook

Sunday September 19, 1954

Arrived at St. Francis Xavier University at 3:00 a.m.

Went to Confession and Communion at 9:30 Mass

Sunday, October 3, 1954

I'm going to try to fill out this notebook faithfully. The Retreat Master brought home some good points.

I

AM

THIRD

God first, others second, and myself third. (Work on humility.)

On the importance of Mass for being good in the world today.

Mr. Business Man went to Mass,

He never missed a Sunday;

Yet Mr. Business Man went to hell,

For what he did on Monday.

Gave two meanings of true love from St. Thomas Aquinas: Love the good of the other and want them to be good and will work for their happiness.

God lets our associates do and say things in order to try us!

[*The four years of undergrad life literally flew by and myriad activities are noted elsewhere in this exercise. But two relationships among the most significant events not included in the rest of this book, but emblematic of the greatest personal value for me and my family, include the following:*

Meeting Sr. Marie Reine, the infirmarian, the first Sister of St. Martha to enter my life to my eternal benefit by engaging me with this extraordinary Congregation of blessed women.

Meeting two roommates, Gerard Holmden Keenan, from Saint John, New Brunswick, and John O'Donnell, of Portland, Maine, both of whom would become life-long friends of 64 years and counting, with never the slightest quiver of tension between us, and/or their permanent roommates for life, Maura McGloan and Judy McGrath.

Homer and Maura Keenan

The late Jack and Judy O'Donnell

Omitted from this Spiritual Notebook are many entries of embarrassing and florid spiritual expressions of such an extreme personal and puerile nature, that I have relegated them to whatever book is being kept by the heavenly accountants, if such a doomsday book there be.]

In lieu of these omissions, I offer a true account of a retreat held in our first year at X. A retreat is a spiritual exercise in which the participants withdraw from their usual everyday activities to concentrate on spiritual matters. A retreat weekend starts at suppertime on Friday evening, and finishes on Sunday afternoon before supper. Retreats are silent affairs, with no talking allowed in-between sessions. A participant is to concentrate on the talks given throughout the day, and to maintain a prayerful attitude for all ceremonies: Mass, benediction, adoration, confessions, question periods, and sermons, etc.

Our first year the retreat was conducted by a "Holy Ghost Father"–that is, a priest of the Congregation of the Holy Spirit, founded in 1703. They wore white garb with a white hood, and were noted preachers. The priest would sit at a little table to the left of the altar in the chapel, with nothing but a crucifix standing on it, sometimes with, for dramatic effect, a single lighted candle. The chapel would be darkened with theatrical spotlighting on the priest sitting at the table. The atmosphere was palpable, because we would all be in thrall to this speaker for the entire weekend.

Our priest turned out to be a rather engaging and entertaining fellow. The talks covered everything of consequence over the space of the weekend, as we young men were warned of the evils that lay in wait for us out there in the big, bad world.

Our man would start out with simple, parable-like stories, and build them up, and build them up, to frenzied conclusion when the evil of the presentation would be condemned in doomsday tones: for example, greed. After covering every possible act of greed, we would surely have committed, the thunderous conclusion, worthy of a mountain top in Sinai, with arm raised high to the hidden heavens, the anathema would ring out, "This . . . thing . . . must . . . STOP!"

Properly chastened we would slink off to our rooms to meditate upon the four final things: Death, Judgement, Heaven, and HELL! For session after session, the retreat ratcheted up the intensity of the message.

A talk on abuse of liquor: "This . . . thing . . . must . . . STOP!"

A talk on our laziness: "This . . . thing . . . must . . . STOP!"

A talk on cheating of all kinds, in school and out: "This . . . thing . . . must . . . STOP!"

On and on and ON, until, of course, SEX: "This . . . thing . . . must . . . STOP!"

And then Sunday and supper, the retreat was over, with an Apostolic Blessing, and we advanced on the dining hall like ravaging Vikings, only to be stopped by grace before eating, a sobering remembrance of . . . gluttony. The tension finally popped, and the entire horde raced down to the Capitol Theatre on Main Street in Antigonish. Nothing like a Hollywood blockbuster to bring us back to our real world.

The film that night was *Ivanhoe* starring two Taylors, Robert and Elizabeth. And it started with some great jousting and bloody medieval combat and the crowd let their emotions loose and cheered and howled in their adolescent freedom. And then the film took a turn, as they oft did in those days, and an eerie silence crept over the rabid audience, for the two Taylors were at each other on a divan like manic otters. Silence reined, until from the back seats came a thunderous shout: "THIS . . . THING . . . MUST . . . STOP!" And no one in that theatre that night ever heard another word of the film, for every time the tittering, laughing, and chortling would die down, the lesson we had learned would burst out from another corner of the theatre.

But, no one who was there ever forgot *that* retreat!

May 21, 1958

I had the greatest time in my life this year. It's the most fun I've ever had.

It's all over now.

Graduation over–heading home to North Adams. Alex MacAdam, basketball coach, drove me to the Halifax Airport. As we drove west out of Antigonish, I took a long, lingering look back towards the campus. Realizing a serious possibility I might never see StFX again, I broke into deep, sobbing tears.

Chapter 4
The Rat Race 1958–63

The half-decade between graduating from university and returning to StFX as a teacher was a whirling, spinning rebirth.

I turned down an offer to become trained, by Billy Roberts the owner, as manager of the Excelsior Printing Company in North Adams, at $10,000 dollars a year, to become a teacher at St. Joseph's High School under Monsignor John P. Donahue and Sister Eleanor Maria, for $3,200 dollars a year ($400 a year higher than the public school scale of $2,800.) In 1960, when Jacqueline and I married, she graduated *summa cum laude* in mathematics and had a job offer in Washington, DC. I suggested that maybe she should take the job, and I could stay home and have the babies. That was a no go.

Then we agreed that we would sign up for the first Papal Volunteers for Latin America and devote our lives to the missions. Jackie ruined that plan by graduating 6 months pregnant, as her university's outstanding example of Christian womanhood. Highly qualified, but PAVLA, in its initial operations, hadn't planned on pregnancy of candidates. Obviously, neither had we.

We then agreed that returning to StFX to teach was a good plan: I really wanted to get back and teach with Fr. MacSween, and also, I thought I was going to die young–and if I did, our children would be guaranteed a college education.

Having left St. Joe's and North Adams after two years, and moved to Worcester so Jacqueline could finish her degree at Anna Maria College, we now had to move again, so I could start work on my Master's degree which would be required to teach at X. I went to meet with Leonard Dean, head of the English department at the University of Connecticut in Storrs. They had a master's degree for only 14 credits and no dissertation. I had to explain to Professor

Dean that my undergrad record was challenged by switching out of Chemistry into English after my sophomore year, but that I had top references from the places I had taught. He bought my explanation and we moved to Connecticut. I got a job at Marianapolis Prep School, had our first child, Mary, and found out that there were problems there.

An even bigger problem was a letter from UCONN denying me entrance to their Graduate program. I drove over to Storrs, tracked down Leonard Dean, and had a to-do with him, and naturally lost. He blamed it on the Committee–my first taste of Byzantine corruption in University administration. Of course, I realize now I was asking for a very tall drink. We stuck out the year at Marianapolis. Father MacSween came down from Canada for a visit and to demonstrate support and confidence that we could work things out.

We did, but it wasn't easy: Jackie got pregnant again. How in the hell was I going to get into grad school if my undergrad switch from chemistry to English was going to spook everybody? We sat down and tried to figure out who we could get to enable us to get into grad school. Finally, I came up with Fr. Desautels, who was Dean at Assumption College in Worcester. I had been visiting Jacqueline every weekend for the past two years while teaching at St. Joe's. Neither the girls nor the Sisters could serve at the Sunday Mass, so whenever I was around, I became the altar boy. Maybe Fr. Desautels could help us. And he did. He suggested that I take two courses at Assumption Summer School in English. This would prove whether or not I had the goods. Assumption English professors had an agreement with Boston College, the largest Catholic college in the country, that any student they recommended Boston College would accept. It was a plan; so without hesitation I resigned from Marianapolis at the end of the spring term. [There would be no pay for the summer months–which meant a return to war-time budgeting.]

Then I sat down and wrote a letter of application for work to 42 Catholic high schools in the Boston area. I got exactly two replies, one school was sorry to have no openings, but the other, a newly opened Catholic Memorial High School, a prep school in the toney area of West Roxbury, just outside Boston, had a third-year opening for an English teacher. Brother Gregory, of the Irish Christian Brothers, invited me to send my relevant credentials to apply for the job. Knowing time was of the essence, I hopped in my car in the wee hours of the night and was waiting for the front door of the school to open. Brother Gregory was amazed since he had sent the letter the previous morning, but my urgency and full disclosure about my undergrad struggles convinced Brother Gregory and I got the job.

Now all I had to do was get superior marks in those two summer courses, and get into Boston College before the kicker in the womb arrived. I was most fortunate to get Professor Ed Calnan . . . of Holy Cross College, not Assumption. I had signed up for two courses: 1) History of the Novel, 2) Shakespeare. After the first class, I cornered Dr. Calnan and explained the deal with Fr. Desautels. Dr. Calnan, who would soon become Ed, settled my fears: Assumption and Holy Cross shared professors, and the Holy Cross Professors had the same privileges at Boston College. And he knew the Chairman of the English Department at BC, and he would recommend me if I did well in his courses.

By this time, I had what I termed "the bloodlust for literature." There is nothing like a summer with no pay, one child and another on the way, and all the hopes of the future resting on two courses to make one drive 80 miles to and from class each day. Result: A- in both courses!

We did manage to eat during the summer. We had shopped each weekend in Putnam at the Weiss Brothers' Grocery Store. Desperate, I approached the brothers who had been very friendly, explained my situation, and asked if they could carry our grocery bill over the summer, and I would send them payments starting with my first paycheck at the new job in West Roxbury in September. They were good Samaritans with no guarantees, but they agreed to care for us. I sent them Christmas cards every year until we moved to Ireland.

So we moved to Roslindale, a suburb of Boston near Boston College and West Roxbury. We lived in a duplex shared with the owners John and Mary Bosscetto. And then, as Yogi Berra said, Déjà vu all over again." A letter arrived that I had not been accepted at Boston College. Shades of UCONN. I called up and found out that the Chair of the English Department Ed Calnan had sent his recommendation to was on sabbatical and there was a new Chair, Dr. John L. Mahoney. I asked to speak to him, and he said he knew Ed Calnan, so have him give me a call. I called Holy Cross and found out that Ed was on vacation at a cottage on Cape Cod with no phone and they had no way to reach him. Where was the cottage? Somewhere near Carter's Crossroads. Another Paul Revere ride through the night. In the early morning light, I managed to find the

Crossroads. The problem: no buildings in sight–just two roads crossing with a sign.

I sat in the car, fighting back the urge to cry or scream, holding the steering wheel with enough force to tear it from its moorings, when coming up one road and turning past me was a station wagon full of kids, driven by, believe me, the TRUTH: the distinguished and beloved professor of the novel and Shakespeare, Ed Calnan of Holy Cross. This coincidence might be considered by some an act of God, by others, merely serendipitous coincidence. When the station wagon kept on driving away from the Crossroads, I realized whatever forces were at work in my life, I was responsible for making sure they succeeded–and I hit the gas and took off chasing the station wagon with my headlights flashing and my horn blaring.

Mission accomplished. Dr. Mahoney accepted me with certain conditions: I would remain on probation and could be dismissed if I got any mark below a C+. And I would have to take 6 credits of extra courses to make up for that messy major in my undergraduate career. In all, that would mean acquiring a master's degree with 42 credits, including a dissertation. [Remember that dream vision of a 14 credit Masters with NO dissertation at UCONN?] Why was the MA so power-packed at BC? Because, being next to Harvard, they did not give PhDs in English Literature; they gave the most difficult MA, and thus sent more people on for PhD degrees in English than any other school in the country.

So Walsh sucked it up, started teaching at Catholic Memorial, and then went over to BC to register for the MA program, on Wednesday nights and Saturday mornings. At the registry window, the little old lady told me that I had to pay the fee or I could not be issued an entry pass to my classes. I explained that I wouldn't be getting my first paycheck until the end of the month. Well then, you will have to get a student loan, at that window over there. At that window over there, I took out the forms and filled them out. On the line for my parents' names and addresses I wrote "deceased." The "at-the-window-over-there" loan lady said you can't get a loan without your parents' signing. I was sent back to the other wicket where I explained why I couldn't get a loan. That's too bad, declared the little old lady with a decided lack of Weiss-Brother Samaritanism.

"But, I have a wife and child and another child on the way!"

"Then drop out."

I was too surprised and stunned to blow my top. I just turned and exited the building and then let the anathemas fly. There was no one present to hear every swear word I could think of cloud the air. Was I whipped? Pretty close.

Then the Lord sent another Samaritan, in the person of my best friend, Mel Mastroianni, home from his naval stint in Morocco and working for Polaroid in Boston. I phoned him up and a loan to cover my registration fee was forthcoming on the spot.

The MA was a doozy to complete. I got the call from Fr. MacSween before Christmas that I would be returning to X as a Lecturer–bottom man on the academic totem pole, but big foot in the door. I would have to go back and forth from Antigonish to Boston during summers. And then a stint as a big-time administrator for two years (Coordinator of Development, Public Relations and Alumni, and Alumni Director) put me on the fast track to administrative glory and doubled my pay. But I figured out fast that my place was in the classroom, free and unencumbered by bureaucratic rules and regulations. My title would again carry no weight by mere alphabetical poundage, and I would be poorer again, but free to keep my classroom rocking. And I finally finished my MA in the summer of 1967. That entitled me to a raise and a promotion to Assistant Professor and a pay hike. Monsignor Bauer told me to get letter from BC, and all good perks would follow. I called the Registrar at BC, and asked for a letter verifying my MA.

After a rather long pause, the voice of doom returned to the phone: "I'm sorry sir, but you do not have an MA from Boston College."

"Why not?" I whispered.

"Well, sir, you are 6 credits short for your degree." He exhaled, I inhaled. He continued, "You have only 36 credits and a dissertation."

Spluttering I tried to patiently asked, "Did I pass the external examination by a Board of Professors?"

"Yes, sir, you did."

"Then how could I be short credits because you cannot take the Extern unless you have all your credits?"

It was his turn to splutter. "Well, I don't know, sir, but you are not listed here as graduating."

"What about the six transfer credits from Assumption College in 1962?"

Long pause.

"Sir, there are no transfer credits from Assumption College."

I slammed the phone down, and spent the next three days slamming it down until some administrator or fixer from Assumption found the letters and notes from Ed Calnan. The excuse given was a change in the office of the registrar, new personnel, etc., terribly sorry about that, etc., etc., we shall rectify this immedi . . . . I hung up the phone before I could say something in the nature of a chargeable offence. It had taken me seven years to get the MA. In the meantime, the qualifications for promotion up the pay scale now demanded all professors have a PhD. The ladder up to the throne of academia kept adding more and more rungs. How long would a PhD take? When you are habitually grading in A country, it takes one wife, five children, and a two-year family study leave/ vacation in Ireland at half-salary.

Mary Ann Walsh, Patrick Walsh, Fran Walsh. All served as Class President at St. Joe's High School, Mary Ann as first girl president and for all four years! The three Walsh children in survival mode: life lessons straight ahead! I was finding my writing to be a useful tool in dealing with my failures to maintain that period of euphoria Fr. Roccopriore has bestowed upon me in 1950 in that General Confession. After our parents died, my sister, Mary Ann turned down a full university scholarship to Manhattanville College, Westchester, New York, in order to keep the three of us together as a family. Instead, she attended The North Adams Normal School for teacher training, as our mother had done. Mary Ann was 16 when my mother died. Yet through the trauma she tried to replace our mother for all of us. I fumbled the attempt, for both Mary Ann and Fran, to replace my father.

So we stuck it out together with my mother's best friend and niece, Angela Cardillo Mullen, Aunt Annie's oldest daughter, and her husband Leo Mullen as guardians. We maintained our little apartment, and I supplied money from my $65 a week starting teacher's salary. Here are a couple of key scenes from the beginning and the end of the play:

THE DAY THE POPE DIED
(Pius XII—d. Oct. 9, 1958)

CAST, IN ORDER OF APPEARANCE:
MARY ANN "MAIME" GALLAGHER: 18 years old, a Normal school [teachers' college] student.

FRAN GALLAGHER: 15 years old, her brother, a high school ballplayer

PETE GALLAGHER: 22 years old, their older brother, a parochial high school English teacher.

TIME: October 9, 1958

SETTING: The kitchen of the Gallagher apartment on the evening of October 9, 1958. Down center, a table and three chairs. Down right, a kitchen area with sink, stove, and fridge and a shiny breadbox on the counter. Up right, an entrance from outside. Up center a table beneath a prominent picture of the Sacred Heart of Jesus. Up left, a door to the boys' bedroom. Left, as far front as possible, 2 separate pictures of the Gallaghers' parents hanging in oval frames. Down left, a small curtain separating the main playing area from a closet with

Maime's clothes and a jewelry box. In the course of the play, the Gallaghers will eat a spaghetti supper and do the dishes afterwards. All actions described may be easily mimed.

[Before MAIME enters, we hear an ash can being bumped into. Then MAIME enters and throws down her books. They spill. She kicks one across the room where it lands under her parents' pictures. She picks it up and looks at them quietly and places her books neatly on the table under the Sacred Heart, which she also, pointedly, glances at as she turns to survey the stove.]

MAIME: Oh, Francis. You make me so mad. No water on, and you'll be in a rush, and Peter will be hightailing it to Worcester.

[She angrily gets out a pan, fills it with water, and puts it on the stove, throwing in salt and oil. She gets out another pan, and from the fridge puts meatballs and sauce on to heat. She carefully counts the meatballs.]

MAIME: 1-2-3-4, 5-6-7, 8-9-10. Oh dear, that's going to be trouble! *[She looks at her reflection on the breadbox and sees a blemish on her forehead.]*

MAIME: Oh God. Why right in the middle of my forehead? *[She starts to squeeze and fiddle with the blemish.]*

MAIME: Stop it, Mary Ann, or you'll end up a Cyclops. I need some Noxzema. *[She crosses to stand before her mother's picture.]* Oh God, it will show. I'll look like an untouchable. That's me, an untouchable. Absolutely untouchable. The untouchable Mary Ann Gallagher.

[MAIME glances at her mother's picture and goes into her closet where she buries her face in the clothing and sobs.]

MAIME: Oh, Mama.

[She cries and sobs violently, then makes a conscious effort to get ahold of herself. She starts to figure out what clothes she will wear if she gets a date for the weekend, and passes freely back and forth from the closet to the playing area in front of her parents' pictures.]

MAIME: What do you think, Momma? What should I wear for Harold? *[She pulls her hair into a ponytail.]* Where are we going? To Lanesboro to play miniature golf. And then to Pedrin's drive-in Burger Palace. *[pause]* Yes.

Pedal-pushers. But what blouse? I need a sleeveless blouse with pedal-pushers. Oh Mother, don't be so medieval. I'll wear a cardigan over it. No, not the white cardigan. I know you like the white one, so symbolic. Yes, everyone in town quite agrees. There goes the noble self-sacrificing Mary Ann Gallagher. Isn't she splendid? But the cardigan has to be dark. *[pause]* Because Harold ends up with his head on my shoulder. It's all perfectly innocent, believe me. Perfectly. *[pause]* On the back road overlooking Cheshire Lake. We pull into the look-out in Farnham. *[pause]* Just talk, I assure you. He tells me all the nightmares he had in the hospital after his accidents. I can understand. He's just like a little boy and I just pet his head a little. *[pause]* Alright. Alright. Pat his head, and he cries on my shoulder. He always ends up crying on my shoulder, so it's got to be a dark cardigan. I'm not sending my white cardigan to Palumbo's after every date with Harold. *[pause. In exasperation.]*

Lots of cars go by the lookout, every 12 seconds at least, and the lights keep shining in on us. It's like being outside a lighthouse. Nothing could happen in a thousand years. He's really afraid of me. I'm too good for him. That's what they all think. *[Rummaging on the rack.]* All I have are flowers and stripes. I need a solid colored blouse. *[pause]* Because it's just not done. The only solid color blouse I have is long-sleeved, you saw to that. *[Kicking her shoes.]* My loafers have dirty pennies. *[She looks in her purse for new pennies.]* Dirty pennies are unacceptable. Harold is so picky. You'd like him. So much neater than Fran, or even Peter. Maybe they'll have new pennies. *[pause]* But maybe Harold won't call this weekend. His car's probably not fixed yet. Maybe Rudy will call. *[pause]* Oh, just to a movie. *[She starts doing her hair in pigtails.]* No, not the Curran Highway Drive-in. Not the passion pit. That wouldn't do for the Mary Ann Gallagher. Just the Paramount on Main Street. *[pause]* A western, *Tensions At Table Rock* or something like that. It doesn't matter, as long as it's a western. Rudy likes the cows, or steers, he calls them. No, Momma. He's very polite and quite proper. And just like the cowboys in the movies, he probably kisses only the horse, or cow. You know those farm boys from Readsboro. *[pause]* Just a blouse, and a pleated skirt. But look at this, *[holding up skirt]* just like a high school uniform. A college girl just doesn't wear a high school uniform. I think I'll give him a treat tonight. *[She holds a widenecked elasticized blouse in front of herself. She pulls the neckline down over her shoulders.]* That should take his mind off the cows. *[She looks at herself.]* Not quite. I'll need a full box of tissues.

[laugh] A pullover would be less obvious, but then I'll have to wear a straight-fitted skirt. And I don't have a clean one. Too many socks and underwear and shirts for Pete and Fran. But, oh God, what am I going to do if it's Larry? *[pause]* I know he's older, but he's a real gentleman. He could be asking 30 different girls out instead of me. *[pause]* But you didn't want me going steady with one guy. Didn't you always tell me to complete my education before getting serious? So I can get married and keep right on doing the dishes and washing and cleaning like I'm doing now–for one husband instead of two brothers. *[pause]* It's none of your business. Not any more. *[She suddenly cries.]* I'm sorry, I didn't mean that. *[pause. Defensively.]* To the State Line in New York. He's over 21, so he can drink in Massachusetts if he wants. *[pause]* I don't drink, anyway. I would never drink. *[pause]* He's not that kind of man. He's real polite. That's where his friends go. He doesn't have more than two drinks. *[pause]* Well, maybe three or four, but I'll make him soak it up with a big steak dinner, and I'll get a lobster dinner, just like you used to like so much. *[pause]* I am not changing the subject. I don't have a driver's license, and I am not going to take my birth certificate to prove I'm 18. I won't order any drinks and besides I look much older when I dress up appropriately. *[She pulls her hair up and tilts her head.]* Just like you used to wear yours. I can even use your combs. *[She locks her hair in place with her mother's combs. pause]* My sheath, with heels and pearls. *[She goes into the closet and takes out her mother's pearls from a jewel box as FRAN rushes in, throws down his books, and begins to get out of his clothes as he disappears through the bedroom door.]* Your pearls and your stole. *[She puts on the stole and spins around, swooping and walking elegantly.] [pause]* Yes, I can in high heels. *[But MAIME stops and puts things away slowly and sadly.]* But I don't have an evening bag. The last time I was there everyone but I had an evening bag. And besides, you're right. He'll want to go parking on the Taconic Trail. And he'd find out I'm half-tissues. And that would be the end of that. Number 31 bites the dust. *[pause]* I hope none of them call. I should have listened to Sister Eleanor Maria and gotten away from all this. *[To her mother's picture.]* But I couldn't leave you, could I? I wouldn't leave. What would people say then?

[*The play continues with interaction of Mary Ann with her brothers. Mary Ann's difficulties are magnified by the shortcomings of her older brother, Pete. (Note: Pete is really Pat, me. I realize now that in revealing Pete's faults, at the time of the writing, I still had to keep my name out of it, albeit unconsciously.)*

Pete is taking off every weekend to Worcester to visit his fiancée, Therese, and is consumed with wedding plans. But the enormity of his selfishness is revealed in the simplicity of a small act. And this small absence of a small act has haunted me to this day, although the ending finds resolution.]

PETER: *[crosses to MAIME.]* I had no idea. You seemed so happy at Christmas.

MAIME: It was the worst Christmas of my life.

PETER: I would have given you a ride home.

MAIME: *[Turning on PETE, driving him back with each retort.]* You were at Therese's house.

PETER: I didn't know.

MAIME: There's a lot you don't know. Any more than you can know about Momma and Daddy being in heaven.

PETE: *[Cursing]* Jesus, Mary, and Joseph *[then changing to a prayer],* pray for me in my hour of need. We're speculating in the realm of psychological imagination. We won't know the truth until we die, and I'm not ready to die yet.

MAIME: I am.

PETE: Don't talk like that. Even fooling around.

MAIME: I'm not fooling.

PETE: Don't say that. That's the unforgiveable sin, despair.

MAIME: You don't really know anything about despair, do you?

PETE: Oh, yes I do.

MAMIE: *[crossing to sit at table]* When did you ever despair in real life, not a dream?

PETE: *[staring out over MAIME's sink]* At college, after Momma died. I flunked math and chemistry, Therese seemed a lost cause, I had a pizza-faced roommate who was so brilliant he did all the math problems in the book the summer before and just waited like a vulture for the Prof to make a mistake. He asked me very embarrassing personal questions about every little motivation every time I said anything. I felt he was seeing my soul naked, and it nearly drove me crazy, 'cause his probing made me look at it, too. I was packed and ready to come home and staring out the window at the moon over the girls' campus thinking about throwing myself to a glorious suicide in Confusion Square below!

MAIME: I had no idea.

PETE: *[lightening up]* It's okay. I didn't.

MAMIE: *[laughing]* Why not?

PETE: My underwear wasn't clean. *[PETE joins MAIME at the table.]*

MAIME: I would have claimed your body. Really, why didn't you do it?

PETE: I don't know. I can't remember any one thing, except I hoped jumping would make Therese take me seriously. I couldn't see living without her.

MAIME: Yes, I think that's despair. *[MAIME jumps up and crosses to the sink.]* But we always get back to Therese, don't we?

PETE: She's going to be my wife. We're going to be married. Why shouldn't I think about her?

MAIME: All the time?

PETE: Not ALL the time. True, most of the time. At least it makes me happy to think of her.

MAIME: And thinking of me makes you sad.

PETE: Yes. It does.

MAIME: There. I knew it.

PETE: It makes me sad to see you so sad and screwed up.

MAIME: So now I'm screwed up. What does that mean?

PETE: *[goes to speak earnestly to MAIME.]* You need help. You need to talk to Father MacNeil when he comes down for the wedding. He'll straighten you out. He can read your handwriting.

MAIME: I don't need to be straightened out. I'm not crazy.

PETE: You sure act it sometimes.

MAIME: How would you know? You're never here.

PETE: I'm here right now.

MAIME: For how long?

PETE: Until I leave for Worcester.

MAIME: There you are!

PETE: She's my fiancée. I love her. I want to be with her.

MAIME: Then go. Go to your damned fiancée.

PETE: Don't you talk about my future wife that way.

MAIME: No. No. I won't. I'm sorry. She's got enough trouble if she loves you.

PETE: What do you know about love?

MAIME: More than you do.

PETE: Oh? What do you call your relationship with the "gentlemen" who come to call for you? What a bunch of misfits. Crackpots. Harold, who has driven four cars into assorted trees and lamp posts. You've driven him to some kind of death wish. And Larry is an adolescent scorekeeper who wants to chalk you up in his little black book. And Rudy, the ploughboy rustic from Readsboro, who would turn you into a milkmaid in the hayloft. When are you going to date a real man? Every guy you fall for has a "problem," he's looking for a mother! You'd be better off with a collection of teddy bears–they wouldn't drive you to despair.

MAIME: *[quietly] You* drive me to despair.

PETE: Me? How? That's the most ridiculous thing I've ever heard. I do everything for you.

MAIME: *[backing PETE across the room with each succeeding accusation.]* You do everything for yourself, you mean.

PETE: How can you say a thing like that?

MAIME: You run off every weekend to Worcester to see your beloved Therese.

PETE: She's my wife almost.

MAIME: You use this place like a hotel.

PETE: I pay the rent.

MAIME: You never go to Fran's ball games.

PETE: I have to prepare my school work.

MAIME: You're at church every day and praying.

PETE: What's wrong with that?

MAIME: Whenever there's work to be done.

PETE: Like what?

[They are now on opposite sides of the table, squaring off at one another.]

MAIME: Like laundry? I'm glad Madelaine Palumbo stripped you naked in study hall, and your roommate did at college. I'd like to see your soul, too.

PETE: Laundry is your part of keeping this family together.

MAIME: Mary Ann's glue. That's what keeps this place together. Nothing has changed since you conned me into playing little maid.

PETE: That was kid stuff.

MAIME: It still is for you. *[mocking him.]* "I'll be the Little Prince, and you be the Little Maid," and I looked up to you so. I did everything, and you took advantage of it, and you are still playing the Little Prince, you . . . you . . . bastard.

PETE: Don't you talk to me that way.

MAIME: *[Crossing from sink side of table, past PETE, to the area in front of the parents picture.]* You've still got me doing everything, now that Momma's not here to primp for her Little Prince, the future priest. Well, what happened? You're not so different from Larry Demarco, are you now? But I took over for momma: the cooking, the cleaning, the laundry, the shopping, the bed making, the dishwashing, floor waxing, even the stinking lawn-mowing. And the Little Maid isn't worthy to be a member of your wedding party. You and Therese deserve each other.

PETE: What are you talking about?

MAIME: You know. Your perfect wife-to-be wouldn't dream of asking a little maid to be a bridesmaid!

PETE: Leave her out of this. She wanted to ask you to be a bridesmaid, but I told her, "no"!

MAIME: You? Why not?

PETE: You don't really like her.

MAIME: Are you crazy? How can you say that?

PETE: You are always so cool to her. I can feel it. You're jealous because I go to visit her. Weren't you just railing about that?

MAIME: Yes, I am jealous. I hate you both.

PETE: Why?

MAIME: Because you have each other. She has you. And I don't have anyone since Momma died. Oh, Peter. I'm so alone. I hate Harold, and Rudy, and Larry–because they're not the one. *[MAIME turns to her parents' picture.]* I'm so alone. Oh, Jesus, God, I'm so alone.

[PETER goes to embrace her. She fends him off.]

PETER: But Mary Ann. I love you.

[Maime slaps his face. He is thunderstruck.]

PETE: You, you, struck me. *[He collapses into a chair at the table.]*

MAIME: *[Very deliberately and cooly like an Angel of Conscience]* You love me? You love me! You miserable bastard, you never, never, never even once have thanked me for one single meal I've put in front of your praying mouth. Never once, not one thank you. Even a waitress at Florini's rates a thank you from a drunken bum, but can you ever remember saying thank you to me? Just thank you.

[PETE is beaten. His head hangs in shame, MAIME gets very quiet. They are both crying quietly. MAIME whispers at him over his shoulder into his ear.]

Just one "thank you" to back up all your praying and preaching. One little thank you. *[Long silence as MAIME sits in a chair opposite him.]*

PETE: *[sobs]* I don't want to be the way I am. But . . . *[Shaking his head.]* It's true. Everything you said is true. *[Silence]* It's no good to say another meaningless "I'm sorry," is it?

MAIME: Try it.

PETE: I really know what I'm saying this time, Maime. *[pause]* I'm sorry. When I see my own rotten mind, there's another thing I see, and it's not a dream, it's real. Daddy asked me to go on retreat with him like we used to every year at the monastery in West Springfield, and I told him, "no," because Therese's family was having a family picnic at their summer cottage. So I went up there for the weekend, and the next week Daddy was dead. And I missed the last weekend with him. And now he's gone, and Momma too, and I was so alone, but, oh God, I'm sorry Maime, 'cause I have Therese, and I feel guilty I'm so happy with her, and you don't have anybody but a thoughtless, selfish, stupid oaf of a brother.

MAIME: That's better than nothing.

PETE: Not bloody much. But I wanted to be like Daddy; I wanted be a father to this family.

MAIME: There's more to being a father than just paying for everything.

PETE: I meant well.

MAIME: So did I. But I know why I'm so miserable myself. *[PETE looks up at her.]* I can't be the mother of this family, either.

PETE: We don't have to go looking for misery. I found that out at Therese's picnic.

MAIME: You didn't have a good time?

PETE: They were having steamed clams. And Therese's father offered me some. I refused, of course. They're nothing but big slimy snots.

MAIME: Oh, Peter. You're making me sick.

PETE: Precisely. Therese forced me to eat some, and when we rode home I got sick as a dog. I made them stop the car on River Street because I would have thrown up in the car. I barfed all the way along Blackinton Street. I swear my toenails came up.

MAIME: *[crossing to sink]* Stop! Stop! That's the best proof of the existence of God I've heard so far. We all get what's coming to us, I guess. I did.

PETE: What do you mean?

MAIME: I could have been out of here.

PETE: That's impossible. Maime, I know you'd never walk out. Never.

MAIME: Sister Eleanor Maria told me I could have a full scholarship to Regis or Emmanuel.

PETE: Why the hell didn't you take it?

MAIME: For your sake and Fran's. We wouldn't have been able to keep as a family.

PETE: Oh, God. Say it isn't true. You're lying.

MAIME: Yes, I'm lying.

PETE: What are you saying?

MAIME: I'm saying I told Eleanor Maria I wouldn't leave you and Fran, that we'd stay together as a family and not to ever mention the scholarship to anyone.

PETE: Oh, God.

MAIME: *[crossing to parents' pictures]* But, it wasn't just for you and Fran. I was afraid to go. And afraid to be something other than what people thought. Everyone has praised me so. "What a wonderful girl. So brave. So generous. Keeping the family together. So noble." I have never been able to do what I really wanted. I've always been what other people expected me to be. *[Turning to Mother's picture.]* And it's all a lie. I am unhappy, and lost. Living a lie.

[MAIME runs into her closet, goes to cry into the clothes. Pete follows her, pacing outside.]

PETE: Maime . . . Maime. You're too hard on yourself. You did it.

You really did do it. It's not a lie. You did keep us together. You have made us a family. You're not Momma, and I'm not Daddy. And Fran is not our son. But we are a family and we can stick together. Come on out. You really did do it. To hell with what people think. You did what you thought was right. That's what we all have to do. Come on out.

[PETE goes into the closet and sees the clothes Maime is hugging.]

PETE: What's this?

MAIME: Momma's clothes.

PETE: I thought you gave them to the St. Vincent de Paul Society?

MAIME: I lied about that, too.

PETE: *[hugging her, and for the first time she doesn't recoil.]*

*

[*The conclusion finds the three siblings ready to face the world, but now united through the TRUTH coming out. Pete/Pat married Therese/Jacqueline, Mary Ann found a real man, and Fran accepted every burden in his short life, with grace and equanimity. And the play, like* The Flowers, *won the Best Production at the One-Act Play Festival.*

There is very little FICTION in this play. This is closer to TRUTH than anything else I have written. The TRUTH here is so raw that thirty-three years later I still cringe when I read it. Richard Chiasson was so close to the reality of being me that it was spooky. The miracle of this situation is that from this confrontation on, my sister and I have had a rock-solid relationship. She did give me Grandma Walsh's ring, and she was in the wedding and she was there again for our fiftieth anniversary recreation of our wedding.]

FIRST PERFORMANCE: October 20, 1985

CAST: Lianna Nasso – Mary Ann "Maime" Gallagher

Francis Flynn [Best Supporting Actor] – Francis Gallagher

Richard Chiasson [Best Actor] – Pete Gallagher

DIRECTOR: Daphne Hamilton [Best Director]

PLAY: Best Production

Pat, grad photo StFX. 1958 Jacqueline, grad photo, Anna Maria College, 1961

The Ballad of Pat and Jackie

There once was a young man named PAT
Who instinctively knew THIS from THAT
But when he met Jackie his mind went quite wacky
And his great heart went paddy-pat-pat.

She was lovely and smart and she captured his heart
For Pat, only friendship she'd had.
He tried four long years to diminish her fears
But the romance was doomed for the lad.

Despite all his affection to change her direction
As a couple they would not live.
Jackie's faith had been calling, so without any stalling
She went to the convent to live.

Their worlds were quite separate and Pat, though not desperate,
For Jackie continued to yearn.
He prayed every day that somehow–some way
His true love to him would return.

At last Fate was most kind, Jackie changed her own mind.
To North Adams she did retreat.

When Pat found this out, he let out a shout,
"My heart never accepted defeat!"

Pat was stalwart and true. He pursued her anew.
And Jackie now gave him a chance.
With sweetness and grace she saw in his face
A life's partner with whom she could dance.

They were "we" years ago and they've danced fast and slow,
Embracing all that Life sent their way.
They've composed their own songs as they've journeyed along:
It's their symphony we honor today.

Happy 50th Anniversary to the most loving, supportive, and loyal couple a family could have. The world is a better place because of you.

Love, Mary Ann [Walsh] Rorke

The Man Who Made Tolkien Famous

In 1957, in one of the first creative writing programs in a Canadian university, my professor, Fr. R. J. MacSween, told us about a novel written by a professor of Anglo-Saxon in England entitled *The Lord of the Rings*, a trilogy. This professor, a friend of C.S. Lewis, had taught W.H. Auden, and inspired him to turn from communism to literature and poetry. His trilogy created a whole new universe of the mind, which swept readers into an epic journey of great moral magnitude.

One of my classmates, George Sanderson, immediately went out, bought the trilogy, and cut classes for three days until he finished reading the novel. I made a promise to myself to read that book the first clear chance I could.

In the fall of 1958, I began teaching at my former high school, St. Joe's, in my hometown of North Adams, Massachusetts. Upon receiving my first paycheck of

$65.00, I hitchhiked to Williamstown, five miles from North Adams, the home of the Ivy League college, Williams. North Adams did not have a single serious bookstore. The bookstore did not have the trilogy, but they looked it up and agreed to order two sets–one for me, and one for the bookshelf.

I started the book and bogged down in the first 100 pages; this journey would be challenging. The following summer, I began again and persisted, and was so enthralled that I began telling my students about this great adventure.

In the meantime, I was having my own epic adventure, becoming engaged to the young woman I had pursued since 1950 when we met in grade 9 (so intensely today it might have been considered stalking, except that she accepted my proposal). She was still attending Anna Maria College in Worcester, Massachusetts, so after my two years at St. Joe's, we married in 1960, and we went to live near Anna Maria. I taught at Shrewsbury Jr.-Sr. High School, and after Jacqueline graduated 6 months pregnant (the top student and winner of the silver medal as "an outstanding example of Christian womanhood"), we moved to Putnam, Connecticut, where I taught at Marianapolis Preparatory School, run by the Marian Fathers. During my wife's pregnancy, I read Tolkien's trilogy to her. Our daughter Mary was born. And my need for graduate study, if ever I was going to be able to fulfill my dream to return to StFX University and teach with my mentor, Fr. MacSween, caused us to move to Boston.

Life was beginning to present challenges. Some of the Marian Fathers seemed to have entered the priesthood to escape the coal mines of Pennsylvania. One in particular enforced discipline by whacking, literally, the boys with a miniature baseball bat. When I broached this subject at faculty meetings, the tension continued to gear up. I went to the local bishop: I got nowhere. I heard that the school was trying to establish itself in the nearby Worcester diocese, so I spoke to the authorities there, and Marianapolis never got a foothold in Massachusetts.

The young men at Marianapolis were fine fellows, although a goodly number were sent to the school to be out of the way of their parents. Five young men seemed to gravitate to the activities in my purview: we started a school newspaper, a drama club, a literary magazine, and they were already at work on a yearbook.

In the spring nearing the end of term, I convinced the kindly Headmaster, Fr. Joseph Dombrowska, to allow me to take the five hardest workers to Boston University for a Saturday convention for High School students, at which the young Ted Kennedy would be the key speaker. We loaded up my car and went conventioneering!

At Boston University, I sent the boys off to hear Ted Kennedy speak, and succumbed to irresistible temptation for me in those days: a gym full of publisher's stands hawking books and giving samples.

And then, the fateful moment. I saw the huge red banner: ANY BOOK YOU WANT IN PAPERBACK, OR WE WILL PUT IT IN PAPERBACK. I charged to the stand.

"Do you have *The Lord of the Rings* in paperback?"

"No. Tell me about it."

So I unloaded my word hoard for the clerk. As my tale tumbled out full of hobbits with furry feet who liked to smoke and eat all day, and Gandalf the Wizard, and the Nazgul and the Dark Lord, and dwarfs and orcs, and Strider and Gollum . . . the clerk stopped me up.

"That sounds like a kid story."

"Yes, it's for kids, and for adults. It's a great story."

"It sounds like science fiction to me."

"Well, if you put it in paperback and get it in the corner stores and drug stores it will sell."

"The only company that would be interested in that kind of book would be Ace Paperbacks."

"I don't care which company it is, it will sell."

"Okay. Buddy, here are the forms fill out the information and we'll give it to Ace."

So I sat down and filled out the forms and they were sent to Ace.

On the way home that Saturday evening, it was beginning to get dark, and I was booting it over the rolling hills between Boston and Putnam, when coming over one hill there was a traffic light, and I was going too fast to slam on the breaks.

Out of a side road came a Massachusetts' State Trooper like a Nazgul swooping down on a hobbit. The scene opened innocently enough. "License and insurance please." A couple of suppressed giggles from the peanut gallery in the back seat. The trooper handed back my papers, and then shattered my confidence, "Would you have a valid license, sir?" That *was* my license. "Sir, that license is expired."

[My Massachusetts license had expired because of the move to Connecticut, and they did not bother anymore notifying people no longer living in the State. My license had run out on my birthday, May 26th.]

The sky seemed to suddenly darken. "Step out of the car, sir." I did. "Put your hands on the roof of your car." He patted me down. Then he leaned into the car. "Do any of you gentlemen have a valid license?" One did. "Step into the cruiser, sir."

"But, but . . ."

"You are under arrest, sir. I am taking you to the station. These gentlemen are free to go, or to follow to the station if they desire." The peanut gallery was eerily silent.

The sergeant on duty at the station said, "Sir, you may pay a fine of $176.00, and you will be free to go, or you can wait to go before a judge and plead innocent."

"I want to see the judge."

"That will be Monday, sir. 9 a.m. You can wait here with us over the weekend." I had about $30.00 in my pocket. I pleaded: "May I talk to the boys in the car?"

"Officer, accompany the gentleman to the boys in the car."

The students came up with the pooled ransom. One of them drove the car back to the school, and then drove me home, promising to pick me up in the morning. Lots of snickers lay in wait for me the next day.

Next year, with a valid driving license, we were in Boston at Catholic Memorial High School, run by the Christian Brothers of Ireland. I started on my master's degree at Boston College, nights and weekends, and at Christmas time 1962, Fr. MacSween called to tell me he wanted me to return to X to teach in the fall. By then, Francis, our second child, had been born. Life was a whirl.

But Tolkien was front and center. I read *The Hobbit* and *The Lord* to my children in succession. The students had a coffee house on campus, an old house on the edge of campus, and I took to reading *The Lord of the Rings* to the students on Monday nights.

And then came the day when the trilogy swept the charts across the wide world and became a classic. And I knew it had happened because of my filing of those fateful forms for Ace paperbacks.

I began to tell my tale of how I had put Tolkien on the charts. In 1989, I wrote and published *The History of Antigonish* and sold more copies than Tolkien had in his initial publication! I couldn't prove my fanciful tale, but it provoked much discussion and couldn't be disproven either.

I have been a reader of *The New Yorker* since about the age of ten when my father bought some secondhand bound copies of *The Best of the New Yorker.* Now 39 years after my infamous arrest reported above, I opened my issue of December 10, 2001, and immediately was attracted to *The Hobbit Habit: Reading "The Lord of the Rings,"* by Anthony Lane, film critic.

Lane was writing about the film of the trilogy: "The film has been a long time coming." After informing that the trilogy will be shown in three separate films a year apart, Lane continues, "No one can say whether audiences will stick with the story, or whether, in two years' time, they will have dwindled to a small band of hobbit wanna-bes, lining up glumly in the rain. All that Jackson [the director] can do is look back at the example of Tolkien himself. *When "The Fellowship of the Ring" came out, in 1954, Tolkien's publisher, Allen & Unwin, gambled on selling as many as thirty-five hundred copies, falling to thirty-two hundred and fifty for "The Two Towers," and so down to three thousand for "The Return of the King," the following year.* [*1956*] *In the event, this estimate proved a little cautious. By the end of 1968, total readership of the trilogy was thought to stand at around fifty million* [emphases added].

Later, Lane continues, "There's no two ways about it, Tolkien fans are a funny bunch. It was, and remains, not a book that you happen to read, like any other, but a book that happens to you: a chunk bitten out of your life . . . The size of the beast is important in this respect. *Tolkien sales remained earthbound until 1965, at which point the three parts of the novel were clamped together and published in America as an unauthorized one-volume paperback; five months later, an official equivalent hit the bookshops, whereupon sales went through the roof and never came back down* [emphases added].

Gentle reader, the unauthorized paperback, was, yes, indeed, the ACE PAPERBACK edition, on the rack of every book store in America. It took Houghton-Mifflin five months to produce an authorized edition, in which Tolkien appended a message in the title pages, decrying the fact "that some people behave as orcs, and take things that don't belong to them. But true hobbit-lovers will read only the authorized version," or words to that effect, as I remember. I suffered a slight twinge of guilt at Tolkien's gentle admonition, but then I felt an overwhelming burst of pride, that, maybe, just maybe, my Ace request turned the tide for sales of the epic. I can't prove it of course, but there are lots of things we can't prove that work.

Afternote: The forces of good behind Middle Earth may have exacted a minor revenge on me for my actions. For two years I was in Dublin, Ireland, studying for a doctorate in Anglo-Irish literature under the direction of Professor Gus Martin. I was Gus's first PhD candidate, and we were the same age, and simpatico. Gus treated me like a colleague, for I had been teaching for some 15 years, and we became blood brothers. I returned to Ireland over the years conducting tours and teaching summer schools, and on one of my last trips, I mentioned to Gus that I regretted not meeting Tolkien before he died. Gus, said, "You never mentioned him to me. Tolkien was a good friend and he was an external examiner for the National University of Dublin. We could have met . . ." and Gus fell silent and so did I.

How Our World Has Changed Since August 20, 1960

Mel and I were lying flat like fallen angels on the grass
in back of your house on Kemp avenue marveling at the shooting stars
in the black sky Leonides flashing as lightning-swift as our young lives
in the still innocent dumb days of the mid-twentieth century
in the comforting embrace of the peaceful Berkshire Hills

we did not know then that Mr. Sterling Clark was burying
masterpieces of world art in atom-bomb proof vaults
in Williamstown or that atom bombs were being stashed

under Greylock mountain or that the Korean armistice
would still be marked by a face-off zone in the new millennium

our universe of young biblical age created by an old white-
bearded man
was bounded by a milky way and galaxy explored only by
Flash Gordon or comic book superheroes until Collier's magazine
published the fantasy art of Chesley Bonestell and Willey Ley
and were taken seriously by Werner von Braun and the military

protected by the hills and valleys of our multi-colored leafy world
with escape east over the Mohawk Trail or west through
Hoosac Tunnel
I pictured in my future dreams a babbling brook and idyllic world
of quiet love in your arms in the placid cocoon of North Adams
a corner of the universe safe from the glooming dark outside our valley

safe in the embrace of holy mother churches French Irish Italian
secure in the solar system of nine planets and an axis spin of Sirius
keeping us within the even-tempered diurnal flow of time and space
with guardians angels and Eleanor Maria Fr. Richard
Monsignor Donahue
caring families in tune with the music of the spheres and
Gregorian chant

we offered our lives to that mini-universe and that unerring church
and pledged ourselves to each other in the garden of Turner's Hall
where Fr. MacSween gave us Ronald Knox's new testament translation
thus armed we left the valley the Hoosac River of the Coca-Cola Ledge
and trusting our Lord and our stars we took off to Austin
Street Worcester

in my groin I felt the thump of your tumble down the stairs
on your graduation morning because I failed to empty the garbage
the old retired couple at your fallen side looked up at me surprised
plunging swiftly into hell I felt the spring of guilt uncoil in my guts
you felt the first of the pains I would hurl against the castle of your love

but you were triumphantly crowned the outstanding student of
Anna Maria
crossing the stage acknowledged by Bishop soon-to-be
Cardinal Wright
mathematics of science in your head erased by the child in your womb
and we became peripatetic from Worcester to Putnam to hill-top farm
to Roslindale branching out like astronauts into farther orbits even
the moon

we voyaged hand in hand to farther spaces in our little solar system
Antigonish Ballybrack Dublin Salzburg Rome Naples the Isle of Capri
and the Blue Grotto the Lake District Scotland London
and Fontainebleau
five children and a life-time later through StFX and *The Casket*
we ended up in Cowtown abandoning the ocean for the mountains

in the intervening years the universe had grown old along with us
from 6,000 to 14 billion-years-old from big bang to black hole
and we from blood clots to stents to colon cancer to new knees
despite the entropy of matter and the metronomic march of time
our wearying flesh cannot stop us from dreaming together in our sleep

in our universe of two lives bound by the cross of Christ
you have been the North Star keeping us centered no matter
what highs and lows joys and sorrows sickness and health
have challenged our path through the reaches of time and space
you are the gyroscope of our journey on land over sea through faith

so that today especially on this day and in this moment of our lives
we have weathered the explosion of knowledge the vale of tears
the new far-reaching magnetic vistas at the edges of our new universe
secure in this most uncertain of times that whatever lies ahead
we are one soul one mind flashing Leonide-like to the gates of eternity

happy anniversary love and light of my life

your Patrick

* * *

During this 'rat race' phase of survival a pattern of life was established for our family. My childhood and Jacqueline's childhood had been stabilized by family support. For instance, because of my mother's illness and the complications of World War II, both my Italian family and my Irish family had stepped up and come to the rescue when our family needed care. Grandma Walsh had come from Boston, or taken me to Boston for care, with my maiden aunts Mary, Alice and Lucy. Day care was often parceled out to aunts Annie or Bessie, uncles Tony or Joe, or cousin Pasquale Cardillo. When we returned to North Adams after the War our family had to be split between aunt Annie and Bessie until we could get into our new house. Angie and Leo Mullen took us under their wing after our parents died.

When Jacqueline and I married and left North Adams we were living in a strange new home with no relatives around for support. This was difficult for Jacqueline not only finishing her college career, but having her first child. A remarkable pattern began in our lives in these circumstances: Seating in Jackie's classes at Anna Maria had been alphabetical. When her name changed from Duguay to Walsh she was seated next to a classmate named Joanne Walsh. We became friends with Joanne who was from a Worcester suburb, Auburn. And with her family, mother and father and brothers. When the birth of our first child approached we were literally taken in to the home of the Walshes and became members of the family.

And that pattern of always having extraordinary generous souls taking us into their homes was repeated throughout our lives. My best friend, Jordan Mastroianni, came to my rescue on more than one occasion, and whenever I was in Los Angeles, his and his wife Yvonne's casa was my casa. When I had to return to Boston College for summer schools to complete my Master's degree, I lived with my uncle Louis and aunt Mae Walsh. When we moved to Antigonish whenever the need arose we were housed by the Curries, the Taylors, the O'Briens, the Milners, and at the cottage of Jake and Marilyn MacIsaac. In Ireland Billy and Eithne Gallagher established an open door policy to any Walsh or friend who needed shelter–a life-time policy of gracious welcome. Ray and Joy Hanley took in a visiting Professor and three children for a full summer school in Charlottetown, Prince Edward Island. In Toronto Terry Green and his wife had an open door, as did Frank Canino and his partner Henry. A similar life-time welcome existed in Fredericton, New Brunswick, where a way station was established for Walshes, parents and children, being halfway between Antigonish and Quebec and Toronto. The gracious proprietors of this home are my roommate of 66 years ago at StFX, Homer Keenan, and his wife Maura. The pattern has continued into our current life with support of Tom and Diane Eason who welcomed us into the Bentley Condominium and are fast friends to this day when we have settled into our final home with our daughter and her husband, Neil White. All of these open doors have been blessings in our times of need.

Ray and Joy Hanley

Chapter 5
Immigrants 1963–71

When I got the call as Christmas was approaching in 1962, just starting my MA at Boston College, I turned to my wife and announced, "Fr. MacSween was just made Chair of the English department, and he is hiring me to start next September. We're moving to Canada." It was not a total surprise, we had been speculating for some time about making the move, although now we were on the fast track.

Jackie and I and Mary and Francis would all need medical exams, which we procured at our local medical clinic. We filled out Canadian government immigration forms, we concluded all our banking and personal affairs and accounts and off we went to Antigonish [The place where the bears knock the leaves off the trees while looking for beechnuts, in Mi'kmaq Aboriginal language.] We settled in to an apartment, one child in each bedroom and parents on a foldaway bed in the living room. We waited for our official landed-immigrant papers.

The official documents were not coming, and the months were creeping by. Fr. Bauer called and said that his office was having trouble getting our papers from the government, but not to worry, former professor Alan J. MacEachen, Deputy Prime Minister [to be], is looking into the matter for us. It seemed about time for a crisis. And sure enough, it came traipsing into our lives as innocently as a Jehovah Witness–but in the person of Monsignor Bauer. He took me aside privately, out of earshot of Jacqueline and the children.

"Pat, the Government of Canada is refusing to allow you Landed Immigrant status. You will be allowed only six months in Canada."

"Why, Monsignor? What's wrong?"

Whispering gently into my ear, Monsignor intoned the news, as confessionally as possible, "You have syphilis!"

I did not tremble, or quake, or get angry this time. I laughed out loud.

"Monsignor Bauer, that is impossible, I assure you."

"I'm sorry, but the immigration medical indicates you have *it*," he said, now that the kids had joined us to see what I was laughing about.

"I'll take care of it, Monsignor, now that I know the source of the information."

It took only three calls to our old medical clinic in Massachusetts to have them discover that they had mixed up my medical file with someone else's. I and my family would all be welcome to Canada. O Canada!

I can never leave the United States of America: it is in my blood and bones, and in my mind and soul. Wherever I go, the USA is in me. And these days it is painful, for my homeland is suffering. I feel that suffering acutely, for I have in a sense been born again into a new land, a new country, a modified mind and soul.

This 'great north' that welcomed me would make my life experiences quite different from what they would have been if I had remained in the USA. The major years of my adult life deeply formed my present being. As I become ever more aware it was not just the activities of my life, but the people in my new Canadian life who formed me anew and enriched my life in so many ways. And the roots of my adult life grew in that place better known throughout the entire world than any other Canadian name: Antigonish–renowned throughout some 195 nations of the world for the Antigonish Movement, a program of continuing education for the benefit of humanity.

In 1989, I wrote a book, *The History of Antigonish*, for the citizens of Antigonish/StFX as an act of gratitude for the blessings of a fine life among fine people.

In the lean years of salary at X, I picked up extra-curricular gigs as a High-School graduation speaker–a useful recruiting tool for my courses at university + expenses. Here is an early sample.

Inverness High School Graduation Address June 17, 1966

Ladies and Gentlemen,

You are here, and I am here, and these people are here today for very special reasons. Six thousand year ago, about 4000 B.C., there would be no need of our meeting together–and most likely we would never meet! I would be in my cave up in Antigonish skinning a bear I had smashed with my stone club. My little girls and boys would be pounding a bear skin to make it soft. And my wife would be grunting her complaints that I never bring home those soft little rabbit furs so she could have a decent coat like Mrs. Ugh-Ugh in the next cave. You boys in the audience would be splitting pine branches and fastening strips of skin around oblong rocks making good hammers for your fathers. You girls would be boiling lizards and snails caught on the banks of the river and trying to get the tangles out of your three-foot long hair with old dried salmon bones. And all of us could look forward to doing the same things day in and day out until gored by a wild boar or eaten for supper by a wild tribe from neighboring Margaree.

In the Middle Ages–the Dark Ages–our lots would not be much improved. We would have lived in little more miserable huts made of wattle or sticks plastered with clay and covered with a thatched roof. Our clothes would be of the coarsest: one long tunic or robe of rough cloth or leather and if we were very fortunate, wooden clogs for our feet. Our furniture would consist of a crude table, a bench or two. And bags of straw on the floor serve as our beds. Our food would be black bread, a few eggs, and probably only cabbage, turnips, peas and beans. Occasionally, we might enjoy a chicken or some pigeons or seagull–normally we could not afford meat. Game and fish would be forbidden to commoners and serfs. Sheep, cows and oxen would be too precious for slaughtering–and they would have to be killed with winter approaching and feed short–then most of the meat would spoil because salt for preserving it would be too expensive. We would plough and plough and plough–and eat a meal under a tree with other ploughmen, and then plough and plough and plough and plough and plough some more. We would go home for supper–as soon as the sun goes down we would go to bed–for our handmade candles give only a flicker and our day would start at sunrise the next morning. We would live in what today would seem unbearable filth–but in such respects even the members of the aristocracy had not developed a cleanliness next to godliness. We would not be able to read or write and would live and die unknown to but a handful. But of course our conditions of existence would be immensely improved by the 1800s, during the Industrial Revolution, say, you could be earning good money–you could all get jobs in the mills working 12 hours a day–starting at age 8 or 9! And the pennies you would get each day would be enough to keep you alive–for at 8 or 9 your stomach wouldn`t be too large and you'd be too tired to eat big meals. You girls, of course, would get out of the mills and earn twice as many pennies a day by working in the coal mines. But of course, any money you earned at the mill would be spent in the company store or the "Tommy shop." The owner of the mill would sell you food for cut rates–or cut-your-throat-rates–depending on how you look at it!

Now–here we are in the twentieth century, on June 17, 1966. The past is like a nightmare which has slipped into the dark recesses of our memories. Today's world is a world full of opportunity–and the thing that has made our world much better than the past is education. The more education we receive, the better equipped we are to continue improving our standard of living and our means of existence. Today, there are over 40,000 different occupations available for you students. But just as the people we examined in our examples had to increase their education to improve their condition–so too, you must be educated in order to obtain a good occupation, a higher standard of living, a better way of life.

Now I certainly understand that it is a struggle–a challenge–to obtain an education in today's world–but I also believe that it is easier than it ever was in the past. We, your parents, your teachers, all of us involved in education hope that your schooling will help you all to find a goal to work for. It is a principle in philosophy that the first thing desired is the last thing obtained. The career you choose is the goal you work for through education–it will be the last thing you get after going through the necessary education.

But you can't have a goal or a career if you have no knowledge of what careers are available for you. For example, there is a man now standing outside the front door of the school handling out $1,000 bills! Oh. 7:00 o'clock. Too late! But, you didn't know about it–so it didn't do you any good. You couldn't take advantage of it!

Your education is designed to give you knowledge, to help you get a goal, to give you what you need to decide what to do in the future. So set your goals as high as you can. There are so many opportunities to get ahead. Plan for a university education. You can get government loans up to $5,000. But certainly all of us are not destined for a college career. If you have special talents in certain fields you can continue your education in Nova Scotia at the Nova Scotia Institute of Technology; the Land Survey Institute; the Marine Engineering School, the Maine Navigation School; or the Fisherman's training Center. In addition, there are Vocational Evening Schools; Coal Mining Schools; and Vocational correspondence Courses.

All of us here have certain talents that must be developed–and somewhere, if you can find it, is an occupation for you. It takes good hard work–no one will kid you that it is a snap–but you can succeed if you really want to.

Many Invernessers have proved that you can succeed. Inverness County has a sterling heritage in great men–men who have served Inverness, Cape Breton, Nova Scotia, Canada, yes, great men who have served even millions throughout 181 nations of the wide, wide world.

I speak of men like the great Angus L. Macdonald, the Honorable Sidney Smith, Father Jimmy Tompkins, Dr. Moses Coady, Doc Pat Nicholson! Truly giants among men, Invernessers who gave of themselves wholly and completely in the service of mankind.

And many of the living carry on in the tradition of these greats–the Honorable Allan MacEachen, Judge Allan MacKinnon, James Deagle, President of the Nova Scotia Teachers' Union, and the man I work for, Dr. Malcom MacLellan, President of StFX University.

Now graduates, it's your turn. Get out there and make the world a better place.

[How obvious in the third millennium is the one-sided masculine bias of this talk. I had a lot, a very lot, more to learn about realizing and acknowledging the contributions of the females of Inverness to the general well-being of society. *Mea culpa, mea culpa, mea maxima culpa.* (Through my fault, through my fault, through my most grievous fault.) My Hoosac Valley myopia definitely needed more broadening life experience.]

Letter to the Berkshires

February 23, 1968

To our dear family members back in the Berkshires:

It is clear and blue sky in Antigonish. We have been having a steady month–long cold spell of crisp but invigorating winter days with no snow. We are all well and awaiting our fourth blessed event.

Monica Anne is three now. She is our local representative for the MAFIA. Her voice is louder than Daddy's whenever she demands a drink of water or juice. Her flashing black eyes can change from anger to coyness and innocence faster than anyone since Sarah Bernhardt. She dances endlessly to Mozart, Beethoven, Larry Welk, or the Clancy Brothers–and she's ever after Daddy to play his one tune on the piano–so she can dance to, as she says, "rot and roll." She has a little pain in her tummy occasionally which she thinks is a baby, in spite of Mommy's explanations. Fran gets a good run for his money from Monica. She is, plainly and simply, a 99 and 44/100% pure WOP.

Francis, age 5, fights a losing battle against the distaff side of the family. He has big soft brown eyes and they often show pain. He doesn't so much get colds or sniffles as triple-pneumonia. At least, from the noise, that is what you'd suspect. He is too good. He is the last of the just–born to suffer for the sins of the rest of us. He is still talking Anglo-Saxon, but he has talent. He is an artist. He draws free-forms which very tastefully fill his drawing papers with pleasing shapes and lines–and he is not afraid to experiment. He has a remarkable flair for colors–and we have hopes he may be able to face the world by the time he's 83.

Mary Theresa, age 6, looks like Daddy, without the beard of course. Her reading ability is at grade 5 already. Daddy is going to have to hide his, ah, um, adult novels. Mary continues in the great family tradition of Law as established by Carmen and Mary Ann Walsh. She starts making a case against going to bed at about 3:30 in the afternoon. At 10:38 p.m. she'll show up in the living room looking for a needle to sew a button on her pajamas. At 10:47 she's looking for a Band-Aid for a hangnail. At 11:02 she needs a drink, and at 11:23 she has to go to the bathroom–well, I mean–she just had a drink, didn't she? The next morning she's home from school with a cold and gets a good day's rest to get rid of the bags under her eyes. Of course, having rested all day she just couldn't be sent to bed until AFTER Green Acres, now, could she? She wants explanations for everything, like "How do they make paper?", "How do records make music?", and "How did the baby get in Mummy's tummy?" Daddy handles the first two and then "has to correct papers, so go see Mummy about that, okay, honey?"

The baby in Mummy's tummy is not really a baby–it's really Alex Karras of the Lions tackling Donnie Anderson of the Packers! Jackie is fine, but the baby coming soon is on a different schedule. He decides to work out every night about midnight. I'm even having trouble sleeping. The bed feels like one of those beds at a motel that will vibrate fifteen minutes for a quarter.

Jackie is as beautiful as ever. She still takes individual orders for the children's breakfasts. She has been handling the family finances for over a year now–and hasn't bounced a check yet. She gives piano lessons to 14 kids, takes sewing two nights a week at the Rural High (Results: one evening gown for faculty parties, one classroom jacket for Daddy, one suit for Francis with left-over material from Daddy's jacket, and 4,383 doll's clothes for Mary and Monica.), types at home for McDonnell Engineering company, Limited, and since she's free from Midnight to 6 a.m. and can't sleep anyway, has applied for a job as a waitress at Webb's All-Night Diner.

I am just great. As happy as can be. I was ten minutes away from shaving off my beard one night and Jackie wouldn't let me! She likes it. To be back teaching after being in administration is just frabjous joy!!! I teach two English survey courses, 2 public speaking courses, 1 weekend course, and a night course in Town in Modern Drama. That sounds like a lot but it's only 12 hours a week. And we just got an $1,800 raise for 1968. Since school opened in September I have lost 52 pounds. That's right. Fifty-two big, fat, ugly, greasy, slippery pounds. (*Who seem to return for visits every decade or so, like prodigal children looking for a place to crash!*) I eat one small meal a day at supper. The family now has the big meal at noon. Not-so-big Daddy goes over to the new gym, the Oland Centre (Canadian spelling, Yanks) and plays handball and has a Swedish

Sauna bath. Ten inches have come off at the waist, 54" to 44", so now my chest is bigger than my waist. I may be handsome again someday. I'm keeping at it, playing seven days a week, religiously.

We had a little fright one Sunday morning near the end of November. I had been to the doctor for a complete physical because of my diet and exercise program. I even had an electrocardiogram because I'm thirty now. Everything was A-OK. I woke up at 9 o'clock with bad charley horse in one leg and I tried to get out of bed and got hit with a charley horse in the other leg. I jumped out of bed to put weight on my feet and felt a bit faint. I started to bend over to put my head between my legs and the pain increased. I never made it. I started to go down–I tried to grab the wall with one hand and turned to reach for Jackie with the other. My head exploded. Colors and lightning flashes. Despite the modernization of the language by Vatican II which eliminated the flowery prayers and thees and thous, I thought I was dying and cried out, reverting to traditional prayer words: "Oh, sweet Jesus!" Blackness.

Jackie never heard me or saw me. I made no noise falling. She saw that I was not in bed, and walked around bed when she heard me moaning as I came to.

"What's the matter, honey?"

"I can't feel my left side and the left side of my head is exploding."

She put a pillow under my head as I lay face on the tile floor. After throwing the bedspread over me, she called Dr. Carmen McIntosh, our family doctor.

I thought, *Thank God I'm in the state of Grace. This is it! And I was doing so well . . . losing weight and all; giving up the pressure-packed administrative job. Everything was working out so well.*

Monica, standing in the doorway, looked at me, didn't understand what I was doing sleeping on the floor, and ran to get the other kids.

"Hey, Mary, Francis, come and see funny Daddy sleeping on the floor."

The three of them stood looking down at me. I remember smiling at them. Monica was laughing and giggling; Fran didn't know whether to laugh or not; Mary was clearly frightened.

I thought, *At least I saw the three of them all together before I left.*

Jackie hustled them upstairs. She returned to my side, knelt down and said, "Honey, there's blood on the pillow." At that moment I felt the top of my mouth with my tongue, and cried, "Honey, my teeth are gone!"

"Where have they gone?"

"There they are!" I cried pointing to pieces of white teeth gleaming on the floor in a perfect arc around my head.

"Oh, they were so beautiful, such nice teeth."

Three and a half of my upper eye teeth had been broken off at the gum line, fanned out on the tile floor, and their roots were what was bleeding on the pillow. A great feeling of relief came over me. I could talk and I knew what was happening. The pain in both legs and head was somewhat less already. A minor heart attack would be not-too-bad to come back from.

I began to rearrange my life accordingly: my dieting would continue. I would be hospitalized for a while. My right side was mobile. I could write and talk. I would be able to teach–or at least write for a living. I would be around to see my new son! (A daughter will be okay, but Fran really wants a brother–to even the odds.)

Dr. McIntosh came into the bedroom.

"Hi, Pat. What are you doing down there?"

I opined I was having some kind of little attack.

I was going to be a problem getting back into bed. He certainly couldn't lift me. He felt my forehead, discovered a nasty lump rising quickly over my left eye. He listened to my back. And then being practical asked me if I thought I could get up, wedged really between the bed and the wall. So Jackie gathered up the pieces of teeth, and I gathered the blanket around my shoulders, carefully raised myself to my knees, charley horses having galloped away, and climbed back into bed, for a proper exam.

The prognosis: I am as strong as a horse! I'm not going to die. Jumping out of bed too quickly caused me to faint. The fireworks in my head came from the impact of my head, now adorned with a huge lump. Two black eyes would appear later in the day, and with my missing teeth and black beard, I would give Quasimodo a run for his money.

But, I didn't mind–being still in shock there wouldn't be much pain until the next day–but that would be a good day–because I wasn't dead, and was unlikely to die. However, the urge to sin faded a little after that day. Poor Jackie thought I was having a stroke. It was harder on her than on me.

By 11 o'clock that morning, my colleague Jim Taylor's father, my dentist, Dr. Omer Taylor had me in his office. He told me there were two possible courses of action: 1) I was obviously in shock, so he could coat the broken roots and I could come back in a day or two, for the second option: the roots were so completely shattered that they would have to come out. No choice there. I said, "Dr. Taylor, if you let me out of this chair now, you'll never get me back into it. This will be your only chance. Rip away!" Out came the fractured stumps.

The black eyes were notable, even in a hockey town like Antigonish. Main gossip question was, "How could he smash his teeth out without getting a cut lip?" The answer that began to circulate to the glee of the locals, was, "He had his big mouth open as usual."

By Friday I had a fine new plate hooked into place, and if I hadn't written this letter you'd never know the difference. But every lunch time now I'm reminded of the thirty years of sensuous pleasure I've had from eating–and I'm thinking it was really clever of a just God to send me this little inconvenience to remind me of my evil habits, Italian-style, of living to eat instead of eating to live.

Now with my plate out, I look like those dirty old men in Ingmar Bergman movies who chase young girls through a dark forest. Wait a minute–maybe a better analogy is–I look like Bobby Hull.

I didn't even get to miss a class. It was kind of rough on the students though–listening to a lecture on "Perthy Bytthey Thelly."

The accident was our big adventure of the year. I had my first poems published in a magazine and I did write a play that started out to be about Renee, Angie Mullins mutt, pardon me, "darling French poodle." But it got carried away. It was put on at the Interclass Play Festival, and may be presented this spring by a professional theater group in Truro, Nova Scotia. [*It was not.*]

Well the kids and Jackie and I are all A-1. Right now the kids are watching Tarzan on TV. They're ready for bed and then Jack and I will be off to a cocktail party.

The general prognosis is *excellent* for the Walsh clan. We have a truly blessed and happy life together. The only thing we could possibly think to ask for would be to be a little closer to our loved ones.

Love and kisses from Jackie, Pat, Mary Theresa, Francis, Monica, and (Boffo the Boxer?).

Patrick X Walsh

The Antigonish Review

One of the most important things I did during this time was to play a key role in making Fr. MacSween's dream of a little magazine come true. The magazine is still publishing but in digital form now–somehow not the same as the printed version. Here is a bit of that story through the eyes and efforts of an up and coming young, accomplished professor.

Excerpt from

Old Provinces, New Modernisms:
Toward an Editorial Poetics of the Maritime Little Magazine

By

James William Johnson

THE UNIVERSITY OF NEW BRUNSWICK
April, 2015

[*Excerpt by permission of the author.*]

3. "Beachcombing in the Twentieth Century": *The Antigonish Review* And Eclectic Modernity in Nova Scotia

I speak of the golden days
now hidden in eastern mist
There I see my youth
in its trajectory towards silence

–R.J. MacSween, "warnings," *The Secret City*

Already by the 1950s MacSween had begun building up a small literary community at StFX among faculty and students. Foremost among his efforts was the cultivation of literary talent through both academic and creative writing courses. In 1956, at the suggestion of student Patrick Walsh, MacSween initiated a Wednesday-night discussion group. The group would grow to include George Sanderson and Sheldon Currie, forming a basis for what would later become the editorial board of *TAR*. [In 1957, at the request of the discussion group,]

MacSween established one of the first for-credit creative writing courses in Canada (Walsh, "For Gert" 116).[1]

Among those students who would later benefit from MacSween's creative guidance were Linden McIntyre and Alistair MacLeod, but in 1957 the class comprised Walsh, Sheldon and Dawn Currie, and George Sanderson [among others] (Donovan 143). Though each student left to pursue further study in the years that followed, they would not be gone for long. In 1962, when MacSween was appointed Chair of the English Department, he began hiring faculty with a view to bringing into the department enough writers to form "a good nucleus for the magazine [he] intended to start" (MacSween, "Interview" 244). By 1969, Walsh, Currie, and Sanderson, as well as future associate editors Gertrude Sanderson, Bill Tierney, Kevin O'Brien, and James Taylor, had all secured teaching positions at StFX. That year, MacSween brought a proposal before the Dean of Arts, Rev. Malcolm MacDonnell, who successfully petitioned the University Council for financial support (Sanderson, "*TAR*" 21).

The first issue of *TAR* appeared in the spring of 1970. With the help of Walsh, who had experience in printing and design,[2] printing of the magazine was undertaken by Jack MacMillan of The Casket Publishing and Printing Company, Ltd., Antigonish's only print shop (Walsh, "Interview").

* * *

Rather than the rigorous and specialized prose of the academic, MacSween advocated for a more eloquent prose style marked by clarity and precision. MacSween's objective was not to replace intellectualism with a populist literature of mass appeal; rather, for MacSween, the aim of the critic was, as MacSween's literary exemplar Ezra Pound had described it, ". . . popularization in its decent and respectable sense. . . to put the greatest amount of the best literature within

---

1 Johnson Note: Earle Birney appears to have established a similar for-credit course as early as 1948 at the University of British Columbia (Mcwhirter xxiii).

2 Johnson Note: Walsh had learned to handset type while working as a printer at a printing company in Massachusetts throughout high school and during his summers home from university. While a sophomore in high school, Walsh also took art lessons from commercial artist Leo Blake in Stockbridge, Mass. These experiences laid the foundation for Walsh's later work with *TAR* (Walsh, "Interview").

the easiest reach of the public; free literature, as a whole, from the stultified taste of a particular generation."

* * *

. . . The first noticeable difference in issue five however, was the visual transformation of the magazine. For the fifth issue, Walsh designed and printed a cover featuring multi-colored flowers, the stems of which comprised the titles of featured poems and their authors. Working with a single-color Heidelberg offset press, Walsh and Jack MacMillan manually applied the colored ink to the roller, washed the roller after twenty copies had been printed, and applied new colors to the roller for the next twenty copies (Walsh, "Interview"). The resulting covers anticipated the organization of the magazine's contents and revealed the determination with which the editorial board attempted to create a magazine that was innovative in both form and content.

Within the magazine, line drawings, pen and ink, and pencil sketches accompanied poems, essays, and short fiction, all of which were intermingled to create what George Sanderson later described as the "literary and visual mosaic that the modern sensibility requires" ("Eclectic" 8) . . .

* * *

Throughout the 1970s, *TAR* retained the eclecticism that had come to define the magazine in its second volume. While Walsh had been chiefly responsible for the magazine's design and layout, and had contributed the majority of the artwork contained in early issues, the magazine garnered an increasing number of visual art submissions in the years that followed.

The editors set a high standard for publication but they espoused a liberal editorial policy that was informed by the magazine's guiding principle of eclecticism. Accordingly, the editors did not discriminate against literature that was not aesthetically or ideologically modernist. In fact, much of the poetry and prose produced within the Antigonish group itself, such as that of Currie, Walsh, and George Sanderson, did not conform to the impersonal and objectivist aesthetic standards of high modernism. . . .

In a 1985 interview with Pat Walsh, MacSween stated that he had two primary objectives when editing the magazine: "the immediate one is to get out the magazine. The other one is some kind of hope that some budding writer gets a good start" (247). . . .

The editorial board 1981: Seated, Fr. MacSween; L to R, James Taylor, Gertrude Sanderson, George Sanderson, Pat Walsh, Sheldon Currie.

The Judge, Part 1

The "sexual revolution" was in its initial stages during my first years of teaching at StFX. I had awakened one Saturday morning about 6 a.m. with a full-blown feature-length drama in my head, the result of a dream. I grabbed the pad and pen kept on the shelf next to my bed and began to write furiously. Quickly jotting down first an outline, I began to flesh out characters and scenes.

Around 1:30 p.m., my wife, who had risen and gone about her usual activities, came into the bedroom and suggested that I might like to stop for a bit of food. She brought me something to eat, and I continued to write in a frenzy to keep the dream flowing in my mind. By suppertime I had a very rough draft of my first full-length play since *Flowers, or Mother Doesn't Live Her Any More*, had won the Interclass Play Festival my Senior year at StFX.

The freshly minted drama was about an idea very much in many minds in the 1960s: survival of the human race. The Cuban missile crisis had set humanity on the edge of self-annihilation. My dream was dark, the situation of the characters was dark: the play, *Splits*, had two acts: "The Coming of Darkness," and "The Coming of Light." The setting was a deep pit in which the characters had been cast for breaking the rules of their government regarding their human relationships. The time was after the Third World War which had returned survivors to primitive conditions of living. Their lives, and their relationships, were ruled by regulations printed on their food labels–and those who broke the rules were cast into the pit.

Here's where the drama gets not just dark, but inky black. The people in the pit have no food, and the realization gradually dawns on the audience that the only source of food is babies. The only way to make food is to create babies. Also in the pit another even deeper pit is occupied by homosexual prisoners, who must raid the upper pit for food.

This whole miniature cosmic world is completed by psychological observers in orange jump suits suspended over the pit, who label the actions of the characters below with the formal titles or definitions of their aberrant behavior.

The drama was constructed to be acted in the school's old band-box gymnasium, which would become the Bauer Theatre after the athletic arena the Oland Centre had opened. The old gym had a balcony/running track around the playing court, and spectators of the drama would be watching the play in 3-D from the running-track railing above the action.

This drama so far sounds pretty grim, but think of Johnathan Swift's classic satire on the poverty of Dublin in the 1700s, *A Modest Proposal*, which proposes that children be bred for food to solve the hunger problem–a revolting idea which powerfully indicts the wealthy and the politicians who, in reality, were already living by "exploiting" and "consuming" the poor!

To add to the challenging human relationships in the quest for survival, the main characters in my drama are named Kallikaks–a famous case study on the inheritance of human intelligence. There were two strains of Kallikaks fathered by one man with two wives: one side of the family was almost all criminal and evil, the other strain was almost all public servants of integrity and honor. The main characters are two couples, one named the Kallikak-O'days, the other the O'Day-Kallikaks. The two couples had been married, divorced and married each other.

Now, believe it or not, there is a great deal of humor in the play, based upon the topsy-turvy married couples, the absurd labels on the food governing how people can change relationships [that is, *split*], and the labeling of the psychological observers who end up with their own difficult relationship about the morality of their work. *Splits* is a serious examination of the question of how far human beings are willing to go to "survive." Of what atrocities are we capable of inflicting on one another to "survive" rather than lay down our lives for our friends.

In the course of rewriting and rewriting and polishing, my first major drama, I showed it to Angus "the Beard" MacGillivray, the artist/teacher whose studio was adjacent to my office, who asked to read it. Angus was the only professor at X at that time who had a beard. Hence the nickname bestowed by Antigonishers, who through desire or necessity had to nickname everybody in a town in which half the people were named MacDonald, and half of the remaining people were named Chisholm. When I mentioned letting Angus see my draft of the play, my perceptive wife warned me, "You shouldn't have done that." I maintained Angus was my friend; it was okay to let him see it. "You shouldn't have done that."

The following Monday morning in the coffee room in Morrison Hall outside the priests' dining room, where the faculty gathered during class breaks, I was having a fine cup of "Joe" amidst the Senior faculty and priests, many of whom had taught me. In the door sauntered "the Beard." He looked my way and immediately turning biblically prophetical, poked his bony forefinger in an accusing stance, and began spluttering, "You . . . YOU . . . your play . . . it's . . . IT'S . . . a piece . . . a PIECE OF S–T!"

Everybody in the room turned to look at me.

"I guess you didn't like it, eh, Angus?" A tough moment for the lowest faculty member on the totem pole.

Nonetheless, *Splits* would win a prize in the prestigious Sergei H. Frankel Playwriting Competition held once every five years at the University of Chicago, and would come within two weeks of a New York production by "Personae," an acting company featured in *Life* magazine: the producer got cold feet and switched to an Ibsen drama.

In the context of this dramatic roller coaster ride, I composed a one-act play, entitled, *The Small-l lord*, and submitted it to the Nova Scotia Playwriting Contest in Halifax, Nova Scotia. This play also is an examination of sexual roles which were beginning to surface in main-stream society. Briefly, here is the gist of the play: The setting is a motel room, with a big mirror over the bed. The room is in darkness. The door opens. A young man and young woman enter. They turn on the lights on the tables beside the bed. They do not speak, but begin to disrobe to go to bed. They get in bed, turn out the lights, and darkness reigns for about fifteen seconds–an eternity in a play! They turn the lights back on again. They begin to speak, the young man in religious terms, and the young girl in sexy terms. Their lines, it was my intention, are spoken in stilted terms–suggesting they are speaking lines in a play. The girl is seeking to entice the young man, who is resisting. They keep fumbling along, and suddenly the door bursts open, and an elderly woman begins berating them for not acting according to the script. Confrontation ensues, and the woman it becomes clear, is not a woman, but a man!

The man exits, and the couple start the scene over. It becomes clear that, according to the script, the young couple is supposed to have sex. But it also becomes clear that they cannot have sex because they have fallen in love–and cannot betray their *true* love for a *fictional* love, that is, for a *lie*. As the tension builds, in frustration the young man hurls a lamp at the mirror, which shatters the mirror, revealing the woman/man manipulating them, who laughs at their predicament. The end–of what I intended to be a serious examination of the tumultuous sexual tensions of the "sexy sixties."

Apparently the judge in the Nova Scotia Playwriting Contest did not see my serious intent. My play returned from the contest, not a winner. That was okay. I didn't feel entitled to win. I would submit it to other competitions or drama companies. No problem. Then I took a look at the script. The judge had written on the script, "I never saw a motel room like this!" As I flipped through the script, the comments continued to flow, ever more fiercely! "Ridiculous." "Stupid." "Inane." "This is unbearable!" "No!" "No!" "NO" The anonymous judge [It was not "the Beard"] was reaching a dramatic high point, "I can't bear this!"

And at the climax of play, came the crowning comment: "I wish the mirror had fallen on the author and KILLED HIM!" [*Caps by the Judge!*]

That last comment really shook me. I penned a letter to the man in charge of the contest, protesting that such a judge be allowed to critique plays. I got an immediate apology and the assurance that that judge would not be selected ever again to judge the contest. The man in charge had not realized that the judge had written comments on my script. Nonetheless, I never again sent a play to the

Nova Scotia Playwriting Contest. *The Small-l lord* was eventually performed by a theatre group in Ottawa, Ontario, the nation's capital, to reasonable acclaim.

The same year, another play, *Everything is All White*, in which I also played a minor role, was performed at the Nova Scotia Drama Festival. The adjudicator, who was artistic director of "Instantheatre" in Montreal, invited us to perform the play there. So we went on the road with a performance in a major venue. My creative career was firmly launched. Dennis Hayes, Drama professor at StFX directed this play, his debut at the University. Usually new professors produce a familiar play, a "plum," to firmly showcase their talents with a polished "winner." True to himself and his craft, Dennis took on a new play, never produced, by an amateur, struggling playwright. For that I am eternally grateful.

But, *The Small-l lord* was not my last involvement with the judge who wished me dead.

To My Daughter Mary

When I think of all the wrongs I have done
the suffering I have loosed in the world
the distractions I have refused to shun
worldly pleasures in which my mind has whirled
I do not want to face my judgement day
what good can tip the scale in my defense
in my emptiness what words can I say
I pray that a merciful God relents
But at that moment of utter despair
an inspiration breathes into my mind
I know eternal happiness is there
goodness I have been searching for I find
dear God, I am washed clean by saving water
you must love me, for Mary is my daughter

Mary and her husband Neil White.

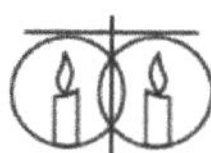

[Many academics may be dull, but a university is never dull. Universities are truly Byzantine institutions always in turbulence. In 1970, StFX was reported to have the most "conservative" student body in Canada. Surely, a challenge, eh?]

ST. FRANCIS XAVIER ALUMNI NEWS

Vol. 9, No. 1 Antigonish April 1971

STRIKE – CRISIS ON THE CAMPUS: CHANGING TIMES AT StFX

(*We present the following article, reprinted from the April 15th edition of The Antigonish Casket, because we feel our Alumni are entitled to an objective narrative of the recent events of the University campus. Mr. Walsh is a graduate of the Class of '58, began teaching here in 1963, was Alumni Director 1965–67, and is currently Assistant Professor of English.*)

Two St. Francis Xavier University graduates, classes of '32 and '46 met in MacKinnon's drug store this afternoon: the afternoon of the STRIKE.

"What are we coming to?"

"What's going on up there?"

"Why, I remember when we were students. We wouldn't think of doing such things. And discipline. We had discipline."

"Yes, I remember one afternoon in 1945 when my roommate got a new car down town and we decided to go to a rugger game in Truro in the afternoon!

The next morning we were up before the Dean, I was sternly reprimanded and confined to campus for one month."

"Was that so bad?"

"I lived through it. And am I any the worse for it?"

Well, Alumni, loyal sons and true-ue-ue! The old StFX you knew, and loved, and still love, is dead. The old StFX!

But there is a new StFX. And it is not dead–it is alive and kicking and this STRIKE will not kill it. This strike is a sign of StFX's life and vitality. A living organism must constantly adjust to the forces and influences surrounding it. StFX has been adjusting. Not fast enough to satisfy the desires of many of its students whose tenure in Antigonish is a brief two, three, or four years.

One example of change is in the liquor regulations. In 1958, liquor was outlawed. No ifs, ands, or buts. No one was allowed to drink. Veterans of foreign wars? No. No one. In practice, however, the casual quiet drinker who minded his own business was tolerated and usually given a stern glare to encourage a blush of shame at least. Everyone knew the rules of the game and expulsion resulted only if a fellow caused a minor riot by appearing in the dining hall in his undershorts, or by punching his fist through a restaurant window!

As the university attendance grew, the rules of the game became difficult to follow and enforce. And unenforceable laws breed disrespect for the law. Ignored by some authorities and zealously enforced by other authorities, double standards soon became recognized as injustices.

The university administration recognized the laws of the province as the proper liquor laws to be followed. And who should police these laws? Why, the students. The students claimed maturity and asked for the right to be "Masters of their own Destiny." So the student discipline system was born.

The priests were to be counselors, able to advise the students, without having to run up and down the corridors at night, searching for liquor. Priests as policemen were replaced, gradually, for old habits are often difficult to break, by Priests as counselors.

And then came permission for automobiles. And representation for the students on all university committees, and the board of governors. And all-night lights. All of this accomplished without the strikes and violence necessary to obtain such representation at other universities.

StFX students are fine young people. Does that sound condescending? Today's students are as keen and intelligent and upstanding and trustworthy as the students of the 1850s 1920s, '30s, '40s, '50s and '60s. They are also as young and inexperienced and ignorant and self-centered as the students of any other decade.

And if the administration of the university has made mistakes and they have of course, the students have also made mistakes. The mistakes of today's students flow from the influence of the media, as McLuhan has informed us.

The StFX students of today watch on TV as their fellow students throughout the world run in the streets; they sit in the flowery new Capitol Theatre and see movies glorifying revolution by the young; they listen on their radios to the rock culture extolling the values of a new age. Youth, young, beautiful, tanned and talented, will bring justice to the face of the earth. As we look at their splendid health and beauty, their idealism and energy, we hope they will. Please God, they will succeed.

So StFX students fly in airplanes to the big cities, they sit down and rap with the students they have seen running in the streets. StFX students at these rap sessions see that they already have most of the privileges that the students of other universities are just now obtaining.

What can they fight for? What do they not have? Open housing. The thought of being left out of the action must have been galling. Open housing became THE CAUSE. Two years ago, open housing was demanded by the students. Open housing means having female students in male students' rooms at designated hours.

The student leaders petitioned the University Council (which has since been replaced by the University Senate) for open housing. The council turned down the student request flat.

Several council members left the meeting in the belief that the matter had been settled. However, in an attempt to offer the student leaders a means of saving face, a proposal was offered just before suppertime. Sunday visiting hours would be granted to students and to the general public. Such visiting hours had been held in the past. Parents could visit in the rooms and see where Junior lived. Everyone would be free to come and go at will.

This proposal was accepted by the students who interpreted it as open housing in principle. The proposal was viewed by council members present as an admirable compromise.

When the decision was announced to the faculty, an immediate and virulent opposition arose, for it was evident that the students thought they had been granted open housing and the council thought they had been granted public visiting hours.

An emergency faculty meeting was convened in the old Assembly Hall, the scene of many a past political debate. After a heated debate the faculty, as the supreme voice of authority under the board of governors, overturned the council decision by an 8 to 1 proportion.

Many faculty members were opposed to open housing at StFX, ever, under any conditions, *per omnia saecula saeculorum*. Some faculty supported the most strongly worded motion in the belief that to uphold the council and let the students think they had obtained open housing when, in fact, they had not, would be a deliberate deceit.

A statement was drawn up and released to the students and the positions were polarized. The students held a mass meeting in the Oland Centre and called in the then president, Monsignor M. A. McLellan and then dean of arts. Rev. M. A. Macdonnell.

The administration carried the day with a one-two punch of direct challenge to the students, and an erudite argument defending the administration stand. The bomb had been defused. The conditions, rules and regulations which caused the confrontation remained.

In an effort to negotiate the open housing question the president established a presidential commission on open housing. Some students viewed this committee as a stalling tactic by the administration. The majority of the committee, which was composed of faculty, administration and students, recommended open housing.

The council, once burned, twice shy, effectively vetoed the committee's report and called for further study and negotiations.

Eventually, a plan was worked out in which students lounges would be constructed in the men's residences. The student residences at StFX had been built with no lounges and with rooms of minimum size, because of a shortage of money, in the days before vast sums of public monies were pumped into rapidly expanding universities.

During the summer of 1969, lounges were constructed. These lounges could be entered from outside, without passing through residence areas. The Students Union Building now nearing completion was begun.

As usual, a few spoiled things for the majority. The lounges in some buildings were wrecked. Property was destroyed. The dean of men closed the lounges. A tense period of negotiations began and administrations of both the university and the students Union changed.

Last year, as the students became more experienced in revolutionary tactics, and in political methods of procedure, experts began to be imported from other universities.

The students established a local chapter of the SDU (Students for a Democratic University). All members of the university community, faculty included, were invited to attend and to join the SDU. After the 100 or so thrill-seekers and curious departed from the Science 14 elevated classroom, 9 students and 2 faculty members formed an SDU cell. The two faculty members were interested in working with students who apparently had a sincere desire to make the university a better community.

A young woman who had been expelled from Simon Fraser University in British Columbia was present as an advisor to the group. She called for an attack upon the "bastards" in the administration. The faculty chuckled and the students from StFX were embarrassed. The students were quick to inform the young woman that while she might think of college administrators in general in such terms, the administrators at StFX were sincere and honest men. The two faculty members were encouraged by such rationality.

The SDU student leaders then began to define the goals of the cell. They said that the StFX cell should examine the relationship of StFX to the Maritimes Provinces as exploited by Upper Canadian Imperialism and American Imperialism in Canada in light of American Imperialism in Latin America. This is not fiction. This is true.

The faculty members suggested that perhaps more practical results might be obtained if the cell examined the problems at StFX first before branching out to cover the hemisphere.

The students agreed and each member of the cell was assigned to investigate a particular problem area; for example academic reform, spiritual life on campus, discipline problems, etc. Several of the current strike leaders were members of the cell.

The cell died of inactivity. The only two members of the cell who brought in their reports were–that's right–the two faculty members [Full disclosure 2019: Pat Walsh and Sheldon Currie]. The student assigned to investigate discipline told one of the professors, "The more I find out about discipline here at StFX, the more I realize how well off we are. I'm wasting my time so I'm quitting the group."

The leaders of the current strike dropped out of the cell or at least never carried on any further activity on the project. The project was dying in the light of facts. The students' pet theories and opinions of the university were being contradicted by the logical pursuit of knowledge, the basic reason for the existence of the university.

The 1970 school year arrived. A student administration committed to open housing was in office. The matter would be pursued. Faculty support was increasing.

The student leaders organized residence councils. Each residence was visited by student leaders led by Dan O'Connor, who advocated that each residence should decide for itself if it wanted open housing regulations. It was an effective way of ensuring conformity among small groups.

The Xaverian Weekly newspaper and the Campus Radio supported the open housing movement. The now vast student body of some 2,500 could not be reached effectively by the administration.

The day when every student knew every other student and every professor knew every student and the president could shake every hand and trace every family tree had long since passed. Many students no longer turn to faculty as friends, or to priests as counselors. Daily Mass attendance is no longer compulsory. Neither is Sunday Mass. Society in general seems to have abandoned such rules and regulations.

Students were sent a letter from the dean of men before they arrived on the campus last fall. The dean informed the students of the council's reaffirmed stand against open housing and suggested that any students not agreeing with such rules consider going elsewhere. Some did go elsewhere. Others moved downtown, outside the open housing regulations.

The new president of StFX, Fr. Macdonnell, established a new Commission in September of 1970. The Commission, chaired by Dean of Men, J. K. MacDonald, was instructed to continue to search for a solution to the housing problems.

The student government apparently had difficulty getting members to serve on the new Commission, but finally appointed three members (matching the three members of faculty appointed) on November 12th. Three meetings were held before the Christmas break.

Dean J. K. MacDonald informed the Commission that it should try to develop options to present to the University Senate, thereby offering the Senate a range of choices in the matter. A timetable was set and the Commission aimed at a presentation to the Senate at a February 1971 meeting.

Dean MacDonald discussed the work of this Commission with Robb MacKinnon, Student Union President; Dan O'Connor, and Gene Deleskie. The House Residence leaders were aware of the Commission's work. The Dean also advised MacKinnon of his responsibility to inform the student body of the work of the Commission. The students were not advised.

At the first meeting of the Commission on January 13, 1971, two student members of the Commission, Donald Gay and John Francis Mclnnis, presented the Dean with a letter bearing instructions from the Executive of the Students Union. The letter demanded that the Dean, as the administrator in charge of residences, immediately declare open housing and so inform the Students Union of his action–WITHIN ONE HOUR!

The Dean's reply has not been recorded, but it was interpreted as negative. He further informed the Students Union that their letter was rude, that even if he made such a decision it would be reversed within three hours, and that the work of the Commission should be allowed to proceed to the Senate as planned.

But Robb MacKinnon made motions which turned the whole matter of open housing over to a one-man committee of Gene Deleskie.

The male students occupied various residences and declared them open and entertained female guests. A number of such occupations were held on succeeding weekends.

Student prefects employed by the university were called in by the dean and given the opportunity to resign if they felt in conscience they would be unable to uphold the University regulations. Some did resign.

The student prefects were told not to physically prevent any students from entering buildings declared open. They were to take names if they could do so without physical force.

Some four hundred male students signed in with prefects as violators of university regulations. The students felt secure for the administration would obviously be unable to expel so many students.

Confrontation politics demand a confrontation. Negotiation ceased. The power struggle began. The student leaders made their move.

The business of conducting university affairs flows in a chain of responsibility under the laws of the province from the people of the province through the Nova Scotia Legislature to the board of governors, to the University Senate, to the administration.

In the area of housing regulations the administration has appointed a dean of men, J. K. MacDonald, who is chairman of the University Discipline Committee (UDC), which is composed of faculty, administration, and student representatives. The UDC handles cases referred to it by the Student Discipline Committee (SDC).

The SDC held a trial for ten or so of the students who had signed up as violators of the university housing regulations. The SDC admitted that the students had indeed violated the university regulations, but that since the general student body through the residence councils had approved the open housing occupation of buildings the students could not be found guilty by the SDC who were, they claimed, responsible to the general student body.

The problem is evident.

In the area of housing regulations, the administration reasons that it has the authority while the student leaders reason that they have exclusive right to determine their own rules and regulations in this area. Who is in charge?

The student leaders claim that they want to test their right to determine housing regulations in the courts of the province. The administration claims it has the legal responsibility in this area.

The administration exercised its authority through the UDC. The UDC brought charges against MacKinnon, O'Connor, and Deleskie for inciting the students to mass disobedience of university regulations.

The students' lawyer conducted their defense at the UDC hearing.

The bane of university life became evident. Legalism is the most serious problem facing universities today. Legalism means that the spirit of the law and common sense are abandoned if a technicality or loophole in the law can be found.

For example, when the letters of the dean of men to the student leaders were introduced as evidence that the students had been forewarned of the consequences of disobedience of the regulations the lawyer objected because letters and documents cannot testify.

When a faculty advisor to the Students Union took the witness stand and testified concerning what the students had said at a meeting the lawyer objected that the professor's testimony should not be accepted because it could not be documented. As Charles Dickens said, "The law sir, is an Ass." (If treated in such a manner).

The students' lawyer also objected that the UDC should not hear the case because the dean of men was effectively prosecutor judge and jury at the same time.

The administration maintains that the UDC is not a court of law but an instrument of administration. UDC decisions may ultimately be brought before the civil courts for hearing in civil court procedure.

Last week, the UDC brought in its decision. MacKinnon, O'Connor, and Deleskie were found guilty of inciting the student body to mass disobedience of university regulations.

The punishment: MacKinnon and Deleskie, both Seniors, would be allowed to write their final examinations but would receive their degrees in absentia. O'Connor, a junior, would be able to write his examinations and would be required to complete his Senior year at another university. Upon completion of that year he would receive his degree from StFX. These students were ordered to refrain from political activities such as they had been conducting.

This punishment must be the most mild ever meted out by a university discipline committee. A slap on the wrists. No degrees were in jeopardy. No careers were ruined. Authority of the administration had been affirmed, but mercy had outstripped justice.

The Xaverian Weekly reacted in a characteristic manner and fanned the embers of revolt. The student newspaper, although subject to criticism from outside the university community, and, as usual, from within, has been attempting to be a lively and functional newspaper.

The faculty advisors have been very sympathetic to the student goals. Faculty advisors just advise. There is no such thing as prior censorship. The advisors do not inspect the paper. Their advice is given only when requested by the student newsmen.

The Xaverian Weekly requested several sessions of criticism with a professor who had professional newspaper experience [Moi, aussi]. His chief criticism, acknowledged by the students, was that in its attempt to provide provocative and colorful articles, the Weekly was full of news stories which were not objectively written, that is, they contained editorial opinions of the writer. Opinion should, as far as possible, be relegated to letters to the editor, signed columns or editorials. The Weekly writers genially accept such criticism.

Then when the RCMP arrested students for drug offenses the frenzy of emotion showed through in inaccurate headlines, mockery of the RCMP, libelous cartoons on the dean of men, presumptuous statements on the motives of people. Objectivity was relegated to the realm of theory.

Another example is the student interpretation that O'Connor has been "EXPELLED." A mere technicality? Expelled means cut-off completely. No degree. No credits. No way to complete a program of study. O'Connor is asked to study one year at another institution. He will then receive his degree from StFX. Expulsion? Not from one point of view. But *The Xaverian Weekly* claimed EXPELLED. A martyr had to be produced.

The students desiring open housing began the chant, "We want justice! We want justice!" A general student assembly was called for Sunday evening, April 4, at the Oland Center. Spring is here, almost, and time for student larks. A cavalier air pervaded the Oland Center. The rites of spring would soon begin.

This was not a regular meeting of the Students Union, for if the Union endorsed the meeting the union leaders would once again be responsible for breaking university regulations. To be absolutely safe, the student union executive is reported to have resigned.

Ballot boxes lined the main gymnasium floor to the north of the Oland Center. The meeting began with an open statement that a strike vote would be cast as soon as the discussion ended. The students were being asked to strike in support of Robb, Dan, and Gene. The University Senate would be asked to reverse the decision of the UDC. The administration would be asked to implement open housing in the fall of '71.

Two Antigonish High School students in attendance remarked that if ever a meeting had an air of a foregone conclusion it was this meeting.

The speakers soon made it evident that the pro-strike supporters were out in full force. Over two thousand students were in the hall. Gene Deleskie in direct violation of the sentence handed down by the UDC called for a strike by student body. He received a standing ovation from most of the students and some of the professors present.

A statement was delivered from the students who had begun a hunger strike in protest of the UDC decision. The administration was referred to as "conniving," the UDC "kangaroo court" decision as based upon "trumped-up charges" for "non-existent regulations."

After some eight or nine pro-strike statements, the chairman of the meeting, Stephen Boyd, requested some anti-strike statements from the audience. When he got them he began to argue the speakers down.

One student rose to decry, "all the shit we have had to put up with here," and the professor sitting in the audience began to have doubts about the letter of recommendation he had given this student who was to transfer to another university next year. When he confronted the student after the meeting the young fellow explained that he really didn't mean it the way it sounded, he was only trying to make a point "like in a debate."

The voting began and a rock band began to play and the joint was jumping. The students were getting high. Emotionally. They were hopping. Kangaroo court analogies leaped to mind.

A faculty member who had been fired floated by. One faculty member was saying, "I'm with the administration." The leaving professor said, with a tint of glee and a not completely serious manner, "I hope the students tear the f–ing place right down to the ground."

Several students approached a professor who had a quiz scheduled for the next morning.

"Will you be having your quiz tomorrow, sir?"

"Yes. You are paying me for being in the classroom and I'll be there."

"What if we can't get by the strike line?"

"Don't cause any violence. Don't risk being hurt."

When Steve Boyd had been asked what could a student expect if he tried to cross the picket line and go to classes, he had replied, "Expect to be hassled."

Some of the students who had been dismissed last year had returned to the campus and were at the meeting. They knew what was going on. They knew what was going to happen. They were here to help it happen. They were here to deliver the goods they had failed to deliver last year.

The students voted 890 to 610 in favor of a strike. The leaders concluded that this majority was not sufficient to justify a strike. They also worried about why so many students had abstained from voting.

At 3 a.m. in the morning, the lunatic fringe struck. A kook was loose. A firebomb was tossed into a reading room in the basement of Morrison Hall. Retired priests living in there had to leave the building.

Over forty years of service to the students and the community, uncounted thousands of kindnesses, repaid with a Molotov cocktail in the dark of the night.

But the leaders who created the atmosphere of tension and hyper-sensation didn't want that to happen. After all, that was madness. The leaders endorsed non-violence.

The professor [Oui, moi aussi] held his quiz the next morning. 69 out of 69, almost all Seniors, showed up for the quiz, including a hunger striker, who wouldn't talk to the professor afterwards.

When the professor returned after lunch he was kept out of the Nicholson Hall office tower; a bomb threat had been telephoned in. In the middle of the afternoon the tower was surrounded by pickets. The strike was on. Go. Go. Go. We want Justice. We want Justice.

The University Senate including its student members, was having a regularly scheduled meeting at the Oland Center board room. The pickets led by Gene Deleskie began to demonstrate outside the senate meeting. A few nervous laughs inside, but the business proceeds.

Then as if by prearranged agreement, one of the student representatives left the senate meeting and when he returned and passed by the campus policeman guarding the entrance, he threw open the door and Deleskie and a number of demonstrators rushed into the meeting and disrupted it. Deleskie's performance of screaming and creating a disturbance was described by a professor originally sympathetic to his cause as "completely ape."

The senators who originally supported the rational stand of Deleskie now reassessed their support.

At the core of a university's very existence is the free and unimpeded right to reason and inquire. Violence interferes with this basic operation within a university.

The senate meeting was immediately prorogued and while some senators left joking and laughing with some of the demonstrators, some, including President Macdonnell, were verbally assaulted and insulted. The true colors of the non-violent protestors began to show through. The regularly scheduled faculty meeting on Monday evening was cancelled.

The strikers blocked off Morrison Hall dining room, a public address system summoned student support for a general strike. Placards appeared. Meetings were held. And the day of the strike dawned. Nicholson Hall was picketed.

Students trying to get in to classes were prevented from doing so. Faculty were allowed to pass in and out freely. When a professor would return to the outside after waiting for students in an empty classroom, the pickets would clap and laugh at him. A police force was established by the students. The police wore armbands, white on one arm, marked POLICE, red on the other arm to signify blood. Symbolic blood. Real blood should not be shed.

Some of the hunger strikers with black armbands began to gather on blankets on the sidewalk outside Nicholson Hall. These students were proving by their actions their belief in the nonviolent methods of Gandhi and Martin Luther King, Jr.–admirable methods, regardless of the validity or lack of validity of the principles they felt so strongly compelled to uphold.

Two faculty members, husband and wife, [George and Gert Sanderson] met a girl who wanted desperately to confer with the wife about her course. The girl was in a state of near hysteria and trembling in fear. The husband had to remonstrate the pickets and tell them, "You're not supposed to use violence."

The girl and the faculty members were leaned on but they got into the building and the girl was comforted and calmed and eventually helped back to her room. Three girls trying to get into an English class were blocked from the classroom building, sworn at by the pickets, cursed and laughed at and they returned in tears to Mount Saint Bernard.

One young lady prevented from entering the Science Hall proved that those interested in studying could employ a trooper's vocabulary as easily as the pickets could. She curled one fellow's hair with a string of epithets worthy of an enraged hockey coach.

As the strike continued during the day, rock music, including a song called "Paranoia" kept the pickets swaying.

The hunger strikers began to be visibly distressed and pale and wan. In the early evening, as they stopped taking even water, one boy declared, "I'm going to get this over with, I can't prolong it." One girl with a weak heart passed out and an ambulance had to be summoned. She was revived.

Kingsley Brown Jr. appeared on the scene to interview Gene Deleskie for "The People's School." Deleskie was urging the students to maintain their spirit by chanting and he led them in "We want justice, we want justice, louder now, WE WANT JUSTICE." He exhorted them to public prayer if they felt so inclined.

Dave Alexander read a telegram from Mr. Goodfellow, the student lawyer, advising them of their right to strike, of their responsibility to avoid violence and to stay off university property.

The pickets were told that they were supposed to keep moving, that they couldn't join arms to prevent people from entering the buildings. So they were told by Alexander how to huddle next to each other and shuffle from side to side, keep your feet moving, to prevent people from entering classrooms. Legalism again. They were effectively by physical means forcing people away from entering the buildings.

So they were told by Alexander how to huddle next to each other and shuffle from side to side, keep your feet moving, to prevent people from entering classrooms. Legalism again. They were effectively by physical means forcing people away from entering the buildings.

The campus radio station was operated by Murray Kelly, a graduate of last year, who somehow reappeared on the campus as the strike broke. Any announcements by the students opposed to the strike were not allowed to be aired, although all of the students have paid a fee for the campus radio. Another bit of "participatory democracy," which evidently means that a student can only participate if he's on the right side of a question, i.e. for the strike.

And the professional agitators were arriving. A former student who had been dismissed. A student from Carleton University in Ottawa.

The two saddest sights of the day were a married student from town who brought his little girl of apparently about three years old by the hand to the group of pickets in front of Nicholson Hall. He placed a picket sign in her hand and then stepped back to take her picture.

The child smiled gamely, obviously unaware of the meaning of the situation and obviously disconcerted by the crowd which began clapping and cheering. Her daddy picked her up and walked back to his car as the little girl smiled wanly as her eyes began to water.

[*I found out later that the married student was against the strike and the sign was to make the point that the strike would be hurting his daughter. I had misinterpreted what I had seen as pro-strike, when the intent had been anti-strike. Judging motives in the heat of the moment is extremely difficult and can easily go astray. I did go astray in my account.*]

And another smattering of applause began as Dan O'Connor and his parents came out of Nicholson tower. Dan zigzagged towards the pickets. He was flushed and obviously embarrassed. A shy individual to begin with, he stopped to chat awkwardly with a couple of students in the swirling crowd.

And no one could know where the swirling would end or who would be swept away in the tide.

The University Senate held a meeting because the student strike leaders guaranteed it would not be interrupted. The senate agreed to let Dan O'Connor return to StFX next year and revoked the $25 fine of the 10 students found guilty of breaking the housing regulations. This seemed to be as far as the senate was willing to go to indicate goodwill.

President Macdonnell stated that reprisals against any student strikers would not be made, nor would any reprisals by individual professors be tolerated. He closed no doors. Deleskie and MacKinnon, because of their continued defiance of university regulations in open advocacy of the strike, would still have to receive their degrees in absentia.

Gene Deleskie stated at public meetings that he needed a mandate of a 1,200 vote majority in order to carry on with the strike. The vote was conducted in the student residences and the voters were signed up for the picket lines at the voting tables. A new type of secret ballot, perhaps?

758 voted in favor of the strike, even fewer than the first strike vote. In spite of his public statements, Deleskie implemented the continuation of the strike.

The university administration, anxious to avoid violence, obtained an injunction against the strike leaders, but withheld serving the injunction until the last possible moment, late Monday evening. The injunction was not served until the last minute in order to give the students every opportunity to negotiate. The strike leaders instead chose to escalate.

Gene Deleskie implored the dean of men, J. K. MacDonald, and special assistant to the president, Fred Doucet, to move their families out of town. Deleskie claimed that he felt he didn't have complete power over the more militant students in his organization and that the families of these administrators were in danger. Once again the forces of violence had been unleashed supposedly against the will of the student leaders, and once again the student leaders disclaimed responsibility, and once again they expected to be free of guilt because they washed their hands in public ritual.

The public stance of moral superiority on the part of the students began to wear thin. The seriousness of the situation and the immense possibilities for loss of life and injury were evident enough to cause the administration of St. Martha's Hospital to prepare for implementation of its emergency disaster plan in case things got out of control. Suddenly, many people in the community realized that this was no game, no student lark, but a dangerous situation. It could happen here.

To ensure that it wouldn't happen here the administration has shut down the university. There will be no exams written on the campus in an impossible atmosphere of fear created by continuing bomb threats. It is possible there will be no graduation ceremony to be disrupted by students on "power trips." There will be order and reason and the democratic process or there will be no university.

Take-home examinations, carefully prepared to test not the memory but the reasoning abilities of the students will be mailed by registered mail to the students on April 22 and must be returned by registered mail dated May 4. Graduation in absentia for three, has become graduation in absentia for all. An awful lot of students were sucked in by few.

The old StFX is dead. The new StFX will live. Who will be in charge?

Men must be judged by their actions. Judge the administrators of StFX. Judge the students of StFX.

The administrators of StFX, President Malcolm Macdonnell, Msgr. Bauer, Dr. M.A. MacLellan, Dr. J. J. MacDonald, and recently, Dr. John Sears, and Dean J.K. MacDonald, have made mistakes. Who has not? But their services to StFX students, have been proven by long service day and night year in and year out. Not perfection, by any means. But they have struggled openly and honestly to translate into a practical reality the dream the student leaders profess to desire.

They have not succumbed to the calls from those outside the community for violent or repressive actions against the student strikers. They have acted with reason, compassion and nearly infinite patience. No lives have been lost. It could have been different.

The student leaders may be sincere, they may be energetic, they may want what is best for StFX, but their actions contradict the dream, for they have brought violence into our community.

StFX will never be a miniature Toronto, or Berkeley, or Harvard. Nor should we be. We cannot compete by mere conditions of geography, wealth, prestige, etc.

It is also a hard reality that we cannot in one fell swoop, yank StFX into the mainstream of the world academic life. The progress toward reform must be performed in the daily grind.

Open housing may be valid in Europe, in the large cities, in other universities, but it cannot be crammed down the throats of the Eastern Nova Scotians by force. When open housing comes, if it comes, it will come because the majority of the people in our total community, the people who pay the bills and support our academic institutions see and believe that open housing is a good thing for our university.

Until that day arrives, I am personally committed to the UDC, the StFX Administration, and the people of Nova Scotia.

P.S. I have been accused by a non-faculty employee of the university of having fed questions and statements to a student who spoke against the strike at the first general meeting. Some people seem to be disturbed by this allegation.

I ask, "So what?" The strikers hired a lawyer, imported "experts" from outside the university, brought back the expelled and suspended to manipulate the students. Have I no right to speak to or advise students on university affairs? I have at least as much right as any outsider who openly aided the student strikers.

However, the fact is that I at no time gave any information to anyone on any side of the strike question. I was taking notes at the general meeting, and I think the reader may judge from this article on my ability to express my thoughts and opinions in the matter. I state my views publicly and with no apologies to anyone.

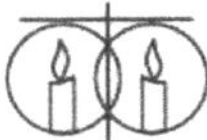

As soon as the Strike was over Fr. Macdonnell called me to his office and commissioned me to write a study of the strike by interviewing all the administrators who had been involved. He gave me a summer stipend for the exercise and hired a stenographer, from away, to type the confidential report for his eyes only. I also interviewed all the student leaders. As far as I know the 1,500-page report has been read only by the president and whoever over the years was hired to be in charge of Student Discipline.

Also, at the outbreak of violence with the fire bomb at Morrison Hall, Fr. MacSween and his cadre of professors had sent a letter to President Macdonnell asking him not to call in police or army forces, based upon incidents in the USA in which calling in such support had led to the loss of lives. Fr. Macdonnell had sent us back word that he had no such intention, "that the University burned to the ground was not worth a single human life."

At my 50th Anniversary of graduation from StFX I visited Fr. Macdonnell in his room in Mockler Hall. We reminisced about the strike. After retiring from his position of President of StFX, Fr. Malcolm had been appointed to the Canadian Human Rights Commission. He became acquainted with a member of the Commission who had been a General in the Canadian Army. The retired General revealed that Canadian Army personnel had been stationed in Truro, Nova Scotia, about an hour away, ready to swoop into the University if matters got out of hand.

As soon as the strike was over, I began to pack for one of the greatest adventures of my life.

Fr. Macdonnell and Dean John T. Sears, both demanded that I obtain a doctorate in order to be promoted any further in rank. So with five children and my wife I was to be off to Ireland to study Anglo-Irish Literature and Drama. The one catch was, the program would take three years, but I would receive only two years of half-salary support [$14,000 CAD per year] from the University–and the third year would be my problem. Another challenge, eh?

*

Man About Town

Antigonish Casket, NS August 12, 1971 Editorial

[*This is an editorial I did NOT write.*]

The phrase, "man about town," evokes the image of the *bon vivant*, the celebrating, care-free bachelor.

Our choice for the man about the town of Antigonish is none of these. He is a dedicated husband and father, a man of moderate habits, and he seeks responsibility in order to serve his community.

Our man about town is Patrick Walsh, who leaves this month for a three-year program of study at the University of Dublin.

Pat is a big man in every sense of the word, and his impact upon life at St Francis Xavier University, in St. Ninian's Parish, and the town Antigonish has been comparably great. He combines a cheerful, outgoing personality with a strong sense of conviction. He is not easily swayed; neither is he blindly opinionated.

For one so young, Pat has accomplished much. On the personal side, he has won wide acclaim and recognition as a playwright. As a teacher he has been variously described as "fair, thorough, and never dull." His English classes are always among the first to be filled. This much, with a lively young family, should satisfy the average man that he is doing his share. Pat, however, is not average. He is a builder, an improver, and a generous giver of his time and capabilities.

He was right in there pitching with the team that brought low-rental housing to Antigonish. The time and work he put into the achievement of the R. K. MacDonald Nursing Home is beyond calculation. His latest sphere of service has been on the Antigonish town council. During his brief term as councilor, Pat has been instrumental in stirring up that body to some much-needed action.

As a successful teacher, he realizes the importance of-well-prepared homework. And Pat, in every undertaking, has done his homework well. This was evident in the preliminary report on the nursing home proposal for Submission to the town and county councils. This careful preparation was evident, too, in his participation in council and school board deliberations.

Another demonstration of Pat's careful weighing of all sides of a question was his assessment of the campus crisis last spring. At that time, he injected a much-needed note of sanity into what was growing into an emotional binge.

No one who weighs a question, takes a stand, and sticks by it is without critics. Pat has his share of these. He has been accused of stirring things up, of rocking the boat. In most cases, however, events have proved that the stirring and the rocking were long overdue.

Pat is a firm believer in the right of the people to know the truth. This is to be expected of a journalist. But when he joined the ranks of those in charge, on committees and on council, his basic honesty did not weaken. If council, or any board of which he was a member, made a mistake, he was not for "covering up" or seeking to sidestep criticism.

He will be missed at the university, in the parish, and the community. Three years is a long time; we know those years will be well-spent. With his industry and capacity for learning, Pat Walsh will emerge with higher academic qualifications.

For our part, we are happy with Pat Walsh as he is right now. He is a well-educated man for whom learning is a continuing process. His honesty, integrity, and generosity have served us well. We hope that he and his family may enjoy their stay in Ireland. We hope, especially, that they will come back to us. By that time there may well be more boats to rock and more things to stir up than ever. This, however, is not the main reason for the wish. We need people like the Walshes as permanent residents in our town.

Chapter 6
Innocents Abroad 1971–73

Our great family adventure of living in Ireland for two years, was, for my wife, as challenging as my quest for the PhD. She had been the leading scholar of our high school class, and the leading scholar of her university class. With five children ranging in age from age ten to newly born, she managed the entire extravaganza with grace, style, and extreme patience—and finally picked up her education by attending Sion Hill Montessori School near our home in Ballybrack, earning a Montessori teaching qualification, with Maria Montessori's son, Mario, being her final examiner.

We had been worried about the children adapting to Ireland. When we moved into our rented house the children were sent out into the backyard ["garden"] to play, and they were soon surrounded by a veritable army of young Irelanders. By suppertime when Jackie called them in to supper, they had Irish accents! Kids catch on quickly how to survive in new settings.

Before long, we were gathered into a circle of Irish friends: a clutch of Irish professors, principally Gus Martin, would become a blood brother, and Tom Garvin and Maurice Manning, political scientists. Outside the ivory tower we became involved with Billy Gallagher and Eithne Collins, who remain to this day close friends, mostly electronically across the wide seas, but actually physically when any Walsh was able to travel abroad.

Billy Gallagher, myself, Professor Gus Martin

At this time, the modern 'Troubles' were exploding, literally and figuratively, in Ireland. Shortly after arriving I heard about crowds gathering at the British Embassy in Merrion Square in the heart of Dublin. I drove into the city to see what was going on. It was evident that when darkness fell, the Embassy was doomed. Who did I bump into in the crowd, but Robb McKinnon, former President of the StFX Students Union at the time of the STRIKE, who was now studying for an MA in Anglo-Irish literature. He had written his Senior Essay for me at X. This time the bombs that would fall around us were real, intentional, and would be part of our lives for the next two years while we were there.

Absorbed into the everyday life in the Irish Republic's capital, we enjoyed Dublin, one of the last great walking-around cities. In this ancient setting, I personally came to recognize that, although I had been raised mostly among Italians, I was not what I thought I was before I got to Ireland, that is, a middle-class American, recently absorbed into a nearly American culture in Canada. I began to realize that I had really been raised as an Irish-Catholic middle-class American. My Catholic roots reflected not the sophisticatedly relaxed Italian Catholicism of Europe, but the strong, fanatic Celtic sternness of the Irish going back to the days of the Irish support that gave the Church the doctrine of the Pope's infallibility of Vatican Council I and the Church's battle against "Modernism." I was becoming ripe for a liberal turn, as you shall see.

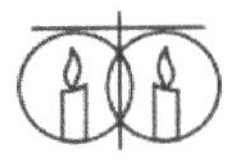

Patrick X Walsh

Irish Letter 1

[*This Irish letter, written to be air-mailed back to relatives and friends in North America, is crammed together, so as not to waste paper, space, or postage—hence the run-on style.* In earlier letters I had written about the "Troubles." You will find slight mention of them, non-political, in subsequent letters. My friend and neighbor, Bob McDonnell, a native of Ireland and a professor in the Engineering Department at X, had written to warn me not to comment in any public way on the politics of the 'Troubles' because to do so would be dangerous for me and my family.]

May 16, 1972. Dear Friends: 'Tis a soft day in Dublin fair city.' (Translation—it's raining.) But here in Ballybrack, the Walshes are content to luxuriate in the gentle rain that falleth from the heavens—we understand Antigonish is still being buried in snow even on graduation day—and the satisfying fact about Irish rain is that that it doesn't have to be shoveled. It was a strange Christmas for us, however. Everything was green and the roses were blooming in the gardens. The children missed the snow and felt occasional tinges of homesickness. Our neighbors, who were originally from Belfast, (for the first time) did not go home to visit their families at Christmas—because of THE TROUBLES, so we had a big gang for Christmas dinner.

January was a relatively tough month. Colds and fevers continued—and during the coldest week of the year our central heating unit broke down—and it took a full week to repair it. We burned a lot of turf (peat) in the fireplace day and night and the situation brought the family circle closer than ever together. We began to appreciate Canadian housing and central heating more than ever. Most of the houses in Ireland do not have central heating. The weather here is, of course, much warmer than at home, but the cold is very damp and penetrating—and I have yet to see even one home with storm windows. Our electric radiators supplementing our one upstairs radiator saved us. But they didn't save on our electric bill. People here use much less electricity than we do in Canada. In Canada lights are put on all day in libraries, stores, etc. Here the lights are kept off and only put on when it becomes absolutely necessary. The lights are not turned on in the libraries until my nose is about 4 inches from my book. The electricity meter-man came to the house to ask me a number of questions and he explained that they thought something might be wrong, for the family who lived here before us used some 300 units of electricity per month–while we were using some 3,000 units per month. When he found out we were from Canada he understood! Also our hot water is electrically heated and Jackie washes every day. Further we are in the habit of showering and bathing much more than the Irish, a North American custom.

My studies are going well. In the second term after Christmas I continued studying Irish Mythology, Folklore, History, and Anglo-Irish Speech, in addition to the regular Anglo-Irish Literature lectures. I also had seminars in Anglo-Irish Prose, The Poetry of Yeats, and The Novels of Joyce and Beckett. I use the library at University College Dublin where James Joyce was a student and I became a reader at the National Library of Ireland, and Trinity College Dublin, The Trinity Library is one of the great libraries of the world and the old reading room strikes an English professor full of awe and silent respect. It is overwhelming. Thousands of old valuable book and manuscripts are in stacks three stories high. The Book of Kells is on display. The Irish, and many others, claim that this is the most beautiful book in the world–and I must agree. (A facsimile of the Book of Kells is in the StFX Library.) I must say also that library service in Europe is not so efficient as in our StFX library: Libraries here open at 10:00 a.m., no services are available (books from the closed stacks, periodicals, etc.) during the lunch hour, 12: 20 to 1: 30; services close at 5:00 p.m. and the libraries close at 10:00 p.m., and have short hours on Saturday, none on Sunday! Xeroxing takes 2 to 3 days! I now appreciate more than ever the superb service we get at the Angus L. MacDonald Library at X.

The Irish live on a different time cycle from North America. Jackie and I were invited to an engagement party. The time, 11:00 p.m. And most people don't show up until after midnight. (The pubs close at 11:30 p.m. Ah ha!) When I was driving home the baby-sitters (a young Canadian couple in the Anglo-Irish M.A. course, Terry Green and wife) at 3:00 a.m. on a Saturday morning (we had left the party early), the streets of Dublin were full of people going hither and yon. The traffic was as heavy as day-time. Young people were hitching home from downtown. At the time I didn't understand these unusual hours, but with the coming of summer, I'm beginning to understand: the sky stays light now (May 16th) until 9:30 p.m. In June it doesn't get dark in Dublin until after 11:00 p.m. We began to notice that our children were in bed while all the other kids in the neighborhood were still out whooping and hollering. Then I began to notice the traffic patterns as I commuted into the University. Lectures start at 10 a.m. A few start at 9:00 a.m., but that is considered by all my professor friends here a fit hour only for milking the cows. We are 10 miles south of Dublin city and the big traffic build-up of working people starts around 8:30 a.m. to 9:00 a.m. From 9:00 to 9:30 the white collar workers jam the roads, and shortly before 10:00 a.m. the executive limousines (Mercedes, B.M.W's, etc.) clog the lanes. After 10 a.m., the Rolls Royces proceed out of the walled estates and tree-lined driveways and float into the city in relative isolation after the working classes are out of the way. In the evening the Rolls Royces head out of the city around 4:00 p.m. and the rest pull out in the reverse order of the morning line up. We eat at 6:00 p.m., an hour later than we did in Canada, but still an hour before any of our neighbors. We have to clear the soccer players out of the back yard in order to eat in quiet.

The pattern of daylight hours has caused the Irish to develop a pattern of living quite different from what we were used to in Canada. The North American early bird finds no worm here. The day starts later and everything–including the night life, therefore starts later–so they sleep longer. The unhurried pace of life is also difficult to get used to. In a leisurely day, time is not important. If you hurry, you'll get heart trouble. The pace of life here is a notch slower than in Halifax, than in Toronto, etc.–and that's great–until something goes wrong and we want to get it fixed.

I have also noticed some other sociological patterns in our neighborhood. We live in the Killiney Hill area. In the 1920s, Killiney was a training ground for the IRA. Now it is a most fashionable burb of Dublin. On the crest of the Hill live people like Roger Moore, of "The Persuaders" series, formerly "The Saint," and Dan O'Herlihy, now retired from Hollywood and the movies and working at the Abbey Theatre. Just down from the crest of the Hill are new luxury homes with 5 or 6 bedrooms, in the $100,000.00 range, which can be purchased by–as the signs say–"entering into a private treaty." (No simple bill of sale at that price!) As we proceed down the Hill we encounter the old estates, the cheaper $50,000.00 homes, then come to the village center Town houses, the Church, and as we descend we reach the estate housing, (where we live) at $20 to $25,000.00, then the council housing, i.e., owned by the municipality, and at the bottom of the valley along the riverbank, the tinkers caravans. From the top of Killiney Hill, you can see the entire social and economic structure of Ireland.

Another interesting phenomenon involves the giving of directions in Ireland. We had trouble telling friends in the city how to get out to our house in the suburbs. Street names, district names mean nothing–but if we tell them, "Go out the dual carriageway (i.e., the divided highway) until you come to the Silver Tassie pub, then turn left"–they know exactly where we are. Directions are given by mentioning the Pubs–or Churches, along the way. What that says about Irish life, I refuse to speculate.

Our only problem in February was a slight case of blood poisoning Jackie got but our family Doctor here quickly took care of that. In March, during the term break, I started work on my dissertation on the Novels of Brian Moore. I began the basic research by compiling all of the bibliographic references to the writer. Joe D. Campbell (Chair of the Education Department at X) and Anna invited all of us over to Oxford University, where Joe is doing a year's sabbatical in the Department of Education. It was a generous offer on the part of the Campbells, but we thought of our five kids joining their seven and quickly decided that I would go alone to Oxford and spend a week doing research at the Bodleian Library.

I flew Dublin to Birmingham, then took the train to Oxford. Joe met me at the station and I hardly recognized him in his dapper mod Carnaby Street styles. We drove home in an ancient but immense van with seats for 12 or so and sliding doors. In the narrow streets of Oxford, Joe D. has become a force to be reckoned with. He dominates the roadway–intimidating all the small English cars. He does give way before lorries and buses. His house is on a hill and he executes a kamikaze right-hand blind dive into a parking space just one inch longer than the van and leaves his passenger staring at a wall he knows he didn't smash through just by the grace of God and Campbell panache. The drink Joe then offers his visitor is more than a social gesture, it's required to get his heart beating again. A tour of Joe's garden is the first duty. His potatoes were in and doing well even on St. Patrick's day.

The Campbells were in good cheer and we compared notes on life-styles in the British Isles. Then I was off for the grand tour of Oxford University. Not only are the buildings magnificent and the atmosphere historic, but I was thrilled to be walking in the footsteps of the great writers I have spent my life studying. I walked in the footsteps of Milton, Wordsworth, and my particular hero, Shelley. I saw Chaucer's working manuscript of *The Canterbury Tales*, Shakespeare's writing, Pope's couplets, Dryden's and Swift's, works of all the greatest writers. I saw Shelley's writing, and his personal belongings. I was able to analyze and see the changes in the handwriting of Elizabeth I from the age of 15 to 50. Joe introduced me to the Bodleian Library and I became a reader in the library, after taking an oath and signing about 7 documents. I had a great week doing research during the day and enjoying the company of the Campbells in the evening. On Sunday afternoon, Anna planned a family expedition to Uffington, about 30 miles south of Oxford to see the White Horse cut in the mountainside by Belgic settlers in the first century BC.

Joe figured 30 miles was about the limit for his old van, which can chug along at about 35 miles per hour on an open straightaway. We got out of the city with little difficulty and wound our way through the pleasant Berkshire countryside. We stopped at the birthplace of Alfred the Great and had our picture taken in front of his statue. We followed the signs to the White Horse and the van was breathing heavily when we turned to start up a hill, which quickly proved to be a mountain, nay, a veritable Everest to the van. The road was exactly one lane wide, no place to turn, winding back and forth, and a crazy green mini was right on Joe's tail, trying to pass. The Campbell kids got very quiet. Joe's neck got red and a flame seemed to consume his fevered brow. As he got redder, Anna got whiter. A brave smile hid her frantic praying. I looked out the window of the van down the mountainside and wondered how many times we would roll over before we reached the bottom. Joe double-clutched or something; the van heaved itself forward, and under Joe's firm grip, steadied down and gently bucked its way slowly to the top of the hill. What Joe was saying under his breath was probably offset by what Anna was praying under hers. My conclusion is that the van was too scared to quit on the hill. The relief we all felt at the top was soon tempered by the fact that *we couldn't see the White Horse.* Well, if we looked at our feet we could see it–we were standing on it. It's just white chalk surrounded by grass. The White Horse can be seen best by taking a train through the valley five miles opposite the mountain. We were too close to it to see it. Joe let the children romp over the Iron-Age hill-fort on the top of the mountain and his disposition was assuaged when he discovered an ingenious gate made with a single spring. He admired the skill of the sheep farmers who made that clever gate. The old van went down the hill easily. The capper on the trip came on the open highway when Joe pulled out on a straightaway and passed a tractor pulling a harrow. The kids broke into a loud and prolonged cheer. "What are you cheering about?" asked Joe. "Gee, Dad, that's the first time you've passed anything since we came to England!" Joe, of course, blamed the difficulty the van had lumbering up the hill on my presence. He said he had instructed all the kids to sit on the opposite side of the van from me–and when they hadn't, the old van nearly gave up. I decided to head back to Dublin, after a fruitful and exciting week.

Studies continued after the break, with seminars now on the drama of O'Casey, Yeats, and Beckett, a seminar twice a week on *Finnegans Wake* by Joyce, and a drama workshop, as well as the regular lectures. I have completed my bibliographic work, and have some 600 references, the most important of which I have ordered from the UCD library and through the inter-library loan. They should start coming in before the end of term so I'll have them to work on all during the summer. Since I shall be working on my dissertation all during the summer we decided to take a vacation to the west of Ireland during the final week of the spring break. This also was the last week of the off-season rates and would save us money. Because the troubles in the North have frightened off so many tourists the big emphasis this summer is on Irish holidays for Irish families. We went to Galway, for a week in a modern hotel, and had room and meals for seven for only 57 pounds. That is only $142.00 Canadian, which is room and board for only $3.00 per day per person. Amazing! And we saw "the sun go down on Galway Bay." We toured through the mountains in Galway, where there are rocks–on rocks on rocks. The children had studied the geography of Galway in school and they said it was rocky–but we couldn't believe it when we saw it. There are millions of rocks. Rock fences are everywhere. Rock fences go right up the almost perpendicular sides of mountains. We visited Anganrach Castle. The castle was out on a point of land and we had some difficulty finding the right road to it. We knew, however, that the road was a *cul de sac*, so I told the children to look for a *cul de sac*. We took one road and it went to a farm along the seashore. We reached the end of the road and had to turn around when Gregory began to shout, "There they are. There they are." We looked. He was pointing at a mound of potato sacks, and he exclaimed proudly, "The *cul de sacs*." We laughed for the next 20 miles.

We went to Ballinklea Castle, saw a burial Cairn, and visited the Ross Errilly Friary. The Friary was the best thing we saw in Galway–and in our opinion is a must for any visitor in the area. It is a ruin of a Friary with many buildings, a cloister, a tower over 100 feet tall. The roofs have fallen in and disappeared, but in one three-story part of the friary the ingenious chimney corner serving all three stories can be seen. We visited Cong Abbey and Ashford Castle, now a modern hotel, and in the most romantic and movie-like setting.

Francis had studied the "Twelve Bens"–that is, mountains–in Connemara, so we drove through them. Farmers were working fields on the hillsides that stood at 45degree angles. I was reminded of the old settlers in the *Keppoch* outside Antigonish. One evening we visited the new Cathedral in Galway City; it is made of Redwood and Connemara Marble and the finest cathedral I've ever seen. We also visited Castles at Oranmore, Dunguaire and Rivanna.

One day was given to a trip of literary interest to William Butler Yeats' tower at Thoor Ballylee. We also drove out to Coole Park, Lady Gregory's Estate, where she hosted all the great Irish writers. We saw the famous autograph tree, on which she invited writers who were in her inner-circle to carve their initials. A young writer knew he had made it when he was invited to carve his initials alongside the Great WBY (William Butler Yeats). If analyzing handwriting is revealing, even more so is analyzing initials in trees. Yeats carved plain square initials, but chose a bad location on a fold in the tree and as the years have passed his "Y" has been swallowed by the groove. AE (George Russell, a paternalistic mystic), has an "AE" enclosed in a triangle, which stands out; Sean O'Casey, with his laborer's muscles and mind, cut a heavy and deep "SO'C"; but the prize goes, undoubtedly, to George Bernard Shaw. Shaw linked his letters together, one over the other, and the sprawling vertical anagram of

G
B
S

over rides everyone else's initials and dominates the whole tree.

We visited more castles and towers, made friends with two families, and visited a Connemara marble factory–about which I may have more news later. We returned home to Dublin, tired but happy. We didn't get to see any plays during the second term, which was quite time-consuming. But as we near the end, and since I'm studying drama, we have seen Eugene O'Neill's *The Ice Man Cometh* at the Abbey, *Fiddler on the Roof*, and Pinter's *The Caretaker* at the Gaiety. We get students tickets at only 25 pence (65 cents).

Last Sunday, we enjoyed a visit with Sisters Madeline Connolly and Sara MacPherson, Marthas from Antigonish, who are studying in Edinburgh, Scotland. We gave them the grand tour of Dublin and the Wicklow Hills and had a fine day.

Last month Ireland had a power crisis. The Electricity Supply Board was hit by a wildcat strike of Electricity workers. The power was off for several days. Then the country was put on a grid which gave 36 separate parts of the country electric current on a rotating basis, 8 hours at a time, once a day. The rotation continued for about two weeks. And now the news is that another strike may come next week. And what about the Walshes' luck? I ran out, bought candles, a small camp cooker and a lantern. Never used them. Our electricity stayed on all the time! It seems that our side of the street is on a hospital line–and what little power they had passed through our line–so we had no trouble at all. Somebody up there likes us.

The children are all well now. Rebecca is cutting molars, Gregory is designing spaceships made out of Lego plastic bricks. Monica is the premier swimmer in the group. Francis is showing a flair for chess and giving me trouble every game. Mary is our Irish speaker and reader par excellence, Jackie is hoping to study for a Montessori International Teaching Certificate next year (if the quota of foreign students isn't cut), and I'm learning to play the tin whistle.

We miss the Stanley Cup Playoffs, and the Expos, but I get the scores on short-wave and was surprised by the demise of the Blackhawks and the departure of *Le Grand Orange!* But the FA cup final in English Soccer was a thriller, and International Rugby saw Ireland in fine form, and Hurling and Gaelic Football still hold forth at Croke Park where I hope to see Muhammad Ali in person this summer.

That's all until the summer break.

Love from Pat, Jackie and the gang-green.

My best friend from high school, Jordan Mastroianni, had been in Morocco with the US Navy when Jackie and I were married. Now we were an ocean and continent apart again when he got married in Texas. But the whole family gathered on the big bed and we placed a phone call to them on their wedding day.

To Jordan and Yvonne: November 26, 1971

Sun cannot look upon us both at once.
Gaps of oceans face our fronts and backs.
A night of blackness intervenes and haunts
The other's day. One waking always lacks
The clasp of hand, the comfort of a voice
When heart is sore, the echo of a good
Laugh, the sharing of pensive moods, the choice
To sit in silence and be understood,
But I have found a patient, loving wife
And a house full of children, while my friend
Has restlessly sailed the face of life,
Floating alone to the edge of ocean's bend.

But separation's rent has now been healed
For joy, as mine is yours. Yvonne has yield.

Jordan "Mel" and Yvonne Mastroianni today.

The Hero

by Pat Walsh from *The Dublin Magazine*

The soldier woke with a start. His head lay against the stone. He sighed and his breath puffed into clouds. Thunderclouds? It was still dark, but as he blinked the stinging sweat from his eyes he could see the glow of the enemy army's campfires across the river to the West. He turned around to see a knife-edge of red in the eastern sky. The turn caused a muscle spasm in his wounded leg. He stifled a moan.

His hand still clutched the knife he had fallen asleep holding. He slid the knife into the grass near the rock. He hammered at the knots of muscle in his aching leg. Pain. He crawled against the rock, pulled himself up, leaned forward with both hands over his head and pushed. The stretch and pressure relieved the ache in his leg but he felt the scab on his wounded thigh crack. Blood trickled down his leg. He was too tired to look at it.

How many days had he been at the ford? What did it matter? Help had been sent for. Worrying about when it would come wouldn't help it come any earlier. Help would come when it would come and if it didn't come in time, what the hell, he couldn't do anything about it. It might come tomorrow. Tomorrow? Tomorrow was yesterday. Today is tomorrow. At least it isn't raining. Cold. But the sky hadn't fallen on him, the earth had not opened and swallowed him, and the sea had not backed up the river and burst over him.

The soldier could hear the burble of water over the rocks below the shallow pool that formed the ford. A twig cracked behind him. He reached slowly for the knife without turning around. He waited. No sound. But he could feel a presence. He leaped around into a crouch with his butt against the rock, his knife cocked up ready to disembowel whoever was approaching. A black silhouette cut through the strand of reddening sky. Puffs of breath hung in the cold morning air.

"It's me." The croaking voice of the farmer.

"Call out to me before you get so close, or you'll be a dead son of a bitch."

Fear shimmered in the old man's eyes. He held out a pig bone with gobs of burned fat and gristle on it. The guardian of the ford felt sorry for the farmer. He remembered with guilt how the old man had suffered because of this goddam war. The whole countryside had been cast back into the Stone Age by the ferocity of the civil war.

The farmer's cattle had been driven off, his home burned, and his wife had been raped and then stabbed to death by a patrol from across the river. And the old man showed up morning after morning with a pig bone. A bloody marvelous pig that. Day after day after day. Until it seemed that the bone the old man held out this morning was the same bone as yesterday. The same–or had the soldier fallen asleep for a second or two? How long had the old man been standing there? The warrior's muscles were so tense he snatched the bone from the old man's hands. The old man trembled. The soldier had wanted to be gentle with the old man, but he said nothing and became conscious again of the pain in his leg. He tore at the bone like a dog. The grease got into his whiskers.

The farmer backed away and disappeared up the hill while the soldier watched him out of his good eye. The other eye was swollen almost shut. Still squatting on his haunches the soldier turned his good eye across the river where the glow from the enemy's fires were fading into the coming dawn. They'll send some again today. Again and again. And again. And tomorrow.

He crawled around the rock to the brook running down into the pool at the ford and let his head fall into the cold water. He washed his wound and wrapped a torn rag around this thigh. He went back to the rock and watched the water below as the light behind him crept across the valley. He watched and waited; he scratched at the lice. As he scratched the sun began to warm his backside and he remembered the last woman he had had. She knew he was going into battle. She offered her body and he had taken it. Gratefully. He had enjoyed watching her face twist in happy passion. She cooked him breakfast. That was when he thought of his wife. Would he see her again? He had long ago accepted the fact the he would die young. The day he had first taken up arms he had accepted the consequences. Death did not frighten him. It would come when it would come. But if he could see his wife again. Once more before the end.

He felt the urge to piss and he was surprised at how loudly the piss sounded as it dug a hole in the dirt. When he finished, silence surrounded his head. The brook and the ford hissed–but there were no birds, no animals, no cattle grazing, no human sounds. The valley was dead. He could feel the hot blood crawling around his brain. He thought of a cauliflower being boiled in a cauldron.

His arms and legs seemed to be sinking into the ground. His eyes were closed, and he knew he was lying on his back. A great weight was pressing him into the earth. He opened his good eye and turned his head to look down towards the river. A soldier was striding up the hill towards him. He was tall, broad, and fair. His hair was close-cropped, blond, and curled. His new green uniform was clean. His silver insignias glinted in the sun. He was armed. He walked up to the soldier and stood over him.

"This is a manly stand."

"It isn't very much."

"I'm going to help you now."

"Who are you?"

"I am your father."

The soldier had to turn away and shut his good eye. His father stood directly in the path of the sun and his face glowed too brightly to look at.

"My wounds are heavy. They need time to heal."

"Sleep a while then. I'll stand in for you."

The soldier opened his eye again and his father was gone. The sun hurt his eye. Had he slept long? For more than a day? Or for a few minutes? A few hours?

He crouched by the rock. He crackled another louse with his thumbnail. A movement across the river. He felt the urge to piss again. Whoever it was, he was coming down the same path as the fellow yesterday. The soldier looked downstream. There was no trace of yesterday. Or was it the day before? He remembered how strange he felt when he killed the fellow. How many had he killed? He lost track. He was a trained killer. It was his business. It was the purpose for which he had punished his body for years. It was all for his country. For his country he had strangled men. The stench after strangling when their bowels let loose was no longer cause for a second thought: in peacetime repulsive; in time of war honorable. But, yesterday? He had spent the morning sharpening a branch into a quarter-staff with one end sharpened. When shortly before dusk the fellow had come leaping at him with a knife he yanked the spear out of the water and lunging, drove it right up through the fellow's stomach just above his cock. The scrape of the spear against bone hadn't surprised him. The jolt of pain in his own shoulder hadn't surprised him. What surprised him were the fellow's eyeball bursting and the blood spurting from his eye and nose as he went up and backwards, riding the thrust of the spear. As he landed in the pool, vomit slid out of his mouth. The soldier had to put his foot on the dead man's hip and jerk hard to get the spear out. It had shattered about three inches from the tip. He stared at a piece of intestine hooked on the splintered spear and then threw the weapon downstream after the slowly twisting body of his dead countryman.

He carved a new spear. It was his duty. To kill the enemy. The enemy. An Irishman. A fellow Irishman, but the enemy.

Today's enemy was standing on the opposite bank of the river. The soldier stayed crouched. The enemy waved to him and called his name. The soldier tried to work up a good spit but his throat was dry. They had sent his friend to do the job. The bastards.

His friend drew out his knife, stuck it in to the riverbank and stepped forward with arms upraised. The soldier left the rock, walked down, stuck his knife into his riverbank, and raised his arms, palms west.

They embraced in the shallows of the ford. The soldier felt the muscles in his friend's back, lithe, not yet flexed. Supple. Until needed in combat. Would his friend be the one? His bad eye beat madly, beat madly, beat madly.

"You're welcome friend," his enemy said.

"I could trust your welcome once," he said, "but I don't trust it now. Anyway, I should bid you welcome: this is my home. You're the intruder. And it's wrong to send you to challenge me. I should challenge you. You have driven out our people our women, our young men. Our cattle. Burned our homes."

"Enough. Neither of us chose to meet here in combat. Why? Why? I remember when we were at school together. You shined my shoes and made my bed."

"True. But I was young. And small. This is a new day."

"A bitter day."

"Because of you and your new friends. I can't let you pass," the soldier said.

"You can't stop me."

"Try me."

"I will."

"I'll kill you if I have to."

"I'll kick the living shit out of you."

The soldier laughed. A good deep laugh. Deep in his guts. He was completely relaxed. His friend laughed too, and they sat down together on a rock letting the cold water wash over their bare feet.

The soldier stopped laughing and splashed some water on his face.

"Remember the matches we used to have at school? We were always together. Camping together. Sleeping together. You were my best friend."

"This goddam war. We have to forget. Those days are gone forever."

"Yes. I suppose it doesn't help to remember. We've chosen different sides."

"I didn't have much choice. I was forced by circumstances. You know . . ."

"The reason doesn't matter. You're on the other side. You're with the enemy army."

"I suppose remembering doesn't help, does it?"

"No."

"Well, then, let's get on with it."

The enemy stood up and faced the soldier. But the soldier couldn't forget. He got up off the rock, stepped back from his friend, the enemy. They embraced again, tripping one another and wrestling in the shallow water. The soldier remembered a day at school when they had wrestled for over two hours and finally had to quit when they were both too tired and too sweaty to hold on to one another. They had lain on the ground panting at one another and smiling like damn fools. That match had sealed their friendship. To the soldier's heated brain that yesterday was today. Nothing had changed. He exulted in the toss and tumble of the match. He pleasured in the twist of flesh on flesh, the grunt and groan and gasp of joy in manly contest. And today as yesterday, they ended up dragging themselves onto a rock and grinning at one another. The soldier squinted his good eye in the glare of sunlight off the water.

"Bloody . . . fooking . . . brawl."

"Aye . . . That it is . . . That it is."

But the friend moved first. The soldier noticed the tired sag in the enemy's shoulders as he headed for the western bank of the river and his knife.

The soldier's brain burst. His bad eye closed and his good eye bulged out of its socket. Every muscle and fiber in his body trembled in anger. His temple beat like a drum and his neck knotted. His teeth ground. He moaned a low moan which grew into a swollen gurgle of rage. His friend was an enemy of his people, his land, his home, his sick and divided country. A traitor. A bloody fucking traitor.

And the friend knew before he reached his knife that the water he felt surging against his thighs would drag his guts downstream before the sun could set: and before Ferdia reached his knife, he felt the flames of Cuchulain's rage in his bowels.

*

[This modernized telling is based upon the ancient texts of Irish literature, and follows closely the details of those venerable texts. Only the last line reveals that this is not a modern story when the names of the protagonists are revealed. But, of course, it *was* about what was still going on in Dublin to that day!]

Patrick X Walsh

The Lüscher Color Test

This is the last item being written for this book, January 20, 2019. This is the date my father was born in 1904. My sister Mary Ann Walsh Rorke is in the closing moments of her 78 years in High Pointe House hospice in Haverhill, Massachusetts, surrounded by her husband and her family.

I have been at my computer since 6:30 this morning having been awakened by a dream: *I was in the company of a group of people I did not know, who were strangely flat and all dressed in beige corduroy clothing. One woman was in obvious distress and I felt she needed help for she was leaving the group. I was pleading with her to tell me about her troubles so I could help her. I became distressed telling her "It will help you to share your problems. Tell me your secrets and you will feel better." She left my presence.*

I woke up and immediately began to ponder what that dream was all about. Gradually it came to me that the woman was my sister, and the advice I was giving the woman in the dream, was really advice my deep unconscious was giving to me, through someone who would know my shortcomings. Here are the thoughts that came streaming into my mind.

At St. Francis Xavier University, my first- year Math professor was Fr. Frank Ginivan, an American from Massachusetts who had graduated from StFX. He became my confessor and I went to confession to him often, whenever I felt the need. He was kind and patient–and he always gave the same penance: "Say five Our Fathers, five Hail Mary's, and five Glory Be's while meditating on the Second Fall of Jesus on the way to Calvary. Jesus always gets up and carries on. He fulfills his destiny. You can too."

And flooding into my memory came *The Lüscher Color Test*. In 1967 I had written a dissertation for my Master's Degree in English Literature for Boston College on "The Psychology of Color in Shelley's Poetry." In the Chinese Library at Harvard I had found a copy of a color test invented by Dr. Max Lüscher in Basel, Switzerland. Max Lüscher believed that sensory perception of color is objective and universally shared by all, but that color preferences are subjective. This distinction allows subjective states to be objectively measured by using a person's preference for test colors. Lüscher believed that because the color selections are guided in an unconscious manner, they reveal the person as they really are, not as they perceive themselves or would like to be perceived. I had applied this concept to Shelley's poetry.

Shortly after arriving in Dublin while browsing in a book store I spied a copy of the color test, now in book form that could be used to analyze people. I bought a copy and when we had friends in for supper I suggested we all take the color test of our personalities for fun. Lüscher maintained subjects who select identical color combinations have similar personalities. So people are shown 8 different colored cards and asked to place them in order of preference. Colors are divided between "basic" (blue, yellow, red, green) and "auxiliary" (violet, brown, grey, and black). I had to go first, and I arranged the eight color tiles in order of preference, best liked to least liked. Green had always been my favorite color, I had assumed because of my Irish background and name. Wow! Was I wrong. I was a "Greenie" through and through:

Green represents the physiological condition of "elastic tension." Psychologically it expresses a will of personality and perseverance, therefore constancy, and above all, resistance to change. Such constancy of viewpoint and self-awareness places a high value on the "I" in all forms of possession and self-affirmation, since possession is regarded as increasing both security and self-esteem. Such a person wants to increase certainty in his own value, either by self-assertiveness, by holding to some idealized picture of himself, in terms of his superiority in physical, educational or cultural attainments.

Symbolically he is a majestic sequoia, deep-rooted, proud and unchanging, towering over the lesser trees, of austere and autocratic temperament, the tension in the bowstring. In emotions, he is often upset by worry over possible loss of standing or personal failure.

Green as "tension" acts as a dam in which the exciting of external stimuli builds up without being released, increasing the sense of pride, of self-controlled superiority to others, of power, of being in control of events, or at least being able to manage and direct them. Control may take many forms: not only directed drives, but detailed accuracy in checking and verifying facts, as precise and accurate memory, clarity of presentation, critical analysis and logical consistency.

This "green behavior" can find expression in a quest for better conditions, in which case we have the reformer, bent on ameliorating conditions. He wants his opinions to prevail, to feel himself justified as a representative of basic and immutable principles, tends to moralize to and lecture others.

But the "greenie" wishes to impress. He needs to be recognized, to hold his own and to have his way against opposition and resistance.

We all had a hearty laugh, and I had to admit the analysis had much to offer as you may surmise from what you have read to this point. Then everyone else tried the test, and it seemed to fit as each person in the group admitted. Finally, Jacqueline was the only one left unanalyzed. She laid out the tiles, and began with Red:

Red represents an energy-expending physiological condition, the expression of vital force, thus has the meaning of desire and all forms of appetite and craving. Red is the urge to achieve results, to win success, to achieve all those things which offer intensity of living and fullness of experience. Red is impulse, the will-to-win, and all forms of vitality and power from sexual potency to revolutionary transformation. It is the impulse towards active doing, towards sport, struggle, competition, eroticism and enterprising productivity. Red is "impact of the will" or "force of will" as distinct from the green "elasticity of will."

Symbolically red corresponds to the blood of conquest, to the Pentecostal flame igniting the human spirit, to the sanguine temperament. Whoever chooses red in the first position wants her own activities to bring her intensity of experience and fullness of living. What form her activities will take–co-operative enterprise, leadership, creative endeavor–will be indicated by the color which accompanies red.

Jackie's reading was not as evident to our company as mine, for her drive and "force of will" was quiet and without a need for the public approval my personality demanded.

Nervously I proceeded to go through the tiles in order of preference until the following analyses popped up for Jacqueline:

She feels trapped in a distressing or uncomfortable situation and is seeking some way of gaining relief.

She wants to broaden her fields of activity and insists that her hopes and ideas are realistic. Distressed by the fear she may be prevented from doing what she wants; needs both peaceful conditions and quiet reassurance to restore her confidence.

Our company quickly dispersed. The party was over: literally over for me.

As we lay side by side in bed that evening, I could not go to sleep. The color test bombarded my conscious mind with Jackie's history: valedictorian/top student both in High School and University, *summa* in mathematics, graduated six months pregnant, awarded highest honor as Outstanding Example of Christian Womanhood, turned down job in Washington DC starting at $10,000.00 a year (my salary $3,200.00 per year), five children in 11 years, took classes to sew clothing for children, took classes to upholster our furniture, taught piano lessons, corrected papers for a philosophy professor, supported my every activity in University, town, and church, especially my quest for an M.A. and now a damn PhD! Every caring thing done to meet the needs of her children and her husband–he, too stupid and unaware and unappreciative of her incredible burdens so selflessly borne. I could hardly breathe, let alone sleep.

I could tell Jacqueline was not sleeping yet either.

"Jackie, you're not asleep?"

"No."

Long pause.

"That test was spot on, wasn't it?"

"Yes."

Long pause.

"Would you like to go back to school?"

"Yes."

"Do you have anything in mind?"

"Well, there's a Montessori Program at Sion Hill not far from here." [We had had a study group with our friends back in Antigonish led by Fr. MacSween and Joe D. Campbell, head of the Education Department.]

I didn't sleep much that night, but I think Jackie did. As had happened with my sister Mary Ann, I had missed the needs of my primary care giver. This was my second major fall on the road to my personal Calvary. How would I get up, and carry on?

Our great family adventure of living in Ireland for two years, was, for my wife, as challenging as my quest for the PhD. She had been the leading scholar of our high school class, and the leading scholar of her university class. With five children ranging in age from age ten to newly born, she managed our Irish expedition with grace, style, and extreme patience. It was my turn to step up,

The next morning I called the Credit Union in Antigonish explaining that I would need more money. Getting it, I hired an Irish nanny to care for the children, and while I got a PhD, Jackie continued to fulfill all our needs, and she earned a Montessori Teaching Diploma with her final examiner being Mario Montessori, son of Maria, the founder of the Montessori Movement.

Yes, after the Second Fall, I got up and carried on. Thank you, Fr. Ginivan. In life, as in spirit and in marriage, you have to get up and carry on: 'caring' being the key and the goal. And it's not easy because for me there would be a Third Fall–nearly costing me my marriage.

NOTE: I wondered why the people in my dream were "flat" and why "Beige" [pale brown]. Brown, especially pale, according to Lüscher, has forfeited the active vital force of red (which contains brown), creating a sense of physical discomfort. And "flat" people are not full and psychologically robust, and thus weak in the face of the discomforting situation. I certainly was repressing this incident that this dream made me face up to.

Having published stories only in *The Antigonish Review* and local papers, I took the opportunity while in Ireland to try to publish a story in an established and prestigious international magazine. Hence the story of Cuchulain above based on the ancient Irish epic, *Táin Bó Cúailnge,* or *The Cattle Raid of Cooley*. I had succeeded on the first shot with *The Hero*, but I knew the critics back home would say I was lucky, so I wrote the story below, based on the one and only live boxing match I have ever seen. Please remember, gentle reader, Pat Walsh is a real, living person, that's the TRUTH; the American Professor is only words on a page that you bring to life only in your imagination, that is, FICTION.

The Knockout

by Pat Walsh from *The Dublin Magazine*

The American Professor deliberately forgot to tell his wife he had bought three ringside seats at the Muhammad Ali–Al "Blue" Lewis fight at Croke Park. He didn't enter the check number or amount in his checkbook; the fight would be over before the bank statement came in the mail. The check had been made out to Conrad Sugrue Promotions, Ltd., for £45. He could claim that that was the name of the copying service and he had needed £45 worth of Xeroxed articles for his research project, "Irish Writers and the Spanish Civil War." But £45? That wiped out the week they had planned at Ryan's Hotel in Galway. He had been looking forward to that. A week away from the kids–no need to wear pajamas, no need to stifle noises in the night, no need to shower separately–and the week had been timed perfectly, during safe days and during a full moon. How could he pass it up? A full moon. He scratched his beard. The Wolf Man. That's what she called him on those special weekends. Her Wolf Man. His Bunny.

And wasn't it doubly difficult on sabbatical in Ireland? No *Playboy* on sale. No. The Irish were intellectually bent. Why every corner store sold copies of *Stern* and other German magazines. The sexiest magazine allowed into Ireland was the *Sunday Times Magazine* with its advertisements for Scandinavian shower nozzles. And, of course, *Titbits*. But that was good for only one purpose which had been discovered by Leopold Bloom on the morning of June 16th, 1904, as he sat meditating behind 7 Eccles Street listening to the bells of St. George's Church. With no porn on sale in the Republic and with the "Troubles" preventing him from going to the "Athens of the North," he had plunged into his research. He got off to such a good start that he would have enough for several articles (really one article–but with a slightly different angle of emphasis he could palm off what would appear to be three or four publications), and even if he never got a book published, the list of articles would impress the Dean. Further, since the sabbatical committee didn't subscribe to Irish periodicals, they would be suitably impressed by exotic titles. The Professor eased up for the summer months.

He took the family out two days a week: to the Phoenix Park Zoo with the MGM lion in quiet repose (he knew the original MGM lion was dead, but the kids wouldn't know the difference, and neither would their friends when they got home to Schenectady, New York); to the passage grave at New Grange, where they ran into a group of schoolboys on a CIE tour who were all atwitter because a girl travelling with two hippies had on a red T-shirt but no bra and her nipples were staring at them like a hypnotist's eyes; to Powerscourt, where the kids kept screaming about the rats in the reflecting pond and he was happy the bus-loads of touring Spanish students were unable to decipher their cries; to the waterfall at Powerscourt, where two days later a fourteen-year-old English schoolboy fell to his death in front of his parents; to the National Museum where his youngest boy had had a traumatic experience when he saw a Paleolithic grave with the skeleton in it and where the Professor had been unable to find the statues Bloom had wanted to examine 'orificially,' so-to-speak. Well, he was entitled to carry home a memory with which to pummel his fellow professors–and Muhammad Ali was it.

None of his associates had seen Ali live. The best they could do was closed-circuit TV at the Empire Theatre in Albany. A ringside seat at Madison Square Garden was out of the price range of university people, except, of course, the football coach and the president, who was not interested in the manly art of self-defense and who had a hideaway in the Adirondacks where rumor (circulated discreetly by the Dean of Science) had it he shacked up on weekends with one of the music professors, the woodwind instructor, some said.

The Professor remembered his cousin who was the first clarinetist in the Boston Pops Orchestra. His cousin had taken him to a concert at Symphony Hall and at the intermission had taken him backstage to meet Harry Dixon, the conductor who was substituting for Arthur Fielder who with Norman Mailer was going to the Sonny Liston-Cassius Clay fight in Maine. The orchestra musicians were worried that the concert would last so long that they would miss the fight on TV. Harry Dixon promised he would step up the tempo and get them back down to the dressing room in time for the fight. He told them they would play only one encore, "The Colonel Bogey March" (2 minutes, 20 seconds) and then take a bow *with* him (unheard of in the days of Serge Koussevitzky!) and beat it to the dressing room. They just made it–in time to see Cassius Clay clobber the Big Bad Bear, much to the chagrin of the Professor, who had wanted Sonny to stick his fist, twelve-ounce glove and all, right down to the Big Mouth's esophagus. Yes, the Professor had hated the braggart Clay, an uppity wise-ass. True, Sonny Liston had had some scrapes with the law, but he had paid–he took his medicine like a man and kept his mouth shut. But Clay and that other big-mouth, Malcolm X, were trouble. They didn't have any manners, they were not gentlemen, they didn't know their place. Sure, change was coming–and should come, of course–but they weren't helping matters by making people hate their kind.

Then the Professor had been overlooked for promotion. The pay scale was tied to rank. He took a new interest in the Faculty Association. He would show the goddamned Administration that a junior professor was a force to be reckoned with. Bureaucracy would pay. He became for the Administration the thorn in the side, the pebble in the shoe, the ingrown toenail. He grew a beard. The first member of the English Department to go hirsute. True, a sculptor in the Art Department had a beard. But that was the Art Department. Everyone knew about artists, and the sculptor, it was rumored, had had his beard from the time he was nine years old.

The Professor remembered with satisfaction that when his beard was only two days old he had been invited to the Vice President's home for a cocktail party and in spite of his wife's pleading he had refused to shave. He showed up looking like William Holden in *Stalag 17*. The Director of Public Relations had pulled him into the bathroom and shouted, "For chrissakes, what the hell are you trying to do? The VP's mother-in-law asked somebody if you were on drugs." The Professor refused to shave with the VP's wife's Lady Sunbeam electric razor and returned to the buffet table to hear the chairman of the Biology Department claiming that he had tried to grow a beard in the navy but that after about a week the itch was killing him and little white pimples had grown under his mustache. The Professor had borne the itch like Job, with justification, and like Job was vindicated by the attention of his peers. He became the spokesman for the maligned and malignant junior professors and, at the same time that he began to recognize that the junior staff was in reality the bum boys of the Administration, he began to recognize the truth spoken by Muhammad Ali, born Cassius Clay, and Malcolm X. He made *The Autobiography of Malcolm X* required reading in all his English Literature courses, the justification being "relevance." The students wanted relevance, and they got it. He and the students agreed at the end of term that Malcolm X and Martin Luther King, Junior, had reached identical positions from polar extremes at the time of their untimely deaths. And Cassius Marcellus had proved that he was not Clay. He could put his money where his mouth was. He whupped everybody–and then the Administration had punished him for being a rebel and refusing to knuckle under and serve in Vietnam. *They* had robbed *him* of his title. The Professor had seen the Fight of the Century on closed circuit TV at the Empire in Albany. Two Undefeated World Champions! Ali had been robbed again. He had too big a lead to be defeated by a lucky punch at the end. And of course the judges, American Legionaries, ex-US-soldiers of Foreign Wars, had given Frazier points for "aggressiveness"–their own personal moral flaw. Didn't they recognize counter-punching, footwork, speed and agility and the beauty of a man using his brains to avoid atomic holocaust? No. Administrations were all alike in their blindness, in their inability to see a man's true moral worth.

Money be damned. A ringside at Madison Square Garden cost $500.00 at least, and a ringside seat here in Dublin cost £15, a mere $37.50. A pittance. To see in person a moral and physical modern-day Cuchulain!

The Professor met his two buddies. A fellow-American, complete with an Asahi-Pentax with which he would get exactly one good picture at the fight: the lovely buttocks of the model who carried the signs marking each round as she indelicately ducked under the ringside ropes after Round Two. The other buddy was an Irish friend, a political scientist. The Professor had admired the political scientist before he met him because the man had steadfastly refused to allow Conor Cruise O'Brien to interrupt him during a debate on RTE.

The three entered a pub on the corner near Croke Park. A hum and buzz were in the air. The locals were sitting back watching the tourists and eyeing one another knowingly. The highlight of the pre-fight scene in the pub was a blonde who towered over her little bald-headed escort by a good twelve inches. She was heavily lip-sticked and eye-lashed and without a word stood her little man at the bar, handed him her pocketbook to hold, and in her white silk sailor-boy pants suit minced into the *Mna* room with her French poodle on a leash leading the way. They were in the *Mna* for over twenty minutes, during which a hush fell over the pub as all ears were straining to hear what was going on in there. The little man drank a ginger ale, desperately chewed the ice cubes one by one, and when the woman emerged, pulling a reluctant poodle behind her, he fell in third in line with her shoulder bag bouncing off his knees. Several fight-goers, feeling no pain, joined the line and gradually the pub emptied of definitely not the usual Gaelic Athletic Association crowd.

Sixth row ringside. The Professor hoped the TV cameras would be able to pick him up. Maybe his brother watching a delayed broadcast on TV in Springfield, Massachusetts, would see him.

The trio felt giddy because the expenditure of so few quid had them elbowing among such notables as John Houston and Billy Conn and The Dubliners. Well, his Irish friend was not as impressed by The Dubliners. He had elbowed them before. The Professor couldn't find Bernadette Devlin anywhere. He informed his Irish friend authoritatively that he needn't look for Governor Ronald Reagan, who was visiting Ireland for President Nixon, because it would be politically *non compis mentis* for him to show his white face at an Ali contest. The Professor chuckled to himself that he could be present at a gala event at which such a conservative Administrator couldn't. That was the trouble with Administrators. When they got tangled up with "principles," they couldn't mix with the common people. The Professor looked at his common people companions. At £15? An awful lot of clergymen, politicians, grey-suited businessmen, and Beautiful People. He began to feel guilty about being at ringside. He had to admit to himself that he was right in the middle of the Establishment.

The Professor quickly dismissed his scruples. He was at ringside as an "outsider." He didn't belong there, so he had every right to be there. He was here to stand witness to the greatest rebel the boxing world had ever known. Wasn't Ali the best known athlete in the history of the world? Better known even than Pele? And Ali was smart enough to talk–and how!–the Establishment into paying top prices to see him mock their system. The Professor smiled at the poor fools who paid £15 for ringside in order to be "insiders." Ali had so scrambled the Administration's values that the only real "insiders" were "outsiders," like himself. The first preliminary was between an American black man (nicknamed Tiger, but who reminded the Professor of the tigers he had seen *in* circuses: old, fat and toothless, who padded around the ring a threat to no one, except the trainer, if the beast fell asleep and rolled off his perch onto the man who undoubtedly cracked his whip just to keep the poor animal awake) and a black Englishman named John Conte. Conte began early to smash the other fellow in the face, and the sound of the blows thumping into human flesh made the Professor sick to his stomach. He became aware that this was the first time he had even seen a live fight. Every other fight he had seen had been in two dimensions, on TV or in the movies, which translated the obscene ritual of two animals mauling one another into mere electrons or photons dancing on a silver screen. But here at Croke Park on a beautiful summer's night he could see three, no, five or six dimensions. He saw the Tiger's flesh gleam with sweat, his mouthpiece float in slow-motion in a gentle arc out of the ring, his eyes look out towards the Hill of Howth as the referee wipes off his gloves after a knockdown. When the bell thunked hollowly for the end of the round and Tiger's seconds couldn't swing his little chair into the ring quick enough to let the animal sink to his haunches, the Professor noticed the rolls of fat hanging over the Tiger's trunks just like his hung over the sides of his gym pants when he played squash.

Mercifully, the referee stopped the fight early, as the Tiger continued to pad around the ring looking glazedly off towards Howth unaware of the beater bearing down on him.

The second preliminary matched an unknown French-Canadian lumberjack against British Champion (former) Joe Bugner, who stomped around the ring like Frankenstein's monster. Bugner could only hammer the Canadian on the head because the Quebecker kept putting his head down and butting Bugner's belly, then grabbing him around the buttocks and trying to lift him up and tip him over. The referee again had to stop the bout because the Canadian would only wrestle instead of box. Bugner clomped out of the ring, shaking his curls like a dog climbing out of the Royal Canal.

The Professor began to reflect upon the personal imagery through which he was viewing events. As a literature Professor he had a tendency to classify images–and he was thinking tonight about boxers in animal terms: tigers, big bad bears, dogs. His closeness to a real fight had reduced his image clusters to the animal level. Previously he had tended to think of boxers in polarized political-psychological-philosophical terms: Joe Lewis vs. Max Schmeling (Democracy vs. Fascism); Floyd Patterson vs. Sonny Liston (Decency vs. Meanness); Sonny Liston vs. Cassius Clay (Quiet Repentance vs. Smart-Ass Arrogance); Muhammad Ali vs. Joe Frazier (Stylish Imagination vs. Plodding Pedestrianism). The real thing from the sixth row at Croke Park had become physically and psychologically repellent. Paying to see two men try to destroy each other's consciousness became almost embarrassing. It reminded the Professor of paying to see freaks at a circus. Curiosity was so strong, but then the embarrassment felt for the freak was sobering. And after paying, he began to think how sick it must make a freak. Day after day he had to look at deformed personalities so insensitive that they were willing to pay money to see living deformities of their own mental condition.

The Professor began to notice how the people around him were all imperfect in some way, One fellow with a birthmark on his face, that fellow with one ear sticking out like a flap, that woman with the heavy hairs on her lip almost like a moustache. The Professor became conscious of how his own suit sleeve had to be tailored and lengthened because his right arm was longer than his left. And he had a mole on his leg, but, thank God, it only showed when he wore Bermuda shorts and he only wore those in his own backyard. The hoopla before the big match distracted the Professor from his morbid reflections. The fans in the far stands began scuttling over the fences and racing onto the pitch towards the ringside seats. The "outside" "insiders" and their *Cosmopolitan* companions found themselves being elbowed aside by Dublin's "travelling people" as the Professor was wont to refer, liberally-speaking, to tinkers.

The Professor was relieved. Here, now, at last, were Ali's people. The people with all their faults on display. They couldn't afford to hide their warts and scars and tailor away their humps and bumps. They wore their humanity proudly, if a bit thread-bare. Their faults were their pride. They were the only people in Croke Park who were openly human. And they wanted to be close to Muhammad Ali. Ali appealed to losers. He lost his title, but by doing so he beat the big shots. They couldn't make him knuckle under. And the tinkers refused to knuckle under. And the Professor had refused to knuckle under. The Professor didn't mind in the least that his fellow "outsiders" hadn't paid their fifteen quid. More power to them.

A painting of Arkle, the racehorse, was being auctioned off for charity in the ring. The Professor knew now how far he had infiltrated the Establishment when a gentleman in a silk red polka-dotted tie eight rows behind him bid £800 for the picture. Ireland's leading Supermarket Mogul, the entrepreneurial champion of the evening, had been topping each bid from £100 up and the auctioneer was nervous about accepting Polka-Dot's bid because he wouldn't give his name. Some aspiring big shots had bid early and had their names sung out to the crowd. They prayed to God they could depend on Supermarket Mogul to top them or else their wives would have their asses. Somebody in the £2 seats in the upper deck was screaming £1,000 !" but the auctioneer didn't seem to hear him. The crowd did. Polka-Dot's friends were becoming angry that their man was not being acknowledged but by that time Supermarket Mogul was in the ring and £1,000 was pledged for real and three big shots at ring side were able to go home with dry trousers.

The crowd roared. Ali was coming. The Professor was sorry his nine-year-old wasn't here. He had wanted the boy to see Ali at least. But at fifteen quid a peek he'd have to be satisfied with TV. Besides, on TV the kid would keep his illusions about boxing for a few more years. Why should anybody grow up too fast in today's world? So his boy would never be able to say to his grandchildren that his Daddy had taken him to see Muhammad Ali in person at Croke Park in "Dubbelin," Ireland, when he was a little boy. But the Professor had picked up a couple of autographed pictures of Muhammad Ali and Supermarket Mogul at Molloy's Delicatessen at the Stillorgan Shopping Center and their signatures were in red ink and Ali was shouting to the whole world while holding Supermarket Mogul's hand aloft, "We're the Greatest!" (Ali gave the £500 fee for posing to a boy's orphanage in Dublin. No tax deduction on that for Supermarket Mogul.)

And now the Professor could see "The Greatest" climbing into the ring, the most subdued man in Croke Park. One bad moment came in an early round. The crowd was quiet and some gobshite screamed, "Knock him back into the pen, Ali." It was the one low blow of the entire fight.

The brutality of the preliminaries faded from the Professor's mind. Those stumblebums had been farmers bludgeoning one another to death with fence posts, but here in living color was a surgeon at work. This wasn't Madison Square Garden, and the crowd wasn't big enough to make any money for charity, but "Blue" Lewis exuded integrity. He was an ex-con, but he wasn't lying down for any man, even the greatest heavyweight boxer of all time. That integrity of the patient saved the day for the Professor. It demanded an honest day's labor from Ali and the residue of memory from the Fight of the Century was enough to give the Professor an image, even though through a glass darkly, of what Muhammed Ali had been before being fouled up in the machinery of the Administration.

Ali won. But the important thing was not that he won, but that he enabled the Professor to think of boxing again in human terms. The preliminaries had reduced the Professor's estimation of himself as a fighter, a fighter against bureaucracy and an insensitive Administration. The Professor's image of himself as a fighter had been demythologized.

After the disastrous preliminaries, Ali had resurrected the image of the fighter as an honorable man. It was like any other profession–there were stumblebums and bum boys. And there are those who rise above it all. Ali rose above it all. And took the Professor with him, floating like a butterfly, stinging like a bee!

The Professor left Croke Park happy. He hadn't even minded that his American friend had rooted for Lewis shouting, "Blue, come on, Blue, you got 'em Blue, atta boy, Blue, baby, Blue, Blue, Blue, hit 'em Blue," in a high-pitched voice, irritating the people around them to whom it had become evident "Blue" was taking more punishment than was necessary to defend his integrity.

They went for a few jars. The Professor stood at the bar contented. He had only one regret: the full moon, which would shortly be going down on Galway Bay.

The Professor unlocked the front door, went up to the bathroom, and sat and thought of how he used to listen to the radio for Joe Louis's fights after World War II. He remembered with pain how he had cried the night Rocky Marciano had beaten Joe so badly. That would never happen to Ali. He was too smart. He wasn't the Administration's bum boy as Joe had been.

The Professor crawled into bed. His wife rolled over. The action was fast and furious. He punished his opponent and he loved it. He lay panting into her ear. She began to breathe slowly once more. The Professor spoke: "It was a tough fight, Ma, but I won."

Irish Letter 2: The PhD process in fantasy mode!

Caricature by Bruce MacKinnon, internationally acclaimed cartoonist of the Halifax Chronicle Herald

TOP SECRET

TOP SECRET . . . TOP SECRET . . . TOP SECRET

FOR YOUR EYES ONLY

SUBJECT: SURVIVAL OF X-AGENT IN DUBLIN: I.E., CUCHULAIN [HERO OF THE IRISH EPIC. *THE TAIN* [Pronounced "Toyn," i.e., turn into Brooklynese, as "bird" turns into "boyd"]]

DATE: 20-12-71

ORDER: X-AGENT IN DUBLIN ORDERED TO PROCURE HIS OWN LIVELIHOOD THRU GRANTS FROM OTHER GOVERNMENT AGENCIES (CANADA COUNCIL (CC), GOVERNMENT LOAN BUREAU (GLB)

RESULTS: X-AGENT (CODE NAME: CUCHULAIN) (pronounced: KOO-KÚL-IN) REPORTED 20-12-71 ON MEETING WITH UNIVERSITY COLLEGE DUBLIN PROFESSOR OF ANGLO-IRISH LITERATURE, ROGER McHUGH (DOUBLE AGENT?) ON 15-12-71.

FACTORS: X-AGENT CUCHULAIN HAS BEEN ASSIGNED TO DUBLIN FOR THREE YEARS. HE HAS HALF-SALARY FROM THE AGENCY FOR TWO YEARS. BECAUSE OF THE RECENT DEVALUATION OF THE DOLLAR AND SERIOUS CUTBACKS IN THE AGENCY'S BUDGET DUE TO POLITICAL FACTORS, i.e., LEFT-WING BACKLASH FROM THE IMPOSITION OF THE WAR MEASURES ACT AND THE SOON-TO-BE-ANNOUNCED CANADIAN GENERAL ELECTION, CUCHULAIN WAS INSTRUCTED TO RAISE FUNDS TO CONTINUE HIS COVER FOR THE YEAR 73-74.

REPORT: CODED REPORT FROM CUCHULAIN DUBLIN 851104 20-12-71.

CUCHULAIN: Believing that Canada Council Grants from overseas students were due in Ottawa by 15-1-72, Cuchulain–a.k.a., CUCH (pronounced "KOOK")–spent the first 3 ½ months here looking for a Canadian author with Irish connections because a request for aid from the CC would be more favorable towards a project involving a Canadian. CUCH read the Dictionary of Irish Writers (FICTION, Vol. I) and found the following:

LEVER, Charles James, b. Dublin 1806. Ed. TCD (Trinity College Dublin), Gottingen and Louvain, where he received his MD. In 1829 travelled in the backwoods of Canada and the US.

These journeys provided the basis for his novels *Confessions of Con Cregan* and *Arthur O'Leary*.

Unfortunately, further investigation showed that Lever's work was not first-rate and further was linked derogatively with the work of Samuel LOVER, b. Dublin, 1797, with the result that Lever is remembered today chiefly as one name in an atrocious Irish literary pun based upon the names LOVER and LEVER.

However, the undaunted CUCH continued to read the entire Dictionary and found the following entry:

MOORE, Brian, b. Belfast 1921, ed. Locally. Served with British Ministry of War Transport as civilian employee, 1943–6. Was in Warsaw with UNRRA mission, 1946–7. Freelance reporter in Western Europe, 1947–8. Emigrated to Canada and worked in a construction camp in northern Ontario before returning to journalism in Montreal. Wrote best seller *Judith Hearne*, widely praised, and has followed it with further successes, both critical and popular; *The Feast of Lupercal, The Luck of Ginger Coffey* (made into a film), and *An Answer from Limbo*. Won Guggenheim Fellowships in 1959 and 1961, and the Governor General of Canada's Literary Award for 1960. Lives in New York, where his *The Emperor of Ice Cream* was first published in 1965.

Since the Dictionary was printed Moore has published *I am Mary Dunne*, about a girl from Halifax living in NRC, and *Fergus*, about a novelist-script writer living in Hollywood who confronts the ghosts of his family and friends from Belfast. (Moore is presently living in Malibu, California, where he moved to do the script for the film *Torn Curtain* by Alfred Hitchcock).

CUCH seized an early opportunity in October to discuss probable dissertation topics with PROFESSOR McHUGH. Preliminary surveillance of Professor McHUGH by CUCH has revealed that although he is small, 5'4", and looks old (65?), he is considered by many to be dangerous. He is known to be moody—one day kindly and fatherly, the next cool and calculating—with the ability to dissect dissertations with the skill and detachment of a brain surgeon. He is reported to be an IRA gunman (retired) with 31 kills to his credit and a slight limp which lends credence to this report. (THE AGENCY confirms McHugh's IRA link, however, THE AGENCY is unable to verify the number of kills. He is currently on the Board of Directors of the Agency established to support the families of prisoners interned in Northern Ireland. His code name is FERDIA.) At the October meeting CUCH found him fatherly.

He is also the author of innumerable articles, books, and monographs on Anglo-Irish Literature over the past 35 years, and has maintained an excellent cover by becoming the founder of the Anglo-Irish degree in Literature and the world's leading authority in the field.

BEGINNING OF OCTOBER CONFERENCE

MCHUGH: Have you thought of a possible dissertation?

CUCH: (Cooly resisting the impulse to pounce.) Well, I have been thinking about someone like, say, Brian Moore.

MCHUGH: Oh, you're better off to think of something that involves more than a single writer. The dissertations on individual Irish writers are pretty well worked out. Overcrowded. Some of them would be good. A theme gives you the opportunity to say so much more than a treatment of a single writer.

CUCH: (Thinking: why was he so quick to put down the suggestion on Moore? Is he a double agent? Or is Moore too simple a subject? He has published 7 novels—they must be good. They won awards so they're above the ordinary—maybe I'd better read one of his books, come to think of it!) Uh. Yeah.

MCHUGH: What subjects do you teach at . . . at . . . ah . . .

CUCH: (Why doesn't he remember the name of my University? He has asked me every one of the three times we've met? Are the rumors of his bad memory true or is he cleverly putting people to the test like a good agent?) StFX. St. Francis Xavier University.

MCHUGH: Yes. That's right.

CUCH: (Of course it is.) Well, I teach the basic surveys in English Literature, the Romantics, Creative Writing, and ah, Modern Drama.

MCHUGH: Modern Drama?

CUCH: (Why did I say that. I only taught it this past summer, 22 plays in 6 weeks, 18 of which I had not read before. I always go one step too far.) Ah, yes. Modern Drama.

MCHUGH: There's a list of possible projects I keep for students searching for a dissertation. And there's one area in modern drama that needs some more work. The influence of Ibsen on Anglo-Irish dramatists. How does that sound to you?

CUCH: (Oh, God.) That's, ah, that's very interesting. Yes, that might be very interesting. (Oh, no. I wouldn't mind doing Ibsen–I really enjoyed the two plays I did this past summer, but that project means doing ALL 30 of Ibsen's plays, and ALL modern drama, and, then, disaster, reading every bloody Irish play ever written! This is only a three-year assignment. That will kill me – absolutely open-ended. I'll finish it in 1984. Sweet Jesus, save me.)

MCHUGH: Well, of course there's no need to decide now. Think it over.

CUCH: Yes, thank you. (I'd damn well better read the novels of Brian Moore, quick, before January 15th.)

End of October interview.

CUCH religiously read the novels of Moore–and because he had confronted MCHUGH with Moore in October only on the basis of seeing the movie, *The Luck of Ginger Coffey*, he now felt confident that he would come up with a suitable project on Moore. I, that is, CUCH, also consulted the three leading members of the Department: Augustine Martin, winner of the Irish Television award as the outstanding person in Educational TV; Tom Kilroy, winner of the Manchester Guardian Award and short-listed for the Booker Award for his first novel, *The Big Chapel*; and Seamus Deane, the Bogside Belfast-born resident genius and editor of the *Atlantis* magazine whose wife`s father was a classmate of Brian Moore, pronounced, so she informed CUCH at a cocktail party, Bree-an, NOT Breye-an.

CUCH, ever alert to the necessity of keeping up in literature, made certain to see on BBC Two an address by Mary McCarthy on "Writers in the World." Her topic was "Expatriates or Exiles?" One of those writers, Brian Moore. Ah-hah!

Then, the BOMB.

CUCH, having dutifully written to the CC for application forms for a Doctoral Fellowship for 1972–73, received them on December 15, 1971, along with the information that the deadline for applications was DECEMBER 15, 1971!

(Why can't THE AGENCY coordinate more efficiently than that–so that at least inter-departmentally, the Canadian Government doesn't screw itself?)

[Reader: Please note: THE AGENCY operates independently and unknown to the CC and Post Office Departments. X-agent CUCHULAIN should have known that fact. Further, his petulant complaints implying incestuous departmental relations in the Government Administration are to be understood as "purple prose" as a result of over-identification with X-agent's cover as a "writer," and the intense pressure he was facing because of his own negligence. And what was he doing at that cocktail party?]

[NOTE: These minor flaws should not prejudice the early evaluation of this usually keen, often brilliant agent.]

2:30 P.M. December 15, 1971

CUCH finds out that MCHUGH is at lunch and will return to his office. He quickly enlists the aid of Ed Daly (Harvard-Agent Code Name: BLUE BLOOD), to cover for his tutorials at 2:30 and 3:30. BLUE BLOOD agrees. Between 2:20 and 2:30.

CUCH outlines two manuscript pages of a project on Brian Moore.

MCHUGH returns.

THE CONFERENCE:

After preliminary greetings and an explanation of the emergency circumstances of the CC deadline, MCHUGH turns side saddle in his chair and says:

MCHUGH: Did we decide on a dissertation at our last talk?

CUCH: (That faulty memory again? Or is he setting me up for a kill?) No. We left it open.

MCHUGH: Okay. Give me what you've got.

CUCH: (Why is this chair so short? His chair is so high compared to mine. I have to look up at him as he gazes out the window.) Well. (CUCH carefully pronouncing Brian and Breean.)

BRIAN MOORE

Expatriate or Exile?

The corpus of Belfast-born Canadian writer Brian Moore offers a unique opportunity for a Canadian student of Anglo-Irish Literature to examine a 20th-Century writer's search for identity.

MUHUGH: What the hell do you mean by that?

CUCH: (Globs of gunk gathering in his throat.) Well, ah, what?

MCHUGH: Identity! What do you mean by identity?

CUCH: Well, yes. I mean, it *is* a word that demands single quotes.

MCHUGH: What does it mean?

CUCH: Well, to be specific, to refer to Breean Moore, he is searching for a frame of reference for his life, I mean he writes all his novels, whether set in Montreal, New York, or Hollywood, with flashbacks to his childhood in Belfast. And he has rejected his past, denied his family and church and Irish heritage but he can't escape them. He's trying to find a structure for his own beliefs, and I think in *Fergus*, with the ending, the final scene on the beach, Fergus waves in a friendly way to his father, and I think Moore is saying, "I have rejected my father's world, my heritage, but I accept the fact that each person has to build his own framework, his own frame of reference, and then live and operate within it. I now accept my father's right to his own frame of reference, and at the same time this gives validity to my own—my own identity." (How the hell about that?)

MCHUGH: Ha, ha, ha! (Chuckle) That's worse than "identity." Oh, so many of these essays are filled with "the search for identity." It's so woolly and vague. And coming at the beginning—it will kill the project with the Canada Council.

(CUCH remembers his application for a Fellowship was turned down last year.)

[Last year's application for Fellowship, AGENCY FILE W142, Project Title: "Shelley in Ireland: An Investigation of Shelley's visit to Ireland and his consequent influence on Irish writing and politics," was rejected, according to

[*The rest of this type-script is missing, obviously due to fire, as the bottom of the page is raggedly singed.*]

The note above is a LIE. It is a FICTION. The TRUTH is that the original script written in Ireland is missing in action. Somewhere in moving back to Canada, and then moving in a new house at 1 Sunset Terrace, then subdividing the plot, and building a palace (according to Mayor Chisholm) at 45 Maple Drive, not realizing that in five years we would move to Calgary and live at 1167 Sunlake Link, then move to the Bentley Condo (better known to Calgary commuters as "The Pink Palace") for five years, and finally as "care" became a factor moving in with daughter Mary and son-in-law Neil in Elboya SW—the vital document was lost . . . or maybe stolen? We'll never know.

I believe I wrote about the negotiations on my dissertation in fanciful form to balance the severe pressure I was under to complete my PhD in two years instead of three. The university was giving me half salary ($14,000 CDN for two years, and the third year we would be on our own.) It may sound tough, but the secret was that compared to about a cost of $40,000 per year in the US or Canada at that time, it cost me 98 Irish Pounds per year for my degree—that was about $200 dollars a year Canadian. We survived, wife and five children, and lived to tell the tale. But I digress.

Roger McHugh had finally agreed to let me write a dissertation on Brian Moore, who had seven major novels at that time, not counting about 5 others written under pseudonyms just to raise money to supplement his journalism income. In the year we arrived in Dublin, 1971, Moore had just published *The Revolution Script* about the terrorist activities in Quebec shortly before. Being a journalist and having some sensitivity for his craft, Moore sensed the spirit of The New Journalism which was in the air, in the writing of some famous novelists, such as Truman Capote, Norman Mailer, Gay Talese, and Tom Wolfe. So Moore wrote a factual account of a true historical event in current history, using novelistic techniques, which at that time had not been fully articulated and published.

In *The October Revolution*, Moore constructed the text scene by scene as if he were observing it directly. He quoted dialogue as directly as possible, or imagined it as thoughtfully as seemed true to him. He referred to the participants in the third person, as characters in a novel. And finally, he described the background and surrounding setting for the actions. These techniques were not the same as in Moore's first seven novels because they were employed to convey true historical events, not imaginatively conceived fictional events.

My examination approached the seven fictional novels examining how Moore used technique as discovery, that is, that the choices of how he used point of view in the books would reveal the essential meaning of his stories. My interim guide through this academic exercise was Professor Augustine Martin. I was his first PhD student, and Roger McHugh would make the official decision on my work, not Gus. Well, Gus and his family–his wife, Clare, and his children–practically adopted me. Gus and I became blood brothers. Our views were similar and compatible. We were the same age, and the fact that I had been teaching for 15 years and had a big family added to our closeness. I would write a draft on each novel, and Gus would put me through the ringer. This was not really as difficult as the metaphor implies. Both of us being busy we found that the best time for us to meet and work was in the evenings. So whenever we could we met at The Leopardstown Pub a hop and a skip from Gus's house. There we would collaborate well past Bartender Barry's final call, "It's time, gentlemen, time please, ladies and gentlemen." That was at 11 p.m. Around midnight, as Barry closed up, he would toss Gus the keys, and say, "Just make sure you lock the door when you leave." This had to be the most pleasurable PhD process in history. More than once after saying good night to Gus, I would drive home over

Killiney Hill and watch the sun rise on the Irish Sea, and go home to bed as a very happy "scholar."

As the funnel narrowed on my two-year self-imposed limit, I was making progress. I read the Anglo-Irish Masters program, taking every class and activity, without having to write exams–surely the most enjoyable way to study. On the side I wrote an Irish novel, *The Cave: A Story of Ireland*, about the burial tomb of the High Kings of Ireland at Newgrange in the Boyne River valley. I had begun to teach my son Francis how to play chess because the Fisher/Spasky Icelandic confrontation was looming. Caught up in chess, on a visit to a Marble Factory in the west of Ireland, I was inspired to design and create marble chess set with gold and silver tops. With two Irishmen, Renton White and Tom Ford, business partners, we formed Irish Marble Crafts to market the chess sets. But now the crunch was on to present my final draft to Roger McHugh.

A further complication arose: I had applied to attend a conference on Modern Experimental Writing at the Salzburg Conference, sponsored after World War II to bring the nations of Europe together. Two representatives from Ireland would receive scholarships; the draft of my novel got me one scholarship, and I mentioned the competition to Gus and urged him to apply. He did, and the two blood brothers would go off to Austria for the Conference–BUT only if I had final approval for my dissertation from Roger McHugh.

I had started well. The first draft of the first novel, *The Lonely Passion of Judith Hearne*, was submitted. I was warned by my fellow students to be prepared for a blood bath: Roger was a ruthless marker. Forewarned, I had taken great care with my draft. I got it typed by a secretary so it appeared very clean. When I got the paper back there was not a mark on it. This caused much conjecture for no one had ever heard of such an achievement before. Exhilarated, I went on to the second novel, *The Feast of Lupercal*. I submitted the draft and slept the sleep of the just–until rudely aroused by the telephone a 6:30 a.m. "This is Roger McHugh." I tried to snap out my drowsy fog. "Be in my office at 9 a.m. I have never seen such a piece of garbage in all my years of teaching." I was instantly as awake as I would have been if thrown into the River Liffey.

For a big guy who had towered over Roger McHugh, I felt pretty small. Roger handed me the envelope with my draft and said, "Explain how you could produce something this crude." I opened the envelope, and out fell the explanation: instead of the neatly typed and impressive draft from the typist, I had given Roger the envelope with my original notes to the typist–a jumble of bits and pieces taped and stapled, with arrows showing where sections should be inserted, penciled instructions–a total disaster of a mess worthy of a first-grader. Adequately chastened, I had to go home and bring back the correct draft. The corrected draft saved me; but the gaffe was a warning to take nothing for granted. The correct draft was accepted and approved, with one sentence in red: when the paper mentioned for the third time that Moore had "ploughed the field of classical allusion," Roger had written in his very tiny concentrated penmanship: "I think that field has been adequately ploughed." The duel was on, and I would have to be *en garde*.

So in July, I met with Professor McHugh and explained that I had the scholarship to the Salzburg Seminar, but if my dissertation did not have his approval I would have to forego the Seminar to make certain I could return to Antigonish by September. Now the fantasy TOP SECRET document met the reality of ROGER MCHUGH: "Well, Mr. Walsh, you have successfully treated the first seven novels, but you have relegated *The October Revolution* to an appendix. You will have to revise that appendix and incorporate it into the main text."

"But, respectfully, sir, *The October Revolution* is more journalism than novel, it is reality, not imagination."

"Integrate it."

The moment of TRUTH had arrived when and where I least expected it. But I had recognized it. With everything in the balance: The Salzburg Seminar, the PhD, the return home in two years instead of three, no funding for a third year. I decided to go for the gold ring.

"Professor McHugh, The October Revolution is not a fictional novel, it is a piece of New Journalism. It is properly placed in an appendix."

"I *say* it goes into the text."

I decided to go for resistance that Professor McHugh, I was certain, had never faced before.

"No." And I began to chuckle. I was in purely instinctual survival mode.

"What?"

"No." (*Bartleby, the Scrivener* lives!) And I began to laugh. A real ha-ha laugh.

"Text!"

Shaking my head "no" now and laughing at the same time, ha, ha, ha, ha.

"Did you say 'no'?"

"No." Laughing now, somewhat maniacally, which could have rattled someone not as seasoned as Roger McHugh.

"Are you saying, 'no'?"

He began to play the game.

"Yes," I managed to say between laughs.

"There you go, you said, 'Yes.'" And Roger McHugh BEGAN TO LAUGH.

"But you 'know' I meant 'no'? Yes?"

"Yes."

"Then we agree?" I was still laughing. And so was he.

With everything on the line, I made my last thrust: "WHAT do we agree?"

"That *The October Revolution* is an appendix, and you should go to Salzburg."

I wanted to kiss Roger McHugh, which I'm sure was a natural instinct in my Italian genes, but that would really cross a line somewhere in the annals of his manly reputation.

We shook hands, still happily laughing gently, and I went to Salzburg, to another traumatic adventure, and then home to my adopted Canada.

Chapter 7
Salzburg Seminar
Summer 1973

This chapter covers only one-month of my life, apparently too short for a full chapter of a biography. But in terms of impact on my life, this story is epic. The major piece below tells a life-transforming story. And in terms of people and true friends, it is a personal treasure.

The Twitch of an Eye - A Memoir

Mihai Nadin

"Memory, in short, is engraved not merely from the life we have led but by the life of the mind, by all the lives we so nearly led but missed by an inch, and–if we grant enough leeway to the imagination–by the lives of others, which can cut into ours every bit as sharply as our own experience."

–*A Guide for Writing a Memoir* by W. G. Sebald

"The world I live in, the objects I manipulate, are in a great part my constructions . . . The worlds the writer creates are only imaginatively possible ones; they need not be at all like any real one."

–*Philosophy and the Form of Fiction* by William Gass

Looking up at the climax of my clever presentation on Robert Coover's short story, "Once upon a time there was a story that began once upon a time there was," etc., etc., *ad infinitum*, I spied a large young man leaning against a tree with his nose hanging over a dour puss of a down-turned mouth. Our seminar was being held outside its normal classroom in the garden by the lake that nestled at the foot of an Austrian Alp. Miffed by the sour reaction–or the lack of a suitably appreciative reaction–I carried on. I had written Coover's story on a Mobius strip, cut the strip in half and, voila, produced not two strips, but one large strip with the story still one and united [ta da!]: sometimes things are not what they appear to be.

The fifty or so participants in the 1973 Salzburg Seminar 148 on Modern Experimental Fiction at the Schloss Leopoldskron–the house of the von Trapp family in the movie of "The Sound of Music"–were suitably impressed and the seminar continued with another speaker.

The young scholars represented nearly all the countries of Europe, including those countries still behind the Iron Curtain. The seminar was established after World War II by Harvard University to bring together potential leaders of post-war Europe and to heal the cultural and political wounds of the battered body politic of Europe.

Distinguished American scholars were the resource people for our seminar: Jarvis Thurston, editor of *Perspective,* a literary quarterly with his wife, Mona van Duyn, National Book Award poet and future Pulitzer Prize winner; Charles Davis, founder of the Black Studies program at Yale; Sergio Perosa of the University of Venice; and finally, William Gass, author with a philosopher's training, professor of philosophy at Washington University, novelist, winner of a National Book Critics' Circle award, and in our eyes, "Father of Meta-Fiction."

The Seminar with Gass was held, perversely appropriately, in the Schloss's Venetian room, which was mirrored on every surface–walls, doors, ceilings, mercifully excepting floors. Gass, a slight man with thick and heavy eyes and thick and heavy hair to his shoulders, was the professor we loved to hate. In those gestation days of deconstruction, it seemed he challenged our beliefs as teachers: that literature had important values to convey to our students; that we were torchbearers of civilization in an encroaching age of barbarism; that literature spoke some kind of "truth."

When Gass shambled into the Venetian room, the electricity in the air was palpable. Whatever alpha waves we could exude from our cauliflower brains imprisoned in our skulls began bouncing off the mirrors. The seminar, truly exciting and obviously a rare experience for all of us, forced us to reexamine our inherited preconceptions about literature. What did we really know about what we read?

There was "fiction," and then the "meta-fiction" of Gass: "The novelist will keep us kindly imprisoned in his language–there is nothing beyond," and "The so-called life in novels is nothing like actual life at all," and "The event [in the world of the novel] may be anything: a twitch of the eye or adultery." We would retreat from the seminar to the *bierstube* and rant about the missing "soul" of "meta-fiction."

How did a 35-year-old lecturer, born in the USA and teaching in Canada, get invited to a seminar for Europeans? I was on leave from St. Francis Xavier University in Antigonish, Nova Scotia, to acquire a doctoral degree from University College Dublin of the National University of Ireland, or else I would never get promoted to full professor. No doctorate, no promotion, no salary increases. The prospect of five children–ages twelve to less than one–clamoring for meals, inspired me to pack the whole family off to Ireland to study Anglo-Irish literature–the seven of us became Walsh's Flying Irish Circus.

The pressure was on: two years of assistance at half-salary, the third year no help. Facing a penniless third year, I had finished the PhD requirements in two years, in my spare time writing a novel "The Cave" about the burial tombs of the High Kings of Ireland [2,500 BCE] in New Grange on the River Boyne. Encouraged by a professor at UCD, an alumnus of the Salzburg Seminar, I applied for one of the two fellowships allocated for Ireland, offering the manuscript of my novel as evidence of my writing skills.

Following the interview, I was awarded one of the Fellowships, and the committee asked me if I knew anyone else who might be interested in the other fellowship. [I feel obligated to mention the paucity of applications, despite the shine it rubs off my award.] Without hesitating I nominated the professor who had guided my dissertation, Gus Martin, lecturer in Anglo-Irish literature at University College Dublin of the National University of Ireland. Gus, who was my age, had become a dear friend, treating me more as a colleague than a student. I had been teaching for some fifteen years and he had me giving public lectures at UCD. Gus had played a major role in introducing Irish writers into the high school curriculum, through seminars at UCD for high school students and teachers from all over the country. He had recently won the award as the outstanding personality in Irish television for his literary presentations employing Abbey Theatre players. He would soon become *the* Professor of Anglo-Irish Literature and Drama at UCD [the Irish have only one Professor per department, all others are of lesser rank], a Director of the Abbey Theatre and an Irish Senator, following in footsteps of his beloved W. B. Yeats.

Gus was a shoo-in and we made plans to jet off to Salzburg, to be followed by a degree-culminating trip to Italy, to be joined by my wife in Milan. After all, having paid respects to my father's Irish forbears, I owed homage to my mother's Italian heritage.

On the plane to Salzburg, I noticed a fellow in the seat across the way, and turning to Gus, said, "That fellow's going to the seminar, too." Gus scoffed, but an offer of a stick of gum led to our becoming acquainted with Gordon Bennett, the American President of New England College. Gordon, an English professor, was in charge of students from the United States following studies in England through the University of New Hampshire. By the time we landed in Austria, we thought of ourselves as three musketeers–instantly simpatico–off on an intellectual holiday adventure.

The three of us moved among the participants like "bull-goose loonies," laughing and joking. The Europeans looked upon us as a three-headed English-speaking dancing dog. They laughed at everything we said, but laughed nervously and with a sideway tilt of the head. We were having a great time–first time in Austria for the three of us–and that the Europeans seemed so relatively reserved and dignified, mystified us.

As we mingled we began to get stories from the Europeans, especially those from behind the Iron Curtain. I got a story from Ioanna from Czechoslovakia: she and her husband had been active in the student uprisings in Prague, and eventually they made a run for the West, and she escaped, but her husband was shot. She and a daughter were living in England where she worked as a translator for the BBC.

Gus was disturbed by a tale he got from Antoinette from Romania. She was a translator and her husband was a member of the Communist Party. He and the government were trying to force her to become a member of the Party, but she resisted and one night her husband tried to kill her with a pitchfork.

Gordon was getting similar stories, and the three of us began to suspect that there were dark shadows in the hallways of the Schloss. The surface air of holiday and bonhomie hid an underlying base of pain and suffering in our new Iron Curtain comrades. We came to realize that these people did not get our jokes, our badinage. Our irony and good-natured banter and attacks on one another–all three of us experienced athletic-trash-talking pseudo-jocks–were inaccessible to our new friends. Our freedom to attack others' personalities and faults was puzzling to them. Weaknesses and personal matters were not to be bandied about in public. We agreed to be more careful and to confer frequently so we could help one another to get a handle on what was really going on with these people.

On the first weekend we had a dance in the main hall of the Schloss. We were giddy with the knowledge that in this very room Mozart had played for the Archbishop; that Max Reinhardt, Europe's foremost theatrical producer, had entertained legendary guests; that Christopher Plummer and Julie Andrews had acted *The Sound of Music* in this palace.

Gus prevailed upon me to dance with Antoinette, the poor woman, to make sure she had a good time. Gordon did his bit, and I did mine, complimenting Antoinette on her sparkling diamond pendant earrings. A long table with nibblies and a dispensing carafe of red wine at one end and white wine at the other was keeping the party loose. After our dance, I asked Antoinette if she wanted a glass of wine, "White or red?"

"White," she replied, and with a classic draw of a finger across her throat, she snarled, "I've had 'red' up to here." I felt uncomfortable and turned Antoinette back to Gus.

Looking around, I spied the big guy with the long, sad face sitting off to one side along the wall. Why wasn't he dancing? Still sad, still dour, still a killjoy at a time of camaraderie. I took a long look at him and decided that a month of having him haunt the seminar would be a month too long.

Sitting down next to him, I shook hands and introduced myself to the young man who said he was Mihai Nadin of Rumania. Possessed of some hitherto unrealized instinct, I said, "I hope you are not offended by what I'm going to say, but you look terribly sad. Is there anything wrong? Is there anything I could do to help you?"

Mihai's eyes immediately teared up. I was almost frightened. This man was going to cry. He told me his story: he was born and schooled in Brasov, Rumania, where he is Associate Professor of Mathematics. He has a master's degree in electrical engineering and a PhD [with honors, I found out later] in Esthetics. This unusual combination got him the job as Assistant Editor of the review *ASTRA*, in charge of the section for arts and philosophy. He was also involved as a dramaturge with several theaters.

Several years ago he had met an American woman visiting Rumania, a translator, and they had fallen in love. Unable to stay in Rumania, she had found work in Switzerland to be nearer to Rumania. The government would not let her into Rumania except on a tourist visa, and would not let Mihai out of Rumania unless on official activity–whatever that meant. They wanted to get married, but for this Mihai had to apply and go through a difficult bureaucratic procedure. Actually the communist government did not want their citizens to marry foreigners because the Rumanian eventually left the country.

So when Mihai won a fellowship to attend the Salzburg Seminar in the summer of 1973, he and his true love arranged to meet in Salzburg. She would be able to come from Switzerland to Salzburg and they would be together even if only for about a month. But, en route, Mihai's true love had an accident and was now in a hospital in St. Gallen and unable to join him. No wonder the poor guy was blue. Mihai's consoling companionship was Andrei, a fellow Rumanian and editor of *ELECTROS* literary magazine. If I felt powerless to help his situation, I could only imagine how miserable he must feel.

As Gus and Gordon and I conferred over the next few days, we began to realize the difficulties of life behind the Iron Curtain. Free travel was extremely restricted, and papers and visas and permissions were necessary between neighboring *towns*. The government could deny people university degrees if they were thought to be homosexual. The government would declare ownership of all homes, allow people to make payments to buy them back, and then repeat the exercise.

The stories of the hard life behind the Curtain began to multiply. I met Dascha and Sonia and Ileana from Yugoslavia, Wanda from Czechoslovakia, Agnieska from Poland. I sought balancing information from Belma from Turkey, Inger from Norway, and Jessie from Scotland. My confusion grew. I began to feel quite intellectually inferior to the Eastern Europeans; they all spoke six or seven languages and had multiple degrees. I had earned my three basic degrees, BA, MA, and now PhD, and could speak English, read and understand enough French to order a meal. Comparing myself to the Europeans, I felt like a fish coming out of water to live on the land.

When I expressed my growing consternation to Mihai who was so knowledgeable in both electronic engineering and philosophy and drama and art, he laughed at me. "Oh, Patrick, if you only knew how much we envy *you*! You can worship as you like; you are on your town council, you can travel freely, you are working in a field you love, you can say and do anything you want, and you were free to marry Jacqueline! You are the one *we envy*! We are huddling so close together in Europe, border to border, we pick up languages like loaves of bread. We leave our chosen professions and go into esoteric studies because the government can't follow us there; they don't understand art and literature. Only in the realm of what they consider impractical ideas are we free." Later, I found out from Andrei that all of Mihai's books had been removed from circulation–only because he wanted to marry a foreigner. One exception was his first novel, which became a runaway success until the government was informed by the Soviet Union that it was an indirect attack on communist Rumania!

This glimpse into the nature of life behind the Curtain came as a shock to me. I thought I had been raised as a middle-class white New England American, with Roman Catholic parents: a father of Irish descent and a mother of Italian descent. During my years in St. Joseph's High School, in North Adams, Massachusetts, I was a fervent supporter of Senator Joseph R. McCarthy against the Red Peril threatening the United States of America: "Better dead than red." "Get the Commies out of the State Department." "Exterminate the atheistic Pinkos!"

I accumulated enough of the US Senate minutes of the McCarthy Hearings to build my own wall to keep out "un-American undesirables."

Our Pastor at St. Francis Church, Monsignor John P. Donahue, also in charge of St. Joseph's school, fulminated regularly in his sermons attacking the Communists and the "garbage pails" known as Ivy League Colleges. I was a gung-ho red-white-and-blue full-blooded American ready to be dead, not red. Then I graduated and went to university in Canada where my views were considerably modified by being in a foreign country.

My conversion to "liberalization" on the road to Antigonish was as instantaneous as Paul's on the road to Damascus. I came under the influence of Fr. Rod MacSween, English professor and autodidact, who converted me from chemistry to English literature. Every Wednesday evening a group of his disciples met for discussion in his digs, a room lined with books and magazines on every wall, desk, table, chair, and radiator. We would begin by reading a page or so from *The Introduction to the Devout Life* of St. Francis de Sales. Then we would read from *The Commonwe*al, a periodical published by lay Catholics, and of a decidedly anti-McCarthy bent. Then we devoured the entrée of the evening's intellectual buffet: a free-for-all discussion of any item brought to the table.

I can never remember any subject raised upon which Fr. MacSween was not more knowledgeable than anyone I had ever met. On those rare occasions if his sources were challenged, he would reach over to a pile of papers or across to a stack of books and pull out the pertinent argument. He could also direct us to any bookcase or table to pull out, "that book with the blue dust-jacket–down there about three from the bottom of the stack" and then he would flip to a page and give us a salient quotation.

On the night in question, a *Commonweal* editorial had attacked Fr. Halton, the Catholic chaplain at Princeton University, who had publicly and somewhat viciously criticized a visiting distinguished professor Jacques Maritain, a Catholic, for being "soft on communism." The discussion group condemned Fr. Halton, and like a trout to a well-tied fly, I rose to the absent chaplain's defense.

"But, Fr. Halton is right," I cried. "The communists are atheists, anti-American, they are out to exterminate us," or passionate words to that effect. After a small scuffle in which I became even more impassioned and adamant, I stated emphatically, "Fr. Halton is speaking the TRUTH. That makes him right. It's his duty to make the TRUTH known and to defend it."

Fr. MacSween, who always spoke quietly, said, "Okay, Pat, let us assume that Fr. Halton IS right–isn't it his duty to make the truth known in a way to make it loved, not hated?" Whatever Rubicon exists between conservatism and liberalism, that was the moment I crossed it.

In the years following, I grew much more tolerant of the right of peoples under communist governments to do as they saw fit. I certainly didn't agree with the communist system. The freedom of America–and Canada–was a superior, a much superior, political system, but foreign governments had to be free to pursue their destiny to the best of their ability. So by 1973, I didn't worry too much about the "Communists" and the way they ran their internal affairs.

But since 1971, I had experienced Irish and English culture, thereby gaining two insights into my heritage. First, I had not received a middle-class white American upbringing; I had received an Irish Catholic upbringing. Second, the social class system based on blood lines was still alive and well and living in England and Ireland, and had influenced my childhood inherited values. My inherited views were being re-evaluated.

Now, here I was in Salzburg, living and breathing and eating and studying with live people from behind the Iron Curtain. Some must have been Communists, but how was I to know? Gus and Gordon and I were caught in a Grade B spy thriller comparing notes on the horror stories of our colleagues. Could life be as miserable as they were telling us? What was the truth of their situation? Of our situation? We were now encountering our life in the Schloss as confusing, evanescent and frustrating as William Gass's world of "meta-fiction." What was "real" and what was "fiction?"

One evening, many us from the Seminar walked into Salzburg to the convent where Sister Maria had lived. The attraction was a concert featuring Vivaldi's *Stabat Mater*. I took a seat near the rear of the chapel, where I usually sat at home. Surveying the congregation, I spotted Aage from Norway and Bob and Tony from England–there was Antoinette standing in the side aisle–and in the front pew, Mihai and Andrei. I watched as Mihai bent over to talk to a little girl sitting next to him. Suddenly he turned away from her and in doing so turned towards me–was he going to cry again? *What now*, I thought.

After the glorious concert, some people headed down into town. We had grown less than enthusiastic about the primary diet of *Wiener schnitzel* at the Schloss. Some pub grub would be a relief. Gordon was organizing a group off to one side. Gus and I went after Mihai and Andrei and invited them to go into town with us for a jar and a bite. They both protested, trying to sidle away from us. We suddenly realized that they had no money. I explained that I was a rich Yank from Canada, and they would please be my guests for the evening. Gus insisted. Still they resisted, looking over their shoulders as the crowd was dispersing. More complications–someone was watching them!

Gordon was headed down the stairs towards town, and motioning for us to follow. I gave Gordon a high sign–a finger across the throat and then to the lips. Gordon caught on, began singing–he was our finest singer–and led his troop off to town like Maria leading her charges to the park. We hustled Mihai and Andrei back into the chapel and then out another door, and being careful not to be seen, headed into town for some good cheer.

We had lost any contact with Gordon, which was probably wise. We ended up in a pub with windows opening right on to the River Salz. Beer and cold cuts and bread and singing along with the locals. We were all in a happy mood. Then the leader of the band, with his accordion hanging on his belly, started going around the room asking visitors to sing their national anthems. Gus bellowed out the Irish national anthem "The Soldier's Song," and I followed with both "The Star-Spangled Banner" and "O Canada." Then we headed home.

As we chugged our way up and down the hills back to the Schloss in the warm summer evening, we kept on singing. The hills *were* alive with the sound of music. Mihai and Andrei were not singing. I called a halt to our march and confronted them. "Why didn't you guys sing the Rumanian national anthem back there at the pub?" They both started to cry–or at least teared up. The explanation: the Rumanian national anthem had been commandeered by their Russian masters and Rumanians were now required to sing the new lyrics "in praise of Mother Russia," which of course these two men could not do. I could just imagine Francis Scott Key's anthem lauding the sickle and hammer. Unthinkable for an American–and I realized I would be an American to the grave. We were now so down we shuffled to a little dive around the corner from the Schloss and closed the evening with some local schnapps of kerosene grade.

That weekend, the seminar scheduled a slight break from Friday noon to Monday morning. Most of the people made plans to go to Vienna, but I wanted to go to Venice, which was not on my Italian itinerary after the seminar. Gus and Gordon were game once I demonstrated the feasibility of splitting three ways the rental of a Mercedes to drive to Venice: the price was steep but bearable–and we would have some small relief from the tales of woe of our study mates.

When I told my Schloss roommate, Harald from Munich, about our plan, he became wistful. He would very much like to go to Venice, having already been several times to Vienna. I suggested he might join us, but he demurred, finally admitting that he did not have enough money to make the trip. He was originally from East Germany but was now living in Munich, and he had driven to Salzburg in his vintage Mercedes that was parked behind the outbuilding.

Being an experienced planner–schemer, some would say–I immediately thought of and proposed that Harald should drive the three musketeers to Venice and we would pay for all the gas and his room and board–why rent a Mercedes if he already had one, albeit an older one? Harald was reticent at first, wanting me to vet the idea with my compatriots.

When I proposed the deal to Gus, he exploded. Gordon was hesitant. Gus had noticed Harald: a handsome young curly-haired Teuton prince, lacking only a dueling scar on his cheek to make maidens swoon, but too quiet and reserved and morose, in Gus's opinion. "He'll put a damper on our party," Gus claimed. "He's a sad sack."

I didn't know why Harald appeared so sad, but I had my suspicions and did not want to pursue the reasons. In our chats before going off to sleep, Harald was personable and thoughtful. I assured my mates that he would be fine and probably easier to live with than someone as pushy and obstreperous as we three. They agreed, harboring slight reservations.

I got a map of Austria, Germany, and Italy and began to go over the route with Harald. The shortest route via autobahn went from Salzburg, briefly through Germany, back into Austria to Innsbruck, where we would hang a left south to Italy. Innsbruck. Innsbruck!

Within minutes, I was huddling with Mihai in private and proposed dropping him off in Innsbruck en route and picking him up on our return Sunday evening. What could be simpler? Quite a bit, as it turned out. Because the highway passed into an arm of German territory dangling to the south, Mihai had to decline. He could not enter Germany on his visa. And, of course, it would not be wise to be seen leaving the Schloss . . . Damn. My scheme was blocked–temporarily.

Friday noon, after picking at our *Wiener schnitzel*, the three musketeers and their driver, Harald d'Artagnan, departed from the front door of the Schloss, with fond farewells from Ioanna, Ileana, and Wanda and Dascha, and Sonia and Inger, and Belma and Jessie. After this elaborate exit from the first stage of our little drama, Harald drove us out the front gate of the Schloss, around the corner and in the back gate to the servants' entrance of the Schloss. A furtive figure as big as a bear came sweeping out the door and down the stairs and folded himself into the trunk of our car. [He may have squeezed into the back seat, but my mind's movie script of this escapade has him completely out of sight in the trunk!]

Safely on the outskirts of Salzburg, our prisoner was allowed into the car with us. We were on our way to Innsbruck. I had found an acceptable route through the mountains, which would keep us in Austria and would skirt the dangling portion of Germany unacceptable to a Rumanian passport–through the Tirol mountains, Saalfelden and Zell am See–and avoid entering Germany. This road, however, was to the autobahn as a footpath to the Trans-Canada Highway. We would deliver Mihai to his Elvira, and he would be able to return to Salzburg on the train Sunday night, in bond, as long as he didn't set foot in Germany on the way through.

I paid a price for my subterfuge: Harald drove the Mercedes like a kamikaze pilot. In the front-passenger suicide seat, my cheeks clenched in terror, as I peered over the unguarded brink of the road at tiny monopoly houses in the valley below, for in true Formula I racing style, Harald *accelerated* into the curves. I murmured an uninterrupted "act of contrition" and resolved to take the train back to Salzburg no matter what the cost–if I lived that long.

In a slight drizzle [that's what the script says] [bit of a cliché] in a square in Innsbruck, we released our passenger. Gus hugged Mihai and slipped a little something into his jacket pocket, Gordon hugged Mihai and slipped a little something into his pocket, and I did likewise. He melted away down a side street and we all headed for our Venetian holiday.

When we hit the Italian border at the Brenner pass, Gus was chortling at me; "Look at Pat: he's darker now, his face is getting oily, and his hands, look at his hands, whirling and flapping like Toscanini–my God, he's becoming Italian before our very eyes." I was. I felt different. I was Italian, although the only words I knew from my grandmother Cicchetti were *spin-otch-a, cambell-a-beans, eye-se-boxa!*

We passed through places that had existed only in my mind: the Dolomites; Trentino, of the Council of 1545; Verona, in a blinding rainstorm that would have put the dampers on Romeo and Juliet and probably saved their lives; Padua, of the St. Anthony of the church where I was baptized. We ended up in a dive of a hotel in the industrial grime of Mestre at one in the morning. Nonetheless, we rose at 6 a.m. to take the train to the Grand Canal and begin our assault on "the drawing room of Europe," as Napoleon had christened St. Mark's Square.

As we glided up the Grand Canal, the morning and everything we looked at was gray. Garbage floated in the gray water and the paint was peeling off the gray buildings. We were down emotionally. Then the first rays of the sun cut through our gloom and barges of multicolored fruits and flowers sidled up to accompany our passage. The red and orange and blue and green houses, lighted by the sun, began to veritably glow. People were smiling, activity blossomed all around us, and the infinite deep blue of the Adriatic sky welcomed us into the tent of glory that is Venice, alive and well and still afloat. We sauntered about the Square, paid our respects to the Doge's Palace, lingered on the Bridge of Dreams, found hidden art treasures in byway chapels, boldly strode into first-class hotel lobbies to avail ourselves of the gentlemen's facilities. We sat on benches to watch the craftsmen of Murano spin webs of glass dreams. Exhausted, we adjourned to stuff ourselves with pasta and wine as the evening turned to night.

When the bill arrived, Gus discovered that his wallet–and the passport it contained–were missing. His first instinct was to blame a light-fingered Italian, but when we mentally retraced our day, I thought he must have dropped it in the little store where he had tried on a pair of pants. The shop was closed of course, but a note was taped to the door advising Signor Martin to telephone the number. We got Harald to place the call, and the owner of the store told us to wait right there, he would come from home and return the wallet which he had found.

Gus had to wait. Gordon and I were absolutely peloothered, but loath to leave Gus in the lurch. Forward steps childe Harald, volunteering to wait with Gus while we abandoned ship. Chilling stare from Gus, obviously loathe to sit in the starlight of Venice with sad sack Harald. But Gordon and I, justifying our action for the good of our families, we convinced ourselves, abandoned the two of them and went home to Mestre to crash in the dive.

To my surprise the next morning, Harald and Gus were fast friends. The transformation was so astonishing that I did not take the train back to Salzburg, chancing the return trip by auto to find out what had created this new friendship between the ebullient Irishman and the morose German.

Harald drove furiously to get back to Salzburg, and on this leg of the journey we took the autobahn. Late into suppertime we pulled off into Bad (pronounced *Bod*, as in 'body') Reichenhall to get something to eat. In a little winery, we had a light supper and enjoyed the music, stirring German songs accompanied by the mandated accordion. The atmosphere was quite exotic and it seemed we were in a movie.

After supper, we took a walk around the town center of Bad Reichenhall. The stylish goods in the shop windows were tastefully and artistically displayed. It struck me that the windows themselves were free of fingerprints and smudges. There were no gum or candy wrappers or leaves swirling about. The white lines in the street were gleaming, literally shining–they were as clean as highly polished tooth enamel! I had a weird vision of janitors kneeling in the road scrubbing with toothbrushes and checking for cavities. It drifted into my consciousness Bad Reichenhall was the cleanest spot I had ever been on this dirty old planet. Bad Reichenhall stood in stark contrast to the grimy, oily, dirty patch of crowded Italy I had just encountered. A sudden chill gave me goose bumps. Was it the night air, or the realization that this was Hitler country? The palpable obsession with cleanliness reflected in this town seemed extreme. I felt uncomfortable and wanted to leave immediately, which we did.

Later I got the story of Harald from Gus. While they waited for the proprietor of the clothing shop to arrive, Harald, prompted by Gus's gentle questioning, told his story. Harald had married in East Germany and both he and his wife wanted to study in the west. The government would not let them leave the country together, so Harald went first and earned his degree, then returned to the East so his wife could go to the west and get her degree. This seemed a reasonable compromise under the circumstances, but when word arrived that his wife was ill, Harald could not go to her side. As her condition deteriorated, no amount of pleading would crack the resolve of the government. Finally, when word came that she might not survive, Harald made the fateful decision to jump the wall. He abandoned everyone and everything to go to his wife's side, but she died before he arrived. And now he cannot go home to East Germany to rejoin the rest of his family. He is marooned in the west, alone, to pursue the rest of his life. Gus never again complained about Harald's attitude.

When we got back to the Schloss, another surprise greeted us. The watchdog for the Rumanian delegation to the Seminar had somehow got word of Mihai's jaunt, gone to Innsbruck and escorted him back to secured residence at the Schloss. We were chagrined. Who was the controller?

Antoinette! She who had given Gus the sob story of her dreadful marriage and had refused membership in the party. We three blind mice had not read the signs. I went to Ioanna and asked her, "How could we know it was Antoinette? She had seemed so put upon and so resolute in her resistance the night of the dance."

Ioanna laughed. "The first clue you missed was that she is a translator; only party members can be translators. Her age was a tip, the rest of the promising scholars are young people with their careers ahead of them; she is on the downward slope. Look at her clothes. They are so much more expensive than the others, and she is wearing jewelry, and not cheap baubles, either." We might profess to be masters of ambiguity and subtlety in our literature classrooms, but in "real" life we were sheep in sheep's clothing.

All of these events, both in the classroom and in the intrigue of relationships in the Schloss, cast me into a heightened emotional state. My beliefs in literature and my knowledge of the political realities of Europe were causing me to reconsider who I was and where I was going. My translucent past was prologue to a very murky future.

I had shared every experience of my life, psychological, physical, and spiritual, with my wife, Jacqueline. We met in Grade 9. From that point on our experiences were shared. In the course of the twenty-three years to the summer of 1973, I shared every childhood memory with her, making our lives shared from our earliest memories.

Jackie was the valedictorian of our high school class, earning a musical diploma on the side. Following a business diploma at a local college, for two years she was secretary to the administrator of a 500-bed hospital. She resigned that position to go Anna Maria College where she was *summa cum laude* in mathematics and again valedictorian of her class. We were married in 1960 after her junior year and she graduated six months pregnant, winning the award as the outstanding example of Christian womanhood. She gave up her career aspirations to create five beautiful children–and support me much more than I had realized, or fully appreciated, in my quest for the almighty PhD.

Now, I was undergoing a traumatic experience without her, bonding to new friends, stumbling about in a mystifying world. She just had to know what I was going through, because my life was going to be changed–deeply and irrevocably.

I telephoned our friends in Ireland, Billy and Eithne Gallagher, who were going to take care of our kids while Jackie joined me in Italy. They generously agreed to take the children a few days earlier. Then I called Jackie and arranged for her to come early to Salzburg before we left for Milan. I got her a room at a little pension near the Schloss and she arrived for the last weekend to see what had happened to her husband.

The final night in Salzburg the participants gathered for a farewell party. We toasted each other, but the highlight was the toasting and roasting of William Gass. He had eventually led us around a corner. We learned to reassess and think more critically about our presuppositions about literature. The lightning in the Venetian Hall of mirrors had cleared the air following our stormy debates.

Adding to our personal gaiety was the arrival of Elvira Palcsey from St. Gallen, Switzerland.

Elvira and Mihai and Jackie and I retreated from the party to the quiet of Max Reinhart's library. We huddled together in a corner surrounded by the rococo carvings on the wooden furniture. The room was dark with a mahogany glow, much as I remember the office of Don Corleone in *The Godfather*–an impression encouraged, no doubt, by the conspiratorial air of our conversation.

I cannot picture Elvira's face in my mind's eye, except that she was petite and lovely. Jackie and I were aware of the blessed ease with which we had courted and married free and unencumbered by the State, while Mihai and Elvira were struggling to establish a union against the shadowy and impenetrable forces of government and ideology. And these forces sought to suppress their desire to unite in the most basic human sharing as husband and wife. They would not be able to marry if they remained in their current situation. I thought of Harald.

Without consulting me or discussing the matter, Jacqueline, who would have to assume the major burden of what she was about to say, said simply to our new friends, "If you want to leave your present situation and come to Canada to find a new life, you will have a home with the Walsh family for as long as you need." She was holding my hand, and I was so filled with joy and admiration for this quiet woman of faith and hope that I could not speak. In that moment, a deeper bond was established not only between the Walshes and our new friends, but between Jackie and me. Some rich vein of faith and hope and love had been tapped–without our having to speak it, for in a sense, such matters lie to deep for words.

The rest of the evening has faded away. We made plans to write, to circulate Mihai's curriculum vitae, to write letters of recommendation. I cannot remember the rest of the party or the parting the next day.

Many years later, I came across a still unpublished manuscript detailing the life of Steffi Hohenlohe, a beautiful young courtesan who had lived in the Schloss during World War II when it was owned by the Nazis. She worked her way up from gypsy origins to be mistress of many powerful men, including some highly placed Americans during a visit to the USA, despite being in the ken of the FBI. One man she seduced was the man who was supposed to be tracking her. Eventually she had been awarded the Iron Cross from Hitler himself–despite the fact that she was Jewish!

I couldn't help thinking about Mozart and the Archbishop, about Max Reinhart and his social set, about the fictional von Trapps of movie reality, about the Nazis and Steffi Hohenlohe–all carrying on in a gray and ambiguous life full of conflicting forces. All of us, for a brief moment, occupied the same space in the Schloss Leopoldskron: matters of import for a few, of insignificance for most. Hadn't William Gass told us, that in a story, "In your story, an event can be anything: adultery . . . or the twitch of an eye."

Back in Canada with my PhD in hand, promotion and building a new house followed. Letters were sent, job hunting for Mihai became part of the routine–without much success. Just before Christmas, Mihai wrote, "After a really long time, I received your letter. Thank you very much! I will explain to you what it means, such a letter and in which way it represents more, much more than a simple answer . . . I don't know if you have received a letter from Europe concerning me. During a very difficult (unexpected!) period of time, I asked a girl that you met once to write you. Now, some things have changed. I am no more so desperate as I was, but am still trying to find an answer." I found this letter a bit confusing.

In January of 1974, we received a letter from Elvira, who had obtained work in Switzerland. "No doubt Mihai writes to you. However, in case one of his letters is 'misplaced,' M. asked me to write you a few lines. He is well, under the circumstances. Our question is again before the State Council, and we pray for the best . . . M. got some disappointing news about a position he applied for in Amsterdam. But we both keep looking. Now we have two applications in–one in Canada, one in Denmark. However, if you should hear of anything, M. would appreciate very much if you would let him know. Better yet, write to me with any and all particulars besides to him. I, at least, will get your letter and can apply in his name . . . When you write to Mihai, please mention only that you received some news from me. Nothing about the contents of this letter. M. knows it already." The State still had them under the heel of its boot.

In her next letter in March 1974, Elvira informed us that she had passed the first phase for a grant to study comparative philology. "And in Rumania, 'they' seem to be leaving Mihai alone, beyond the usual petty pressures.

"It's no surprise that Mihai's letter confused you. He confuses even those who've known him for a while. Just remember, his letters must pass the censor's inspections, and in confusing them, he doesn't realize how he confuses others. It's a peculiar system, but you develop a 6th sense for it. Just keep in mind the joke: An old rabbi in Rumania was on a train bound for main stop in town A. His acquaintances on the train asked him where his final destination was, to which he replied town B. A close acquaintance and travel companion asked him, 'Why do you say you're going there?' To which the old rabbi replied, 'I say I'm going to town B so they'll think I'm really going to town A, when I'm actually going to town C.' Actually, once you sense the system, it's not so confusing."

Clarity arrived when, nine months after our Innsbruck caper, Mihai and Elvira were blessed with the arrival of their first-born son, Ari Michael Nadin!

Following the Salzburg Seminar, a group of us wanted to keep our new relationship alive, so under the driving force of Gordon Bennet's leadership we formed the International Society for Contemporary Literature and Theatre (ISCLT) and had our founding meeting at Arundel in Sussex, England, in July/August of 1974. The group still meets every year as a moveable feast throughout Europe and even once at Salt Lake City, Utah.

In October of 1974, Mihai wrote, "You'll be surprised (I was no less), but after being refused to go to the follow-up seminar at Arundel, I am now in West Germany for more than 2 months (yes, months!). I am trying not only to use this extraordinary occasion, but also to look for something in order to change the course of my life . . . As you know, we–Elvira and I–have a son, but the situation concerning our civil status hasn't changed at all. Elvira is now in Rumania (believe me!), with a grant in philology. She told me that she wrote to you about my intentions to move wherever I'll find an opportunity, more or less in accordance with my competence . . . Please answer me at the following address [in West Germany]. You can say anything you like and don't have to worry about the consequences. Isn't that wonderful? Or have you never discovered what that means?"

Yes, I had discovered what it means to be able to write without censorship. My life was following my dream: teaching at St. Francis Xavier with my mentor Fr. Rod MacSween, surrounded by deep friendships, involved in community and church. And on the home front, an indefatigable wife and a thriving family made possible by a writing career as playwright leading to promotion to full professor and the salary that goes with it. That summer that we moved into our new home overlooking Brierly Brook Valley we got a message from Rumania:

Ari Michael, son of

Elvira Tereza Palcsey and Mihai Nadin

is overjoyed to announce the marriage (finally)

of his parents on 23 July, 1975

Reception cocktail to be held at Blvd. Dimitrie Cantemir 45,

et. 8, apt. 52 from 17:30 to 19:30,

Casual dress, please.

We sent a telegram of congratulations. The government had finally allowed Elvira to enter Rumania permanently to live with her man, as far as we could guess, because of the commitment to the union in the person of Ari Michael, and perhaps that they would be gaining an American scholar. In Antigonish we would still be pursuing opportunities outside Rumania.

Then, one last postcard:

"Dear Pat and Jackie!

(as usual) I hope my letter (postcard) will reach you on St. Patrick's Day, so that I will be present in your house, but only in order to wish you good luck and to see you for an instant.

Sometimes I miss you very much so that I look at your picture and enjoy Pat's smile. Let me know, sometimes, how you are.

Yours faithfully,

Mihai"

And that was the last we heard from the Nadin family. Our letters to Rumania came back undelivered or they "disappeared." One night I was thinking about our lost friends and I said to Jackie, "You know, one thing puzzles me." She didn't find that unusual, but decided to humor me.

"What puzzles you, dear?"

"Well, I have never really understood why the government was picking on Mihai and Elvira so much. They weren't committing any crimes against the State. They just wanted a normal life. Why were they persecuted so persistently?"

Jackie was truly surprised at my ignorance.

"You really don't know?"

I waited in silence rather than affirm my ignorance again.

In gentle exasperation, Jackie enlightened me.

"Patrick, they were persecuted because they were Jewish."

I thought I was back in the Venetian room as the lightning struck. Had I really perceived any significant degree of reality of the Salzburg situation? I had no inkling of the faith of our friends. They were just people like us, but not as fortunate, caught in a painful situation.

Down through the years, I often thought of Mihai and Elvira and Ari Michael, especially when Rumania was in the news, or *The Sound of Music* drifted into my consciousness, or an article appeared on the persecution of Jews. I had to wrestle with the question of the persecution of Jews in the name of my own faith. But not just these stimuli from the media and my reading and study of scripture brought my friends to mind. In the dark mahogany shadows of a room in a library, or the quiet corner of a chapel, even a color, a musty smell of furniture, a deep silence, could bring our last meeting to mind, and I would utter a prayer for my lost friends.

When the wall fell, I thought, *Maybe they will surface now*. I waited in vain.

Twenty-eight years after Salzburg, Jackie and I were empty-nesters. Jackie retired after twenty-five years as editor of the newspaper in Antigonish. I took early retirement after 37 years of teaching at StFX. We moved from Nova Scotia to Calgary, Alberta, in the foothills of the Rockies, to be with our oldest and youngest daughters and their families, with two grandsons each. Also I was the first professor of English at a brand-new Catholic college, St. Mary's, now in 2003 in its 6th year of full-time operation. Following some heart complications, I am fully retired but remain writer-in-residence. The college gives me an office, a phone, computer and printer, and invites us to all the parties.

In December of 2002, I had to move all my files, some unopened since leaving Antigonish, to my new office at St. Mary's. I came across the last post-card above. It brought back the flood of memories, much of which I have shared with you.

I also began to think of how deeply my Salzburg adventure had affected me. The memories here have been writing themselves in my mind for a quarter of a century. For nearly twenty years, I gave public lectures to assorted Lions, Kinsmen, Rotarians, teachers, and religious congregations about my Salzburg experience and the indomitable Nadins. Often the last lecture of a course was devoted to my life lessons in freedom, faith, and commitment at Salzburg.

Sitting at my computer–a technicality not available in the 1970s and 80s, I decided to reactivate my search for Mihai. I went to the computer and Googled the name: "Mihai Nadin." The result: 1,550 hits! Mihai was on that many sites! How could this be? I tracked his home site to Wuppertal University in Germany, and fighting my way through the faculty listing found an email address.

> "Mihai, is it you?" And it was!
>
> "To: "pat and jackie walsh" <walshpj@shaw.ca>
>
> Subject: Re: friendship
>
> Date: Sunday, December 29, 2002 3:47 AM
>
> dear pat and dear Jackie,
>
> once again: beautiful! This is an event I want to acknowledge. Finding you again, or better yet: you found us. and we are, my wife and I quite happy.

well, after the marriage (4 1/2 years of waiting for approval is already a test) our lives unfolded in exciting though taxing ways. Details (if you really wish to hear them) once we meet again. The short of it: I was out of Romania, my wife was in Romania with our children . . . and it took again patience, love, luck, Gods blessings until we got back together . . . and here are our stations:

Germany, Humboldt grant; Rhode Island School of Design, Providence,

Professor for almost 5 years; THE Ohio State University (Columbus), endowed chair . . . etc., New York city, Wuppertal . . . And come February 28 I will be retired (mandatory in Germany). . . and see how I continue my professional life.

Our home base is Rhode Island (USA), but we are not enough there . . . My wife is the better half of the entity we constitute, and the children are grownups . . . some more challenging than the others.

Let us know more about yourself. I am sure there is a lot to find out. And let us stay in touch . . . let us plan to see each other and eventually meet.

Life is wonderful and precious. It is up to us to make the best happen.

We wish you well."

So, we are now planning to get together as soon as our situations permit. I have sent Mihai some poems and we have bought a couple books: *Jewish: Does It Make a Difference?* by Elvira and Mihai Nadin; and Mihai's nineteenth book, *The Civilization of Illiteracy* [888 pages], reviewed as follows by Amazon "a reader"(San Francisco) July 9, 2001:

"Dr. Nadin's cultural critique is a remarkably erudite and incisive tour-de-force. The author is at his best when examining contemporary culture through the lens of semiotics; his comments on Peirce are particularly insightful.

It's difficult to critique a book that is obviously the product of decades of intense study. While the terms 'masterpiece' and 'genius' are tossed around all too frequently nowadays, this is one instance where their use might well be justified. An extraordinary work from a unique mind. Bravo, Nadin!"

We shall meet again, Nadins and Walshes. Thank God, thank HaShem!

Patrick Walsh

Calgary, Alberta 2003

*

We did meet again–at least I did. On a visit to my sister in the Boston area I drove to the Nadin's home in Little Compton, Rhode Island, and stayed over for a few days so we could get caught up on our lives since Salzburg. It was a touching and satisfying reunion. I was stimulated now by Mihai's brilliant work. We are now still connected electronically through emails and phone calls. His magnum opus, *The Civilization of Illiteracy,* was so powerful that I established a small study group at the University, and Jackie and I and the group spent an inspiring year studying the book chapter by chapter. The highlight of the Salzburg Seminar was the mind-expanding confrontation with a deeper understanding of the way the world really is. As the years slip by, my worldview continues to be enlightened by Mihai's work. And my study of scripture with Michael Duggan and the relationship of my Christian faith with the First Testament of the Jewish faith, continues to draws us closer together. I have passed from my childhood world of an angry and punishing God (which I now believe was a distorted and false image) to understand through the historical/critical method of Scripture study that the Creator/God of the First Testament is the same Creator/God of the Second Testament. And that God is a loving, caring God, and the act of Creation, of calling into being, is an act of love.

*

In Salzburg, my encounter with the mind of Mihai Nadin would flower into an enrichment of my faith, and in Calgary, my encounter with the mind of Michael Duggan would pollinate through his great opus, *The Consuming Fire: A Christian Introduction to the Old Testament*, and bring me to a deeper understanding of the underlying unity of, not just the Abrahamic faiths, but of the Spirit working in all humanity. To reach this point in my personal faith, a journey my wife has made with me, I owe a great debt of gratitude to these two outstanding teachers. They advanced the liberalization of my mind begun by my mentor and friend, Fr. R. J. MacSween. How fortunate my wife and I have been to make this faith journey together. *Deo gratias*.

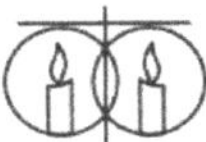

William Gass was one of the leading postmodernist writers of the second half of the 20th century. His work established what is often called 'metafiction': work that self-consciously refers to its own storytelling and the writing process, and whose form eclipses the importance of plot. His seminar was a challenge for all of us to reassess the limited methods of literature; really to understand the limits of language in conveying the reality of the world around us. He dragged us by the scruff of our necks into the coming postmodernist world.

Toast to Professor William Gass

Fellow Salzburg Leopoldskronschlossers,
Let us recognize our gains and lossers–
We arrived as boys and babes "in the woods"
At Austria's "Gingerbread House" of goods
Both literary and philosophical–
The hills were alive with the sound of worms

Eating away our conventional terms:
The mountains were figments no longer there–
Mere fictional constructs made of hot air!
Monsters named "Meta" crawled out of the cracks
And clawed at our minds and jumped on our backs.
And some of us ran through the "forest of fear"–
And some of us tried to escape in our beer.
One Fellow who tried to escape to the moon
Was dragged back to earth by a "flying raccoon."
Our nightmares were caused by ideas we ate,
That Prof William Gass had served up on our plate.
We balked at his menu, we shouted, "Nein, nein!"
Yet swallowed his diet of "worms" name-ed "Klein."
A new Luther was loosed in our minds,
Hammering theses on our shuttered blinds.
He kicked open windows, he let in the sun;
None of us shriveled–it turned out to be fun.
Seminarilly digested without any squawks
Were Barth and Barthelme, Coover and Hawkes!
Natural gas is supplied with a smell
To warn us of danger if all is not well–
But when struck with a spark, it burns bright
Supplying us equally heat and light:
Transformed by chemistry into a friend.
Philosophical Gass who seemed to offend,
Burned with the heat and the brightness of stars
That led us to planets far beyond Mars:
He freed us equally from time and from space–
Our guide through the "Funhouse" of fictional faith–
And setting our goals in infinite thought
Drove us to strive for what cannot be caught!
If intellectual challenge and gall
Were wed in the Garden of Adam's fall–
Then William Gass is Professor supreme
Who makes us dream the impossible dream:

I ask you Fellows, to charge your glasses,
And drink to the health of the finest of Gasses:
"The End of Everything" was his claim;
But "Beginning" is a far better name:
Proof lies in the fact that we are all here,
So join me in drinking a glass of cheer–
To William Gass, Professor extraordinaire;
We drink to your health–IF you're really there!
PS:
That writers create like God we've been told,
We witness Bill Gass's mimesis bold:
His Mary is kindly and full of grace,
Beauty and charm which temper his pace.
But his Trinity shows his artistic sins:
Instead of a son, he creates female twins!

Chapter 8
Antigonish in Earnest 1973–83

Earning a PhD was a relieving achievement. My life had been full of tension since the death of my parents. Everything that seemed demanded of me was always a struggle, and I was not sure I could succeed. But I wasn't going to fail through lack of effort. At the age of 17, during Christmas vacation from StFX, I had to be hospitalized for excision of polyps. I had been subject to rectal bleeding for some time, and while the polyps were not cancerous, they could become so. Over the years I had to be tested continually and the polyp situation carefully monitored. When I came home with my PhD, my life's plans seemed successfully enabled. The bleeding mysteriously ceased. It had been a more than twenty-year span. Nonetheless, the doctors warned that I should keep up regular testing. So I did.

When I walked into the coffee room with my newly minted PhD, people seemed to look at me differently. Was it my imagination? My mentor, Fr. MacSween, did not have a PhD, but he was most likely the most imposing mind on the campus, an autodidact with an ability to range freely through any topic of discussion. Whenever famous visitors came to the University, the administrators would seat them next to Fr. MacSween at the President's table. He could hold his own in any conversation. Being nowhere near a MacSween, I survived on a flamboyant dramatic style and a dogged, never-say-die indefatigable work ethic–I still had the "bloodlust" for literature despite the cessation of polyps. So, now, when the discussions in the faculty lounge began to vibrate about how important a PhD was, or how everyone who taught at university must have a PhD–having to bite my tongue and remain silent for twenty years, I could speak freely because now I had the good old union card. The actuality was that the PhD was the easiest of all the degrees of my life. After 15 years of teaching experience, the challenge was without tension, a great joy, and a pleasure. So when my colleagues started going on about the almighty, absolute need for a PhD to be a professor, I could say (and they never knew how serious I might be), "All it takes to get a PhD is to gnaw like a rat. If you gnaw long enough, they'll give it to you." That was often my exit line.

Of course, that line is flippant and a gross exaggeration, but there is some truth in it. Over the years I observed many graduate students, who, when they would encounter difficulty, would quit. To succeed, perseverance is necessary.

For a number of years, I served as Chair of the Honorary Degree Committee. The Committee's job was to vet people nominated for an honorary degree and compile a background dossier for the use of the University Senate, the conscience of the University, which would vote on the nominees. One of the most famous nominees I presented to the Committee was Bobby Orr, not just a hockey player who had single-handedly changed how the game was played, but also a humanitarian, who having had his career foreshortened by injury, established a number of institutions to help prevent and treat injuries to players. He inspired the following poem.

For Bobby Orr

Achilles stares into his silver shield,
The Metal eyes reflect blood turning cold;
Muscles, sinews, tendons, tortured, now yield
An Ore tempered in a warrior's mold.

Achilles sees the statue in the shield
Step down in fluid grace, and raise a spear
In challenge to enemies on the field.
He shouts an unheard war-whoop loud and clear,

And races across the blood soaked ground
To smash old idols down. They fall beneath
His relentless blows, and without a sound
They pass in shadows from the shield's dark heath.

Victory cups, crowns of leaves, fill his eyes,
Which close–before he sees a Hector rise.

A classical sonnet framed and built for my buddy, Jim:

The Master Builder

He frames a house and raises high a roof.
A master carpenter hammers and saws
Building from preconceived plans and laws
A human habitation. Yet the proof
That he has succeeded cannot be found
In watertight joints and hand-hewn oak-beams,
In carpets laid without revealing seams,
Nor stuccoed walls and workmanship renowned.

Rather are larger plans of life fulfilled
In making of that house a friendly home
Enclosing space where those in need find rest:
The world thus built will prove the builder skilled.
For my carpenter friend I shape this poem
To celebrate the room in which I'm guest.

For James Deagle's birthday, March 16, 1975

As the years passed, I often thought about a famous picture of Jesus crying over Jerusalem that Aunt Annie had over her piano. He sure wasn't thinking happy thoughts. Someone suggested that Jesus was thinking about the justice that would be meted out on Jerusalem for what it was about to do to him. Here is a story about my brother, and an injustice I visited on him. The TRUTH underlying my actions, I see only now, was gnawing away on my very deeply buried guilt.

My Kid Brother

"My God, he's got a big nose."

That was Mrs. Chartier speaking. None of us kids would say "my God." Dad would have given us a backhander.

The kid was dark, too.

Mom pulled back the baby blanket and he started to scream. He was pretty lusty for a new baby.

Naturally, he turned out to be handsome. And I with all my curly locks turned out to be unpleasingly plump.

* * *

Dad used to tease Black Diamond. The little guy was just learning how to waddle about. Dad would get a grapefruit and put it in his overalls so it hung down in back like a big job in his diapers. The poor kid couldn't get the grapefruit–but he would turn around, switching from side to side, trying to get it out.

Then he'd jump up and down.

We'd all laugh until tears were running down our faces. I'd get sick and once I even wet myself I laughed so hard.

The game ended when he would stand in the middle of the living room and begin to cry. He never screamed. Just kind of whimpered a bit. He'd look so old with the wrinkles all over his brown face.

* * *

He was a real pain when I wanted to play with the guys. He was just too small and I was just too big.

He couldn't run fast enough–and he'd cry. And we were too old to put up with a kid crying like that.

One day, though, when I tried to ditch him . . . well, when we all tried to ditch him, I got punished good for it.

We wanted to go down to the railroad tracks and see if anybody dared to put his tongue on the tracks right after a train had gone by.

Your tongue would stick to the track if you did that. Jimmy Feder's uncle had done it when he was a kid, and they had to cut his tongue off to get him off the track before another train came by.

The guys were going to get the kid to do it. But I got scared. I started to run, and so did the guys and when the kid started to chase us he fell down and skinned his knees on the sidewalk. He was bleeding something awful. He reminded me of that picture of the little Chinese baby in Singapore before WWII.

I ran like hell.

He went home bawling.

I thought I'd get beat up bad when I got home for supper, but he never told on me.

The very next day I was playing hide and seek and there were lots of boards lying beside the goal, which was the electric meter on the side of the house.

My grandmother had sent us a piano cause she was moving to California and didn't want to take it with her. The boards were from the packing case and had big nails in them.

I snuck around the corner of the house and saw the goal was free. I had the guy who was "it" beat by so much I ran and jumped way up and shouted triumphantly "My goal, one, two, three," and came down on the boards and drove a nail right up through my shoe through my big toe on my right foot. I didn't even feel it. But then I tried to walk.

Mrs. Chartier had to hold me down while Mom pulled the board off my foot. She was kind of mad that she had to pour good Canadian Club on the toe.

I sat there screaming my fool head off.

My kid brother just stood in the doorway smiling at me.

* * *

When the kid was a freshman at the local parochial school, St. Joe's High, he got the starting assignment to pitch against the big public school in the city–Drury High. He beat them 1–0. That was in 1958. The last time St. Joe's had beat Drury was when my father beat them 1–0 in 1927.

They made a big flurry over that in the papers. They even put in the lineup of my dad's game and told what all the players from then were doing now. Only my Dad and one other guy had died.

One of the living was Dr. Ramsey our dentist. Then I understood why my Dad had always made us go to him even though he was drunk most of the time and never used any Novocain.

* * *

The night we–I mean St. Joe's, 'cause my kid brother was pitching for them, and I was teaching chemistry there, and I used to travel with the team and keep score–well, the night we played at Wahconah Park in Pittsfield against Pittsfield High who were the defending state champs, I will never forget.

It was the biggest crowd ever at Wahconah. We got beat 2 to 1. The kid pitched a one-hitter, but the other pitcher pitched a two-hitter and we lost on an unearned run: an error by Sandy Whitmore, the first baseman. He was usually dependable. I still have the score sheet in the glove compartment of my car.

The kid who played shortstop for Pittsfield was Mark Belanger. That's pronounced Bell-*ange*-er, not Bell-an-*ger*, like the announcers on the radio pronounce it. He plays shortstop for the Baltimore Orioles. I was not too sad when they got clobbered by the Mets.

Anyway, the thing I remember best about that night was that when it came time for the team to run out on the field, the coach put the ball in my kid brother's hand and said, "Now, it's a night game, kid, remember, when you get to the mound, turn and face the crowd and smile so they'll know you're there." We all laughed. And he smiled.

* * *

I was home from college one summer and working at the High School for the old monsignor, painting the classrooms and stuff.

I found the debater's tape recorder in a closet and I took it home and messed around with it. My buddy and I were just fooling around one night when my kid brother came in.

"Let's make him say something, George."

"Okay," I said.

We grabbed the kid and held him down. He was kind of strong, which surprised me, but we were two to one. And I was plenty big even then and was lying on him with his arm up behind his back in a hammer lock. The kid was really shy. He never said too much, and he really didn't like the idea of being recorded.

"Say, Puck, puck, like a chicken."

He said, "No."

"Say puck, puck."

Silence.

"Puck, puck, c'mon."

No sound.

I kept it up for a long time. I don't know how long. But my buddy got real quiet and the kid was moaning a bit but he wouldn't say "puck, puck."

I was really surprised when some sweat rolled into my eyes.

It stung. My eyes started to water and when I looked at the kid I thought: *My eyes must look just like that.*

He never did say "puck, puck."

Even today, he likes to remind me that he never said, "puck, puck."

* * *

My dad wouldn't let the kid pitch until he was 10 years old.

He said he might ruin his arm trying to throw curves. So all he did was pitch to me.

I was in high school then, and even though I was 8 years older he used to sting my hand, but I was afraid to admit it. I used to call off catching on the excuse I didn't want him to hurt his arm.

* * *

The kid won 27 and lost 2 in Little league. He won 32 and lost 5 in high school. Baltimore offered him $15,000 to sign a contract after high school.

But I put pressure on him to go to college. Our folks had died when he was 12 and we kept the family together. I knew my folks would have wanted him to go to school. So my sister and I really worked on him.

The coach clinched it.

He got the kid a scholarship to Providence College. Now, he couldn't go and ruin it for all the kids who would come after him by turning it down. Not after the coach went through all that trouble and everything. So he went.

And he didn't lose a game. And he flunked out. His heart wasn't in the books.

Baltimore wasn't interested anymore.

He sold clothes in Florida to be near Spring Training camp. But you can't get in without a scout to get you in. Not even the Mets would look at him. And they could have used him then.

He worked construction and kept trying.

He worked at Green Mountain Race Track as an usher. One night the local sports announcer, Bucky Bullet, brought two guys out to the race track to see him: Frank Malzone and Ted Williams. They weren't scouts, but they'd get him into spring training camp. No bonus of course, but he'd have a chance.

He knew he was better than many of the bonus babies. But they had scouts pushing them and the club had money tied up in them. He pitched real well.

But on the last day of camp, the manager, Dick Williams, came over and the kid kept throwing hard and not looking at him or letting him catch his eye. But he had to stop.

"I'm sorry, Fran, but we've got to let you go."

"But, you know I'm better than some of the guys you're keeping."

"Yes, but the club has money tied up in them. There's nothing I can do. I'm sorry."

"Sure."

He knew he wouldn't be able to try the minors. He had been engaged for four years, and it wasn't fair to her.

Now or never had become never.

The kid was the last man cut from the Red Sox the year of the miracle 1967.

* * *

I remember how after Dad died this insurance salesman came to town looking him up. He ended up selling Mom a policy, lying about her heart trouble. He wouldn't let her answer any of the questions. He did all the lying for her.

She paid the premiums for a few months and then let the policy lapse. Guilty conscience. She died about a year later.

I remember though, she told me that the salesman (I don't remember his name) had played ball with Dad. I guess that's why he lied about the policy. Anyway, he had told mom that he was a stringer, a scout for the San Francisco Giants.

I often thought about trying to find him to get the kid another chance, but he was from Springfield, Mass., and I didn't know the name of his company even, let alone him. The kid's too old now, anyway.

* * *

I saw my kid brother on New Year's Day. We got together at my sister's for a little family reunion. We watched all the Bowl games together.

That night, late, we were sitting around drinking and chatting and reminiscing about the family– about Dad during the Depression. Mom used to tell us how tough it was because Dad never said too much about it.

The kid was finding out what it was like. He's been out on strike at the G.E. for six months now.

His wife got kind of startled when he all of a sudden turned to me and said. "You know, George, I'd be playing ball today if you hadn't pushed me into college."

He didn't say it mean. Or bitter. It was just the truth coming out. My sister wouldn't look at me. She knew. And what could I say?

Nothing.

So I just looked at his eyes, and I thought, *It's amazing how the son-of-a-gun manages to keep a tan even into the New Year*.

Although often looking back, I likewise looked ahead. At around age five, my son Gregory was in St. Martha's Regional Hospital for an inflamed appendix. Greg was stuck in the hospital, so I brought him a board and colored clay to play with to while away his time.

For Greg

Our son has magic hands

magic hands take clay of many colors
fashion little men in little space ships
soaring through the convolutions of a Brain
perceiving patterns past the edges
of the universe of thought
spaces outside the boundaries of art

tiny dinosaurs attack pygmy villages
in St. Martha's hospital
while a reluctant appendix refuses to burst

hands:
bone sinew cartilage nerves extensions of a soul
searching for beauty in a wilderness of mediocrity

fingers
fly over the keyboard computing
in microseconds relationships
Euclid spent a lifetime pondering

Bartholomew might have been but Gregory is

we try to mold the child hoping this time
to get our own lives right but
in the double-helix of her chromosomes and mine
create patterns of genes unique to the finite moment
of creation what springs forth

from the mind of subsisting existence
confounds us

no way could we imagine
the ready smile the keen glance
the willing spirit the helping hand

we see perfect nails
tiny fingers wrapping around my little finger
squeezing and unfolding like a spring fiddlehead

today flicking a badminton racquet
tomorrow perhaps flinging a satellite
beyond our galaxy to the fourth age of middle earth

hands capable of cuddling a shivering bird
like Francis of Assisi

hands
to steady the weak to be strong support
to grasp the truth to paint to mold and shape
to carve to write to pray–

in wonder and joy we watch amazed at the way–
the hands of our son transform the world we live in

*

In the interest of TRUTH, my wife informs me that Greg was in the hospital for pneumonia. But I allow the FICTION of his "appendix" to stand, for it fits the memory, faulty as it is, that inspired this reflective poem, written years later.

Poems contain common symbols available to all readers in a common culture. But some personal symbols known only to a few, may need explication. For instance:

Bartholomew might have been but Gregory is

When our second son was born, we asked Sheldon and Dawn Currie to be his godparents, and Fr. MacSween to perform the baptism ceremony. So on a Sunday afternoon, the two families trooped to the baptistery in St. Ninian's

Cathedral. I had carefully pondered a name for this child, and came up with Bartholomew; Bartholomew Walsh, in everyday use: Bart Walsh. A lovely lilt in the formal name, and a strong manly name for common usage. Bart Walsh. Wasn't Bart Starr the best quarterback in the NFL?

Dawn Currie held the child over the baptismal fount as Fr. MacSween turned to me and asked, "What are you going to name this child?" "Bartholomew Walsh," I replied. A beat of silence. "Bart–Bart Walsh," I repeated.

Dawn muffled some kind of snicker and speaking to no one in particular, said, "Bart? Bart? That rhymes with fff. . . !"

Fr. MacSween said, "Bartholomew? That sounds like a fart in a wind tunnel!" and turning to Jacqueline asked, "What do you name this child?"

And without hesitation she replied forcefully, "Gregory Peter Walsh."

"I baptize thee, Gregory . . . [pour], Peter . . .[pour], Walsh . . .[pour]."

Gregory it was, and Gregory it is.

Tracey Snider with Greg Wals

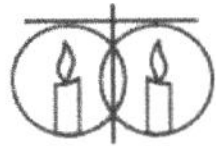

My wife is the only person who has influenced my life more than Fr. Rod MacSween. I met him three months before my father died, and he stands in my pantheon of inspiration as an artistic and creative father and mentor. The interview below brought Fr. MacSween more mail than any thing he ever wrote. In it you will find the spirit that informed my commitment to teaching and writing.

Patrick X Walsh

MacSween Interview

from *The Alumni News*

R J MacSween In conversation with Patrick Walsh (Summer 1980)

Walsh: How did you get to teach at StFX?

MacSween: I sneaked in when nobody was looking.

Walsh: I know that.

MacSween: No, I think Dr. Nicholson [*President of StFX in 1948*] picked me because of my library. He'd come down to where I was staying and looked at my books, at a time when I was only a young priest. There was a look of envy in his eye. I'm serious. I think he believed that my books should be up at StFX, not down in New Waterford, where they were. So, he just figured out some way of getting them up here. He concluded that I had to go along. He used to come into my room, again and again, and walk around looking at my books. Then he told a friend of mine that a man with such a library should be up at StFX.

Walsh: When did you start building a library?

MacSween: When I was two.

Walsh: That's awfully young to handle a hammer.

MacSween: No, I suppose the year I left college. I began to buy books, as many as I could. I got a job, laboring in Glace Bay. Hard work. I'd go down every payday and wander around the only bookstore, unable to make a choice. Finally, I would make a choice and buy a book. So, by the time I went to the Seminary, a year later, I had a nice collection–that is, nice for my age. When I was in the Seminary, in Halifax, I discovered the Penguin editions downtown. Paperbacks were practically unknown at that time. When the Penguins appeared, I realized I could get a very good library by spending a few dollars every once in a while. That was the beginning.

Walsh: So you were a priest out in a parish then for a number of years before you came to StFX?

MacSween: Yes, seven years. Two years in Pomquet, and five years in New Waterford. During that time I bought many, many books. I mean, as many as I possibly could buy. The books I bought while I was in the Seminary, of course, were mostly theological or philosophical and, after I was ordained, I got in touch with a very fine book store in New York–the Gotham Book Mart. You and I were there one day, weren't we?

Walsh: Yes, we were.

MacSween: By reading their catalogues and magazines that I bought from them, I got in touch with the most important currents of modem literature. By the time I came here to teach, I had a good start on a collection of modern avant-garde books, *really* avant-garde. And a good collection of magazines of various types. Many of them were oddities that you couldn't pick up anywhere. If I had known enough at the time, I would have bought many more, because these go out of circulation very quickly. They're worth a fortune now. Anyway, that was a good start.

Walsh: You were facing quite a change, coming from a parish, and being thrown into the academic life here: When you arrived on campus, what was it like teaching?

MacSween: I wasn't prepared at all. The administrators thought I was prepared because I had read a great deal. But I hadn't read many of the things that came into the curriculum. A great deal of the work was new to me. First of all, the teaching of grammar was new. Also, that first year I taught what is now English 350 [Modern British and American Poetry and Short Story]. Many of the things I had to teach, I hadn't seen before. I had read many important works that were not in the textbooks. So, I had to work very hard the first years I was here; the first two or three years, I guess. Once I learned grammar, the rest was easy.

Walsh: You got on-the-job training?

MacSween: Sink or swim!

Walsh: What kind of teaching load did you carry then?

MacSween: Well, at that time, the average load was four courses, one of them being religion. The problem wasn't that there were so many courses but that we were too busy prefecting. We went to bed late every night. We couldn't go to bed until everyone else was quiet. The old strict regime was still in force in regard to prefecting. And we got up early in the morning. We priests all got up at six o'clock and said Mass at seven. And then we didn't get to bed until twelve or so, so I was always tired, terribly tired. Also, Dr. Nicholson kept me busy with various jobs which prevented me from doing more reading and preparation. It wasn't his fault; he was that kind of man, but it didn't give me much time. But about three years later, I found everything rather easy.

After a while, the prefecting ceased to be so strict. To some extent, through my own efforts and those of a few other young prefects, we got rid of the old discipline that was just killing everybody. The need for change, of course, was in the air. Everybody knew it. At that time the veterans were on the campus, older men who didn't want to take any kind of discipline, for which I don't blame them now. But even those who weren't veterans were already infected with the modern idea of liberty in all things. So, we had to relax the discipline and we did, almost completely, except for that matter of open housing. The discipline became very relaxed. When I spoke to Dr. Nicholson and Fr. Macdonnell [then Dean of Men], they agreed that things should be relaxed but that nobody was doing anything about it. They needed a push and I've always been a very good pusher. The Mounties are going to arrest me for pushing!

Well, that's the way I found the campus. I found it very, very difficult.

The prefecting, especially. Also not having enough time to prepare for my classes.

Walsh: What year did you arrive on campus?

MacSween: 1948.

Walsh: What changes do you see since 1948? First of all, in English–the teaching of English, and then maybe in regard to the campus life?

MacSween: I don't see many changes. It seems to me there has been a very gradual increase in everything, as far as quantity is concerned. But I don't really see much change in quality. There are some people who claim there is a very great change in quality. But I can't see it.

Walsh: You mean quality of students?

MacSween: Yes–and the quality of professorial staff. The quality of the actual teaching. I don't see any improvement. In our own department for example, Fr. Bannon was teaching the important courses and he taught them very well. Fr. Kane, also, was here when I arrived. In his own field of grammar he was supreme. We'll never have another grammarian to equal him. And that's about it.

Walsh: Could you explain why grammar isn't taught at the university anymore?

MacSween: Well, we found this matter of grammar impossible to control. We felt it should be taught in the early grades and that it was too late to change the habits of a lifetime at college age. We felt that grammar should be taught in grammar school (after all, it's called "grammar school") and in high school. In dealing with students, we wanted to do a little polishing, but found that the fundamentals were not known. There are a number of other reasons, too. We discovered that most of the students who had to take grammar did not finish their degree. They dropped by the wayside. So, we were placing a tremendous burden upon people who did not finish. We were teaching grammar to the lowest third of those who wrote the English Usage Test, and that lowest third, for the most part, did not graduate. And, we were missing the two-thirds who continued to work for a degree. We felt that such an effort to teach grammar was just a waste of time. So, we dropped it.

Walsh: But do the students today have to cover more material than they did in those days? I mean, the range of material or the depth of material?

MacSween: They have to do more writing at the present time. The number of term papers demanded is quite large.

Walsh: You don't see any great difference in the students of the '40s, '50s, '60s, '70s?

MacSween: No, I don't. They seem the same to me. Today they are more free in their way of life, but as students, they seem just the same. Their life on the campus, of course, is much freer than when I came here.

Walsh: What changes in university life did you see from 1948 through the '50s, '60s, and '70s?

MacSween: I can't say much about that, but it seems to me that a good many of the faculty are cut off from the life on the campus. You know, when I came here the faculty was rather small, and for the most part, made up of priests. We discussed everything, we went to everything, we saw all the shows, all the games and so on. The students knew us. But now, you could go right through the year and hardly know what extracurricular work is carried on, on campus. You might not see a movie, you might not see a play, you might not see a game; whereas thirty years ago that was unthinkable–you attended everything. So there is a rift between the faculty and the students which wasn't there before.

Walsh: Is that just a function of size? There were about 600 students when you arrived to teach.

MacSween: Around that; yes.

Walsh: And now there are four times as many.

MacSween: Yes, rift is principally a matter of size. Also, a great diversity among the professors. They come from different backgrounds, and are accustomed to different things. For example, I think the early faculty was for the most part sports-minded. They took for granted that they went to every game. But, I don't think that is true anymore. The faculty go their own way. They live their own lives more so than in the past, I think, naturally enough.

Walsh: Your life has been related to books and magazines and so on. You served on the Library Committee in the early days and saw it grow from a small library to the one we have now. What can you tell us about that experience?

MacSween: Of course, I was very much interested in the library, and interested in every book that came in. Often when the packages containing books came in, I'd examine every book. I think, the majority of those books were ordered by myself. For years, I think, I ordered, I would say, about 90% of all the books. And at that time, too, you could order in any field you wanted. After a while, I was constricted to ordering only in English. But I ordered everything in the early days and the orders got through. So, hardly a week went by when I wasn't presenting something to the librarian. I marked countless catalogues and brought them over to the library. I think I spent many a weekend marking catalogues–every hour. I'd go through 50 catalogues at a time. Or I would compile lists from catalogues or from magazines, copying down titles reviewed there. This work went on for quite a while and I still continue it to some extent. But I haven't got the freedom of ordering for other departments. I used to order everything–even economics sometimes, if the book was a classic. I did the same for music, art, history, psychology, philosophy. There were other little areas of learning that were not very well marked out, and I ordered for them, too. At the same time, I was buying as many books as I could for myself. Most of the money I ever made went into books.

Walsh: You are a full professor and you reached the highest rank without getting a formal PhD and you have been something of a rebel. Can you say something about that?

MacSween: Well, not very much. I don't consider myself a real rebel, but I didn't want to go to graduate school and I got away with it. Nowadays I wouldn't get away with it. I just came at the time that it was possible to avoid the drudgery. I think what happened was they probably intended to ship me out to a parish. But I was teaching four courses and doing it passably well, I guess, and was indispensable. So, rather than send me out, they delayed. I was here for so long that I became a fixture. On my 25th anniversary as a priest, they made me a full professor. But I wouldn't have become a full professor if it had meant an increase in salary. All priests on campus get the same salary. Making me a professor caused no great upset. They gave it to me as an honor at the time; it was not a financial matter at all.

Walsh: Still, it's an honor. Do you know how many full professors there are here?

MacSween: About 13! I like that number!

Walsh: Actually, 17 out of 179, which means it is a pretty exclusive honor.

MacSween: Well, I guess it is an honor. I'll agree with you rather than argue. That doesn't cost anything.

Walsh: Why didn't you want to go away to graduate school?

MacSween: Well, I'm a very private sort of person. I don't believe in going anywhere I don't have to go. And I felt an element of coercion which roused my stubbornness. I figured, "I just won't go." They could have ordered me to go, but they didn't. Dr. Nicholson told me to go and I told him I didn't want to go. Then I think he washed his hands of the whole affair, and he must have decided, "The first chance I get, I'll get rid of him." But the chance didn't come, so I just stayed here. I don't think I had missed anything by not going to graduate school. It's different in the sciences or any course that requires a great deal of training. But in the matter of English Literature, I don't feel that you need a PhD at all. I think there is almost nothing in English that you can't learn by yourself. It may be good to have a well-trained professor give you a few courses, but I don't think you have to go through that drudgery so long as you like to work by yourself. And I like to.

Walsh: Well, what kind of work do you see an English professor doing? What do you think his responsibilities are?

MacSween: Well, first of all, I think he should try to make his subject loved by the students. He can't be dull, and he can't have views on life in general that do not elevate the life of the student, do not increase his spiritual vitality. In every aspect of life, his views must inspire and incline towards spiritual freedom. And if he hasn't got these, it makes no difference what his learning may be, because he will be a failure as a professor. The actual matter of what is taught in the classroom is no mystery. It can be assimilated by any energetic person. This is dangerous ground, of course, anyway, the teacher needs broadness of vision, a vision that to some degree resembles the visions of the great writers he deals with. He can't go into the classroom and talk like a dolt about writers who aren't and weren't dolts. He can't teach like a reactionary about writers who are always forward-looking, and he can't teach with cruelty in dealing with writers who always taught kindness, generosity, and so on. So, it's a big order, but most of that order is not concerned with literature alone.

Walsh: You have done some writing yourself. Have you been writing throughout your career?

MacSween: Yes, to some extent. When I first came here I was too busy to write. I think that 15 years went by before I had a chance to begin to write again. Even then, I found it very hard to produce anything of length because there was never time. There was time, it is true, but it wasn't time when I was at my best. Often I couldn't write because I was tired, or mixed up, or had something on my mind. But those moments of peace and clarity that you need for the creation of good writing–I didn't have them too often, living in noisy buildings and teaching crowded courses. But in the last 14 years, I've had more time. For example, we used to teach summer school every year in the early days and we got very little for it, but it did absorb our time and energy. It takes quite a big chunk out of a summer. When a work of some size is contemplated, something that requires long constant writing, a single month or two months is not enough. But, of course, as time went by I got more skilled and faster; I think I could write a great deal now if I felt so inclined. It's a craft, and I didn't really learn how to write until I was 57 or 58. I started to write seriously when I was about 50. Before that it was just little scraps of prose, or the occasional poem. But at 50 I began to write more seriously, and produced quite a few things. I was learning all the time; at about 57 I began to know something about writing. I believe nobody really enters that magic field of literature until he produces three or four books.

Walsh: So, you have to practice and make quite a few mistakes before you learn how to do it correctly.

MacSween: Yes, you have to practice in writing, as you do in everything. In sports, for example. Moreover, I think when you write you teach much better. You understand things from the inside. A teacher can be very valuable in transferring knowledge to students, but I don't believe he'll ever know what a poem is until he's written one; and it's the same for short stories or novels or almost anything else. Every professor should go through a period when he writes for himself, just in order to know, not to sell or make money, but to know what he is talking about.

Walsh: So, if there are a lot of things that don't get published, at least you've gone through the process and learned from it.

MacSween: Yes, the writer learns a great deal from simply writing. Not a bit of it is ever wasted. The danger lies in writing academic things; most of these are stultifying and must be avoided if possible. Then the writer must have good models. Some critics write beautiful essays; such men are very few, but these constitute our models for that type of work. If a person is going to model himself on anybody, he mustn't model himself on the general run of academic critic– because if he does, he'll never develop. All he'll know at the end is how to write a poor essay. He should know that without trying very hard.

Walsh: Yes, that's almost natural. You have published several books of poetry; the poems are very often concerned with death. Why is that?

MacSween: Well, I think death is a great and terrifying thing. If you don't realize that, you're not alive. We're all heading towards death as fast as we can go. And it doesn't take away any of our love of life. If anything, it intensifies it. Even if you do enjoy life a great deal, the enjoyment doesn't, in any way, take away the power of death. But, I think, an amateur poet, as I am (I was even more the amateur in the early days) only writes when he is moved by something unusual–and he's generally moved by death, the death of somebody else, or the sickness of someone else, or disappointment, or a feeling of depression in his own life. So, if he writes in that way, he'll end up with a collection of poems with the emphasis heavily slanted towards depressing things like death. But if he is a professional poet and writes about everything in sight, I think that poems on death will be just a comparatively small portion of his output.

Walsh: You mean the theme of death fits with the limited amount of time you had to write?

MacSween: Yes. A professional poet writes poetry very often, perhaps every week. He may not publish it and he may destroy it, but he's writing a great deal, and he writes on every subject. He could write on death only occasionally–if at all. So, at the end of the year the professional may produce 30 poems; perhaps only one or two would be about death. The rest wouldn't be, and as the years went up, fewer and fewer would be, because he would have worked out the subject. But the amateur would only write when extremely moved. He may write only five poems in a year and perhaps three of them would be about death, a high proportion of his work. He only writes when he's moved by personal disaster, like news that a brother or cousin has died, or someone has gone permanently away, someone he'll never see again. Every separation is a kind of death. But, I think, everybody thinks about death a great deal but only the poet writes about it. His next-door neighbor, who perhaps never wrote a laundry list, thinks about death just as much as the poet does.

Walsh: I'd like to ask you about an activity at the University that took up a great deal of your time and energy. You've been chaplain at Mount St. Bernard [women's college] for a long time.

MacSween: Well, I still am in a way, but in the early days I was wanted over there as a sort of guidance counselor. In fact, the first year I was there I refused to be that and was almost dropped because I did no counseling. So, after a while I gave in and saw anybody who wanted to see me. By using my knowledge of graphology, I had a kind of key to character. For about twenty years. I went over every evening after supper, and would stay there for as long as anybody wanted to see me. Now, I have stopped that for a number of reasons; I was getting old and finding myself strapped for time. The establishment of a guidance center on the campus took away the great need for my presence. There may be other minor reasons, but these were the two principal ones why I just stopped going. I began to get impatient with sitting in an office in the evening, getting tired and bored with it all.

Walsh: You had a period as chair of the English department. How would you assess that period in your career?

MacSween: Well, it meant a little more work, I suppose, although I didn't notice it because I've always been inclined to avoid simple administration. I did not feel it necessary to lay down many rules and regulations, only the very, very essential ones. Then, Mr. Pat Walsh (do you know him?) used to do a lot of the bull work for me. The setting up of schedules and so on. There wasn't much extra work except at the beginning of the year during registration–where Pat Walsh and I helped register students. My ambition, when I was chair, was to bring into the department people who longed to write, and I thought that if we could get, say, seven or eight who were oriented that way, we would have a good nucleus for the magazine which I intended to start later on. And so, for that reason, I was anxious to hire men like Pat Walsh, Sheldon Currie, James Taylor, Kevin O'Brien, and perhaps a few others. That was my main object in being head of the department–to see if I could influence the hiring in that direction.

Walsh: What about the magazine now: *The Antigonish Review*.

MacSween: Well, I had the notion from the time I came here; I was very interested in these little magazines, many received through the Gotham Book Mart and through seeing them advertised in magazines. I had begun to collect many of them early in my career. It seemed to me that this was about the only way we could break into what you'd call the world of culture. In this region we haven't the wealth or the population to break into that world. But we could start a little magazine with a small outlay of cash, and everybody knows how to write–not write well, but everybody knows how to write, and with a little bit of finesse we could get a group here who thought as I did. It wasn't a question of achieving fame but of producing a good magazine. When I was very busy, in the first part of my career here, I knew it couldn't be undertaken, but later on things began to look up. I knew that the Canada Council would help after two years of our publishing if they approved of our work, but it was up to us to produce eight issues that would be of a high quality. And so, we made a move. I forget the year.

Walsh: The year we started was 1969–70.

MacSween: So, I went to see Father Macdonnell, who was Dean, and he approved and told me he'd give me support. Then, I went to see Msgr. MacLellan, who was president, and he told me he had to bring it up before the Council, which was the governing body at that time. I appeared before the Council and gave them my case, and they approved, too. That must have been the spring of '69. And then we started it in '70. At that time, we hired Fr. Brocard Sewell. He had been editor of a magazine in England–*The Aylesford Review*–and later on we made him editor. I actually appointed him myself. I put him in charge of everything. I felt it was mean not to do so, since he had experience as an editor already. But I think I made a mistake because it cut me off from the rest of the editors. I was on the editorial board, but it cut me off from the old group, like yourself, Pat, Sheldon Currie, and George and Gert Sanderson, who had been in at the beginning.

Walsh: The idea is to give new writers a chance?

MacSween: Yes, although it is open to the general public, to those who want to write, but the real hope is that we'll get more and more from Nova Scotia. We'll never make it just a Nova Scotia journal; it will be international, if possible. But we hope it will affect those of a literary bent in our area. It already has to some extent, but not so much as we'd hoped for. Well, the fact that, in this last issue, we published two students whom I taught here, John Rogers and Richard Marchand, is indeed very encouraging. One has a short story and the other has two poems. And it seems to me they are of high quality. Now, those two boys could be famous someday. Without the magazine, I don't think they would even have tried. And there are others, too. And, if we could get one or two like that, say, every five years or so . . .

Walsh: Who would you say are the major people the magazine has introduced so far?

MacSween: Well, we haven't introduced any great writers. I think that's certain.

Walsh: Any good writers; or writers who have achieved some degree of success outside the local community?

MacSween: I really don't know those who achieved great success. Because in most cases, those who write for little magazines don't become famous. Yet almost every important writer started away in little magazines. But, there are a few. Those who seem to shine are Bela Egyedi, who's a Hungarian d.p., and Peter Van Toorn who, it seems to me, is certainly headed for greatness, if he continues. We published him first and then we published most of the stuff he produced after that. So, there must have been something–we were open-minded enough to recognize the talent of these people. They're both very grateful that we gave them a chance but neither one of these men is famous. They could be someday. And there are all kinds of others who are fairly well known. A fellow named Ralph Valgardson, whom we printed a few years ago, put out a collection of short stories last year. And a few others are on the way, and have produced books after we published them. I haven't a very complete list of them. If any of these becomes well known, it would be to at least be in a large center like Toronto. Personally, I'm not very anxious to get the writers that are considered important. Say, the best ten writers in Canada or the best fifty in the States–I'm not anxious to get those people at all.

Walsh: Well, they're going to be published elsewhere anyway, so you want to give other people a chance to develop?

MacSween: Yes, that's right. Those people crowd out the lesser-known writers, they write a great deal and they dominate in a few of our magazines. You ll see them all the time in the *Tamarack Review*, and when they're in, they are well represented. They might have ten poems in one issue. I'd rather give five people two poems.

Walsh: So, actually you see the responsibility of running the magazine as something which looks very much to the future.

MacSween: I suppose there are two goals. The immediate one is to get out the magazine, to pick the best writing we can get. The other one is a kind of hope that some budding writer gets a good start.

Walsh: Over your career here at StFX, what has given you the most satisfaction?

MacSween: The most satisfaction is teaching. I don't know if anybody realizes how much fun I get out of a class. In fact, it's the nearest thing to a Charlie Chaplin show. We do so much laughing that–well, I'll give you an example. I walked into the last class one year, it must be ten years ago now, and I saw a student in the back row whom I hadn't seen before. I thought he had been skipping class all year and had come to the very last one, so I told him to get out. He went out. He waited for me after class and he said, "I'm not in your class at all, but I was in the class next door, and all year long we were listening to this class laughing, so I decided I'd come in to find out what it was all about, and you kicked me out." That was Professor Joseph; he now teaches at the College of Cape Breton.

Walsh: Oh, Brian Joseph, yes.

MacSween: I never taught him, but he was in Fr. Dougie Campbell's class next door and we were laughing so much it could be heard. I think there's more laughing now than when I started, oh! much more. But for one thing, when you, Pat, were in English 350, the class was too large.

Walsh: Yes, 112 people, I remember.

MacSween: But I would say that for the last 15 years, the classes have been great fun for me. I enjoy them. It's as if I were taking a holiday. And I think I teach much better than I ever did, and I get a great deal of work done at the same time. Yet, I've learned in the course of the years to develop an atmosphere of humor in the classes. So that's where I get my real fun–in the classroom. And very rarely do I get a class that's dull or that I feel is dull.

Walsh: What do you expect out of a class? What do you want them to get out of the literature?

MacSween: First of all, I expect them to be pleased with what we're doing. No, I expect them to be wide awake, and that's the purpose of the fun. And I mustn't exaggerate this. It's all spontaneous, spur-of-the-moment stuff. It keeps them alive. But then as for the literature and its effect upon them, first of all, I try to make them see the joy of it all, that there is a pleasure in doing a poem, but not pleasure that gives a laugh, but a kind of passive enjoyment in seeing something well done. The same pleasure you get from watching a horse gallop or a deer go across a pasture. They are both fine works, well-organized works. The poem is well-organized too, it's beautifully put together, and there's an aesthetic enjoyment in the reading of it. As for the subject matter of the poems and the stories, it should always be something that hits you vitally. It should touch life; it should teach life. You should always have to stop and say, "My God, that's true." And so as long as you get the aesthetic pleasure from it, plus the idea that these things are not toys but pointers to thoughts and emotions, to the vital areas of life, then you've got it. The two must go together. The importance of these things is most obvious in the stories. Almost every short story we do is concerned with something dreadfully important. The writer interprets his age, as if he were a sounding board for his age, he vibrates with that age. He produces the short story to interpret some aspect of that age for his readers. And in story after story, this can be seen. In poems, too, but poems are much more difficult, much more subtle in their presentation, and in expression of their ideas. But if you stop and think for a while, you'll find poems doing the very same thing as stories: interpreting the age for the reader. Not that the writer is sitting down and saying, "I' m going to interpret this age," but he'll say, "I'm appalled by this war," and he'll sit down and write his impression of the war, and a hundred years later you read it and you say, "My God! Isn't that true! For that age, for every age." Or a writer feels terribly sad because he's lonely and he doesn't say, "I am going to interpret my age," but, "This loneliness must be expressed; I feel that it must express itself." So he writes about his loneliness. A hundred years later, somebody reads it and says, "Oh! He was like me!" The reader looks back and sees this person, in the early 19th century, being lonely in the middle of a different kind of world. It's like a message sent from a hundred years ago, telling us how human we all are. So, all these works, literary works, are pleasing in their order and arrangement, they're pleasing in the message they give us and they are pleasing in the way they interpret the world. Do you see that?

Walsh: Yes, I believe it, too.

MacSween: The students are most taken up by what the writer is telling, and almost always it's something that intrigues them. Because the writers, being greater men, men of great intellect, they don't waste their time on matters of no importance. They hit home hard; the student must see that this man is writing about something of dreadful importance to him and to everybody. Often it's in the short stories that they get the sense of universality most easily because they are more available to the young mind. Poems have to be interpreted, and I interpret all the poems as well as I can. Students can give their own interpretation if they want, provided they give mine, too. They don't ask me about that now, but years ago they used to ask, "Why can't

I interpret this in my own way?" and I'd say, "You certainly can. Also you can put your interpretation down in the examinations, but then you must put down mine. You're not here to just indulge yourselves without discipline. You'll get my outlook on things first, and then you can have your own. When you're through here, you can throw out all my interpretations and hang on to your own. But if you want to pass, you'll remember mine while in this class."

Walsh: Also, you've spent your life studying these things and practicing the writing and doing this reading and, therefore, I suppose, you speak from the point of view of experience. They should know that as a starting point.

MacSween: It wouldn't hurt them to know that. But, sometimes they add a bit to my own explanation. They do have insights that I miss. Every year, you learn a little bit more about something because a student speaks up. In a class of fifty, you're liable to have five or more, say fifteen, who will add something to your interpretation and in the course of ten years your own ideas are very much enriched. But they individually couldn't do a very good job.

Walsh: Who are your favorites of all the poets or fiction writers you've taught about?

MacSween: Well, at this stage of the game, Ezra Pound is my favorite poet. He was a difficult man. He was very often wrong. But nobody has given literature such dedication as he gave to it. From his early youth on until he died, he was simply swimming in literary matters. It was his whole life and he regarded literature as being of supreme importance. He gave it everything he possessed. The result is you could make an anthology of pieces from Ezra Pound's work, which would loudly proclaim him a great poet. He's so difficult and at the same time so interesting, you could spend your whole life on him and not exhaust the subject at all. With other writers, a half a year on them is enough. They surrender all that they have to give. But with Pound fifty years is not enough time to exhaust his riches. Now, he's the one that interests me most. His life is interesting. He's written a great deal. It's hard to be finished with such an amazing man. And I like Eliot, too. He was a very great poet, a man who always said the important thing and in this matter he surpasses Pound. There is a heaviness, a gravity, about everything he wrote that brands him a man who thinks deeply about everything. But Pound didn't have that ability. Eliot surpasses him there; his words have an impressive gravity, as if he were quoting the Bible. Pound is much more difficult, much more various, in the work he produced, and much more far-reaching in his cultural allusions. His work is like a heavy, thick broth. You bump into mediaeval troubadours, Chinese philosophers, anthropologists, the Greek and Roman classics, the mediaeval classics, oh! Almost everything. The richness of Pound's learning is just amazing. He opens all kinds of avenues. And if you study him, you get interested in Chinese literature, for example, and Japanese literature, and you get interested in anthropology, you get interested in the history of money, and banking, in the mediaeval bankers, in the Provencal troubadours, the works of Dante, Homer, Catullus, Francois Villon. The list is endless. And then he produced music. He wrote a number of musical works that are considered to be very good, and are just coming into their own. You never finish studying Pound. Now that wouldn't be enough, except that every once in a while you come across a poem or a piece of a poem that is so beautiful that you adore it. He's my main interest.

I enjoy many prose writers: But the one who gives me the most pleasure is Evelyn Waugh. I like him much more than other writers who are considered greater, like James Joyce or D. H. Lawrence. I enjoy Waugh more; I read him for fun. But I don't read the others for fun; I read them for work. I may enjoy a piece now and then, but every bit of Waugh is a joy, every letter, every essay, every story, every bit of his diaries. And his letters are coming out soon, I hope. There is nothing about Waugh that I don't enjoy and that's because he's a supreme artist. He couldn't write a short note without its being an artistic triumph. He did it, I believe, without thinking. I read a few years ago a selection of his letters, most of them short notes, making arrangements for dinner, for example, every one of them a masterpiece. And there is a great joy in reading a person who has no failures at all.

But I read everything; I can't even remember at the moment who else I enjoy. I enjoy him–always–and I can read him over and over again.

I enjoy Muriel Spark and Beryl Bainbridge. Also Graham Greene and William Trevor. Most of the novelists I like are English. Among Americans, the one I enjoy most is Walker Percy. He's an important writer because his thought has deep, cultured roots. As far as thinking is concerned, he is above Waugh, but he's not the artist that Waugh is. Yet, he's a very good writer and he writes clear, simple prose, very much like English writing. But very few Americans have the ability to produce novels that are works of art. They write good books, and very often enormous ones, but, so far, they haven't the artistic polish of the

English. They will get it someday. My real pleasure is in reading English novels and American poets. Those two great poets of the century, Pound and Eliot, are American and many of the minor ones are American also: Robert Frost, Wallace Stevens, and some more I can't think of. They are American. They dominate modern poetry. They dominate fiction too, but they haven't the artistic instinct for the novel, so far. It's hard to name more names, there are so many. The table is always spread for us. There are the gross along with the delicate; the fine and the refined; the cultivators of the earth and the searchers of the heavens.

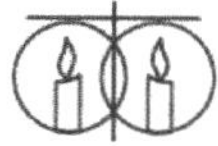

A Classical Sonnet

FOR BISHOP POWER–
on the occasion of his twentieth jubilee
as Bishop of the Diocese of Antigonish

Jesus warned Peter, "They will tie you up
And lead you where you would rather not go."
Centuries later, Ninian was slow
To drink quickly or deeply from that cup.

To leave his Irish home and sit and sup
With Highland Scots, was God's demand to show
His priest what every Saint must come to know–
That this world's joys are destined to corrupt.

Some twenty years ago, our Irish priest
Left his French home and came to pastor us.
Like Ninian he saw his duty clear:

Compassion, kindness, deep and inner peace.
He has kept his priests' and his peoples' trust;
We count as blest the ropes that led him here!

December 3, 1980–the feast of St. Francis Xavier
Presented at the Casket Banquet, 1980

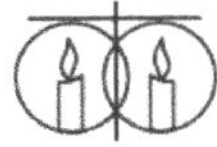

Politics

I served two terms on the Antigonish Town Council, one before going to Ireland for my PhD, and a second after returning from my studies. Serving on Council was a profound learning experience. Council was never dull, and it was often a contentious exercise. I loved it. When defeated for a third term, it turned out to be a liberating experience–life went on, and I was freed up to go on for new adventures; having learned much through Council, I was ready for the challenges within the University.

*

The leaving of Council led to perhaps the greatest one-liner of my teaching career:

The first term I had been elected to Council, my youthful exuberance led me to go door to door to every home in Antigonish. I got the highest vote of any Councilor ever, and was immediately tabbed as a "comer." Then I had to interrupt my political career to go to Ireland for my PhD. When I returned again I was re-elected easily for a second term and ended up on significant portfolios of Council. Tough decisions were demanded. As Chair of the Town School Board, along with my entire Board, we made a decision to restructure the system which entailed eliminating one principal when we amalgamated the two town schools. The principal went public and ballistic, and the CBC and CTV came from Halifax to cover the brouhaha. My children were harassed at school, I became the bad guy, and under instruction from the town solicitor, the Board was told we could not speak publicly about internal personnel matters. The total Board was summoned to Halifax by the Nova Scotia Minister of Education, who told us we had to reverse our decision. We told him in conscience we could not that. I told him, "Mr. Minister, *you* can change the decision if you want to," and pushed the files across the table to him. The Minister immediately pushed them back, and the meeting was over. It became clear that I did not have the chance of a snowball in hell of surviving in the election. Against advice of friends, and to the delight of opponents, I refused to resign the seat. Having done what was right, I would let the people throw me out, rather than quit. I bounced pretty high when they tossed me out. Among eight candidates, I narrowly edged a little old widow lady for seventh place.

The next evening I was due to face my large film course of some 150 students, all of whom had followed the campaign with great interest. I entered the auditorium to an unusual silence, as if I had entered a wake at MacIsaac's Funeral Home. No chatter as usual. With my head down I trudged slowly to the center of the amphitheater, stood silent with my head bowed. Then I slowly slipped off my shoes, stepped back and took off my hat and placed it tenderly on top of the shoes. Building the dramatic moment I stepped to the left, tilted my head, and surveyed the hatted shoes. No sounds yet from the crowd. I stepped to the right and surveyed the scene again. Nobody would ask the question–so I asked it myself, pointing dramatically to the hat on the shoes: "Do you know what that is?" No one offered a response, some beginning to think perhaps that I had been unhinged by such an ignominious defeat. I answered for them: "That, folks, is Pat Walsh–with the shit kicked out of him." The roar of laughter wiped out the election results, freed me from pity, and let me throw my freed-up schedule into a year of art work. As Satchel Paige said, "Never look back–they might be gaining on you."

This bit of doggerel was inspired when Donald Gillis, the publisher of *The Casket,* suffered a heart attack and was dead on the slab at St. Martha's Hospital. But after his bout of cardiac arrest, his revival, and triumphant return to work, his birthday party was a bit emotional for his staff. We thought of it in fateful, cosmic terms.

The Story of Donald in the Dell

Our publisher, Donald Gillis, a fearless man in print,
Is quite a spiffy dresser, with ne'er a hint of lint.
Thick silver locks adorn his noble brow,
A hue inspired by his daughters and his frau!
He used to huff and puff like an engine on a track–
Until one day on Pill Hill, he woke up on his back.
He thought the warnings to desist were nothing more than jest–
'Til he woke with Doc O'Brien pounding on his chest.
Our friend, stretched out, dead and cold as cod,
Found his bare and naked soul, face to face with God!
We know the four last things we all shall have to face,
And Donald Leonard shivered over where he'd find his place:
A golden palace in a heavenly little dell?
Or a bubbling pool of s___, in a putrid fiery hell?
Donald Leonard trembled like a goose before a cook,
For the Maker checked his entries–but Huntley'd kept the book!
The Maker looked through Donald like humans look through glass–
And saw a Man o'War–or at least a horse's . . . class!
So Donald took a gamble, grasped the one last desperate thread,
And asked his fearsome Maker, to check the final spread!
The Maker shook his long white hair and laughed,
He considered such a rabid bettor daft.
So He motioned Donald Leonard to what looked like a deep well,
And when Donald looked down, he was gazing into hell:
And there was Jack MacMillan, in his office chewing nails,
And there was Eddie Gavel, piling greasy rags in pails.
And Tommy Glen was cutting mile-high stacks of stock,
And hirsute Derrick Landry driving Heidelberg amok!
There was Valerie shooting eight million PMTs
[Photo Mechanical Transfer]
And Linda wrapped in masking tape from her eyebrows to her knees.
Paula Lowe was setting Chinese type for TAR,

[*The Antigonish Review*]
And John DeCoste was slugging doubles at a bar!
Bonnie was at Town Council for a meeting of 16 years,
And Dawn's crossword puzzle was driving her to tears.
Ann was in the chapel, praying for one and all,
With Darlene on line 2, with her thirty-thousandth call!
Margie was correcting the Deacon's punctuation,
And Huntley was moaning for a Christmas-tree vacation.
The bindery crew was wrestling with a 43 section issue,
And Joey was folding a Michelin job–on tissue!
Rita couldn't move, stuck to Donald's rug with gum,
And when she cried for help, Mr. Chadwick only hummed!
Gail MacDougal was frozen in the ice up at the rink,
And Eileen Cameron Henry was bathing in the sink!
Blaise was off, with you know who, in costly Halifax,
Poor Terry's fingers caught in Robertson's damn fax.
The most frightening sight and sound that made Donald even paler–
Was Jackie Walsh–cursing and swearing like a sailor!
The Maker said to Donald, "I can send you down there, too,
But you'll have to stay forever in your office with–guess who?"
And Donald, he was tempted; it might be a busty babe–
But Donald hesitated, when he thought of trusty Gabe!
But then the crafty Donald, made a pitch to God on High,
And, his argument completed, brought tears to the All-Seeing Eye.
For the poor souls Donald saw in their suffering and strife
Were no different in hell, than what they were in life.
So God sent Donald back to us, that is the simple story:
And thus he still is dead–but just in Purgatory!
The moral lesson of this little piece of verse
Is just "Don't worry, folks–it can't get any worse!"
There's no sense in complaining, in blowing out your gasket–
We're all stuck here together, in this living hell: THE CASKET!

Happy Birthday, Donald!

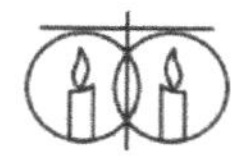

Chapter 9
Retreat to the Mountains 1983–84

I had just purchased cross-country skis for winter exercise and had tried them out on the flat field at the high school. No problems. Here I was at a psychological low—the weather was contributing to my psychic state: a severe ice storm was due. Hadn't I learned about the great simpatico of weather and emotional moods in Emily Brontë's great novel, *Wuthering Heights*? Looking back on the situation, it now appears overly dramatic, but for me at the time it was bloody real. With the best of intentions, I had done something to help a friend in trouble, but the result was to put my wife and family in difficulty—because I had not considered the repercussions of my actions on them. "The Little Prince" was still alive and as stupidly selfish as ever. I had betrayed my professed values and responsibilities. This was the Station of my personal cross: Jesus Falls the Third Time. Three Our Fathers, three Hail Marys, and three Glory Be's wouldn't do it this time.

As the ice storm loomed near, I packed my cross-country skis in my van and took off for the 12 km. BEAVER MOUNTAIN CROSS-COUNTRY course. No one else was so foolish that day. Alone on the mountain, I strapped my skis on and launched myself into the wind. If I was to die in this storm, it would be my just reward. And the possibility was there, I realize now, more now than then, that I might have fallen and not been found in time. So, on I forged, up hill and down dale, across little bridges over streams, like Macbeth, "stepped in so far to go back t'were twice as BAD"—and another marvelous possibility emerged, when I returned to my van having conquered the 12 km. without falling even once! A feat never to be remotely approached again.

Surely it was a sign? Not really. But I left Beaver Mountain, and returned home determined to change. And to prove the earnestness of my changed state I decided on a sabbatical year of exile to separate myself from all that I had nearly lost.

You will note that this year of retreat gave me ample opportunity to write: not just on a major play, but on a personal level exploring deeply through poetry the relationships I had endangered. Exile and/or retreat, Nelson, British Columbia, proved a reformative renewal of my commitments, in faith, hope, and love. The point: relationships must never be taken for granted–they must be retained, revived, and renewed every day of one's life.

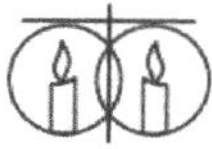

separation

The rain is dripping on my window sill
and Elephant Mountain is hiding in the night fog
while I am hidden from my lovers
in a distant paradise they cannot see
either in their waking or their dreams

Yet in my solitary cell
my mind's eye sees them in familiar places
walking up a grassy walk
pressing buttons on a new dryer
turning up the TV when the dishwasher whines
lying in fresh green rooms
wending through the jungle rec room in the dark
picking steak and lobster from their teeth
counting heads in an early Casket
lounging lizards lured by blaring videos
locked in high-rise castles overlooking Bedford Basin

I know every broken bush struggling red maple
dripping clothes line dirty sock and
muddy boot print on white tile

to them I am in darkness beyond the horizon
in a paper land of shiny brochure
in a brown blotch in the big atlas under the TV

but I am like a God the father
for though invisible to them they are visible to me
in wakening reverie and tossing dreams
living in my every thought and prayer
What I do I do for them and spend my 40 weeks
in exile for their sakes and my own
for when I return mimicking Moses
from Mount Sinai and Jesus from the desert
I will have faced my maker on the mountain
and my temptation in the sand returning
to try to love my dear ones better than before

so every day I rise and bless the sun
that has seen my lovers earlier and warms me
with memories of where they are

and I climb the hill to pray
so the winds hearing my sighs
will blow some memory of me
across mountains plains and lakes and marshes
so my lovers will know the rain from the west
falling on them is salty with my tears

September 15/83 12 a.m.

The father/son theme appears again, this time in relation to my oldest son, Francis.

for Fran

"When they came to the place which God had told him about, Abraham built an altar and arranged the wood on it. He tied up his son and placed him on the Altar, on top of the wood. Then he picked up the knife to kill him. But the angel of the Lord called to him from heaven, 'Abraham, Abraham!'" Genesis 22:9–11

You kicked your way out of the womb
restless then as now impatient with your lot
railing against restraint believing
you can grasp any star you can see.
I your father wild-eyed in panic
scattered early morning commuters on 128
maniacal in the calm face of your mother

remarkable in her understanding quiet wisdom
of Mary about to share a miracle of creation

the nurse held you up squished bawling
still bloody screaming at me
for the crime of fathering you

so you get even by being like me
in your blood impetuous
in your forays against the world vulnerable
in Dublin your hypochondria faked me out

racing again against destiny trying to snatch you away
the pain of your appendix bursting
screaming frightening me

did Abraham feel this fear
when the Lord ordered him to sacrifice Isaac

heart aches when the Lord asks us to die
in ourselves or in our sons

did Abraham feel this joy
when the angel stayed his thrust
as I when Mister Kelly pronounced you saved

my constant companion in every byway of Ireland
you did not cumber me you lighted my life
exploring a strange new country
of filial communion my boon companion

crossing from Stephen's Green
to the quays for my lost buttons
leaving a frightened boy returning a young man
somewhere on Grafton street severing
the umbilical cord of my paternity

now an adversary kicking to be free
once more knowing all the answers
when so shortly before you had clung to me
a little monkey chained to an Italian organ-grinder

by wiliness alone I survived two days
on the racquetball court
in former days you would have slain me
the king is dead long live the king

instead you smile quietly looking suddenly
like your mother understanding how defeat
is enough
loving me seeing my vulnerability
loving me seeing my need
loving me for what I'd like to be
not for what I am

when I see your room I grieve
for how much you are like me

but when you analyze the StFX basketball team
in the backseat on the way to Fredericton
or spend long nights studying
instead of lazing about
I rejoice in how much you are like your mother
for she has made you whole as likewise me

my greatest gift to you
the potential to be realized by her gift of life
like Abraham I praise my Lord for the miracle
He has wrought allowing me to share
in His creation of a son
asking me to surrender you to His will
I do so content
the Lord shall do good through you

my joy my boy my son

happy birthday–today you are a man

"I make a vow by my own name–the Lords is speaking–that I will bless you because you did this and did not keep back your son from me." Genesis 22:16
Patrick Walsh 11 p.m. Oct. 11, 1983

I am struck by the nuts and bolts detail of a life alone. When I am in the rough and tumble of a rich family life at home, I don't have time or inclination to deal with such particulars, as begin to fill the absence of family.

Saturday, September 17, 1983 11:20 a.m.

From the laundry room of the Lombardy Court Apartments:

Dearest Jacqueline and Mary, Francis, Monica, Greg, and Becca—love you all so much—think of you so often—here are the latest notes from the Kootenays. Got your first letter yesterday afternoon, Jackie. Thanks muchly. In spite of your nasty cartoon about baseball [inexplicably, she is a Yankee fan]—and you didn't have to explain that it reflected your views—I got the point immediately.

Glad to hear everyone is well.

Jackie—if you want to get rid of the Ford—just don't let it drop—let me know—I'll call Ronnie MacGillivray at Keltic Motors—and put it on their lot to see if they can sell it—we might make a little something on it.

Well, the walking is going great—I'm seriously thinking of going in the Terry Fox run tomorrow morning (I'm walking, though). I'm back on the handball court now—they have only one here—tough to book. I played a little warm up with an older fellow Wednesday, just easily coasting—no challenge. Then I played a faculty member Thursday—he was no contest. BUT there were two young fellows from town: slim, wiry, quick, etc., who were really pounding the ball. Set up a match with me. They watched me play the other fellow and left after a couple minutes thinking I was a pushover. Yesterday (Friday) I got warmed up—very carefully—(slight hamstring pull in the left leg Thursday) felt good, psyched up—and blew out to a 15 to 0 lead on the young fellow with a dazzling array of hard, soft, fast, slow, dipsy-doodle serves—and coasted (well not really—I had to work hard) to a 21–10 victory. In the second game, I let down a bit and he got a 16–4 lead—so I was raging back and the score was me 15, he 19, when the time was up! I was feeling good—the hamstring was well warmed up and feels great today. I play the other young fellow Sunday p.m. After that match yesterday, I gave Colin Browne a lesson—he and Fred Wah, the other full-time writing profs are going to play. Colin has all the natural moves and instincts—he should progress rapidly and be quite good. Fred will be good because he's a very intense poet—and they are both in shape.

Met Clarke Blaise, the novelist. Very fine fellow. We had lunch together—he's a real baseball nut—so there! And he lives at a motel and has satellite TV—gets every ballgame broadcast—we intend to get together for some of the playoffs.

Everything is going well at school. I've made good notes for the students from my studying—a good secretary—but nothing like the services at StFX—my God we're spoiled, I realize now.

Today I pick up my new table–and attach the legs and get my bedroom set up for work. Colin may put off my colloquium presentation 'til later–but I'm very flexible. My classes have gone well–so I'm not the least bit worried any more.

The weather has been great–rain sometimes at night–but days as gorgeous as any ever.

Saw a girl with a JAZZ-X sweater–she got it from a friend of a friend at X. Nice girl from Calgary in the writing program.

I think I mentioned that Sr. Grace and the Sister from Antigonish are going to have me to supper some time. Called the Sisters of St. Martha in Kamloops the other night. They're going to take a weekend off when I go up to visit–which will be some time before the snow flies.

They have a strange bug here–looks like this.

I saw one in the hallway–stepped on it and kept walking. They live in cedar trees–and I was warned about them: they are STINK BUGS–smell just awful. If they get on your clothes, they must be washed–just as bad as skunk, so everybody lets them alone. I saw one in the office yesterday and just let him wander around. He eventually left. They say this is going to be a bad year for them because it's been so wet. None in the town or apartment, thank goodness, but lots at the school which is up the mountain in the forest.

I make my lunch now everyday–getting down the meals. Bought a cheap Korean thermos–guaranteed five years for $2.99. Realize now I should have bought a better one. It's plastic–that's why it won't break–but it doesn't keep anything hot or cold either! I'm living with it.

Bought some pumpernickel this week. Also broiled myself salmon steak–3 pieces one night for a treat–$1.65–cheaper than hamburger here! Also had a little steak after my Tuesday 3-hour class–$1.50–catching on Ma!

Am enjoying Mass every morning at the Cathedral–remember you all of course. On Mon. & Wed. I have to leave before communion, but on the other days I stay–no bus to catch–enjoy the singing–communion under both species. I sit in the back and get up last and empty the chalice.

This morning at Mass I saw a little old lady who lives in my apartment block. She has very quietly and privately been passing me at the apartment. She looked sad and lonely. After Mass I smiled at her and said hello–Ian, one of the people I met after Mass at coffee, invited us over to the Chancery/rectory this morning–and the little old lady went, too. Well everybody left early because there's a big youth conference on this weekend–so we were left alone. Her name is Clara Tinklebank, born in Greece of English father, Greek mother. She's a writer, so from 9:30 to 10:30 I got her life story: fantastic, & sad. She's going to invite me up to tea someday. She lives on a pension of $435 a month and pays $310 at least for her apartment. Tough life. More to follow I'm sure.

On Saturdays, 'cause Mass is at 9, I don't get up at 6 and eat breakfast as I do during the week. So at 10:30 I walked home via Johnny's Bakery, where they have a rack of marked down goodies! Last week I had two stale Danish for 30 cents. This week two apple fritters (fantastic) with 4 broken cookies for 70 cents. I saved the cookies for dessert tomorrow. First sweets I've purchased. Hope it's not the beginning!

Got my black shoes repaired–$20–but they're in top shape–guy did a good job. And the Welcome Lady gave me a $2 ticket. Also got some waterproofing for my boots. They're really into that stuff here–it's pine tar and beeswax mix–no animal fats or any synthetics: you grease up the shoes by hand–the rubbing hard from hand rub makes the stuff penetrate–then you bake the shoes in the oven set to 150 degrees. When the oven is ready, shut it off, then tuck the shoes in the oven–out they come beautiful. I'm going to double-coat–then keep it up as necessary to preserve the waterproofing. The stuff is great–doesn't stink and is not greasy.

I'm on a one-a-day vitamin now–just to make sure my eating doesn't do me in. I follow the nutrition clinic pattern–I find I'm really at the proper pace: I feel hungry in the a.m. Then I get hungry at noon–then I'm hungry when I get home.

Don't have any snacks at night–lots of juice (I did have popcorn one night for a football game). Think I'm going to have eggs and beans with pumpernickel tonight. Have a half of a salad for snack tomorrow.

I'm going to get my brown shoes repaired, too. (By the way, the Welcome Wagon Lady got me $2 off on my vitamins, too!)

I signed up for a hiking program in the recreation committee here. First organizational meeting Thursday night. NO climbing, just walking. There's a glacier just up the road from here–the ice-capped mountains I see in the distance up the valley.

I'm really learning a lot of things about drama–that I didn't have time for before. I know it's going to help me rewrite *Dieppe* and improve it immensely. I plan to get that done before Christmas.

Colin is going to pick up my table this afternoon–so my writing at home here will be beginning in earnest shortly.

Results of my walking and controlled eating are showing results already–and I feel good–my wind is improving.

I'm anxiously awaiting the other pictures of the family. Wrote to Jim and Mary twice. To Sheldon. To Fran & Mary Ann.

Four kids killed here in a car crash last weekend. Went off the road–and that's fatal here cause of the mountains. People from the hills really race their cars around here–no mufflers–nor Hollywoods–so lots of roaring up and down the valley.

A guy named Larry lives next door. Works some kind of strange night shift. He's built–works out lifting weights and has his head shaved like Kojack–and wears shades–and is soft-spoken. He used to have the apartment I'm in–and a procession of beautiful young girls keep coming to the door asking for Larry–when I answer–they run away. Tell Kevin O'Brien, this being a writer is not as glamorous as it's cracked up to be–I'm in league with Clara Tinkleback!

The bus is great for getting to school–and there are only about four drivers–I know them all now. They are polite, too–they wait for little old ladies–never start up until the people who get on are seated. Very civilized!

This is NDP country–hard hit–no employment–no construction. Lyle Christiansen is our Member of Parliament.

Went to a faculty forum–this is not a University–but a bastarditic creation of Selkirk College (in Castlegar) and the University of Victoria. It resulted from the government's deliberate policy to get rid of the old Notre Dame College that was associated with StFX and gave their degrees from StFX. They are now trying to survive the Bennet government cutbacks. They were mixed happy/sad this week because the Minister of Education didn't shut them down–but no increase in budget for next year. Pressure is to accept technical students, computer students, etc., and get rid of writing, music, theatre, fine arts, etc. The Philistines are roaming in the mountains. Colin wants me to talk to their faculty forum about StFX's fundraising. I've been discussing such problems with him.

At lunch I met the "Fine Arts" Fellows who teach graphics and art work, etc. They're having a show–and we're simpatico.

The more I see of the world, folks, the more grateful I am to a bountiful God for all the blessings and riches of spirit and body we have in Antigonish. I pray for you and love you all with all my heart and soul. Your loving husband and father, Pat

The news from Antigonish of friends who were separating shook me up in my exiled state of mind in Nelson. "Separation" meant so much more to me, being separated. I was beginning to realize how painful the loss of a healthy relationship can be.

On Receiving News of the Separation of Friends

4,453 miles separate us
even the sun spinning through space
and earth twirling on axis
cannot catch us in the same hour

I sleep while you rise
you sleep while I gaze at the setting sun

tossing in a half-empty bed
I turn to nothing instead of palpable flesh
a train whistle winds down the valley
drowning the imagined hum of your breathing

am I fevered I cannot tell what is hot is hot
only in contrast to a cold foot jolting me from a dream

conceived half-male half-female Duke and Carmen
body and soul ripped asunder cast from womb again
born to a loneliness better borne in days
of unknowing youth when dreams lay ahead

today I live on memories of happy moments
the curve of your cheek an eyebrow askance
the glow of love in your eye your quiet laugh
your hand clasping my hand during Mass

sweet agony empty fullness deep-felt numbness
glowing darkness spinning stillness happy sadness

metaphors of a love more deeply felt
because impossible to express in flesh

a love metaphysical stretching
across a whole country

a love unable to be taken for granted
never passing away
because unable to be fulfilled

seemingly conquered by space defeated by time
subject to the laws of nature
days and nights passing never to be regained
one day closer to the end never able to be relived
lost opportunity begetting lost opportunity
in perverse birth of love not made

lost days dying darkly into history
never to dawn again

yet I am not unhappy nor am I victim
unmanned by tears of self-pity

for I am waxing strong facing the late-rising sun
gliding down morning mountain in glorious joy
for time cannot defeat me

I climb a hill each dawning day
no matter if shrouded in gloomy cloud

for I enter a blessed spot
in the Cathedral of Mary Immaculate
or the Church of the Blessed Sacrament
on 4th Street Nelson

I seek these morning meetings
Because living alone facing my self
I know my need my weakness my emptiness
turbulent visions stalk my dreams full of violence
a kraken clamoring to surface
breaking waves on the placid mirror of my mind

yet in a miracle of quiet ecstasy
through the blessed mutter of Father Wilson
or *paisan* Santopinto or the punctual Fr. Malone
I am united to the Mass
and to the life of God in man

there is no time no nor space
to keep me from my love
time ceases to exist I am in the ineffable eternal
I am who am with Christ ever on the cross
dying that I may live
that my darling wife may live

that my sons and daughters may live forever
to be together

I float free of space and time
to the oneness of eternity on my own cross
Christ's cross
in His timeless act of love forever present
to the subsisting existence
beyond the before and after of mere mortals

and at that moment of communion
I am with you Jacqueline and darlings
in eternity and love
strengthened by your strength
made whole by your goodness
comforted by your concern
buoyed by your thought of me
on my finger a gold ring etched with two candles
glow intertwined bound by the cross of Christ

on the paten the priest raises the bread and wine
earthly work and toil
my thoughts my words my work
my failings my walking my very breathing
offered up for you my wife
my miracle of goodness and loving flesh

for you my children arrows in my quiver
love of my love flesh of my flesh
blood of my blood dreams of my psyche
life of my vitals living on
an image of our love hers and mine

all that I am and have and do
are offered up to God each morning
and in return not to be outdone
He gives me his own son

his flesh to eat his blood to drink
elemental act and I have life in me
that will never die a life we can share
so I am with you and therefore happy
because my happiness
lies in wanting what is good for you

I am in penance here in the mountains
climbing to peaks sacred places
telling it on the mountain
Olympus of Zeus Ararat of Noah Sinai of Moses
Snowden of Wordsworth Mont Blanc of Shelley
and appropriately Toad Mountain of Walsh

I shall return to you across space through time
able to love you better when next we meet
more understanding more diligent in service
more patient more giving more tender
more loving

'til then be happy dear wife and dear children
for I am with you whenever I enter
the timeless miracle of the Mass
and it is every moment of every day
somewhere in the world

my puny human efforts are made infinite
in glory peace and love
through Christ our Lord amen

these things I believe
your happy husband and father
Patrick

10:40 p.m. Sunday October 2, 1983

Going home for Christmas break!

Thoughts on leaving Nelson to be with you again

joy follows pain as flowers follow rain
after black night I welcome daylight's blue
crying because I live as one not two
questioning why my loneliness is pain
each dream becomes a technicolor stain
laying before my sleeping eyes purview
intimate memorable visions of you
nightly forming a connubial chain
enchanting thoughts of seeing you once more
warm the coolness of the miles between us
as lightning leaps from cloud to mother earth
love of you creates poetic metaphor
so my love flows into your animus
happiness melds our souls' eternal birth

to Jacqueline December 8, 1983

[Freud and any first-year English Prof could have a field day with this sonnet–shades of Duke's sonnet to Carmen.]

Back into exile.

Sunday, February 12, 1984, 5:15 a.m.

from the Laundry Room of the Magnificent Lombardy Court in the Sno-Fest Capital of Beautiful British Columbia

Nelson may be Sno-Fest [sic] capital–but we have no snow in the valley. Temperatures of 11–12 degrees Centigrade. The snow is back in Antigonish: -16 Centigrade this past week. And I saw on the American weather forecast for Chester, Massachusetts, in the good old Berkshire Hills–the coldest place in the United States at -40 Fahrenheit! It's great to be here in the tropics, but up on the mountains all around there's lots of snow!

I put off writing for a week and a half–but I'm running out of underwear and socks–so I had to do the wash today–so here's your letter. I was hoping my fingers wouldn't be so numb, but that neck arthritis is still giving me trouble. My second and third fingers and a bit of my thumb on my right hand are numb most of the time now. I'm still getting therapy, which is helping–but one nerve appears to be pinched. It feels queer and tingly when I write–but I have to–I'm a writer. So here I am.

The skiing is giving me trouble. I fall on the slightest hills. I guess I'm just too afraid–too heavy–can't control the skis: when I start to fall I go into a slide like Jackie Robinson going into second base. So now my left hip is aching. My feet are so wide–I get stuck in the cross-country track and stumble forward. I did manoeuver one big hill perfectly–that's what gives me hope. But the little ones give me so much trouble. I think I'm going to try snowshoeing instead. I won't get as far, but I should get there in one piece.

Now I've started working out again in the gym, playing basketball with Jim Hoffman who used to play for the University of Victoria Varsity. I can't stop him from driving on me, though: he's taller than I am–and in shape. I have begun to deny him the baseline, but when, if he gets me under the basket, he puts up a backwards layup. I really get frustrated. He's too nice to foul flagrantly, but sometimes I have the urge to give him my considerable hip! Yesterday I drove by him myself for the first time–maybe there's hope. I gave him a scare when I got hot from about 16 feet out–now he guards me closely all the time.

I can hold my own at foul-shooting (21) and the perimeter shooting game around the key–in fact I have the record at 32 pts. In 21–and shut him out yesterday without a single win–although he has won every game of one-on-one!

I do get to watch the NCAA B-ball on TV and today the Celtics vs. the 76ers will be my weekend recreation. I'm pretty busy these days. The Theatre department is putting on three of the student scripts from my seminars–so I have to go to some of the rehearsals. They are also doing two radio plays by my students.

The government Minister of Education has agreed–after terrific pressure from the Mayor of Nelson and many other mayors and councilors of the interior of BC (representing 160,000 voters)–to go back to the Cabinet for reconsideration of a two-year moratorium on closing DTUC–so there's hope in some quarters the school may survive. I don't think it will. In three months, everybody will go home and the Cabinet will just say "NO"–and that will be it. However, I say this to only selected people!

The Sisters of St. Martha in Antigonish are clipping the job ads in Maritime newspapers–and my friends, the Johnsons, are operating a consulting service to help people even 5,000 miles away! Their mail pouch with the job ads gives the people here some hope: somebody somewhere cares! But the unions–I am afraid to say–are wrecking BC. Seven Safeway grocery stores closed last week–couldn't make it go–to the stock clerks: the guys putting cans on a shelf were wanting a raise. They are currently [1984] getting $18.36 an hour with 45 days off per year. That's $38,000.00 per year! Un-be-leeve-a-bull! [*Thirty-four years later in 2018 the BC Provincial Government minimum wage is $12.65!*]

Last Saturday night, "Johnson" Johnson turned 40 and had a big party. I went. Had a fantastic feed of Mexican food–enchiladas of all description–exotic fruits–and vegetables–and drank Tijuana Sunrise: a tequila and orange drink. Dancing on the first floor–the students were there. It all sounded to me like Michael Jackson's hair was on fire! So I went upstairs where the DTUC faculty were jamming. Kevin, you would have loved it.

Went home early, though–tired–but full. My own cooking is developing. I am into T-bone steak, long grain rice, and, of course, another gigantic 3-bean salad. Cooked Chinese food, chicken chow mein, Friday night–did the noodles myself–pretty good: but I don't think Wong's is in any trouble! I'm learning to use the broiler better. I caught on that I should move the rack down a notch: I'd be sitting there listening to my barbequed chops, or chicken, or steaks sizzle, and I'd hear funny little puff sounds. I began to peek and the stuff was catching fire, exploding and going out, then doing it again. Now I have moved the rack down and things are better: I don't have to open all the windows and the door anymore. The dogs in Nelson don't come hanging around me anymore at the bus stop.

I blew last week's reading at the Nursing Home. Tried to read them J. D. Salinger's story "The Laughing Man," one of my favorites–but they couldn't follow the New York lingo. I had been encouraged because they had responded very enthusiastically to Frank O'Connor's story "My Oedipus Complex" a week before. But now I know what they can handle: they need a simple story line, not too idiosyncratic, so I'll try Ring Lardner this week.

It's great having breakfast every morning with the Sisters and Father Malone: great fun. I'm working like a beaver on my next project–a story line given to me by one of my superior students here. If I can get some funding from the College I would love to collaborate with him on a screenplay. The gist of the story is about a young man who is studying computers at college. He falls in love with an aboriginal girl who is modern and trying to break away from the old ways by becoming a public health nurse for her people. But the young fellow's father, a fisherman, is disabled in an accident at sea–but saved by the whales! The son has to go home to take over and save the family fishing business. He gets friendly with the girl's grandfather–a Kwakiutl chief–and has an experience in Porrier Pass in which he communicates mentally with the whales. He becomes fascinated and works out eventually by computer that the whales' songs & the aboriginal chants are related to the old creation myths about the Thunderbird from the Skies! It turns out that extraterrestrials are communicating with the whales (whose nervous system is closest to human beings) who will survive the atomic holocaust humans are bringing on themselves. (All that from that Kwakiutl smoked salmon Jim Hoffman fed me!)

Love, Pat

*

Footnote to the above: When I got home to Antigonish, I applied for a summer research grant to work on the "Kwakiutl" screenplay. A few days later, up in the coffee room, the Dean of Arts was holding forth on the summer grants. He gleefully reported that the Research Committee had received the most cockamamie request in the history of the Committee: someone had applied to do research on whales instead of humans being contacted by aliens to warn the earth of immanent destruction. Again I was ahead of time: any Star Trek fan will tell you to Google *Star Trek IV: "Whale Probe."* The rejection might be related to the fact that the Dean of Arts was a Harvard Business School graduate.

Terry Fox, the young Canadian who lost a leg to cancer and set out to run across the country to raise money for cancer research, passed through Antigonish. I missed meeting or seeing him or cheering him on. He became a national hero. I felt I owed him a bit of a run in Nelson. The problem: I thought the race started in the city and would go out to Taghum Bridge outside of town. When I went to the race site on Baker Street, they informed me that all the runners were already at the starting point at Taghum Bridge and were going to run INTO town, not OUT of town. To just give up and go home was not a moral choice I could live with. Here's what happened.

The Terry Fox Run
Nelson, British Columbia

good in ten tions
good in ten tions
good in ten tions
good in ten tions
as my feet pat-
ter on the main

streets of Nelson
B C my mind
racing because
I have not planned
how to get to
Taghum Bridge six
miles outside of
town down a long
the Kootenay
river winding
toward Castlegar
*
too late too late
to hitch a ride
so I decide
in perverse pride
to walk the route
in *reverse* and
set out down Bak-
er Street toward Gov-
ernment Road pass-
ing empty tab-
les waiting for
cups of water
for weary run-
ners later in
the morning
clev er think ing
clev er think ing
*
so up the hill I go alone against the traffic
out of town looking back over my shoulder
to see more and more of Nelson the further I go
along the river gliding peacefully
below the snake of railway track to my right

*

clumps of waiting women stomp the ground
in turnouts by the side of the road
like wading birds shifting feet in shallow water
fighting off the chilling air
*

I glide along alone conscious of the tune
of a different drummer
into a silent world of God's grandeur
*

sounds of humans sink rumblings of nature rise
the drip and drizzle of water off jagged rocks
looming far above me
far below on the mirror of the river to the right
a gull skims along the surface looking for a fish
*

I feel a master of paradise until the honk of goose
snaps my gaze from down to up
and I see the skein of geese above
laboriously keeping formation with a short-stemmed V
missing those geese fallen by the way
and above them even gray clouds swirl in unseen movement
shrouding the peaks of mountains
scraggy with trees sentinels in silence
on the slide-scarred sides of mountains
hovering unseen but felt far above
my now humbled thoughts
*

I turn my gaze to the rocks
hanging above me to my left man-made cliffs
mountains blasted away to fill the valleys
paved with roads of good intention
*

I see where wind and water and tenacious roots
have cracked new wrinkles in the cliffs

the sign beware falling rock
warns we cannot stem the tide of time
*
the pattern of man-made blasts
are mere scratches on the face
of lava-lined diagonals telling how eons ago
these rocks were heaved toward the heavens
with subterranean force more powerful
than our atomic toys
*
giant slabs overhanging
listening for the some-day summons of gravity
loom over my head notions of mortality
heavy heavy what hangs over
my lonely soul so far from home alone unknown
with a card in my wallet "I am a catholic
in case of an accident please call a priest"
*
coming down the long hill ahead
the flash of cruiser lights
heads appear over the crest
and two lithe young men in prime side by side
float by hardly seeming to touch the heavy earth
muscles glistening aware of one another
as partners yet foes in quest for laurel
only one of whom will bear the prized leaf
they do not see me intent on future days
they slide through the present
like spring ice toward a restful ocean
*
now a straggle of also-rans knocking more loudly
on the impassive earth feet plumping plodding
slapping the pavement
chuffing breaths like frothing horses
more angular than the leaders flailing at unseen forces

dragging against their forced urge to flow
ripples in their bodies more violent
than those on the timeless river
flowing below them the opposite way–
my way
*

then a woman arms akimbo
next a rush of runners who begin to notice me
going the other way cap in hand
their eyes searching aware of not winning
wanting to but knowing their mortality
hearing it hiss out of themselves
like tires going slowly flat
*

now children some having fun
not knowing why they run away from cancer
larking their way chatting challenging one another
in sudden spurts as though the finish line
was not four miles down the road
*

then a man and woman walking dogs
a young girl blonde hair whipping side to side
in Dionysiac frenzy
military type stiff-backed beer-belly hanging over belt
aide-de-camp wife in plus fours with
cap pulled low over eyes keeping step keeping up
*

then afro-rainbow-haired white-faced clown
in wildly checkered pants honking his horn
like Clarabell as he passes
running forward yet seeming to run
backwards at the same time
they're sure to get him on TV at the finish
even though he won't win tricking his way into
an Andy Warhol fifteen seconds of fame

*

a blind man head tilted sideways up toward a dark heaven
his dog ahead of him by stiff leather halter
a young woman with dog at his elbow
looking for unseen pitfalls

*

now the wheelchair people wrapped in blankets
pushed by cheery folks chattery bouncy
who probably will walk the same way
through the pearly gates

*

and then the stragglers the trudgers
the father urging the son at his waist
to maybe run a little now
the woman who yells
“hey you’re going the wrong way”

*

but suddenly I’m alone again
aware of the quietness feeling my feet
realizing I am flowing down the hill
going down like the river to an endless mother sea
like the mountains to a resting place below
but quicker

*

did Terry Fox still feel the pain
in the leg that wasn’t there
was it greater than the pain in the bleeding foot
he hobbled on

*

I’ve seen the pattern of human life
in my race-in-reverse
the quick and the last who shall be first

*

the starting line my finishing line
the tattered banner Annual Terry Fox Run

flapping in the breeze of passing trucks
on the near side of Taghum Bridge
I don't feel the pain in my feet anymore
unknown unseen by the TV cameras
but happy because I've walked
some BC miles Terry never reached
and because I didn't see him
when he passed through my hometown
but now I feel I've met him
tired and elated I revel in the morning sun
the clouds have lifted
the breeze grows cold because I've stopped
I walk to the middle of the bridge
stare at the green water swirling below
then hitch a ride back to town
happy because Terry Fox
really won the race
and gave us all
a chance
to win it too

St Patrick's Day – Whales

(8 p.m. – From the quarterdeck of the Canadian Princes in Ucluelet, BC, on Vancouver Island facing the pacific rim of North America, March 16, 1984. (Happy birthday, Mr. Jim Deagle). Sorry, it's been on the absolute flat-out since last writing, and I shall attempt to give you a brief summary of some of what has transpired since then.)

Thursday, March 15 – Up at 4:45 a.m. to get [a] bus to Victoria on Vancouver Island. Due to arrive at 9:30 a.m., cross on ferry boat (1 ½ hours) – beautiful crossing. See a skein of Canadian geese: over 80 in one long single line about a foot off the water. Upon landing, rent a car–another deal from my new ENCORE card–whip over to the provincial museum to see an Alan Hoover in the ethnology department, a friend of Colin Browne's. He puts me into their archives, and by 12:30 p.m., I've Xeroxed nearly 200 pages of material for my screenplay. Dash out to University of Victoria for the departmental meeting, which goes till 5 o'clock, and during which I report on the demise of DTUC. They are not sympathetic. The boss man takes me to supper at Pagliacci's Antipasto (I even ate the hot green peppers–having been so rushed I had not eaten yet that day) and Ernest Hemmingway Pasta (stuffed tortellini with bacon and cream sauce), followed by marble cheese cake–New York style. Bill Valgardson (the boss) talks me out of driving off that evening as I had planned. So, I go home and get a reasonable rest.

Friday, March 16 – I take off in my Nissan Sentra and head up Vancouver Island to Nanaimo and then across the island to the west coast–to Ucluelet (folder enclosed)! The trip is like driving up and down Mount Greylock for 5 hours! Good thing I didn't leave the night before–I couldn't have made it. I checked in at suppertime aboard the *Canadian Princess*, a ship driven ashore and turned into a small hotel. Lonely supper on board–bacon wrapped scallops as "hors d'oeuvres"–followed by seafood casserole and cheese cake. (None compared with yours, Jackie!) Then up to the quarterdeck lounge where I started this letter. Pouring rain all night! But Saturday was St. Patrick's Day, and it turned out to be a beauty. Friday before going to bed, I took a shower on board. Cramped quarters, but okay. Then stuck a scopolamine button behind my left ear (I remember only too well how violently seasick I got on my trip to Saint Pierre and Miquelon near Newfoundland!).

Saturday, 7:30 a.m. – All-you-can-eat breakfast on board the *Canadian Princess*. I had a great big breakfast, very daring on my part, then boarded a 43-ft fishing boat, the *Barkley Princess*, and off we went under a RAINBOW as the sun came out. We went to a series of islands–"Broken Islands"–in the Pacific Rim National Park to a feeding ground of the great whales off–believe it or not–WALSH Island. The sea was relatively calm that day–only 10-foot swells. We saw eagles perched in trees, seals on a reef and along the shore, then the whales, great grey whales, feeding inside the reef. We heard them blow. Then they'd surface and dive all around the boat—very friendly, so no life jackets. (Too cumbersome, interferes with cameras and binoculars, etc.) We would run from port to starboard, fore and aft, and the captain of the boat and his deckhand could spin that rig around. We were spinning and bouncing, jumping around in circles like frenzied leprechauns! After about an hour of this, our captain said: "The whales usually take turns coming inside this reef to feed. Let's take a run outside the reef to see if one of the big boys is lurking out there." So off we went outside the reef. Everyone was keen-eyed, straining to see a telltale spout, or a circle of bubbles. I was alone on the land-side of the boat. We were about 100 feet offshore. I had just tucked my camera inside my jacket because my hands were getting cold. I looked up, and about thirty feet in front of me a great grey whale breached the water in an arching dive that took him virtually completely out of the ocean. He was as long as our home in Antigonish, bigger than the boat I was standing in. I shouted: "There he is! My God, there he is!" By then, he was under again, but the captain fired the engines and we took off, lurching into the swell after him (when they breach once, they usually breach again). He breached a second time, twisting sideways, his flukes slicing into the sea. Up again, mouth open, I looked up at his open jaw like a giant saw-toothed pair of scissors. Then he slid back into the sea. Six times he breached. We were like a stadium full of spectators shouting and gasping and cheering touchdowns, interceptions, fumbles.

It was truly an exciting experience. The adrenaline was pumping furiously. I was witness to one of the great creatures of God's fantastic world in his natural habitat, and the word which fits it best is overworked today. But in its original meaning of filling one with fear and admiration in the face of beauty, it was truly AWESOME! Back to dull land, I hopped into the car, hightailed it back to Victoria in time for 5 o'clock Mass. Then went to the theatre to see *Amadeus* by Peter Shaffer about Mozart—very well done.

Sunday, up early—flew into Vancouver at 10:30. Rushed over to the aquarium to buy a gift for Jackie. Hadn't had the money [my] 1st day there. Then over to [the] Museum of Anthropology to buy the Indian books. Then back to airport to board plane at 1 p.m. for Castlegar. That was thrilling, too! *Last* landing at Castlegar, the clouds were smothering the mountains when we finally broke through and saw the ground without having hit the mountains—everyone on board cheered! It's that kind of experience flying into Castlegar. One point: I usually write when I'm doing laundry, right? Right–I haven't done any laundry since my last letter. I hope to do some soon! Good news, I'll be through with my duties here in April 6, and I'll be back in Antigonish on April 7th–God willing. Love to all.

Patrick!

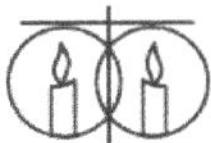

For Monica

it is the middle of the night

I lie awake in the shadow of Elephant Mountain
in a strange bed in a strange room in a strange land
but am I really alone

am I a memory to the ones I left behind
as if I had died because I cannot be hugged
or kissed or scolded or exasperated at
for turning off the stereo's incessant thump

but I am not dead yet I crawl up and down
the hills of Nelson with aching muscles
seldom used before

I look in store windows
seeing the same old pots and pans
spying myself reflected in the window
a shadow of my self

and I know I'm still alive
so in my little cage in Nelson I pace about

peopling my mind with remembered reflections
of the ones I love

strange as it may be I'm closer now to my Monica
Italian beauty so like my mother
with your cameo cheeks and dark darting eyes
that wound so many fine fellows
your lovely brown skin kissed by the same loving sun
that even now glides through the ethereal gloom
towards Elephant Mountain

thus I live four thousand miles away
with shadowy reflections haunting my mind's eye
like the hole in the ceiling of your bedroom
I did not fix before I went away

but know this darling daughter
as I stare into the window of Hipperson's hardware
on Baker Street in Nelson thinking
should I buy that toaster
the warm and loving sun strikes the pane of glass
a glaring blinding flash and you are standing there
beside me

so I thank the loving God who made the sun
that warms us both though we are far apart

I know I shall be warm in distant mountains
because no matter how cold or dark or lonely
as long as I'm alive I can summon up a memory of you

my Monica

Monica with husband Jamie Oatt

Nelson had been a beautiful land of exile, but my soul was more deeply touched by the people, new friends, I met who nursed me back to renewed life ready to face the homestretch of the race, the human race.

Thoughts on going home

to Nelson in exile living alone
seeking relief by climbing mountain tops
stretching toward Creator climbing stone
to heights where earthly matter stops

trees blossoms mirror-lakes cragged peaks
the beauty of Eden lay all about
to questing heart and mind prime mover speaks
the green hills echoed with my joyful shout

yet daily chores and duties dragged me down
to earth to toil in the lowly valley
fearing the lonely night walking the town
seeming lost soul chained like slave in galley

but our Father can never be outdone
He sent me you my friends to be His Son

12 Noon – Monday – April 2

Excerpt from a letter.

March 22 – Read lots of poems at the nursing home–better than short stories. Friday night invited to Jim and Evelyn Hoffman's house for supper. Had English teacher friends in. Lots of interesting talk. Also, we listened to the whale records I picked up in Vancouver. Great food. Great company. Great fun! Up early Saturday am to attend the Awareness Festival held at DTUC–an annual event. The hippies come out of the woods and have conferences on all sorts of exotic subjects–tarot, astrology, foot massage, neurolinguistics. The local ministers group wrote a letter in the Friday paper warning people not to attend. I ignored them, went to hear Gray Wolf talk about harmony: the old Indian wisdom of life through the universe. The batteries on my little tape-recorder were dead (Haven't used it for a long time–but took 8 pages of notes and chatted with Gray Wolf in the cafeteria after.) He came in, spread his buffalo skin on the table, burned some moss (sweet grass, I found out later), and spoke magnificently. He was simple yet profound, and extremely literate. Explained Indian religious beliefs–related to why [the] Achilles heel was vulnerable. Explained why men dominate women, etc. A lovely man. In the conversation afterwards, I found out he had been a Catholic, died in a hospital–was outside his body. They pulled a sheet over his face and left the room. The girl in the hospital serving lunch didn't realize, left his tray. So, he re-entered his body, sat up, and ate lunch! That's a neat trick. Keep a tray handy, Jackie, I <u>do</u> come to eat!

Had a macrobiotic menu with Yvonne Trombley at the Festival. Pretty flat stuff for an Italian–TOFU is POO-POO! Caught some NCAA B-ball & special Mass at Blessed Sacrament Saturday night. Followed by a special meal in the church hall. Had a group of singers in. They were not Catholics, but go around singing at various churches. Sang our songs, though! This is really Mission Country–hard to get music in church (there has been no musical accompaniment at the Cathedral since Marin Brown went to hospital!).

Sunday morning – 8:30: Met a truly fantastic person and personality, Jill Fairchild–the whale lady who spoke about her experiences with the whales. She's blond and beautiful. Very interesting speaker, and when she imitates the whales, you can't tell the difference. Showed amazing slides–and thank heavens I had recharged my batteries. I got her all on tape. She began playing with whales when 9 years old. She didn't know enough to be afraid. Her mother on shore thought she was being eaten. Helicopters came out to rescue her, etc. She was hooked, so to speak. She got a degree in marine biology from University of Washington and has been involved in filming whales, etc. Full of the most incredible stories of whales and she'd love to come to St Francis to speak. She's never seen the Atlantic whales. So, I'm going to work on that! Right now, she lives in the mountains in Montana because the whales told her to go there. They are currently (the whales) in a period of purification. She misses them terribly. She showed pictures of herself cavorting with two dolphins and you have to look hard to tell which one is her! Life is full of the most interesting things!

Thursday: March 29 – was a great day in the life of one P. Walsh, Esquire. My landlord, Bill Murphy, a retired chiropractor took me up to Whitewater ski resort outside Nelson. We went up on the ski lift in glorious sunshine. Hooked on snowshoes and tramped all over the peaks in 400 cm of snow (that's about 13 ft. deep for youse Americans!) Took all kinds of slide photos. Then went over the side and down the mountain. What a wonderful new world I've been introduced to–no practice, no tension, no fear. I'm selling my skis. Snowshoeing is fun. I'm just thrilled because Jackie and I can do it right away–no learning. I learned how to cut out a niche in the snow and arrange the snowshoes into a chair to sit down and have lunch–like a new duck discovering a pond! Alleluia.

Peace and quiet and splendor in the mountains! Traversing down the mountainside, we ended up about halfway down under the ski lift. I asked Bill to stop so I could watch some skiers come down the precipitous slope. They spin and stop

(I would keep going over and over to my doom, like that poor bastard on ABC's *Wide World of Sports* introduction who falls off the jump every week, week after week–you'd think he'd catch on). As the two of us stood there, looking up the slope in our snowshoes with back packs and ski poles, etc., 2 young fellows floated by on the ski lift in their skin-tight Gucci yellow ski suits, blond curls, bronzed by the sun, mirror sun glasses. As they drifted away up the mountain, one fellow looked at me gazing up the slope and shouted: "Go for it!" I laughed very hard. It was a great line. Bill shouted, "We don't have the right wax!"

Friday–the final colloquium is 10:30–Plane leaves 12:55. See you soon.

Love,
Patrick "Bigfoot" Walsh

PS: One of my students was thrilled the other day. He got a story published in the *Canadian Fiction Magazine*–very prestigious, much celebrating. He had a pre-publication copy. I took a look at it, and–lo and behold–a story by Sheldon Currie. Congratulations, Sheldon–good work.

Boo! Who?

Who comes gently tapping at my morning door?
Rebecca
Who criticizes how my tie and jacket match?
Rebecca
Who do I ask to straighten out the front hall floor?
Rebecca
Who delivers the nasty colds I catch?
Rebecca

Who's a budding actress on the A.V. stage?
Rebecca
Who thinks cleaning the table is a guilt trip?
Rebecca
Who treats coming home from school like entering a cage?
Rebecca
Who is *sometimes* willing to share a sour-cream chip?
Rebecca
Who tries to do her homework by TV?
Rebecca
Who swims like a waterbug?
Rebecca
Who buzzes around the house like a bumblebee?
Rebecca
Who is reluctant to vacuum a rug?
Rebecca
BUT
After all is said and done–
Who has a smile that lights up my day?
Rebecca
Who touches my hand as she passes my chair?
Rebecca
Who is a daughter for whom I pray?
Rebecca
Who is as special to me as moon-dust is rare?
Rebecca
Who would I take on a trip anywhere in the world?
Rebecca
Who do I miss here alone in my room?
Rebecca
Who can keep me about her little finger twirled?
Rebecca
Who's as pretty as a rose in bloom?
Rebecca
Miss you, honey. See you soon. Dad.

Rebecca with husband Derek MacDonald

Chapter 10
The Home Stretch 1984–97

I returned home from Nelson a new man, and set about planning a perfect palace of a retirement house for my wife and myself. The palace began to thrust itself into the sky on Maple Drive–kitty corner to our PhD house on Sunset Terrace. I researched and plotted and designed and redesigned everything that could possibly make my wife's life easier. This time I engaged Dale Archibald, local prizewinning architect who had designed the National Philatelic Building in Antigonish. I wanted the house to flow down the steep hill overlooking Brierly Brook valley–done by having one level down over the hillside, and entry to the ground level via a bridge large enough to park the car, and having a third level.

We needed the house to be airtight for clean air, so we had windows designed by an allergy specialist in Halifax. We had a balcony off the dining room, a sloped ceiling in the living room, full house music-video-intercom system, a water furnace for geo-thermal (underground) heat, alignment with the sun for summer shade and winter heat. And the crowning architectural feature a three-story open stairwell for air flow. I began to conceive of a three-story waterfall for that stairwell–but Jackie quickly stepped in and squashed that idea with her small foot. So I conceived of the main central wall that ran unbroken from the kitchen through the dining room and into the living room as an ideal place for my books. Jackie said nothing, but looked at my big foot and shook her head.

I self-contracted the house, and Jim Deagle, master builder, and I began touring houses under construction in the town and county. At St. Joseph's on the lake, we came across Joe MacDonald's new home. We knew Joe, who was on staff at the university. We got the grand tour, and Jim, having seen no better workmanship anywhere, urged locking this builder up a year ahead of time. So

Jody MacDonald, a former musician, who was saved from a dissolute career on the road by his wife, got the contract. Jody's crew was mostly family, including his brother and his wife. She was a striking woman who looked familiar–because she was the evangelist who had come to the door with two children–but I had dismissed her summarily, but thank goodness, politely. What a prodigious worker she was; even when I stopped by to chat in my contracting hat, she would keep working while answering all my queries. The house was so perfect and so beautiful Jackie wanted to keep Jody in a closet downstairs, to pull him out in any difficulty.

We had two gala affairs in the new house. The first was an open house for the public to pay to view the house, a fundraising project to the new hospital (Jackie was secretary of the committee). This put us in the elite circle of important house owners who also took part. We set the house up as if the Queen were dropping by for tea. Everything sparkled. But one thing was missing: when the time came to install my great wall of books, Jackie had put her small foot on my big foot and declared: "No dust gathering books in my living and dining rooms; I believe they'll be perfect for the shelves in your new office." What could I say to the woman who has to this very day prepared some 67,000 meals for me? Very few visitors would see my marvelous collection of books.

The other gala event was the most wonderful engagement supper we hosted for our goddaughter, Rachel Currie, daughter of Dawn and Sheldon Currie. Although it was the hottest night of the year in August, the air-conditioning kept everyone cool.

The golden years ahead looked enticing. I had been appointed full professor, our retirement was secured, so the pace of life would begin to relax.

Or so we thought.

How Film Studies Came to X

Here is my story (the traditional opening of an Irish *shanachie*-storyteller):

When I returned to X to teach after five years of teaching in prep schools in New England, I had to teach three public speaking courses and two introductory English courses. In my second year back [1964], I addressed the Students Union banquet. The new President, Dr. Malcolm MacLellan, heard the talk and pressed me to be his assistant with the imposing and blathery title: Coordinator of Development and Alumni Director responsible for Development, Public Relations, and Alumni. Two years of administration and travel convinced me to go back to the classroom.

So I went back to teaching full-time in the English department under Father MacSween. Finishing my MA in English with a dissertation on Shelley, I taught basic surveys and introduced a course in the Romantics. In my Senior year at X in the first-ever Canadian university credit course in creative writing [So we thought, but we were beat to the punch by Earle Birney in British Columbia, we found out later.], I had written a script for Fr. MacSween that was performed and won the prize at the StFX One-Act Play Festival. I had been writing plays since then and was getting them produced in the Festival while teaching.

In the 1970 summer school before leaving for Ireland for PhD studies, Father wanted me to teach a course. I suggested the Romantics, but he wanted something new to better attract students, and suggested I introduce a drama course. I really didn't want to teach drama, arguing I had no formal academic training in the field. I also had the Romantics under control, and was not looking forward to preparing a new course.

Father was adamant, giving the arguments that reflected his philosophy of teaching: "Any good teacher can prepare an undergraduate course on general genres; you have been writing, acting, and directing plays for over ten years; the best way to learn a subject is by teaching it." I taught drama that summer.

Of course, teaching drama was a natural for me. Further, teaching it opened another whole genre supplementing my Romantics courses and my Irish courses following my doctorate from University College Dublin.

In those days, with the student population exploding, professors had to alternate courses each year so as to cover the full offerings in the English department. So one year I would teach an introductory English Survey, the Romantics, and an Irish survey. The next year I would teach the intro Survey, Modern Drama, and a seminar on Irish fiction and Joyce. That is a lot of preparations necessitating constant updating and shuffling of files.

As a former art teacher in high school [I had private lessons from Leo Blake, the highest paid artist in the USA during the depression, before studying at X], I was strongly visually oriented. This visual approach was extremely useful in my drama activities.

My approach to teaching drama was to treat the written script as if it were a score for a symphony. Who enjoys Beethoven by reading his scores? A drama must be seen as acted in a performance. The electric communication between the actors and the audience is the essence of drama, the art form closest to real life, in living time. So I started by making students attend all live drama on campus.

In covering modern dramatic works, how could I enable the students to attend live performances? Impossible, especially in small center like Antigonish. So I turned to the StFX Student Film Series, which showed films every Sunday and Wednesday night in the auditorium under the chapel. I had succeeded in getting the students to book films useful to my English courses, for instance, *Romeo and Juliet* and *Wuthering Heights*, and turning them into compulsory "workshops" for my classes.

An important step to film studies occurred when the new Nicholson Hall classroom complex opened in 1969. The lower auditorium, B33, was an ideal 300-seat classroom with stadium seating perfect for film projection. The students wanted the auditorium for their Film Series. The administration said no. The classrooms could be used only for academic purposes.

- I wanted to get my large classes into B33 for the visual facilities, so with agreement of the student executive I went to Dr. J. J. MacDonald, Academic Vice President and my former chemistry prof, and made him an offer he couldn't refuse:
- The Film Series would become a joint project of the English Department and the Students' Union.

- The Students Union and the English Department each would order half of the films.
- The Campus Police would be hired for order and security.
- The projection would be done by Media Services.
- I would take responsibility for film orders, posters, advertising, tickets, scheduling, etc.
- This arrangement would keep slasher flicks and trash out of the series.
- The movie series represented the largest extracurricular liquor-free activity outside of sports events.
- This activity would be non-profit and self-supporting.

J. J. accepted the deal, and it remains in effect today over 30 years later.

Once I got into B33 and got such input into the film series, it dawned on me that film, and later video, were worthy disciplines in themselves. The interaction and relationship of fiction, drama, and film interested me. I was writing plays and getting into doing video scripts for the Sisters of St. Martha.

In the early 70s, a part-time continuing education instructor named Charlie Palmer was interested in teaching a continuing ed course in film, in which he was experienced. He approached Sheldon Currie, now Chair of the English Department. Sheldon liked the idea and approached Dr. John T. Sears, Dean of Arts, to sound out the idea. Johnny, with his PhD in business from Harvard, promptly booted Sheldon out of his office.

I was secretary for the Department and involved with drama and the Film Series, so Sheldon and I discussed ideas for getting a film course past an intransigent Dean.

By now, *The Anatomy of Drama* by Martin Esslin was my bible for theory of drama, and as I realized later, for film. Our logical step was to develop an English Department film course. Film, and of course, video by technological extension, were by then the primary art form of the twentieth century. And the end of the millennium was approaching without StFX having a film course in its curriculum.

Our mentor, Father MacSween, was most positive about our plans. He and I had often spent time in his apartment discussing the dramatic merits and faults of films and TV programs. Although our teaching styles were polar approaches, he always encouraged me to teach in my own style, not his [I couldn't have approached his style if I had wanted to]. He believed that students are engaged in the study of a subject if the professor can convey a "passion" for it, which leads to an engagement with the subject so as to become deeply and thoroughly knowledgeable about it. Father was always encouraging me to explore new ideas and fields, so as not to become bogged down in trivial minutiae of over-specialization. Knowing he was with me, even though he was not Chair at the time, gave me the courage to face any kind of opposition.

So Sheldon and I decided to try an end run, and to make it unofficial, I approached J. J. and explored the possibility of getting a film course on the curriculum. Long gone the days when Fr. MacSween would order a new course dished up. New course proposals would have to be approved by the Committee on Studies. J. J. opined that I would have trouble getting film on the curriculum. My courses were already huge, with an average total enrolment those years hovering in the 300-student range. Members of the Committee would consider film a "bird course" or "fresh-air course," lacking in academic rigor. [If the Committee had checked the Dean's statistics, they would have seen that I had the highest failure rate of any professor in the English Department–no birders allowed!]

These objections were a welcome challenge. As I devised the course, it would lead from what the Committee knew to what they had to learn. The course became not merely "film," but "Narrative in Fiction and Film." The course would deal with the nature of fiction *and* the nature of film through an historical survey of film to the present.

We would examine the techniques of fiction writing and learn the techniques of filmmaking, and in the comparison come to understand that they are two different art forms, and two different ways of telling stories. I presented a list of over a hundred great novels that became movies. The Committee had to be impressed with the novels of which they knew, if not the movies. The course, despite opposition from the Dean, was approved.

I was most fortunate to have the backing of Fr. MacSween and Sheldon Currie, and later, Jim Taylor, as chairs of the English Department. They always encouraged me to experiment, and I could count on their support in any arena. In the proof, the film course was a runaway blockbuster, breaking the box office records for arts courses. In the end it became, and still is, under my successors, a McLean's Hot Course!

In 1990, I made a trip to Hollywood to interview Brian Moore, on whom I had written my doctoral dissertation. Moore invited me to work on his latest script, *Black Robe*. Moore forwarded several of my suggestions to the director, Bruce Beresford, who incorporated them into the final film. On that same trip, I met with Daniel Petrie, award-winning Hollywood and TV director, who had graduated from St. Francis Xavier University. When Danny was awarded an Honorary degree from StFX, it was my privilege to squire him around the campus. He generously took time out to view and critique the video I had done with the National Film Board about the Sisters of St. Martha.

Danny was always loyal to his *alma mater* and willing to help Xaverians. Every time I traveled to Los Angeles, Danny would take me out to lunch on Rodeo Drive and then chat about StFX and film, in that order. Danny made arrangements for me to spend the day at the American Film Institute–with the guidance of the vice president. I sat in on classes and script discussions. I returned to Antigonish knowing that although we were in a rural setting, our classes on film had the necessary technology and support to study and understand on a par with the Institute in the heart of filmdom.

That 1990 trip gave my morale a great lift. I knew that my instincts and actions in film at StFX would stand up to scrutiny from professionals in the field as well as from academics.

As the course continued to develop, I realized that the Fiction/Film nexus was perfect for my background. The congruence with fiction kept my film efforts from flying too far from terra firma. As I reached the final years of my teaching, I was happy to discover that I had headed in the same direction as my most influential critical source, Martin Esslin. His latest book, logically developing his earlier *Anatomy of Drama*, had become *The Field of Drama*, incorporating film and video into the core concepts of drama.

When I left StFX to go west, I turned the course over to two professors I tutored in film. They have taken the course to new heights from my groundwork.

Note on Danny Petrie

When *Bay Boy* (Petrie's film based on a real-life incident in his youth in Cape Breton) came out, it enraged a number of priests at the University. They were angry that Danny, a true blue Xaverian, who had received an honorary degree from X, had included in the film an incident of a priest abusing boys. The scene was pretty tame even for 1984, yet highly prescient.

The present-day troubles of the church would indicate that Danny was courageously ahead of his time, and not so hard on the abusing priests as he might have been. He always wanted to make a sequel to the *Bay Boy* but died before he realized that dream. The *Bay Boy* introduced Kiefer Sutherland to movies. Donald Sutherland refused a role in the film, telling Danny that he didn't want to upset the balance of the actors. Sutherland Senior felt he would have been a distraction from the ensemble of actors.

I don't know who suggested Danny's honorary degree, but I suspect it might have been Senator Al Graham, who as an undergrad lived with Danny upstairs over McKenna's Restaurant in the forties. The apartment was kept by Mary Deagle's mother, who respected Danny very much.

The new house would take many years of planning and financial managing to bring to fruition. Little did we realize that we would have such a short time to enjoy the house, as we had been warned by Robbie Burns, *The best laid schemes o' mice an' men / Gang aft agley* [go oft awry]. Yet, I planned for the ages and had a slab of a standing stone erected in front of the house with the spiral from the burial tomb of the High Kings of Ireland in New Grange on the River Boyne carved on it by Arsenault's Monuments of Antigonish. Surely such hutzpah was a challenge to the gods.

The Symbol in the Garden

no one else was there
to know how it was–
the supple stretch to pluck a peach
rainbows raging in the eye
silence languishing in the inner ear
sympathetic drum-beat of blood and breath

our Garden of human delight
until the hour of truth falls

had Adam not brought
the sword of death into the world
what I had done to you
was sufficient to the deed

as Adam's tree/Christ's crucifix so I/your cross
beauty to bleakness trust to dust
pleasure to pain sun to shade

the art and poetry of a life-time study
hollow at the core
the gap between index fingers light years apart
no vital spark to leap the infinite void

philosophers reason the way it should be
prophets predict the way it will be
poets strive to tell it like it is
but the words cannot be hammered into clarity
between "then" and "now" and "then" again
a gap in the brain
with more circuits than molecules of matter
in the universe

bodies in exile from birth must be wrapped in wrinkles
molt to constituent elements in a wink of eternity

but inexplicably unfathomably incomprehensively
"*felix culpa*" of Adam/me
impregnates the void with infinite fullness for the race

then you—new Adam's Eve/Mary—fill the void
love incarnate reaching out forgiving giving
living loving transfiguring
a soul generous enough to embrace me
that though bodies separate and die
souls unite and live forever

you breathe your life into me
I wear the triple spiral of our wedding band
thee and me and He speaking in silent primitive carving
the mystery of our eternal love

Letter to Family and Friends

November 25, 1985

Dear Family and Friends,

Well, it certainly has been a long time. I apologize for getting so busy that I haven't been able to rally my energies to sit down and write—but here I am, with a full report on the life and times of the Walshes of Sunset Terrace! First, the biggest and best news: The premier of Nova Scotia has given the go-ahead for the new St. Martha's Hospital, so Jackie's long hard grind has paid off and the people of the area are ecstatic. Everything is going ahead full steam and ground should be broken in the spring—a $40,000,000.00 job of which Jacqueline's committee had to raise $6 million and at last count were at $8 million and still going! The only problem is that the more than $4 million in cash in her name in the bank has been turned over to the hospital board and our chance to see the world in style has been lost forever. Ah, well, Jacqueline in Tahiti with a guilty conscience would have been a party pooper. Still, with the cold weather arriving, it must have been a little tempting to her . . . .

We had a friend living with us for two weeks: Frank Canino, a drama director who directed my Louisbourg plays and my TV film about the Sisters of St. Martha. He was in town from Toronto to direct *Macbeth* at the University. The play opens tonight, and Jackie and Rebecca and I will be there, as will all my freshmen and drama students. Oh, by the way, my new play, *The Day the Pope Died*, about the Gallagher/Walsh kids after their parents died did pretty well at the One-Act Play Festival; the review in *The Casket* is enclosed. I am happy to report Jackie liked the play, and survived the references in the play to Pete Gallagher's fiancée, Therese, the ex-nun.

A couple of weeks ago I adjudicated the One-Act Play Festival for the regional high school–Junior High on one night, Senior High the next. A hard job to say something about every child in every play. One was easy, though: Rebecca Walsh in the Grade 10 play as Mrs. Hill the wife of an amateur spiritualist in the play, *A Mad Breakfast*, was beautiful, charming, always in character, and delivered her lines with a great sense of comic timing, although her petulant whine of "Oooh, William" sounded suspiciously like "Oooh, Daddy." A fun job to adjudicate but a pressure job to watch three plays a night, and the minute they are over to run up on the stage and start talking, yet having to be truthful and critical without hurting anyone's feelings. (I love it. I'm at my best under pressure–that old debating experience at St. Joe's still stands me in good stead.)

Also at the Casket company, as a board member, we have just completed a $240,000.00 expansion and remodeling project. Jackie has a new office and a much nicer atmosphere to slave away in. I have always succeeded in helping her to be more productive. What a nice guy.

At school, I had 202 students write some 15 pages each (total: 3000) of midterm examinations. The correcting nearly drove me over the bend. It's the only part of the job I mind. Also, the freshmen are doing a term-long research paper I am checking at 7 stages along the way. Add in seven Seniors doing Senior theses under my direction, and you know I'm not wasting too much time.

At the nursing home, I have been preparing the counter-proposal for negotiations with the new Nurses Union and their first contract. Having been the chief negotiator for the Board with the CBRT&GW (Canadian Brotherhood of Railway, Transport and General Workers), I am now the chief negotiator for this new union, without benefit of a consulting lawyer. (We've never had, a strike, or the whiff of one. We treasure our workers as much as we care for our patients.) Nonetheless, it takes a lot of careful thinking and talking to sort things out. Negotiations are scheduled for all day Nov. 27th & 29th. Our installation of $200,000.00 of new boilers at the nursing home this summer was completed, but the boilers keep cutting out and the manufacturer is not responding to our requests for help, so it looks like I'm going to have to dip the pen in fire and threaten disclosing their lack of cooperation to the media. More to follow on this one.

Also at the University, my latest fight is to get an audio-visual TV reserve room in the new library. The librarian and the academic vice president don't understand what we're doing in drama, so I'm mounting support from the faculty to try to force them into the 20th Century. Our regular film series on Sundays and Wednesdays, of which I am the advisor and overseer, is doing quite well with popular films. The students are quite cooperative in the selection of films, so we have no trouble avoiding real bummers like *Police Academy* & *Porkys*. However, there is a place at University for more serious and challenging films, so last night we launched a new ALTERNATE FILM SERIES, with *Clockwork Orange*, which, in my opinion, did not stand the test of time, and which, in my old (or older) age, I find a flawed and offensive film.

Last Sunday afternoon, I did the first of two workshops with Lectors at the Cathedral, and missed Refrigerator Perry and the Chicago Bears football game. Another touchy job because a system has to be set up to encourage some readers who can't be heard to retire. The group has agreed to set up a review committee, but guess who's going to have to be the Public Speaking authority? We'll eat up half-a-dozen Saturday afternoons with training sessions, after Christmas.

Also last month, I designed and produced pamphlets and brochures for Recovery House, a drug addiction center which was headed by our friend Judge Donnie Tramble. It was a rush job which I couldn't turn down because of Donnie's passing and the disarray the group was in. The Westville Heritage Project is underway with brochures and posters designed and being printed.

The book being published on the History of Westville, Nova Scotia, is being published by Scotia Design Publishing Company (Jackie and me). Our second edition of *English Essentials for Students and Teachers* is doing well and is being adopted, it looks like, by a school district in Prince Edward Island. We're being invited over to the island to do a workshop with the teachers, probably in the spring break if we can arrange it.

Also, I did not get the editorship of the drama anthology for high schools in Nova Scotia–the editor can't have a play in the anthology. So I wanted to get my Louisbourg play in the book, then I found out it couldn't be in the anthology because it is already published by Playwrights Canada, so my hopes for the anthology are riding on *The Day the Pope Died.*

As Vice President East of the Playwrights Union Of Canada I took part in a Cross-Canada Conference call a couple of Saturdays ago. I have been deputed to see if our national convention can be held here in the Maritimes. Should be fun.

I have a meeting Monday with the author of a book, *The Fire Spook of Caledonia Mills*, a story of a poltergeist experience in Antigonish County that made headlines all over the world in 1922. The CBC wants to do a radio play of the story, so I may be making a deal to do the script. However, you don't count on anything in this business until the deal is signed on the dotted line. [The deal was never signed.]

An interesting evening last week: met Omar Pound, son of Ezra Pound the most influential poet of the 20th Century. A very nice man and a translator of Persian poetry who teaches at Princeton. Also, we had two young priests to dinner, and I really am getting along because one of the priests who was a student of mine at University is now the Chancellor of the diocese. I thought it was strange to teach the children of my classmates at college, but I hear I'm going to be teaching the child of one of my former university students next year. When I look at the new faculty I realize I'm a member of the Old Guard. I wish I'd get a little wiser as I go along.

Here's a rundown on the children: Rebecca worrying about schoolwork and pulling down honor marks. Had to take her up to out-patients at the hospital this past week with vomiting and severe stomach cramps. Appendicitis scare, but all is well, merely a rather severe gastroenteritis, and she has recovered well. Gregory, the new trim slim model, is taking part in badminton tournaments and came home with a new digital solar clock as doubles champion in a tournament in Halifax last week. The new car posters continue to sprout on his bedroom walls. Monica is doing well in Toronto and is looking forward to coming home for Christmas, and we're sure looking forward to seeing her. Fran was home for Armistice Day for a home-cooked meal. He got a great mark in his anatomy course and he looks well, although he admits there are a few more distractions in the big city as compared to Antigonish. Mary is surviving the winter in Calgary and has also managed to arrange to get home for Christmas, so we should all be together for the holidays, and if our celebration is as good as last year we shall consider ourselves to be blessed indeed.

Well, how about one last item for the entertainment section: Near Antigonish is a historic town, Sherbrooke Village, which is a heritage town with its old buildings maintained. A call went out for extras for a pilot for a new TV series being filmed there. I ignored the urge to take part, although the filming will be done during the term break. Well, son of a gun, they called me. They need someone with an American accent, who can be pompous (great acting skill needed there), to play the role of the father of the heroine. He doesn't want her to marry the hero, the inventor of kerosene. They took photos of me, and believe it or not, the wardrobe lady took all my measurements and snipped a lock of my hair and I'm waiting for a call from the director. Nothing guaranteed–but it would be fun, although I get petrified when the cameras begin to roll, and I know there's money on the line if I mess up. What price glory? I'm not holding my breath. [Good thing! I would have been long gone.]

Love to all, and remember, Jackie and I are remembering you personally at Mass every day.

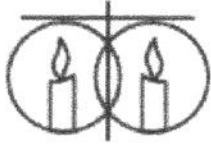

Mavor Moore

Mavor Moore, among the pioneers of Canadian television in the 1950s, was the creator of the CBC National News: The National. He was well known for his contributions to drama, having created more than 100 plays, documentaries, musicals, and librettos, for stage, radio, and television. From 1970 to 1984, he taught theatre history as a professor at York University and chaired its theatre department (1975–1976). He was named to the Canada Council in 1974 and was the first artist to chair the council (1979–1983). He received three Peabody Awards for his radio documentaries produced on behalf of the United Nations. Moore received Canada's highest honor in the performing arts in November 1999.

Seeking support to try and get my Dieppe play produced, I asked Angus Braid, Director of Continuing Education at StFX, for whom I regularly worked, a former student of Mavor Moore, to intercede with the great man on my behalf. Angus sent Moore a script of *Dieppe: A Quarrel with Destiny*, the ill-fated raid on Nazi-occupied France in 1942, Canada's worst ever military disaster.

Here is Moore's response:

mavor moore

3815 West 27th Avenue,
Vancouver, B.C. V6S 1R4

13 July 1984

Prof. Angus Braid,
Continuing Education Program,
St. Francis Xavier University,
Antigonish, N.S. B2G 1C0

My dear Angus:

I am ashamed to see that the date on your letter to me, accompanying Pat Walsh's play, is dated 16 April. But it's not all a matter of procrastination. By the time it reached me I had already left York for all practical purposes (I retired at the end of the academic term), and was in the midst of a total move to Vancouver with my family -- where, as you will see from the letterhead, we are already ensconced.

There was not a hope that I could it read before the move or immediately afteward, so I decided that instead of returning it I would simply keep it until time permitted. I have now read it and am impressed. Coincidentally, the new Nanaimo Festival ("Shakespeare Plus" -- one of the pluses being a new Canadian play every summer) has just been launched with great success. I'm one of the patrons. And I would like to give the play to Leon Pownall, the Festival's director, to see if they mightn't be interested in it for next summer.

Pat Walsh has hold of a most interesting idea, and has carried it through skillfully. I might have some ideas for his consideration, but it is much more important at the moment for him to get it into the hands of a potential director -- who would have rewriting ideas of his/her own. Would you be so kind as to let him know my plan? I'll return it if he prefers.

Sandra is to teach in the music faculty at UBC here, while I (mainly) write -- though I've taken on an adjunct professorship at UVIC, very part-time. I want to finish some of those damn plays I've been shoving over the hill!

With warmest best wishes to you both -- and even though we've moved farther apart may we meet again.

As ever,

Mavor

3815 West 27th Avenue,
Vancouver, B.C. V6S 1R4
13 July 1984

Prof. Angus Braid,Continuing Education Program
St. Francis Xavier University
Antigonish, N.S. B2G 1C0

My dear Angus:

I am ashamed to see that the date on your letter to me, accompanying Pat Walsh's play is dated 16 April. But it's not all a matter of procrastination. By the time it reached me I had already left York for all practical purposes (I retired at the end of the academic term) and was in the midst of a total move to Vancouver with my family -- where, as you will see from the letterhead, we are already and ensconced.

There was not a hope that I could it read before the move or immediately afterward, so I decided that instead of returning it I would simply keep it until time permitted. I have now read it and am impressed. Coincidentally, the new Nanaimo festival ("Shakespeare Plus" -- one of the pluses being a new Canadian play every summer) has just been launched with great success. I'm one of the patrons. And I would like to give the play to Leon Pownall, the Festival's director, to see if they mightn't be interested in it for next summer.

Pat Walsh has hold of a most interesting idea, and has carried it through skillfully. I might have some ideas for his consideration, but it is much more important at the moment for him to get it into the hands of a potential director -- who would have rewriting ideas of his/her own. Would you be so kind as to let him know my plan? I'll return it if he prefers.

Sandra is to teach in the music faculty at UBC here, while I (mainly) write -- though I've taken on an adjunct professorship at UVIC, very part-time. I want to finish some of those damn plays I've been shoving over the hill!

With warmest best wishes to you both -- and even though we've moved farther apart may we meet again.

As ever,
Mavor
(letter retyped to fit publishing format)

Later that summer, while teaching drama at a Prince Edward Island University summer school in Charlottetown, I spotted Mavor Moore in a restaurant. I introduced myself and had a brief chat about our future undertaking. I was in, if not Seventh Heaven, at least Fifth Heaven, knowing how the gods of drama were so often fickle. Mavor, no longer Mavor *Moore*, intended to ask the Board of Directors to mount a production of *Dieppe* under the theatre's mandate to produce one new Canadian play each year. I began to plot how to finance a trip to Nanaimo to take part in this giant step forward in my playwriting career. But, but as I feared, those fickle gods struck, and it was not a mere theatrical tap on the cheek.

Brian Mulroney, class of 1959 at StFX and a person I knew both as an undergrad, and later worked with on financial campaigns in support of the University, was elected Prime Minister of Canada. For most Xaverians, this was good news–for me it was not. Mulroney's government pulled support from the arts, cut the Nanaimo government grant, and as a result the theatre could not mount a new Canadian production, and my attempt to get Dieppe performed was quashed.

And I never had a chance to deliver the speech I had prepared to deliver to my pal, Mavor, following the anticipated opening of *Dieppe*.

The Judge, Part 2

The evaluation of academic prowess at StFX continues constantly. Each year, two departments are chosen for internal evaluation every decade or so, one in science and one in the arts. About a decade after the debacle with the Nova Scotia Playwriting Contest and my play *The Small-L Lord*, the English Department came under an additional external scrutiny by the Association of Canadian University Teachers of English. A team of three professors from other universities showed up in Antigonish to evaluate, one each from the University of Ottawa, Mount Allison University of New Brunswick, and the self-acknowledged queen of universities, that of Toronto.

The evaluation would cover all phases of English Department activities: teaching, research, creative activity, departmental procedures, resources, facilities, and interviews with all the members of the department and administrators of the university: a thorough vetting of approximately two weeks. As secretary of the department at the time, I got to squire Professor Harvey Kerpneck of the University of Toronto about his rounds. A memorial tribute to Harvey Kerpneck from his University described him thus: *"If Harvey was a man of personal unexpectedness, he had a high level of social and professional predictability. He spoke his mind, even when it was inopportune; infelicitously, even when diplomacy would have been advisable; hastily, even when it may have been premature; publicly, even when discretion would have advised privately; sweepingly, even when discrimination of discretion would have been more effective. In other words, Harvey often thundered like a Hebrew prophet to Philistine bureaucrats who originated policies that he vehemently disagreed with."* In other words, we got along splendidly. We spent one whole day in the Angus L. MacDonald Library bonding while examining all the books and journals in our English Literature collection for strengths and weaknesses.

As the scrutiny proceeded, Harvey enjoyed particularly the company of the MacSweenites, and on the last day of the committee's stay on campus, we invited Harvey only to a party hosted by the Department Chair Sheldon Currie and his wife, Dawn. It became a rip-roaring Down-East do, and in the midst of it all, Harvey said, "You may be small university, but you guys are good, really good. You could all be teaching at Toronto. We should bring some of you in for summer schools." We were feeling pretty good, and somebody brought up the tale of my encounter with the "hanging judge" of the Nova Scotia Playwriting Contest.

Harvey listened intently, and then announced, "I heard about that. I remember that."

Incredulous, I asked, "How could you know that up in Toronto? Only the people in this room know about it here in Antigonish."

"I know, because the judge told me about it."

Silence prevailed for a rare moment, and I asked, "Would you mind telling me, who was the judge?"

Pregnant pause.

"Mavor Moore!"

The judge who nearly squashed me like a bug, was now one of my strong supporters. Fickle indeed, the gods of drama.

That was the night I began to formulate the speech I would give to my friend and advocate Mavor, who failed to quell my urge to write. Feeling that somehow Mavor's attack had steeled my nerve and my commitment to prove him wrong, his approval of my later work would be pleasing to us both. Unfortunately, our paths never crossed again before his death in 2006. I think we both would have enjoyed a hearty laugh together.

By the by, in the ACUTE final report on the state of English Studies across Canada, by internal evidence we deduced that the StFX English department was the model for teaching on one hand, English students majoring and desiring to go on for graduate studies, and on the other hand, general students from other disciplines studying for general enlightenment. *Finis coronat opus.*

December 3rd each year is the Feast Day of St. Francis Xavier, the Apostle of the Indies, for whom the University is named. Through the years, particularly following World War II with the sudden growth in enrollment and the creation of the X-Ring, the day has assumed more and more popularity as the day the Seniors receive their X-rings, rather than the religious holiday. In the hopes of providing some balance between the Ring Day and the religious holiday of our namesake, I wrote the following religious monologue:

St. Francis Xavier Speaks - Stfx Day 1992

[*At the appointed time, Xavier, appropriately garbed in a cassock with crucifix tucked in his belt, should make his appearance entering the chapel through the front doors and progressing through the audience shaking hands with students, and greeting them with the invocation, "Peace be with you."*

Moving among the people, he should retain a humble demeanor, ask personal questions, and fix people with a bright and intense eye, giving them full attention while engaging them.

With appropriate pace, and a sense of how the attention of the crowd is developing, he should then assume the podium, eschewing use of a microphone, and treating it as a strange piece of technology.]

People of An-TIG-on-nish, I am honored to be among you today. I never thought in my life that a University would be named after me. Yet, I must confess

I am very pleased that you should invoke my name for your beautiful University. It reminds me of the College of St. Barbara in the University of Paris where I studied and then taught philosophy.

Ah, yes, I was born in Spain, but the seat of my family was the castle of Xavier, near Pampeluna, very close to the French border. I see you have adopted portions of my family crest in your own crest. My mother was an heiress of the house of Xavier, and my father was a counsellor to the king of Navarre. Unlike many of you, I gather, my family had the resources to provide my education. Yet, later in my life I learned to appreciate the difficulties many of you may be facing.

But, first of all, with all due respect, let me say, without the intention of being ungrateful or unappreciative of the honors you have done me, by adopting the name of Xavier, I must be truthful and declare that the bronze statue in your sparsely decorated chapel, does not look like me. On the other hand, the white marble statue outside the chapel, is at least a recognizable human being, and for that I am humbly thankful.

I hope you all realize how fortunate you are in being able to attend a University. When at St. Barbara's I never dreamed I would end up in Goa on the west coast of India, or become popularized as the Apostle of the Indies, a title obviously the creation of publicists for the church. We know not the day nor the hour when we shall meet our maker. I never contemplated during my college days that I would meet my Lord and maker, alone, deserted and delirious on the tiny island of Sancian off the coast of China. Only today do I understand the generosity of God in allowing me to discover the life he called me to lead.

It all started at the University of Paris about 1530. Spain, yea, all of Europe, was caught in the fever of the recent discoveries of Cristoforo Colon, you call him Christopher Columbus. I think you know of him now principally through paintings–your new kind of paintings that move, that show action–they are called–how do you say it–ah yes–moo-VIES.

Providence brought me under the influence of a former high-spirited military hero, a fellow nobleman of Castile, Ignigo, known to you as Ignatius of Loyola. He was older than the rest of us he gathered about himself. He had been valorously wounded in the war with France–in, of all places, Pampeluna, when I was a child. While recovering Ignatius was converted to an active union with Christ. From that moment he dedicated the rest of his life to pursuing an ever-closer union with Jesus by carrying on the work of Jesus in the world.

The story is too long to tell you today. Ignatius founded the "Society of Jesus," which you may know as the "Jesuits" a term we never used. I was one of the first seven who founded the Society with Ignatius as our General, and the military obedience and rigorous discipline was perfect preparation for the missionary work we would undertake to bring the good news of the love of Jesus Christ to all the peoples of the new worlds being discovered.

The work of our Society you may know through your . . . moo-VIES–one called *The Mission* and another called *Black Robe* here in your own country. But, ironically, instead of sailing west, where I might have come to An-TIG-on-ish, I sailed east. Many Spaniards sailed west–for wealth, for glory, for possession of your continent and its riches! But, I sailed east to win souls for Christ. Ignatius had impressed all of us to give up our noble inheritances, our titles, our courtly influence, our saunter through the halls and chambers of power, for the work of Jesus. He put the question to me, the question that reached the depths of my heart and soul: "Francis, what doth it profit a man to gain the whole world, and lose his soul?" My dear young friends, I have seen the whole world, and Ignatius was right.

My University days were very happy. I hope you are happy here in your university days. But I am here to tell you greater happiness lies ahead. But it may not be the happiness you expect. I never knew anyone, and I would challenge you to find anyone in this world today, from royalty to political leaders to those who accumulate vast wealth overnight through entertaining the masses with bread and circuses, who achieves a pure and unalloyed happiness.

True happiness rests in love, and infinite love rests in Jesus and the will of his Father. I am proud that here at your University, named in my honor, and seeking my patronage, you are dedicating yourselves to seeking "whatsoever things are true, whatsoever things are good, whatsoever things are beautiful."

What I see here at Xavier University is the opportunity to achieve what I myself worked and died for: a community of peoples from all over the world who come together to learn and help one another make this world a better place, a place where all can know and love one another as sisters and brothers of Jesus Christ under the Fatherhood of God Eternal.

There on your crest are the black people of the Indies I labored to love as Christ would love. Today I see people coming from all the nations of the world to this place named in my honor. You wear my initial proudly on your rings as a sign and symbol of the "Xaverian Family." You have continued my work and made the Xaverian family's home the entire planet of every nation under the sun. Xaverians labor for love, and goodness, truth, and beauty, in my name. All who do so are true Xaverians, and true to my spirit.

What fills me with great happiness and hope for the future of this common home, our planet Earth, is that you have openly embraced all those who share in the quest for love. Not just Catholics committed to Rome, but Christian brothers and sisters, and Jews, and Muslims, and searching agnostics, and, yes, even atheists, who despite denying our heavenly Father, work for the values we espouse in His Name: truth, goodness, beauty, and above all–love! A love Jesus expressed in his supreme sacrifice for each and every individual human soul. As long as you work together for these things, my dear sisters and brothers, the Xaverian family will bring the living love of Jesus and His Father to be a living reality–to the day when all will be fulfilled in union with Him.

As long as you do this, Xaverians, I shall be with you. God bless you all. May you find true and lasting happiness in your life's work.

Not only in books do we find answers to the mysteries of life and death, creation and destruction, love and hate, being and not being. A simple walk, hand in hand, experiencing a page in the book of nature can lead us to appreciate the deepest joys of human relationships.

walking together

walking together we face the sunset
gnawed by curious silhouettes of black spruce trees

we turn left off Hawthorne Street sidewalk
to Brierly Brook Road gravel
lured on by tender evening

nature's bagpipes the peepers shriek at us
from oozy green mirror bristled with swamp grass

the crescendo of their cry
metronome of temperature
blots out logic of our inner ear
symphony of hidden forces

we cannot see the source of the sound
the word of mother nature speaking to us
like a voice from a burning bush

we go home wading through darkness
no longer able to hear the peepers
oblivious of our absence

the memory of their tenor drone
haunts our aural memories
like shrieks of suffering children far from home

where were they during icy winter
where will they be in decaying autumn
or when Brown's Mountain lies on harbor bottom

the patterns of evolving time elude me
mystery of life beyond my ken
for I am rooted in the here and now

I turn to you daring to keep knowing you
you who have conquered time
giving me eternal life

mother of my children souls never-ending
called forth from the word-made-flesh
by your gentle *fiat*

in these silent nights of your summer
do you hear peepers of joy or pain

are you in vale of tears
or
mystical moment of *ave*

because you share with me
your miracle of life I am a father

together let us hear
the song of the unseen peepers
reminders of unspoken human tears

yet promises of present happiness
exploding into timeless joy
my wife

Mother's Day

As life passed by and the children aged, they always loved stories: at first about my childhood and "the olden days." Then they began to enjoy stories about their own childhood days – which gave them entrée into the adult world– then we all began to discover the quizzical relationship memory created between TRUTH and FICTION.

Francis Stories

The Story of His Life:

Monica, five-year-old Fran's younger sister, had a bag of lollipops that cost one cent for five lollipops. Fran asked for one. NO. Fran begged for one. NO. Fran offered one cent for ONE. NO. He offered a nickel for ONE. NO. He offered a dime for ONE. NO. Finally, he offered Monica a quarter for ONE. She refused.

Mother, who had been watching this attempted transaction, intervened. She said, "Francis, you could get five lollipops for a penny, or over a hundred for a quarter! Why don't you take a few minutes to go to the corner store for your own lollipops?" "Because," answered the desperate lad, "I WANT IT NOW!"

Facing Death

One night at suppertime, everyone was called for supper, but five-year-old Francis was nowhere to be found. As we sat quietly contemplating where he might be, we heard the familiar whimpering from the bathroom. We knocked on the door to no avail. The whimpering grew louder. Our concern grew stronger. Finally, Father, at the decibel level of a 747 jet taking off, threatened to bust the door down. The door clicked open from inside, where Fran lay curled up on the floor holding his stomach. Of course we thought appendicitis. Upon questioning, though, Fran revealed he was dying. How did he know? The neighbor kids had cruelly told him so. How did they know he was dying? Because they had poisoned him. How? They told him the red berries on the huckleberry bush were good to eat–and when he ate them they then laughed because they were poison and he was going to die. Without waiting for any explanations or retractions, Fran scuttled home like a wounded dog to curl up and die alone in the bathroom. But he didn't, 'cause he's here today, isn't he?

The Tummy Ache

The first week we arrived in Ireland in 1971, Francis began moping about a tummy ache. We let him lie on the couch, fussed a bit over him, and gave him a blanket. He complained some more and whimpered a bit, so we allowed him to stay home from school. Mother took a close look and asked Father if he didn't look a bit greenish. We decided it was not just because we were in Ireland, so we called the doctor we had signed up with the first day in Dublin. He came out to the house, took one look at the whimpering green boy on the couch, and declared we did not have time to wait for an ambulance. We bundled him into the front seat of the car, and Father set out at breakneck speed for the Children's

Hospital in Dublin, which he knew was next to a building James Joyce had lived in. The mad dash took twenty minutes with Fran scrunched on the floor in front of passenger's seat, whimpering softly to himself. At the hospital, the waiting attendants grabbed him and whisked him away. Within fifteen minutes, the surgeon had removed an about-to-burst appendix. Another ten minutes and it would have been too late. We learned that Fran could take a lot of pain, and if he were whimpering we should take it like a five-alarm fire!

The Future Priest

One day, we asked little Francis what he was going to be when he grew up. Not for him the usual fireman, policeman, or hockey player, but he would become, he announced proudly and firmly, a priest. Desiring to know how he had developed this deep faith from the example of our many priest friends among the professors at the University, Fran declared, "Because they don't have to work!" How did he know that? "Because they are always just walking around the campus or visiting our house to eat!" I guess that career choice is out today, eh, Fran?

The Big Question

Fran always had a deep affection and love for his parents. This was demonstrated when we were to go on vacation when Fran was about three years old. He didn't want his mother to go, which we thought was very charming, until he kept up his resistance beyond what was reasonable. Finally, Mother talked him down to a normal tone, and asked why he was so worried. Fran finally blurted out his primary concern, "When you're gone, who will feed us?" He didn't know anyone but his Mother could cook.

Catastrophe Script

Knowing Fran would be hyper whenever we went out, we would try to explain where we were going and how good the babysitter was, etc., etc., etc. But Fran had a perpetual cloud over his head. His logic went something like this: "But what if the babysitter spills the orange juice, and then Mary slips and falls and knocks over the high chair, and the high chair hits the lamp, and the lamp falls over and breaks the television, which catches on fire, and then the firemen come and put so much water on the fire that it goes over my head and then I float out the window and down the gutter in all that water and go into the manhole and through the sewer and then into the Dublin Bay where a big shark will rip me to pieces, and then you will be really sorry at my funeral that you left me home, won't you?" We didn't get away on too many vacations trying to wrestle with that logic.

Concern for Food

Fran's concern for food had been revealed earlier that summer. We took him to his first movie at an outdoor theatre to see *Snow White and the Seven Dwarves*. We felt he was getting on quite well, watching the screen intently while sucking on the two middle fingers of his right hand. He never said a word, and survived the scary scenes with the wicked witch, so we thought he might go through the entire film without a word. But, in the climactic scene at the end, we realized what he had been watching most carefully–when the seven dwarves pursued the wicked witch up the mountain and she dropped her basket of apples, Fran began to cheer wildly. We thought he was overjoyed at the death of the wicked witch and the triumph of good over evil–but then he blurted out, "Hurray, hurray, now *we* can get all those apples!"

The Big Decision

At age seventeen, Fran was a member of the Nova Scotia Provincial Badminton team, and he and his partner, Kevin O'Keefe, were silver-medal winners in the national championships. Fran was also a member of the Provincial Board and was organizing tournaments and traveling all over. After his first year at StFX University, he sat down to talk to his father. Fran revealed on his report card that he was 151st in a class of 300. His marks were okay, but he felt that he couldn't get a good biology major and entry to graduate school, so of his own accord he had decided to quit the provincial team and concentrate on his studies. He did. And when he graduated, Francis was second in his class of 300. He had learned to work hard, and play hard, and in proper proportion. So he got into graduate school, became a physiotherapist, and met Lucie. He knows how to make good decisions.

Speaking French

To play all that badminton in his high school years, Fran eased up on his studies, and in grade ten dropped the study of French. He realized this might not have been a good decision when Lucie took him home to Quebec City to meet the family, and Lucie's grandmother asked, "Does he speak French?" Fran realized how bad dropping French had been when he visited Lucie's family one week later and Grandmother inquired, "Does he speak French, YET?" So Fran learned French, *vitement*, motivated by both love and that previously noted sense of survival.

[*Stories prompted by the imminent wedding of Fran and Lucie Gagnon of Charlesbourg, Quebec.*]

Fran with wife Lucie

Leavening the many joys in our lives were moments of great sorrow, this time caused by the untimely death of my nephew, my sister's oldest son, Danny Rorke.

[At the funeral Mass of Daniel A. Rorke, III, Specialist Fourth Class

b. September 5, 1963–d. April 6, 1986 mountain climbing, River Canyon, Fort Jayne, Alabama]

a leap of faith

we rage against the darkness
for death has ripped the bud
of youth's bright promise
and we can feel it in our blood

our minds are flooded with regret
a pall of fear hangs in the air
feeling ourselves in heaven's debt
our cry assaults the sky it isn't fair

but at this mass we celebrate
the death of God's own son
his mother standing at his feet
injustice seemingly has won

that wasn't fair when perfect love
took on our whole world's weight
but earthbound reason cannot see above
trapped in time cut off from future fate

Jesus himself begged to be relieved
but in a loving leap of faith
he taught us how to live belief
and hang suspended still in space

and each of us must brave the step
from the cliff of this fond world
for every life no matter how adept
will from this earth be hurled

as Jesus leaped and left all flesh behind
so we must trust and trusting conquer death
by casting off all ties with earth we find
our fevered minds will rise to endless rest

but if we cling to aught of earthly worth
our leap of faith will certainly be flawed–
our Daniel slipped the surly bonds of earth
and soared to "touch the face of God"

and when we each step off this earth to final end
we'll rejoin our Danny and the living word
son brother grandson nephew comrade friend
will welcome us to the bosom of the lord

all flesh must fall to free our souls to soar

Uncle Pat Walsh April, 1986

We lived with incipient fear concerning my brother Fran's health: following the early death of our parents, and Fran's first heart attack at age 29.

To Francis

my brother from the same womb
from another miracle of life
the cycles of time spin on
through the endless universe
Carmen and Duke are no longer with us
nor will *we* see day follow day year follow year
generation/generation eon/eon

even this world shall spin to rest
and stars flicker out
yet I do not grieve I rejoice in you my brother
to know your love your valiant suffering
your enduring spirit
to laugh with you and cry with you
to sport with you and agonize with you
to face the mystery of pain with you

to stand by you to witness
yet unable to explain why you hurt
why you are besieged from without and within
why why my brother O Lord
we have myths and revealed truths
stories to explain the inexplicable
Adam and Eve serpent and fall
Jesus and blameless lamb crucified and risen
give us patterns to deal with our human experience
but they do not give us understanding
do not give us now and here unalloyed happiness
they do however
reach into the very pattern of our humanity
the cells of our beginning the beat of our hearts
and call forth a humble faith beyond reason and logic
beyond darkness beyond everlasting quiet

we are not men of note nations do not cheer
nor crumble at our roaring
and who remembers Duke and Carmen
we do yes we do

they live in us and in the time to come
they live in our memories
of how to deal with the enemy of love and life
they lived in each other in joy and in pain
in happiness and in suffering

in faith and in us their sons
they lived and died
for that ineffable mystery
beyond this vale of tears

yet we remain you and I brother
flesh of their flesh bone of their bone
blood of their blood
and though separated by miles and time zones
from each other by their leaving us behind
from them
you and I brother recreated their pattern
by finding women of uncommon mettle
of strength and courage and generosity and faith
who took us on in flesh and spirit
who gave us strength in our weakness
patience in our folly joy in our flesh
children in our time faith in our doubt
fullness in our emptiness
these remarkable women gave us love
to the farthest possible reaches of human capability
so Black Diamond (precious stone of many facets
formed by immeasurable pressure upon delicate plants)

upon this your 40th year your tenth birth day
I send you my prayers from the Mass of February 29th
from the first letter of Peter:
You have been obedient to the truth and purified your souls
until you can love like brothers
in sincerity; let your love for each other
be real and from the heart–
your new birth was not from any mortal seed
but from the everlasting word of the living and eternal God.

my love my hope my faith
that "He's got you and me brother" in his hands

Pat

In the summer of 1990, on a sabbatical leave, I was invited to Los Angeles to work on the script of *Black Robe,* Brian Moore's novel being made into a film directed by Bruce Beresford. In the course of that exercise, Brian Moore told me that Ted Kotcheff, the director of many Hollywood hits, had spoken to him about making a film of Dieppe. I called Danny Petrie, my StFX benefactor in Hollywood, who put me in touch with Kotcheff's assistant, who arranged an appointment for me to pitch my script to the great director.

At the appointed time I drove to the meeting, passed through security, and ended up in a lobby with palm trees growing in it, and an impressive waterfall. I had driven in very early and very nervous from my friend Jordan Mastroianni's home in Rancho Palos Verdes. I had to wait for the appointment, and my bladder needed relief. I could not see any public washrooms in the lobby, so I approached the lone security man at the welcome desk. There were no public washrooms, but the fellow could see that I was in difficult straits. He directed me to go over to the elevators and continue to the end of the corridor where I would find a door to a stairwell. "Just go up the stairs and at the top you will find a washroom. Just be quick about it, and get back here, pronto." I did as instructed, entered the washroom, and realized I was in La La Land! Gold sink, gold toilet, gold everything. Now, I was really nervous. It did not take me long to do my duty and get the hell out of there and back to the lobby before "the quick brown fox jump[ed] over the lazy dog!" I said to the man at the desk, "That is one helluva washroom!"

"Yeah. That's Harvey Weinstein's washroom, but he's not here today." TRUTH, FICTION, LIE? I'll never know.

The pitch went well, and couple days later, I submitted the fax below and went home to Antigonish to await my fate.

"Just the Fax"

TO: Mr. Ted Kotcheff, Penta Productions, Los Angeles.
Fax: 477-* * * *
FROM: Patrick Walsh
RE: screenplay based upon The Dieppe Raid
DATE: Sept. 4, 1990
PAGES: 1
INCOMPLETE? call (213) 396-* * * *

Dear Ted:

Following our discussions last Wednesday at your office, I shall submit to you on or before Oct. 31, 1990 a 6–10 page treatment for a feature film set against the "Dieppe Raid" of August, 1942.

Sincerely yours,
Patrick Walsh

*

RAIDERS

IN THE DARKEST DAYS OF WORLD WAR II, TWO YOUNG CANADIAN SOLDIERS AND THEIR COMMANDING OFFICER DISCOVER THEIR GREATEST CHALLENGE IS NOT THE GERMAN ARMY—BUT THE ENEMY WITHIN.

SEPTEMBER 1939, CANADA

Marcel Renaud, 20, a young French-Canadian addicted to making home movies, films a magnificent sunset at his family cottage at a lake in the Laurentians. [We will often see scenes from the POV of his camera.] His prominent Quebec family dynasty is gathered to watch a short home movie Renaud has made with his siblings and young cousins, the story of THORD FIRETOOTH, a crippled caveboy who wins renown in his tribe by hollowing out logs with fire so they can be used in darkness to raid the enemy tribe across the lake. Renaud's father attacks his son's obsession with movies. Renaud claims a camera's pictures get at the truth of events. They fight and Renaud's father impugns his son's manhood.

Peter White, 19, nicknamed Calgary, is called from the corral to the house by his uncle Malcolm. The family room contains a picture and the military medal of his father, a soldier killed in WWI. His uncle challenges Calgary's intention to enlist in officer's training school and abandon his widowed mother. Calgary affirms his intention and storms out to the corral.

Horses flash by–an international polo match, pitting Canada against Germany. Norman Nelson Holmes, 30, the most dashing player for the Canadians, scores the winner in the final chukker. He congratulates his opponent, Klaus Kretschmann, expressing regret the political situation in Europe will prevent future matches. A kerfuffle develops when someone announces war has been declared. Holmes, excited, dons his captain's uniform.

Renaud, packing to go off to officers' candidate school, grabs his bag and his camera equipment, leaving as his father berates him for joining the "goddam Anglais."

Calgary says goodbye to his angry uncle, aunt, and stoical mother, who gives him his father's medal to take with him to officers' candidate school.

Stalking through a woods [Renaud's POV] , an attacker springs out of the bushes, machine-gunning him with a wild cowboy "Wahoo!" It's Calgary who stands laughing over Renaud's body. The "dead" Renaud leg-whips the westerner and holds a knife to Calgary's throat. As they argue over who killed whom, they look up to see they are surrounded. Holmes, the officer of this obvious exercise, plunks a red badge on both, declaring them dead.

Later, at the Officers' Mess: Fine dinnerware and cutlery, white-gloved hands, splendid red uniforms, drinks, with Holmes observing our two cadets from the officers' head table. Renaud and Calgary, taunted by upper-classmen must behave civilly in spite of their obvious aversion to each other.

Holmes, in the classroom, waxes eloquent about the innovations of the great military leaders of the past. He decries the stupidity of politicians who refuse to fund the development of tanks, the key to modern warfare. Renaud argues for air power, Calgary for tank power. Holmes challenges Renaud to investigate tank strategy; Renaud would–if he had a tank!

A serene and silent countryside, shattered by the howl of grinding gears. Two shell-plated trucks simulating tanks careen into view, and battle each other, one finally broad-sided into a ditch. A jeep with Holmes and a civilian in it pulls up as Calgary leaps out of the victorious "tank" and rushes to help his victim. Renaud fends off his help and gets out by himself as Holmes congratulates them. Holmes introduces the irate civilian as his brother-in-law, Tom, the largest Buick dealer in Toronto, who is so kind to supply the "vehicles." Tom carries on, but Holmes ignores him, reviewing strategy with his two charges. Renaud charges the strategy may be perfect, the machines are not. Calgary claims the difference is the man who drives the machine.

Blackness–sounds of a truck laboring. From Renaud's POV inside a military truck bouncing cross-country, blindfolds come off Calgary and other cadets, as Holmes unceremoniously dumps them into the wilds of Canada's north. Departing, Holmes tosses them a fragment of a map. They must find their way to the destination on the map–but they don't know where they are. Darkness threatens, tempers flare. Renaud realizes they have been tricked: trained with maps scaled 50,000 to 1, the fragment is scaled 250,000 to 1. Everything is five times further and will take five times longer to reach. They come to a train trestle across a raging river, but it is washed out. One foolhardy cadet attempts to cross but falls to his death in the turbulence below. Renaud figures out a method of using their ropes to swing across the stream. The intrepid Calgary volunteers to go first and tie up the swing line. He gets into difficulty and has to be saved by Renaud. When they are all safely across, Renaud expects some thanks, but Calgary is furious and they come to blows. Their mates force them into an uneasy truce.

Calgary and Renaud are locked in a struggle to be top cadet, Holmes pushing both to the limit. In the final competition, an obstacle race, both are leading, but, concentrating on each other, fall together into a mud pit. The only way out is for one to help the other, but the one left behind will lose! Renaud, seeing Calgary's father's medal, decides Calgary needs to win more than he, so he boosts Calgary out. Calgary starts off to victory–but turns back, helps Renaud, and they both lose. Their enmity is not over, but is at least honorable.

Renaud and Calgary and their mates, more skilled than earlier, move through the woods at night, capturing–the nurses quarters! Only the beds are empty, and they face an irate matron of nurses, Miss Tate. She conducts the embarrassed raiders out through the girl's gymnasium, where they are forced to run a gauntlet of nurses armed with tennis and badminton racquets, etc. Matron sends the nurses to bed, and returns to her own, greeting Holmes, who claims the first essential of a successful raid is reliable intelligence. Miss Tate adds, "Complete surprise, Benedict Arnold!"

An elegant officer's ball, Renaud shooting home movies, Holmes escorting Miss Tate. After the dance, the cadets and their dates [are] drinking and toasting one another, for they are shipping out for England. As the camera pulls away, we see they are in a graveyard.

1942, ENGLAND

An English pub. Renaud asks a local beauty, Susan Archer, 19, for a date. Canadian troops live it up. Calgary and his outfit enter. All vastly entertained by a local performer singing an anti-Hitler comedy song. The Canadians follow with a ribald song of their own, and, taunted by the locals and Second Front agitators, respond crudely. A fight breaks out. While Renaud tries to break it up, Calgary rescues Susan and escorts her safely home. She has both lads on a string.

Renaud and Calgary [are] on the carpet for the womanizing and diminishing morale of their troops before their new commander: Col. Holmes. He expects them to convert classroom theory to reality in their new context: don't be afraid to be creative and unorthodox in keeping your troops in fighting trim with high morale.

After drowning their sorrows, the two men meander back to quarters, arguing about the Toronto Maple Leafs and Les Canadiens. They get an idea:

their platoons begin a series of stick hockey and rugby competitions–disastrous, for the frustrated troops maim and disable one another.

Calgary, invited to dinner by Susan, faces the resentment of her parents who have a son in North Africa. As Calgary leaves Renaud arrives. Susan's father has to intervene, advising them to save their fighting for the Huns.

Market Day in Horsham, England. Renaud shooting home movies. A Ladies Auxiliary is holding a greased pig contest to help British troops abroad. One of Renaud's men puts up the fee, enters the contest–madness and mayhem–and wins the pig. The locals claim the pig must be "blind" to run to a Canadian, and Renaud, grasping the value of the affair to morale, adopts the pig as mascot, and "The Order of the Blind Pig" is born.

An elegant dinner party. Holmes discusses tanks with Canadian General Crerar. They meet British General Montgomery, who advises Crerar to dump the old fogies in Canadian command ranks; give young officers a chance. Crerar pitches for action for Canadian troops and Montgomery suggests playing up to Lord Ismay, Churchill's Chief of Staff. Holmes volunteers to make the pitch; he played polo against Ismay.

Calgary, at Susan's home, finds she has gone off with Renaud to make some kind of propaganda film for "the war effort," her mother says.

The "Blind Pig," ensconced in mock-royal splendor, is wearing sun glasses. Calgary, trying to arouse the morale of his men, leads a frontal assault and they spirit away with the pig. Calgary's men, apparently "born again," frequent the local church. Renaud's men raid the church, find the pig in ecclesiastical splendor in the church's bell tower. In turn, they hide the pig in a "safe place." Calgary, putting the pieces together, devises a devious operation to recover the pig from its seemingly impregnable hiding place: the Combined Operations Headquarters of Lord Mountbatten. The raid arouses the ire of the COHQ staff and the raiders are dragged off to the stockade. Calgary and Renaud are hauled into the presence of Col. Holmes, but before he can chastise them, Mountbatten enters with a fuming General Crerar in tow. Mountbatten opens the three files of the two raiders and an embarrassed Holmes and reads the riot act. He summons an aide, who brings in a home movie produced by Renaud: a mock-drama of Allied Generals gambling with Hitler with little model tanks, airplanes, and ships, for the prize of a symbolic French maiden played, to the chagrin of Calgary, by Susan Archer. Mountbatten, fending off Crerar, says the men must be punished: Renaud is assigned to work with Noel Coward on the propaganda film *In Which We Serve*, Calgary is assigned to the Calgary Tank unit for a little party Combined Ops is planning for the Nazis, and Col. Holmes will be assigned to planning with Combined Ops. Initiative and creativity and action are to be rewarded, with the approval of Gen. Crerar, of course.

At Combined Ops, Holmes appreciates the plan of the Dieppe Raid for General Roberts, Force Commander of the Canadian division assigned the raid. Tanks in frontal assault appeal to Holmes, as well as the plan's classical "simplicity." Over the objections of Major Reginald Unwin, who cites overrated optimism about Dieppe's minimal defenses, Holmes recommends the Canadians accept the British plan. Unwin is transferred out. Mountbatten enters to inform both bombing and shelling before the assault have been withdrawn. Holmes insists the raid can still succeed, for "surprise" is their chief weapon. The raid is ON!

Rehearsals for the raid: Calgary having trouble on the beaches with the tanks. Renaud observes Mountbatten's masterful public relations moves, including parading the Royal Family on the set of the Coward film to silence critics. Renaud films Mountbatten's review of the chaotic exercises. Mountbatten, undeterred by the mistakes, claims having been made they can now be avoided. Holmes concurs, and the raid will proceed–but for security reasons, treated as a mere "exercise."

Calgary and Renaud pursuing Susan at the same time, each seeking advantage without telling her they are leaving for an "exercise." When she goes into her home, they begin to argue about the weaknesses of the "training exercises." Calgary is gung ho for the tank assault; Renaud is wary of a frontal assault unless the intelligence is accurate–remember the raid on the nurses quarters–and even more serious, remember the trestle disaster. Calgary is for going; Renaud cautious, and they are at odds again, with Renaud's fighting spirit questioned once more.

The final briefing of 300 officers includes Calgary and Renaud, who films Mountbatten's patented inspirational speech. Holmes continues the briefing, unveiling a model of the target and explaining the raid. Troops will not be informed of the destination until after boarding the ships. The junior officers react negatively to the plan, and the Canadian Generals have to quiet them down. After the meeting, Renaud, in the presence of Calgary, confronts Holmes with his doubts about the plan. Holmes pronounces the plan "a piece of cake." Renaud bitterly infers the raid is politically motivated to keep the Russians happy and shut up the Second Front agitators.

On the headlands of Dieppe, an angry Colonel Klaus Kretschmann orders his desultory troops that although the invasion alert has ended, they will remain at their posts for the night and be fully armed for first light, as if the Allies were really coming.

AUGUST 19, 1942

The ships for the raid lie in port with the troops on board. A grenade explodes accidently. Some troops have brought empty ammunition boxes, thinking this another useless exercise. Rifles are still packed in grease–uncleaned and unfiled for action. But the raid will go! The ships, disguised as harmless merchant vessels, set sail. During the night-crossing of the Channel, a German patrol appears, a fire-fight ensues, and the patrol disappears as mysteriously and silently as it arrived. Here, the perfection of the plan begins to unravel. Landing craft have been scattered. Confusion sets in. [The raid takes place in fog and smoke of various colors, for markers and for hiding movements: a surreal journey into the inferno that will be the Dieppe Raid.]

The commando flanking attacks launch. No news. Calgary is anxious to go. Renaud is not. They part, disappointed in each other. Renaud, confirmed in the disintegration of the raid, confronts Holmes–who orders him to transfer off immediately, or take up his place with the backup battalion of the Fusiliers Mont-Royal. Renaud salutes and joins the FMR with his camera, to film for Mountbatten the glorious return to Fortress Europe.

Troops in the first waves of the assault are dismayed by the air attack of mere seconds. Never told of the withdrawal of major air or naval bombardment, they are slaughtered in cross fire from the cliffs and headlands.

Calgary gets into his tank landing craft and departs for the main beach at Dieppe, where all hell is breaking loose. One of the tanks runs over a mobile radio unit set up in a dip in the pebbles on the beach. Col. Southam, instead of going himself, sends Calgary to assess the situation.

Radio operator David Hart sends a message received by Holmes: "three Essex Scottish" are in the town. Holmes misinterprets the message as the Essex Scottish have taken the town, and he launches the FMR to reinforce them. In the FMR craft approaching the beach, Renaud films the disaster. Calgary returns to inform Southam of the failure of the attack. No one has brought materials to blow the seawall, an oversight on the part of Holmes and the planners. Calgary's tank is disabled, and he sits on the turret directing fire at the enemy installations. Driven off the tank by a direct hit and a fire, he crouches down behind it, looking out to sea. He sees the FMR coming out of the smoke and is struck by the beauty of the scene: "Christ, aren't they pretty?"

Radio Operator Hart can't believe what he sees. He radios Holmes to stop the FMR, but Holmes has no way to inform the landing craft–and he must watch them go to their deaths. The lead officers are killed at the prow of the wooden crafts, even before they hit shore. The troops sit numbly frozen, until Renaud draws his pistol and forces them ashore. Calgary behind the tank sees Renaud corning. Renaud tries to help the troops reach the cover of the seawall. The signal comes that the withdrawal from the beaches will begin early, and the two young officers end up hauling wounded to the landing crafts come to take them away. Some landing craft are swamped by too many men, [and] mass attempts to cross the beach to escape result in most men being cut down like wheat. The tide is now 200 yards out, and the beach is ringed with a solid line of bodies. Calgary and Renaud are heroic in cooperating to save men. Waiting for the last landing craft to take them off, the two sit in the shelter of the back of Calgary's tank and make their final peace. They are both free of their fathers now!

Renaud wants to shoot as much film as he can before leaving, but Calgary insists he must move immediately. Calgary asks Renaud to take his father's medal as a sign of their new bond. He drapes it over Renaud's neck. Renaud keeps filming. Calgary insists Renaud must get off the beach and tell the truth with his film. Renaud keeps filming, so Calgary slugs Renaud, hauls him to the last landing craft, tosses him on board, and as he tries to crawl on himself, is wounded in the leg, and falls back into the water. With the reviving Renaud we see Calgary fading into the distance, and plucked out of the water by the Germans. Renaud stands up to take one last long pan of the inferno that is Dieppe, and the rising sun coming over the headlands catches the medal around his neck and glints in the sights of a German sniper, who squeezes the trigger–Renaud falls back dead as the camera spins out of focus and the scene goes black.

A magnificent military parade. Brigadier Holmes is decorated for his brilliant planning of the Dieppe raid by Lord Mountbatten. A reception follows. An aide brings a package to Holmes from a prisoner of war camp in occupied France. Holmes opens it to find a black moldy hunk of something with a piece of cardboard with writing on it: "It's just a piece of cake."

A beautiful sunset over the lake at the Laurentians. Renaud's father opens a package, and takes out Renaud's own posthumous Victoria Cross, won on the beach at Dieppe.

Postscript: On the vicissitudes of playwrights.

[*This pitch is quite different from my play about Dieppe. When I got the OK to try to develop an outline for a film for Kotcheff, I enlisted the co-operation of a Nova Scotian aspiring writer-director who had been squiring me about Hollywood. Delaying my return to Antigonish, the director, Rick, and I retreated for a week to his retreat in Bear Mountain, California, to collaborate. We hammered out the above and finalized it. Rick, in the end, did not want his name on the effort, but gave me permission to submit it by myself. Rather than abandon the project after so much work, I submitted the FAX above. Rick's intuition proved correct–but I am most grateful for that exciting week of collaboration and the generous hospitality of Rick and his wife.*]

After a month of waiting, I phoned Mr. Kotcheff's assistant and found out that Mr. Kotcheff had been ill and would be unable to deal with the script. Shortly after, he became a producer and director for *Law & Order SVU*, the second longest running prime time show on TV, and he is still with it as executive producer at age 87.

By this time, I was well aware of the difficulties of writing plays. It takes money and personnel and facilities and programs to mount plays. All you need to produce a finished script of a novel is a pen and some paper. Okay, a computer and some paper. The point is you, an individual, are in control of your work, and it will be in its final form as you so choose. Not so with plays. To paraphrase Betty Davis, "Playwriting is not for sissies."

My first full-length play won an international award 49 years ago: never performed; in production off-Broadway when canceled.

A play on schizophrenia took 23 years to get performed.

Chaucer play 21 years to get performed

MadShelly play over 20 years to performance, won the National championship.

Feature-length screenplay: 29 years; never performed.

Never say die–and keep on scribbling.

In 1975, the Sisters of St. Martha were preparing to celebrate their 75th anniversary of being founded. At such times, the Sisters often put on entertaining skits at such celebrations. They asked me to write a little play for the affair. I said yes. Then I thought, what a piker, the Sisters have been so good to me, I should write a full-length play. So I called, they were honored, but who could direct such a thing? Why, I'll get you the best director in Canada, Frank Canino, who had won the Louis Jouvet award for his play based on the Wakefield Cycle of medieval plays and performed by StFX to win the National Championship. Then I thought, what a shame such a talented team effort would disappear after a single performance for the Sisters. So I called the National Film Board of Canada regional office in Halifax to see if they might be interested in making a video of the affair. I could not get to talk to anybody, and after several futile attempts, I finally called and declared to the receptionist, "I have an idea for a film."

"Don't we all? What is so different about your film, dear?"

"It stars 29 nuns and a bishop."

Four days later, I was in the NFB office in Halifax pitching the idea of celebrating the Marthas. The pitch: two girls join the Marthas, one stays and one leaves. We weave in the exciting story of how the Marthas were trained by the Sisters of Charity in Halifax, but when the time came to go to Antigonish to serve the boys and priests at the College, they were not released. So we would have their struggles at the beginning, and the difficulties of vocations in the new age of Vatican II changes in the Church.

Okay. They had offered the film to a young director.

"What next?" I asked.

"How about the script?" [Not a word of it yet written!]

"Okay. When do you want it?"

"Next week."

(Silent gulp, and panic in my empty head.)

"Okay."

I was used to writing under pressure at the University theatre, and as a part-time reporter for *The Casket.* Deadlines were my motivator. No time sitting around musing.

Put the pen to paper. *Thecla's Choice* premiered at the Bethany Motherhouse in 1977.

Now having good relationships at the NFB, I sought materials from them that would be useful for my film course. The Film Board had engaged a Czech director to do a workshop with five young Maritimers who wanted to become directors. They had taken a script called *Bargain Basement*, supplied equipment and sets, and each of the five had shot scenes from the script. Thus, at the beginning of the course, we could evaluate and compare different techniques for the same scenes by five different directors-to-be. And we could rate them. An added bonus was I knew several of the actors because they had been in some of my plays. The one condition was that the material not be used in public, only in class. We ranked the five directors and debated the reasons for our choices. What a valuable resource. One drawback was the crude language in the script, [the] overuse and repetition of which we found to be a fault.

The film was about a woman shoplifter being apprehended by a store detective. Her pleading led the detective, a Czech, to take her to his apartment instead of back to the store. Eventually he tries to rape her, but she shames him, and he allows her to depart.

This script was eventually rewritten by an NFB director named John N. Smith, who was named co-author of a half-hour film, still named *Bargain Basement,* but set in Montreal. John N. Smith is a magnificent director. He turned a basically raw and crude script into a masterpiece of a human document with sensitivity and compassion. Our workshop sessions concluded with Smith's rendition, and revealed how the crude language was not at all necessary. The characters became alive and both were sympathetic, both suffering in their individual ways. This guy Smith was impressive.

Thus began my telephone campaign to contact John N. Smith to take a look at my Dieppe script. He was in Montreal. I didn't know he was about to make the major film *The Boys of St. Vincent* about the orphanage scandal in Newfoundland. After half-a-dozen phone calls, his assistant rather brusquely severed any possible relationship with me: "Stop calling. Mr. Smith does not care to make a film about Dieppe. He will make films of his own choosing, and will not accept any script from anyone else. Please leave us alone." Another avenue cut off.

A number of years later, I was awakened by a phone call at *12:30 a.m.*, by an excited voice. It turned out to be Brian Loring Villa, an American professor at the University of Ottawa, in the nation's capital. He explained, "Your contact at the Directorate of History gave me a copy of your play on Dieppe. I just finished reading it. My God, you got it! You figured it out before I did! I just published a book, *Unauthorized Action: Mountbatten and the Dieppe Raid.*"

Still a bit dazed, I replied, "Well, um, thank you." I paused.

"Oh, I'm sorry to be calling so late, but I am meeting tomorrow with the CBC-TV to make a film based on my book. You should write the script. You know Dieppe and have the feel for what really happened."

I was fully awake now.

"I am going to propose to the CBC that you write the script. I'll call you tomorrow."

It was already tomorrow and I got the feeling I wasn't going to sleep much anyway. I thought that, at last, my ship was coming in.

The phone call came around noon the next day. No need to go down to the dock. Brian Villa informed me that the contract for the script had already been signed yesterday. No problem getting a good sleep now.

I waited anxiously for the film and watched it with great interest. Not bad. Then came the credits, "Directed by John N. Smith."

Here is my farewell on the passing of Brian O'Connell, PR Director at StFX and columnist in *The Casket.*

*

Mission Accomplished

per*i*scope, n. *an optical instrument for viewing objects that are above the level of direct sight or in an otherwise obstructed field of vision.*

"The Periscope" was an apt name for the columns that appeared in this space for the last quarter-century. Like a submarine commander zeroing in on a ponderous aircraft carrier, the author with finely-tuned journalistic skills sank many a pompous and ponderous ass. None of us were safe, enemies or friends, especially friends, including even his personal friend the Prime Minister [Brian Mulroney].

But how could any of us complain, when the members of his own family, past and present, were targeted for the eloquent tongue of his wit? The measure of the man, Brian O'Connell, was honesty and his sure grasp of the ironies of life.

That we live in a vale of tears, no man knew better than Brian. He carried his ill-health, his one-lung, his isotope-invaded body, as a badge of honor in a human family of all-too-fragile flesh. He fought to the end with a fierceness affirming life, pounding out columns full of humor and compassion and amazement at the absurdities of life.

Let us take a moment to reflect upon the sea of the subconscious this master submariner sailed. Behind every laugh is a bite of pain. When the pretentious man slips on a banana peel and comes a cropper, we laugh, when we see it from a distance–and looking up from below. But when we see the fall up close, we see the pain, and because we are close to it, we feel its potential in our own situation. As a columnist Brian could play us like a fiddle, with a comic insight, and like a Stradivarius with a sense of deep compassion, as the occasion demanded.

Brian O'Connell's great insight, through his own suffering, and his own basic decency and honesty, was to help us bear patiently and with quiet dignity, the pain and suffering, and to remain humble and composed for the occasional fleeting joy and triumph of our ordinary lives. His carefully crafted deceptively simple words, reached out to our community, and grabbed us by the heart in moments of tragedy, and by the funny bone in moments of human foolishness.

Brian, with immense passion, could defend the weak and underprivileged while asserting their human dignity. Brian, with equal ferocity, could attack the ignorant and mean-minded while revealing their shallowness and venality. In doing so, he enabled us to see below the surface of things, to have a better feeling for the right thing, the right word, the right act of friendship–yes, the right impulse to love one another.

Beneath the hidden depths of the laughs and the tears he shared with his own family and many friends in the words of this column beat a tender heart and a lively mind, both enclosed in an all-too-human frailty. He served all of us so well, so faithfully, and so skillfully.

Can't you see him now, at the Pearly Gates:
St. Peter: Aha, Scribe, we've been waiting for you.

Scribe: I had a few guys I wanted to outlive. And I had to make that fiftieth wedding anniversary. I wasn't sure if this elevator was going up!

St. Peter: I know, my son. I was a bit impetuous myself, in my own day. We've been saving this white robe for you.

Scribe: Hold on, Pete. I'll look like a scarecrow in that thing.

St. Peter: I'm afraid that's the way things are here. Besides, we saw your knees in 1953, when Mother Veronica and Dr. Somers got you to wear a kilt for the hundredth anniversary of the University.

Scribe: A temptation to the Virgins on the Frozen Lake?

St. Peter: No, no, no. We couldn't keep our haloes on for laughing.

Scribe: Halo? No way.

St. Peter: You don't really have a choice, old boy.

Scribe: We'll see about that. I'm not going to look like a damn fool. Where the hell is my typewriter?

St. Peter: Miiichaelll! Security to the Pearly Gate . . .

Thanks, Brian. We're going to miss you. All of us.

Take it on home. Mission accomplished. Periscope down.

Another year, another ceremony, but this time I got to speak for myself.

The X-Ring Ceremony - StFX Day 1993

Fellow Xaverians:

I daresay no one of you was forced to come here tonight. You all want the ring. Why? What's the big deal?

A small item of jewelry serving no useful purpose, my ring cost a mere $19.25. Why did I wrap an ounce or so of precious metal around a finger–especially one with the 24th letter of the alphabet on it?

I was on an airplane and the man next to me kept surreptitiously eyeing my ring. Finally, he leaned over and whispered, "Are you a member of the Ku Klux Klan?" Recently someone asked one of my colleagues, "Are you a supporter of Malcolm X?"

How can the X-ring be mistaken for two diametrically opposed meanings? Because the X-ring is a symbol–that is, a concrete object representing an abstract idea, an idea deeply invested with feelings and emotions. Let us examine for a moment the history, and thus the idea, behind the X-ring.

The X-ring was born about a half-century ago during the Second World War. In the early decades of this century, each graduating class at StFX appointed a pin committee, and that committee designed a ring or pin for the graduating class. In the twenties and thirties pins were very popular, and each class had a unique pin with a unique motto engraved upon it. In 1942, a student named

Willie Locker MacDougall was chair of the ring committee for that class. For whatever reason, he neglected to prepare a design, and desperate for something to present to his class meeting, grabbed a paper and pencil and drew a design for a ring–a circle with an X in it. Necessity being not only the mother of invention, but the easiest path to a destination, the simplicity and stunning uniqueness of the design was welcomed by the class of '42. The class of '43 could not improve upon the classic beauty of the X-ring, and a tradition was born. As a result, we have a most recognizable and unique ring.

Originally, the X-ring was bought individually over the counter and later in bulk by students arriving on campus for their Senior year. There was no ceremony. In 1957, an American student was Secretary of the ring committee. He talked the class of '58 into ordering the rings before leaving in the junior year so he would have the ring to give to his girlfriend in the summer. The Senior class objected vehemently, but when the Junior class ordered the rings and announced their distribution, the Seniors went hairy! You weren't a Senior till you returned in the fall, they argued. The Juniors countered, they became Seniors when they got enough credits. If symbols are invested with emotions, you would have needed a chain-saw to cut the tension on campus. The Juniors voted to carry on; the Seniors howled in anger!

The night the X-rings were to be distributed, they disappeared–all 300 plus of them! Supper in Morrison Hall that night was a madhouse. Fights broke out between Juniors and Seniors. The RCMP came to investigate. The next evening, the President, Dr. Hugh Somers, addressed the student body, and offering an amnesty, gave the culprits 24 hours to return the rings or else a fate would descend upon the campus worse than that visited upon the Pharaoh of Ancient Egypt. The next afternoon the rings mysteriously reappeared and peace was restored. The American got to give the ring to his girlfriend–and she refused it. So much for love! [Full disclosure 2019: *C'est moi.*]

Around 1967, when I was Alumni Director, deep feelings divided the campus again. One group contended the X-ring was for graduates only. The other group contended many worthy Xaverians had to drop out of school for various reasons, including lack of funding, and were entitled to wear the X-ring! Every so often, one of the dropouts became a highly successful and wealthy donor! Obviously, the symbolic X-ring meant different things to different people: was it a graduate ring for academic hoop jumpers? Or a sign of spiritual bonds of a collegial community? Or a symbol of membership for benefactors?

In the end, the graduate status was enforced. Rules and regulations for the X-ring were instituted with a solemnity worthy of the tablets of Moses. Today the X-ring is an exclusive, copyrighted symbol that has to be earned.

So here you are ready to receive it, having earned it. What does this passionately longed-for symbol mean to you? Why do you need this ring? Why do we confer this ring to you in this sacred house of prayer and worship some of you have never before entered?

We do it for the same reasons couples stand before altars and promise eternal fealty with rings, for the same reasons bishops and popes and kings and queens are invested with rings, for the same reasons heroes are bestowed Victoria Crosses and Medals of Honor. Because this moment is an important moment of commitment in your lives. We are trying to put into concrete terms those inexpressible emotions and feelings we have toward the experience we have shared by coming together in this community of scholars to pursue "Whatsoever things are true." When you came to StFX, you set a goal to graduate. While striving to that goal you have made and lost friends, explored new and often disturbing ideas, been challenged by and suffered through professors. You have been happy and sad, excited and bored, prodded and led astray, triumphant and defeated–but most of all, you have endured. But, having passed through "X", you will never be the same. No one on this earth can know how deeply or how profoundly you have been affected. You may not realize how deeply yourself.

We do know that the first graduates who wore the X-ring loved this place, the people who labored here, and the Catholic tradition that formed the philosophical basis of the community. StFX entered the modern era and began its rapid growth only after World War II when the veterans arrived to spark our growth from a small school to a larger national institution. They were people facing a troubled and changing world with traditions and faith challenged on every front. They gave themselves to the battle of life, fortified by their experience here at "X", proudly wearing the ring that symbolized their membership in the Xaverian family, in the values espoused by St. Francis Xavier himself, a fierce faith and a willingness to sacrifice for the good of others.

Today that tradition of the past as symbolized in the X-ring has changed significantly. The priests and sisters, both Notre Dame and Marthas, no longer dominate the campus scene. The faculty is more non-Catholic than Roman Catholic. Latin, theology, and religious rites are no longer mandatory. The rules of social intercourse and quality of life on campus have evolved sadly in the manner of the rest of the world. Some elder Xaverians are disturbed by these changes and feel that the X-ring today does not symbolize the same experience they lived here. One of my dearest friends from those days refuses to wear his X-ring.

I, too, am disturbed by the current situation. But, because of my experiences here, which now have covered forty-years of my life, I am honored to participate in this ceremony. I believe that the X-ring and its value as a symbol has never been more important. I was so moved by my undergraduate experience I vowed to return to *alma mater* and spend my life sharing the gifts, joys, and benefits given to me here at "X". I remain fully committed to the Catholic heritage of StFX and the goals of this academic community of scholars. I may have trouble living them as fully as I might intend, but I am committed. I also recognize that while the past was full of many glorious blessings, being a human institution, it was also subject to faults and failures. This institution still is human–and it still has noble goals it must strive for more effectively. But, that is precisely the strength of the Xaverian family, as it was the strength of Francis Xavier. He never quit, dying on a barren island named Sancian off the wild coast of China over three hundred years ago. We shall not quit either.

Today the Xaverian family includes Catholics and non-Catholics of every ilk: Protestant, Jew, Muslim, agnostic, atheist. Every single one is capable of pursuing "whatsoever things are true." They do pursue it. They may not have grown up in the Catholic tradition, they may not even be familiar with it, but if we Catholics present our goals with clarity and good will, all Xaverians–Catholic and non–can see the wisdom of the path. Here in our small community on the fringes of the weary world, like Francis Xavier on the shores of Sancian, we should all work together to help one another to peace and fellowship and love in the Lord.

So, here this evening, I say to you about to be invested with the X-ring: bolstered and strengthened by your undergraduate experience, make this ring the symbol of your commitment to face a weary and suffering world and make the best of it. Make this ring a symbol of the values this community of scholars stands for. You have earned the ring, but the right to wear it must be earned every day of the rest of your lives.

The true value of your undergraduate years here will be meaningful only some fifty years from now, when you are standing on the shores of your own Sancian. If, when you look at the ring on your finger, you can say to yourself, "Yes, Lord, in this troubled vale of tears I have been faithful to the values and goals of my

Xaverian heritage–I have sought whatsoever things are true, whatsoever things are beautiful, whatsoever things are good," then, dear friends, your X-ring truly will symbolize a peace and a happiness beyond all understanding.

God bless you all.

*

This is the original talk I gave in the chapel at the 1993 X-ring ceremony. It was later edited and revised for *Prayers for the Xaverian Family* prayer book published in in 2003 for the 150th anniversary of the founding of the University.

Bur-Mac: Keeping the Spirit Alive

A story from *The Xaverian Weekly* February 7, 1996

As he proceeded in his metronome-like amble along the sidewalk, of which he knew every lurking frost heave ready to trip him up in front of Xavier Hall, Fred's bypassed heart quickened as he approached the Geology building. He remembered the day the Sisters of St. Martha had vacated the place in procession two-by-two to their new home in the south wing of the new Morrison Hall. They were happy to leave the building where so many of their predecessors had died of overwork and exhaustion in service of the boys and priests. Fred had been happy to set up his new digs as lecturer in geology, proud to have an office to himself and a room to display the rocks he had assembled for demonstrations to his introductory classes.

Could it really have been forty years he spent tapping on rocks, and tapping on the heads of students in there? His wife had never visited his office there, and he was glad she had never seen the clutter of his daily routine. Order was to be found at home, in the regularity of both meals and children being born.

Order was to be found in the college in the mutter of the morning mass he used to serve for Fr. MacLean in the "catacombs" under the old Somers Chapel, the daily pattern of classes, and the seasonal exams and commencements. His nose was lifted from the grindstone by the eternal pattern of sports at the college.

Rugby matches, basketball in the bandbox that is now the Bauer Theatre, baseball–now no more–and the long lost races and field events of interclass competitions. And, of course, the crowning glory of hockey in Memorial Rink, built and named to honor companions and classmates lost in the Great War no longer remembered by the students.

In Fred's days, the life of the college seemed to revolve daily around sporting events. The whole student body and most of the town turned out for games. Of course, the whole student body and most of the town actually fit into the rink.

Even growing up Fred had remembered stories about X's winning the first big hockey trophy in the twenties. The little school could be noted for more than producing priests; it could turn out fine young athletes: remember Ronald John MacDonald's world-record victory in the 1898 Boston Marathon! More vivid in Fred's memory bank were the hockey deposits of the era following World War Two. The hockey team reigned supreme. After venerable Fr. Poppy McKenna led them to new heights, feisty Fr. Andy Hogan raised them to Olympian standards. The Xaverians could have represented Canada in the '48 Olympics, but they couldn't arrange for classes–there were rules and regulations then.

The college had two teams–the Varsity played in the APC league against the reviled New Glasgow Rangers, whose coal-miner players did not, definitely not, want to lose to a bunch of snot-nosed college dandies. After the incredibly fierce and bruising playoffs in the APC League, the varsity players would drop down to the Junior Varsity level and thump the bejabbers out of the collegiate playoff opponents with double-digit, often shut-out, victories. Dal and Acadia and St. Mary's never paid any rent past the StFX blue line. Why one year the team, holus-bolus, was inducted into the Nova Scotia Hockey Hall of Fame.

Hockey, however, was the second great religion on the campus. Mass, evening prayers before supper, retreats, Tenebrae–three days of prayers before Easter–in the Cathedral, paying respects to the source of this mini-paradise came first. Hockey was a close second. Fred recalled the Sunday in the Chapel, Vice President Monsignor Mike MacKinnon had turned to greet the congregation, solemnly intoning *Dominus vobiscum* in Latin followed without pause in English: "StFX 4, Acadia 3!" The chapel had reverberated *Et cum Spiritu tuo!* The Xaverian family prayed together, and stayed together.

Mostly Fred remembered the difficult case of the WWII vet, George Mc___, who, nearly penniless, had come to X unable to bring his wife and five children to Antigonish. Weekends of loneliness and academic despair drove George to take a nip or two. After a fateful bout in town, he wobbled back from The Main, passing through the doorway in Xavier Hall toward Confusion Square. George, accosted by an unpleasant light in his sore eyes, gruffly uttered a threat–"Put out the fucking match." Unfortunately, it was to Fr. John Angus Rankin, Dean of Men (discipline), holding a flashlight in George's face. Goodbye George, goodbye degree, hello world.

Alcohol was totally banned on campus, and even the vets who had fought at risk of life and limb in "The Big One" were not exempt. Of course, the few priests who took a nip or two too many and avoided public scandal were protected by the brotherhood. Their private indiscretions were tolerated, but if their sins became public and created problems with missed classes and dereliction of duty, they were transferred out to singular suffering in some isolated country parish.

Fred recalled with a sense of justification the even tenor of the public life at the University in those days. "Whatsoever things are true" and "good" and "beautiful" were thought upon and openly espoused and preached to the world. The rest was consigned to the secret alleys of the night. More than lip service was given to pronouncements of "goals and priorities." Decency was observed–publicly.

Fred loved the students. The vast majority were so wholesome and inspiring, actually. He was often struck by their basic honesty and sensitivity. They had kept him young for so long. Being around them was life-enhancing. They glowed with energy and enthusiasm for the future, feeding him with the urge to carry on, unlike some of his colleagues who seemed to tire of classes and who burned out. Fred had looked younger than his years–until he had retired. He had begun to notice, however, the *small* minority of students who were mean-minded and vulgar in his day when the enrollment of the University was in the several hundreds were now a *large* minority among a giant student body of several thousands. Antigonish, although previously tucked safely in the isolated corner of north-eastern Nova Scotia, was now plugged into the main channels of the Global Village.

Fred lamented the lack of decency that had followed. It had been so rare to hear the "F" word in those days gone by. Sure, everybody knew "the word," and the vets had known how to use "the word" with élan, but people did not ever spout them in public, and even in private they could be fatal. Witness poor George.

These days on his way across or through the campus, it was the rare exception to not hear the "F" word erupting from the mouths of the students as innocuously as "Hi!" Fred, himself, of course, said the word–when he hit his thumb with a hammer or lost a parking space to an aggressive driver on the way to a doctor's appointment. But in the privacy of his workplace or the interior of his car. Never in public, nor in a place where strangers could overhear.

Just the other day, he had been shocked in the library periodical reading room. He liked to drop in, on days too cold to walk very far on his constitutional, to read the out-of-town papers and magazines his meager pension did not allow him to subscribe to.

He had been admiring the students. As he had always joked, the older he got, the younger they got. The students today were so tall. Being of average height in his own college days, he had never considered himself lesser than his mates or colleagues. But today's students! So many were so tall, so fresh, so full of vitality. They seemed to tower above him. He seemed to be shrinking back in time as they were growing into the future. They seemed to be evolving minute by minute rather than generation by generation into a higher form of human race, healthy, vital, ennobled.

Then, as he was browsing in a photography magazine, he overheard two beautiful young women talking in normal voices, seemingly oblivious to the context of place and the presence of others. And there it was, ringing in his ears–the "F" word. They were f-ing this and f-ing that, and f-ing some him, and f-ing some her, and f-ing . . . He had carefully, with a nearly palpable quiver, placed the magazine back on its rack and turned away. He wondered, as he walked down the steps, if his own daughters were f-ing someone somewhere.

Walking around the corner of the Geology building, Fred saw the Philosopher's Bench erected by the students in honor of Fr. Edo Gatto, and he recalled the reverential mid-day masses, now no more, of Fr. "Porgy" Kehoe, the former Athletic Director, yes, and Dean of Men in his day. Two stalwarts, albeit not without their faults, of the Xaverian family and the spirit of the place, tragically killed on an icy hill in St. Peter's. A huzzah of sound interrupted his reverie.

As he turned to pick up the sidewalk directing him to the chapel where he would attend the daily 5:05 Mass, Fred opined what the noise was. This Friday, February 2, 1996, is the eve of the great Bur-Mac hockey game, pitting the two residences, Burke House, named for Bishop Burke, the first pioneer bishop of Nova Scotia, against MacIsaac House, named for he-couldn't-remember-which glorious Mac benefactor. Who could keep track of all the Macs? They took up two-thirds of the local phonebook.

This Bur-Mac thing was a sign of life. A continuation of the spirit of the place. The students really got up for this. Fred remembered fondly the Massachusetts-Maine hockey match of the late fifties. The inept Americans, of which there were more in those days, got together for unbridled mayhem and massacre in an annual match which unleashed considerable testosterone in harmless play. The rink was always packed: the priests in their box at the end of the rink near the door. Students hanging over the balcony around the rink, newly reinforced after the collapse of a section had spilled people on the ice in the late forties, or was it the early fifties?

Recently, hockey had fallen on hard times. Not many championships these days. Football, the new Canadian game, not hard-scrabble rugby, had nearly been erased, making the glory days of Coach Don Loney a fading memory. How many students even know why the lounge in Oland Center is named the Loney Lounge?

Basketball had won the Nationals a few years ago and given the whole school and the town a big shot of adrenalin and spirit. But this Bur-Mac game, Fred thought, seems to be the sporting equivalent of the X-ring ceremony, which in turn seems to make commencement anti-climactic–tradition alive and well, if modernly modish. Fred was not aware that the women students, in imitation of the male Bur-Mac clash, had initiated their own hockey match. The nature of a possible feminist comment in this act would have escaped him anyway.

As Fred stopped to let a cat pass before crossing the main entry road leading to Morrison Hall, the sound of shouting re-entered his consciousness. He saw a large group of some thirty or more young women students in front of Cameron Hall, named for Bishop Cameron whose statue guards the entrance to Xavier Hall, facing the world outside the protected enclave of the University.

The young ladies were all dressed alike in some kind of gray carpenters' overalls. They were the women of TnT residence, an acronym for Tompkins and Thompson Houses, named for the co-founder of the Antigonish Movement, vice president Jimmy Tompkins, and Fr. A.M. Thompson, rector, as we used to say, of the college at the turn of the twentieth century. These young ladies, Fred thought, wouldn't remember when girls from the Mount used to go to downtown Antigonish two-by-two with escort battleships of pairs of nuns fore and aft. These young ladies were plunked on campus after the notorious student strike of 1971 when the students won the right to open housing—that is, girls on the lower campus—after forcing the University to close.

Opposite the festering group in front of MacKinnon Hall, a similar if smaller group of young women was quivering like a flock of restless pigeons. The women of "Chillis," an acronym of Chisholm and Gillis Houses, named for more illustrious rectors of the college: Fr. Hugh Gillis, who also played a major role in building the Cathedral, and Fr. Daniel Chisholm, who was instrumental in bringing the Sisters of St. Martha to the campus in the 1890s. The two groups were shouting at one another and gesticulating wildly.

Fred thought the TnT group the more voluble and explosive, in keeping with its nickname. He observed some rather unusual actions by the young women. Yes—one TnT-er was giving the Chillis bunch the finger. Now she began gyrating in an epileptic manner. Fred twigged—she was imitating the sex act, bumping and grinding.

The roar and buzz of the high-pitched exchange began to coagulate into words Fred could understand, which at first he didn't believe he was hearing: "bitches," "cocksuckers," "dykes," "Fuck you!" Fred put his head down and kept his feet moving, one in front of the other. He reached for the railing of the stone steps and literally pulled his tired body into the sanctuary of the new Somers Chapel, trembling with relief as the huge wooden door clicked shut behind him.

The ten adults and four students there for the evening Mass were just beginning to pray. Fred flopped into a pew and felt his palms begin to sweat. He tried to focus his mind to join in the prayers, to listen to the readings. But his heart seemed to race—his pulse quicken. The candles beside the altar became a blur of streaky light clusters.

Breathing deeply, Fred began to focus on the Mass, the moment of transubstantiation was approaching. The Son of God, the body and blood of Jesus, the Spirit transformed into flesh to suffer the ignominy of humanity, would be called to this altar, this table of sacrifice, in this place, in this time, to offer his broken body again for the souls of the people of this University family, the old and the young, the beautiful and the deformed, the brilliant and the stupid—*All of us, even me*, Fred thought.

But the noise was too loud. The young women outside the walls now had bullhorns, and like troopers were broadcasting their vocabulary of obscenities and vulgarities and barbarities through the thin glass windows into the haven of the chapel. Fred would not hear the words of the consecration. And as he looked up at the elevated host the words of a young woman smashed into his mind–"Fucking bitch cunt dyke cocksucker."

*

This story with its graphic language caused a significant stir on the campus. Within hours of the publication of the student newspaper, several students were at my office door, some in tears, apologizing for the behavior of the students in the story–for they knew this FICTION was the TRUTH. The juxtaposition of StFX tradition with the crassness of modern culture drove a spirited dialogue among and between students and staff. The "language" disturbed some, enraged others, and others read it as honest reflection. Fred was modeled on Dr. Bill Foley, my first year chemistry professor. All the other people named were real people. I was "Fred." The incident was factual.

At the besmirched consecration, despite my wife's attempt to calm me, I left the chapel and rushed directly across the main university entrance to MacPherson House. I had lived there my sophomore year. In the third floor hallway window were two large speakers broadcasting to the quadrangle below. I flew up the stairs and the students shrank back into their rooms, looking at the "mad" man–they knew I was angry. I grabbed the speakers from the window and threw them down the corridor. To the students peeking out their doorways, I let loose with my most thunderous voice, decrying the fact that they were despoiling my "home," that I would be here after they were gone, and they were turning it into a pigpen. The only reason I never incorporated my fit into the story was twofold: first, Fred would never have done that, and second, the real ending would detract from the sense and impact of Fred's disappointment.

And, more significantly, my actions revealed my sense of being unable to change the evolving nature of my beloved *alma mater*. The final Bur-Mac game was played in January of 2016. In 2017 planning was under development but the student organizers were unable to create a success plan, something the University and Students Union required prior to any support for the game to continue. The final game of 2016 had resulted in $5,400.00 in damage to the Antigonish Arena, and that was the end of Bur-Mac.

"Farewell, Mr. Mayor" - from The Casket

Mayor Colin H. Chisholm

A few days before his own Passover and resurrection into eternal life during Holy Week, I had the privilege of saying goodbye to the man I can truthfully say was "the most unforgettable character" I ever met–Colin H. Chisholm, Mayor of Antigonish. In his home and in the presence of his lovely wife and daughter I was able to enjoy one last joke, one last compromise, and one last peaceful farewell.

I met Colin H. Chisholm first some thirty years ago when he hosted the reunion of his StFX classmates on his island in Lochaber Lake, and I was, at the time, Alumni Director of the University. He was a gracious host, a lanky homespun Lincolnesque character, with the quiet charm of a Gary Cooper. This public persona hid a wide-ranging, inquiring mind–any subject or scheme broached–he had an angle on it. At first glance the angle might seem far off the point, but the deeper into the subject, the more pertinent and apt Colin Chisholm's view became.

Until then I had known Colin Chisholm only by reputation, and that was considerable: Soldier, MLA, and probably the best Minister of Agriculture the province ever had. I had listened on the radio anxiously to the Liberal convention at which he became ill and the window of opportunity for the premiership of the province slipped away from him into the darkness.

We became political adversaries in 1970 when he was elected Mayor and I was elected a town Councilor. I opposed the tax write-off for the mall of which he was Manager. Ever since through two terms as town Councilor, and twenty-five years as Secretary of the Board of the R. K. MacDonald Nursing Home Corporation, the Mayor and I were often on opposite sides of many votes. Through it all he became for me, "Mr. Mayor," and I never, ever called him Colin.

His position allowed him to be called "Your Worship," a title smacking of the deity unsuited for such a rustic character–he deserved and wore with impunity, in my mind, the moniker "Mr. Mayor." We have had some dandy Mayors in this town, men of great character, honesty, and integrity, but I don't think any of them enjoyed the job as much as Colin Herman Chisholm. The town was his personal Monopoly game, and no one ever beat him at it.

Provincial politicos were astounded by some of his moves–like the million-dollar tax write-off–but they were most respectful of his abilities, for they had seen him in action in the provincial legislature. When the Mayor spoke, they huddled with their advisors to make sure their pockets hadn't been picked for the benefit of Antigonishers. I was present at hearings in Halifax and witnessed the awe and reverence accorded Colin H.

He was "Mr. Mayor" around the clock, and on every corner, street, lane, and byway of the town, as well as throughout the province. He toured the town every morning, driving every street, noting every pothole, every fence, every new home being built. If there was a trick he missed it wasn't worthy of note. He could tell you to the penny the value of the fencing around the old dump-site on Brierly Brook Road.

Mr. Mayor knew how to make things happen, and when he wanted to solve problems he could tap the people to make them happen–even if the people were not particularly enamored of the idea. One of the most astute projects ever put together was the Sewage Treatment Lagoon, which failed as a unified project, but which the Mayor was able to bring into being in stages.

His notebook was his ever-present cigarette pack. When he got it out and jotted something down, you knew it was important. Sometimes the results like the Sewage Treatment were successful, and sometimes they were not. But if those cigarette packs had been catalogued, they would make a good book on municipal management do's and don'ts.

Last summer we met and he asked what I was doing. "You know perfectly well I'm building a new home, Mr. Mayor–increasing your tax base." He cocked his head and drawled, "I heard it was, ah, a Caw-thee-drall!" *Touche-aye!*

In the first days of our opposition back in 1970, I noted that although the Mayor and I might argue different sides of questions, he never had a personal grudge against me. When a meeting was over, no one could ever tell from his demeanor whether a debate had gone his way or not. He treated his Councilors with fairness and personal respect.

Even in the mid-seventies when we had some real donnybrooks and the council meetings were entertaining enough to draw people away from their TVs, the Mayor never got personal. The Mayor would lean back in his chair and apparently fall asleep, until someone slipped, and then one eye would open, he would lean forward in his chair, flex an eyebrow, ask for a clarification, and before the speaker realized, his mouth was full of shoe leather and the Mayor would be tacking on a new pair of heels. If you underestimated the Mayor, you were a cobra who thought a mongoose was a nice little pussycat! He played the activities in the council chamber the way Pablo Casals plays the cello–plucking the strings with perfect virtuoso control.

One hot night I made a motion, and the usually calm and laconic Mayor nearly flipped out of his chair, declaring, in Jehovian tones, my motion was "the most stupid %$#@*&(^#@!%&@(+^$ motion ever put before a council in the province of Nova Scotia." Before the exchange was completed I had been reduced to a mound of simmering pork rind, and my position lost. But, Mr. Mayor had not attacked me personally–just my motion.

Many of the proposals I brought forth, which he deemed worthy, Mr. Mayor supported unequivocally. I shall be eternally grateful that he not only made possible but encouraged my writing of *The History of Antigonish* (a project for the town's 1989 Centennial of Incorporation) and never intervened in the slightest manner in a single word I wrote.

At various times while in Council, and over the intervening years, I had to intercede with Mr. Mayor for various groups and causes. It was always a most interesting adventure to go up to his home on Hillcrest Street. He would hail me in from the back door. I'd sit down at the kitchen table where he was pouring over the *Globe & Mail*; he'd light up a fresh cigarette, and the political education of Pat Walsh would begin. Those sessions were as stimulating and interesting as many a seminar in graduate schools on two continents.

I came to appreciate that in many of the questions that had divided us, Mr. Mayor had a rationale that made his position worthy of serious consideration. I remember, especially, one thorny problem we had wrestled with for over twenty years. He asked me to interpret a document, pretending for the occasion I had been called as an expert witness and English professor before a court of law under oath. When I interpreted an ambiguous passage not only in my way, but as also possibly interpreted in his way, he was pleased and said, "I have always believed you were honest, and now I know you are." That we could mutually arrive at the belief in each other's honesty after so many years of opposition, was a joyful moment for me, and I hope, for him.

Sometimes, Mr. Mayor would enlighten me with history of the town and the county; sometimes he would amaze me with his freshness of insight; sometimes frustrate me with a blind spot. Throughout the three decades of our friendly rivalry, however, I can say that I cannot think of a single instance in his presence when I was bored. The Council meetings he conducted, on occasion until 5 a.m., were never dull, because he was always up to something–and the way he would make things unfold was truly astounding. People would come in loaded for his hide, and leave polishing his boots. He was charming, he was clever, he was pig-headed, he was enigmatic, he was shy, he was a politician's politician, he was "Antigonish's first citizen." He loved this town with a deep and abiding passion, and gave a major portion of his life and energy to the benefit of the people in it.

Colin Herman Chisholm was my adversary and he was my friend. He was unforgettable, and I shall miss him–he was truly "Mr. Mayor."

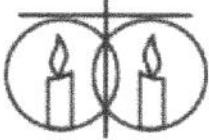

This exchange (*From The Xaverian Weekly student newspaper*) is not a cause for alarm; this is what I call a "teaching" moment in civilized and respectful dialogue.

From The Xaverian Weekly student newspaper

"Why I Don't Go to Church" by Sean Barrett

There is a common notion that Christians are organized groups of people who gather together once a week or so to profess their faith in Jesus Christ. If you happen to be a Roman Catholic, meeting this criterion is a simple task. You merely show up to church for approximately forty-five minutes each Sunday and repeat a sequence of learned responses throughout the mass. This entails very little effort or thought as the responses remain essentially the same week after week, year after year, and once enshrined in your mind become a natural reaction.

For example, when I hear the phrase "The lord be with you," I automatically respond by saying, "And also with you." I don't think about the meaning of what I say, I just say it because I've been taught to respond in such a way. Nevertheless, it is a common belief that to be a good Christian you must learn such responses, use them at least once a week, and conform to the teachings and beliefs of the organized institutions of worship (i.e., Roman Catholic Church). In my opinion, such actions do not reflect Christianity and the organized institutions of worship may be "de-Christianizing" its members.

In my opinion, to be a good Christian, one must only follow the teachings of Jesus Christ. As far as I can tell, the essence of Jesus' teachings in the following:

1. Love all humans and accept their differences
2. Act as a pacifist and avoid all conflict
3. Do not be judgmental
4. Greed is terrible thing and material possessions are not important
5. We should strive for equality among all humanity

Wouldn't the world be cool if all alleged Christians followed these principles? There would be no fights or war, racism, sexism, and homophobia would disappear, and without greed or emphasis on material possessions social and economic equality could prevail. Unfortunately, organized forms of Christianity usually make the task of being Christian extremely difficult.

Churches act as institutions of moral guidance to their members. The attitudes of the members of a particular church usually reflect the position of the institution. For example, the Roman Catholic Church sees all practicing homosexuals as being sinful. As a result, members of the homosexual community are denied many rights (such as adopting children through so-called "Christian" agencies) and face discrimination from those who judge them through the Church. So much for the Christian principle of having and accepting all humans and not being judgmental towards others.

Another major difficulty with the Roman Catholic church is in the way it accumulates and allocates its resources. The Vatican has literally billions of dollars' worth of assets in the form of gold, art, and collector's pieces. As well, the Roman Catholic church spends millions of dollars every year renovating their buildings. Meanwhile, millions starve. So, what about the Christian principles against greed and possessions and of helping those in need?

It has been argued to me that you cannot be a good Christian unless you go to church and follow the church's teachings. I argue that you cannot go to church and follow the church's teaching and be a good Christian.

*

A response to last week's commentary on "Why I Don't Go to Church" by Sean Barrett

"Why I Do Go To Church" by Patrick Walsh

As a Roman Catholic graduate of StFX '58 who worked for *The Xaverian Weekly*, and who has taught here for some thirty-two years, I read the letter from Sean Barrett in last week's paper with much sadness.

Sean's reasons for not going to church may be heartfelt but seem to me often illogical. His understanding of the Roman Catholic Church differs from my lifetime experience in it.

However, as a practicing Catholic, I can understand some of the anger and frustration Mr. Barrett vents because of the all-too-frequent difference between what Christians profess and the actions they perform. This understanding is based on an awareness of my own shortcomings in living fully and faithfully what I believe are the truths of Christ.

Because of my own faults, I do go to church–to the StFX chapel and to my home parish, St. Ninian's Cathedral. I go to Mass because I need to and want to and like to.

For me, the Church is not as monolithic as Mr. Barrett states. Within the teaching guidance of the Church, there is a lot of room for debate about exactly what Jesus taught and exactly how things should be interpreted. That's why we still have theologians, and even bishops, debating things. Peter and Paul had a great debate at the birth of the church, and Vatican II is still hotly contested among Catholics.

Yet, in spite of obvious divisions among Christian churches, and within the Roman Catholic Church itself, there are more things that unite us than divide us– Jesus being the bond and model of love for us all.

Let us make no mistake about it though. Jesus commended some actions (the Good Samaritan) and condemned others (the Pharisees, and those who would harm children). We can love the murderer but hate the murder. We can love the sinner, as He taught us, but hate the sin.

Yet, as Mr. Barrett implies, peoples' actions are not often easy to label black or white. Human actions are often gray, often difficult to label sinful or not. Yet, the abortionist and the bomber of clinics seem equally evil and harmful, despite the good intention of each.

For me, the Church has a divine nature which is eternal and spiritual, and a human nature which is temporal and physical. Its human nature is embodied in an administration, which, like all human institutions can make human mistakes. We used to burn heretics at the stake. We acknowledge we know better now. We still have a lot to learn.

The Mass is a living symbol of the love of God for humanity: Jesus offers his life for us, once and forever. The Mass is a ritual of a Christian community. In celebrating Mass, people worship God, thank Him for His many blessings, ask Him for help. We need rituals to carry on our lives, as may be seen in funerals, marriages, celebrations, and even graduations. Rituals help us witness the underlying values we place on our lives and experience–those values so difficult to put into words.

That's why we have an X-ring ritual which puts into action a public expression of the values we attach to our StFX experience. For some, the X-ring is a valued symbol of a deep and heartfelt experience. For others, it may be an empty and trivial piece of jewelry.

Some graduates may wear the X-ring as an expression of faith and fidelity to the values of this institution and try to live up to its meaning. Others may put it in a dresser drawer. Those who wear it do so to express a unity with the meaning that lies behind the ring. However, some may live the values, and others may only advertise that they passed through here.

That's what the Mass and going to church is like: for some people it is a source of inspiration and commitment. For some it is a meaningless ritual, practiced out of habit. For some "The Lord be with you" expresses a living spirit of love, and "And also with you," a recognition, acceptance, and reciprocal response to that love. When some find these words empty, I am sad, for they are missing what some of us find a deep and satisfying experience.

Yet, at the same time, I acknowledge an important point implied by Mr. Barrett. Some who go to church do not live out the reality behind the symbol. And I acknowledge that many who do not go to church live out the reality of Christian belief, just as many members of the Xaverian family who do not have X-rings live out the values of StFX.

As I said in an address at last year's X-ring ceremony, "Today the Xaverian family of students, faculty, and staff, includes Catholics, and non-Catholics of every ilk: Protestant, Jew, Muslim, agnostic, atheist. Every single person is capable of pursuing 'whatsoever things are true.' They do pursue it. Some may not have grown up in the Catholic tradition–they may not even be familiar with it. But if we Catholics present our goals with clarity and goodwill, all Xaverians, Catholic and non, would be able to see the wisdom of the path."

These thoughts touch on the reasons I go to church: to follow the teachings of Jesus that, properly understood to the best of my ability and training, will lead me be a good Christian and thus a decent and loving human being. I hope and pray I'm right.

Kingsley Brown, Sr. was Director of Development at StFX. He was shot down over Germany in WWII and spent four years in a stalag prison camp. He had been a newspaper man before and after the war. I delivered this eulogy at his funeral in the StFX chapel.

Kingsley Brown Sr.

Goleb Plasov, a steel-worker from the rolling mill of the *Vereinigte Stahlwerke* in Liegnitz, was born in the little village of Latulia north of Sofia. In 1943 while transferring from the Liegnitz plant to a new steelworks in Strasbourg, he was arrested in the Chemnitz train station by the Gestapo.

Goleb Plasov turned out to be Kingsley Brown of the RAF, who, after being shot down by Prince Egmont zu Lippe-Weissenfeld and imprisoned there on July 3, 1942, was attempting to escape from Stalag Luft 3. Kingsley wanted to leave his German prison and return to his wife Marion, for as he dedicated his memoir, *Bonds of Wire*, he was the prisoner in her heart.

The man we have come to honor today at this memorial mass was guilty in war-time of *namentausch,* the switching of names. He became expert at *namentausch*. But switching names and identities was dangerous. On one hand, you could become confused and forget who you were, and on the other, the authorities might actually believe you, and you would become the other, officially.

I respectfully suggest that we take a closer look at the man we hold in our memories as Kingsley Brown. Who was he, really? And who did he pretend to be? I shall base my conclusions on two sources: my own observations of Kingsley as colleague and friend, and a close reading of his written texts.

First, it was my privilege to log many thousands of miles traveling with Kingsley. Imprisoned together in our train compartment or automobiles we shared experiences, rich material for short stories–and tall tales. Kingsley was obviously a very married man, and Marion was never far from his thoughts. He was a proud and devoted father. He was a tireless worker, a true friend, and an impeccable gentleman. The miles melted away in his company, and hours seemed minutes, as he recounted stimulating and thrilling adventures of a rich and satisfying life. He was a man equally at home in the groves of the academy, or the forests of his seaside estate. Kingsley truly reveled in life: the man was incapable of surrendering to moaning of the naysayers and doomsters.

A most vivid image lives in my memory. One spring I drove down to Dunn's beach to check on how much ice was left before I could start walking on the shore. There were mountains of ice yet, worthy of the brush of Loren Harris. But rising out of this desolate remnant of winter, rose a goggled apparition: Kingsley, in his eighth decade, wet-suited, as vital and frisky as a new colt in a spring meadow. The man knew how to live fully wherever he landed.

Yet, wherever Kingsley went, he eschewed the spotlight. He served quietly, efficiently, generously, in his gray suits and autumn tweeds, with that life-celebrating splash of a yellow tie–the color of life and hope. To meet him was to like the man, to work with him was to be assured, to know him was to be privileged. Could such admirable qualities in a man be an assumed identity? A charade of a prisoner of the world? The persona of a master of *namentausch*?

I suggest that to see the true nature of the man Kingsley Brown, we should subject his writings to analysis. Writing is the most truthful fingerprint of the mind. Ideas a man sets to words for his readers are the blueprint of his soul. To read the writing of Kingsley was to see a mind of reason, of clear thought, of generous understanding, of simple and direct statement, of honesty and honor.

Having learned the journalist's need to be accurate and direct and sharp as Occam's razor, Kingsley's prose was a model of clarity and precision. No purple prose please. Balance, restraint, harmony, thank you very much.

Oh, yes–he professed a rosy revolutionary youth, an agnostic's doubt's, a rationalist's demand for proof. But in all his actions, his thoughts, his manner, his compassion, his service to country, community and college, Kingsley Brown was the epitome of an ideal Christian gentleman. He put to shame many who professed to be what he did not claim, but was–a loving and caring man.

I defy anyone to read his memoir, and not see the perfection of the Christian ideal of love. Kingsley could see the pain and suffering in his mates–and in his enemies. He could not be blinded by the evil of war to the goodness manifest in the enemy. It is easy to love friends–but Kingsley truly loved and appreciated and was enriched through the enemies he loved. He was capable of that miracle of what he called the Spirit of Man. He saw it in men, women, and children, friend and foe, nobleman and peasant.

When you read Kingsley's writing you encounter a truly religious spirit, not professed, but lived. His writing betrays his true identity. We see the man behind the man, the *namentausch.* We see a good Samaritan of the twentieth century's darkest moments. In the end, this noble prisoner of life, was run to ground by the Hound of Heaven. A Christian gentleman of happy memory, Kingsley Brown, has been called to rest in the bosom of the Lord he could not resist.

The Annual Interclass Play Festival was short a one-act play, and the Artistic Director of Theatre Antigonish called me up and asked if on short notice I might have something to fill the empty slot in the schedule. I didn't have anything, but I could whip up a play about a subject dear to my heart. What follows are excerpts from a one-man show, written and performed by yours truly, with minimal set [a small table and easy chair surrounded by books and papers, a couple chairs side by side on which I would sit as Pat Walsh, the driver, and slide over to become Fr. Rod MacSween, the passenger]. The tech crew rose to the occasion. I present here the opening of the play, a poem by Father about being born, and a poem at the end, about the nearing death. Sandwiched in the middle is an actual homily Father preached at a wedding.

*

Father MacSween - a one-man play

[Stage in darkness: the cry of a newborn child. A pool of light up on a stool. Enter and sit.]

just born

I think of myself just born
blood and filth on my mouth
air scorching my lungs
and my cry quivering in the air
uttered not for nurses or doctors
through the great spaces of the sky

and even up to God
my fierce cry
demanding an explanation
why this rape from the infinite
into this question box of a world
why this imprisonment in time and space
and in this animal body
made for limitation and suffering

to be nothing and then suddenly something
to hardly feel and then to be in pain
to be in an envelope of flesh
and then to be open to sound light and air
to be pricked by numberless stimuli

to be all alone and then to be the center of touch
circled by voices and eyes

much later in my crib
I reached out to catch the birds
that flew above the trees
when I opened my hands
they were empty
I saw only my empty hands
those symbols of captivity
as I grow shall I capture
and retain

*

[Don a priestly the stole and glasses for the wedding homily.]

Homily for the marriage of Maire (Sheldon & Dawn's daughter) and Donnie:

You better sit down. It's going to be a long sermon.

In the name of the Father, and the Son, and the Holy Spirit.

A good place to start is at the beginning. In consideration of marriage, that means beginning with original sin.

Now you know the story in the bible of how Adam and Eve sinned in the garden–and there is nothing there but an apple. One of our great writers said it certainly wasn't an apple–it was an orange, and we've been slipping on it ever since.

But, what is behind the story is that our minds are darkened, our wills are weak, and we're inclined towards evil.

The story of original sin is trying to tell us what condition we are in, that in this world, things are not easy. And the story is dramatized to show us how consequences follow from our actions, and that we're not a smart as we should be, we're not as strong willed as we should be, and we always, unless we are very careful, we end up in evil.

Like a man who walks along the side of a hill, when one foot is lower than the other, even with all his might, he can slip down the hill.

Now, have we got a chance to win in life with fate so strongly against us? And the answer to that question is: No. That we'd have no chance–if it wasn't for the grace of God.

If it wasn't for this grace, not only for Christians, but for everybody, humankind would never make it through life. He would stumble along somehow, but he wouldn't live a really good life.

The things that make this life possible, give us a measure of success, is that we are able to use that grace that's all around us.

Just as we walk through the air, the air is all around us, and so the grace of God is around us, too. But it will not become part of us, it will not enter us, or change our souls unless we make use of it, and we make use of it ordinarily through the sacraments.

And here is where we come to marriage. Because marriage is a sacrament.

There was always a form of marriage. Even with the animals there is a form of it. But ours is special and that is why it is surrounded with so much ceremony. Why we dress up in these garments. Why the people concerned are dressed up and look so handsome.

Because marriage is special. Not only the church, but all of society says that marriage is special–and precarious. Therefore, we surround marriage with every bit of ceremony you'd find. We speak about it in terms of happiness, but we also speak about it in terms of fear. Because this thing that is so important to us can be lost, or it can be ineffectual, or it can break up.

Is that important? It is that important. Marriage is the way most people save their souls. There are other extraordinary ways. Some not at all likeable, like martyrdom. If you want to pick martyrdom, you're free to do it. But there are other ways, like the priesthood, which is not to be confused with martyrdom.

But, the ordinary way to save your soul is through marriage. All good people here are going to save their souls through marriage.

I was thinking of a few things that I think of whenever I speak about marriage. I think of snow; going through the snow to attend mass on Sundays. I think of shoes; the children putting on their shoes, especially in winter. I think of hamburgers, hotdogs, dirty dishes, dresses, trousers, socks, lots of socks; always singles, never two. But the socks themselves are a symbol of how mixed up marriage can be.

All of these things remind us of the dayliness of marriage, the eternity of this world, the routine: how we move on from day to day, from night to night, without a letup, until we die.

Marriage is not only for the couple, but for the children. Parents are asked to do daily things for them. Not only to feed them and clothe them, and make them go to school and church, but also to teach them the simple virtues of honesty, truthfulness and loyalty. They will fail, and have to start again. All these trying daily things belong in marriage. And so, we do try to the utmost to be proud of that dayliness.

A few years ago I read about the death of Einstein. Even Einstein had to die. And they filled magazines with essays. One woman wrote in and said he used to pass her daily on his way to teach, and he used to stop every once in a while and chat with her. Not about physics or some strange secret formula. He spoke to her about the weather, about her own health, and trips she had taken. And the writer said that it's a wonderful thing to think of when great men die; all we can think about is that they have the simple virtues of the poor.

In marriage, the simple virtues, the ordinary ones, the daily ones, come to full bloom, and by them you can save your soul.

In the name of the Father and of the Son and of the Holy Spirit.

*

[To the desk to write the last poem.]

Jerome

[St Jerome was a priest/theologian who translated most of the Bible into Latin at the turn of the third century]

now that I have reached the end
      I speak openly to others
why should I not speak openly
      to myself

sitting all alone
      in preparation for my last journey

I am like Jerome
his lion glowering behind him
all the monsters of fancy
peer from the surrounding darkness
to see the spectacle of my fall

people have watched me live
for many years
but I have been dead
I have come to life
like a hungry bear
in the springtime
its winter hibernation done
how it tears at the grass and the bushes
how it rips at the city of the rodents
and slaughters the inhabitants for food

I have emerged from my den
chains clinging to my limbs
not the chains of church and state
but the invisible bonds
of my heritage
the corruption of my time
the animality of my nature
the leaden things
of my personal being

I should like to scratch
the body of the church
as a woman scours out a pot
so that the genuine metal
shines from within

I should like to throw the scrapings away
as worthless
as a waste of time to linger over
as a blind for the shining core

I should like to call to the officers of the state
    to give an accounting
not that they shall hear my voice
    or read my words
but so that I shall know where I stand
    and in what silence I live
    wherein I have connived at evil
    or neglected to call out from the wall
    when the enemy has captured
            part of our town
I should like to die in the knowledge
    that at least I have called out

so I say to myself retire into a cave
    to think to the end
blot out the sun and moon
they remind me of my days
    of foolish optimism
call up the snake the bat the lion
    fit companions for solitude
then let the judgment of my life
    begin

Much of my life was spent in dramatic endeavors in the Old Gym, which became the Bauer Theatre.

The Bauer Theatre

[A talk to welcome visiting Scottish dramatists.]

The ancient Greeks, trapped between the rock of the cold, hard, yet tantalizingly beautiful world they were born into, and the hard place of death and the world of the gods they aspired to, invented drama. In amphitheaters where the population of four or five Antigonishes would gather, they celebrated the human experience and all the mysteries life contains. As the closest of all the art forms to the realities of everyday life, drama continues to thrive, because both life and death remain mysteries–mysteries that continue to challenge people of faith, and people of no faith, alike. Life forces all of us to make choices based on how we "believe" the universe is destined to unfold–to a glorified eternity free of sin–that is, pain and suffering and dislocation–or to entropy at last into a black hole of nothingness beyond our comprehension. These two possible fates you saw in the masks of joy or sorrow you passed on the way in. My one contention: drama is important to all of us, and will continue to be important as long as we remain human–for the function of art, especially drama, is to help us break through the barriers of this earth and to give us a window to the infinite.

My privileged task here this evening is to welcome our guests from Scotland, and to introduce our main speaker. To make them feel at home, I shall briefly describe the space they will perform in–for drama takes place in a living, three-dimensional space, which many still consider a site of sacred and religious function.

As an aside, we might mention that some people, unaccustomed or untutored or inexperienced in the techniques of the theatre, sometimes consider what may happen here in this space to be anything but sacred, in fact, sometimes blasphemous. And I must admit, that sometimes, performances in this space have disturbed people of religious faith, and likewise, people of secular faith–my own dramas among them.

But if we stop and think about the nature of the exploration of human experience, even the teachings of Christ, which are an attempt to guide us through the vast gulf of gray between the extremes of black and white, can be misunderstood: witness the excesses of the Inquisition. This week's readings in the Mass are from Matthew, in which Christ confounds the establishment by dining and consorting with prostitutes, tax-gatherers, and other low-lives.

I have been consorting in this space, now known as the Bauer Theatre, for some 44 years. Forty-four years ago this space was a gymnasium, and I was the manager of the StFX basketball team. I was in this place almost daily for four years. We won Maritime and Atlantic championships every year, and one year a Senior C national championship–although the final game had to be played at the parish center across from the Cathedral, because this space had a running track around the second floor, and opponents couldn't shoot from the corners–for us, a distinct and unchristian-like advantage. Because lights went out at 11 p.m. every night in residence, I ensconced myself in the equipment room–now Addy Doucette's office–and with blankets over the window, had all night-lights, a record player and radio for music, and so I wouldn't be reported to the authorities, a hot plate for making hot chocolate for "Jack the Cop" MacGillivray, the one-man campus security force.

We had some great sporting dramas here, including a miracle three-quarter court basket by Dr. J. J. MacDonald in a student-faculty game. The Harlem Globetrotters played in this space. Student initiations were committed here, until such events were moved from dramatic to realistic by a number of broken limbs.

This building became dramatically sportless when the new temple of sport, the Oland Center was opened in 1966–67. So shortly thereafter, twenty-five years ago, Theatre Antigonish was founded and established as its sacred playing space, here where you are sitting. And that's all it was then–a space.

The University had enjoyed a great golden age of drama under the direction of Monsignor Cyril Bauer, who had studied drama at Catholic University of America. Fr. Bauer produced major musicals and Shakespearean dramas of overwhelming success–some taken on the road to major cities in the Maritimes. Dramas were performed in Immaculata Hall at Mount Saint Bernard College, where the good Sisters of Notre Dame had introduced dramatic culture to Antigonish in the 1880s. After 1950 performances were in the basement auditorium of the new chapel next door. The life of drama flourished, including a One-Act Inter-Class Play Festival, which hijacked me into a life in drama in 1958.

In 1963, when Fr. Bauer's duties as Vice President of the University became onerous, drama fell into the hands of another Catholic U. grad, Frank Canino–who dropped modern drama on campus with a vengeance. Frank's play, a triumphant adaptation of the Wakefield Cycle of medieval mystery plays, starred, among others, Addy Wintermans and Lionel Doucette, and won the 1967 Canadian Dominion Drama Festival. The next year the two principals appeared in *Romeo and Juliet*, and as they say, life imitates art. Well, not perfectly, for they are living happily ever after. When Frank Canino left, the drama department was eventually entrusted to Dennis Hayes, of CUA, and John Rapsey. Modern experimental drama of the "Living Theatre" variety abandoned traditional musicals and classical drama, and entered an age of improvisational group productions, centered in a coterie of a dozen or so devotees of drama as a way of life. As a result, in 1973, the University closed the drama department and looked for someone to re-introduce the community to more traditional forms of drama. Thus, under a series of creative artistic directors, starting with James Colbeck, through Jeannie Smith, to Addy Doucette, Theatre Antigonish burst on the scene. Drama was again alive and well and appealing to wide audiences, with not only experimental drama, but traditional, classic, and Shakespearean productions. Furthermore, the theatre now involved the people of Antigonish and the surrounding communities, who supply continuity and stability to the operation in the face of constant student turnover–students insist on graduating.

I have not the time to name all the talented people who have contributed to Theatre Antigonish over the years. A couple of weeks ago I was surfing the TV and saw three TA alumnae on three different programs. I began to write out a list of TA people who have gone on to exercise their talents in the wider world, and within a half-hour, I had a list of over 50 people who were active that week in the entertainment and media industry. As distinguished representatives of all these talented people, I might mention just two families–the Murrays, Bob and Mavis and progeny, and the Alcorns, the clan of Dianne and the late Russell–for whom Theatre Antigonish has named it highest honor. One of the most pleasurable features of my long association with Theatre Antigonish was to watch Russell Alcorn, not merely as the sensitive and loving person he always was, but to watch his growth into a most accomplished and distinguished actor, who brought out the best in everyone around him.

Theatre Antigonish has not only survived for a quarter century, it has thrived. It has given birth to an imposing child, Festival Antigonish, a ten-year-old professional repertory company under the indefatigable Addy Doucette. Theatre Antigonish has become an astonishing scene of any place on, over, under or beyond this earth, under the talented designs of Ian Pygott. It has been promoted tirelessly by the always upbeat Marjorie MacHattie.

Most appropriately, this home of Theatre Antigonish, this sacred place, this place of wonder and delight, has been renamed the Bauer Theatre, in honor of the spirit and accomplishments of the beloved priest-director who fostered our life of drama. All who toil in this marvelous space are his direct descendants.

In silver celebration of what we do here, we are most pleased to welcome this evening the troupe of the University of Glasgow, Scotland. We, the children of the diaspora, are happy to share with our comrades from the homeland these hallowed boards. We look forward to the magic and mystery of life explored by your author, your players, your director, and your entire crew. Theatre Antigonish is fortunate indeed to have you initiate a truly international expansion of our search in drama, "for whatsoever things are true."

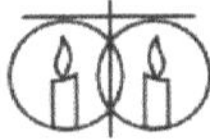

House

the empty house sits silent in the sun
towels limp on racks bananas sunning
your cook books stand in white birch garrison
dead fly in kitchen light no longer humming

in the upper chamber a high bed waits
children leap-frog years in formal photos
below a rose of Renoir radiates
and lower yet a cycle nowhere goes

gray walls enclose a universe thereof
as you did bear our children in your flesh
creating for them life and soul and love
then set them free in worldly wilderness

a mother fills a space with love and life
a house is made a home by you my wife

happy mother's day 1996
your loving husband

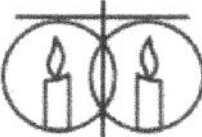

Sheldon Currie stole the show at the 1999 University Convocation with this brilliant mocking praise of my teaching.

Outstanding Teaching Award

By Sheldon Currie at the Convocation of 1999

As every Cape Bretoner knows, mockery is the highest form of flattery. I have known Pat for over thirty years, and as far as I know, I have never missed an opportunity to make fun of him. And it's not that hard. Pat is the master of so many arts, crafts, skills, and like Ulysses, Aeneas, Beowulf, like Superman, like Xena and Marg Delahunty the Warrior Princesses, and like God, everything he does is of such epic proportions, everything he does is so visible, audible, tactile, olfactory, tangible, palpable, tangy, zesty, so full of . . . flavor and savor, that he presents an easy target for any pygmy with half a brain and a blunt instrument. Readers of Frank Magazine will already be familiar with the epic exploits of **FRONT PAGE PAT**, so I don't have to tell you everything. I'll try to tell you something you don't know about Pat.

PAT THE ATHLETE: Lots of people know about Pat's encyclopedic knowledge of sports. He has read and memorized every issue of "Sports Illustrated" since Fred Flintstone beat Alley Oop MacDonald in the one wheel horseless chariot race. Pat could tell you who won the Tour de France in 1968. Those of you who have attended basketball games in the Oland Centre, especially the referees, know of Pat's prodigious knowledge of the rules and customs of the game. But very few people know of Pat's stature as an athlete, and the reason is, Pat's choice of game. Pat was a handball player. Handball, like squash and racquetball, is a game played in a rectangular box with a hole in the upper back end wall for the referee. There is no space for spectators, which makes you wonder why Pat, of all people, chose this game as his sport. I believe he did it because his friends played the game, and it gave him an opportunity to punish us. In handball, when you hit the ball, your opponent is in front with his back to you. Pat hit the ball so hard that it disappeared and was out of sight until it hit the front wall in front of you or grabbed you by the back of the neck and lifted you an inch off the floor. Then you had to serve the ball to him so he could do it again.

But I'm here to tell you about **PAT THE TEACHER**. Teaching is an art, a craft, a skill. As with any skill, most people can learn to do it; but only some are naturals. Some people couldn't teach a dog, or even a pet rock, to "stay." Some people could teach anything to anybody, and Pat is one of those. When Pat and I were young profs we shared a space, and one day the phone rang and Pat answered it and said, "Mmm, mmm-umm, mmm, mmm-ummm, no problem." He hung up and said to me, "Father Charlie wants me to teach his philosophy class while he's on retreat."

"Why you?" I asked.

"I don't know, Pat said. "I guess he can't find anybody else."

"What's the class on?" I asked.

"Aristotelian Metaphysics in the *Summa Theologica* of Thomas Aquinas," he said.

"What do you know about that?" I asked.

"Nothing," Pat said.

"So what are you going to teach them?" I asked.

"Whatever I can find out in the next 24 hours," he said. And he did. Imagine Father Charlie's surprise when he discovered it was Pat Walsh of the English department and not Pat Murray from Philosophy who taught his course. And imagine his chagrin when his students began to hint that Pat's was the best lecture in philosophy they'd ever listened to.

Pat has been a printer, an artist, an actor, a politician, a poet; he has written plays and short stories, he is a film script expert and script doctor for Telefilm Canada, he is a specialist in 19th Century Romantic Literature, Modern Drama, Film Studies, Anglo Irish Literature. He is a master of many trades. Pat is a great teacher because he brings such a variety of experience to his classes. Pat is a great teacher because he believes in the redemptive power of literature and because he genuinely loves his students.

I'd like to read you an e-mail Pat received from a student this year at the end of the term. Pat gave me a copy of this. He let me read it if I promised not to tell anybody about it.

"Dear Dr. Walsh,

I was a student in your English 250 class this year and I just wanted to say thank you for giving me the opportunity to realize that I really do have a passion for English . . . Your style of teaching and your motivation proved to me just how passionate you are about what you do."

Yes. That's the word. Passion. Pat is passionate about everything. About sports, about literature, about teaching students, about hitting me in the neck with a handball, and about his friends. Pat has been a friend of mine for over thirty years, and I am delighted to have this opportunity to make fun of him one more time.

Most Reverend Chancellor, with pleasure and pride I present Dr. Patrick Walsh for the Outstanding Teacher Award.

*

And that citation, I believe, will go down in the annals of the University's archives as the most memorable, humorous, and delightful citation of all time. Thanks Sheldon.

A Shocking Revelation at 60 Years of Age

One night at "Monday Night at the Movies", my film course in B-33 Nicholson auditorium at StFX, a girl about 20 feet to my left asked a question. When I turned to answer her, I noticed she had a bruised chin. Oh, God, I thought, I hope Shannon is okay–looks like she was in an accident or somebody struck her. About ten minutes later we took a break, and Shannon came up to ask me a question, and her chin was fine! After break when the students returned to their seats I took a look at Shannon–her chin was bruised again! I began to look at other students around the auditorium–and pale girls with dark lipstick all had bruised chins! I squinted hard and realized I was seeing TWO chins! I knew something had happened to me.

After class, about 10 p.m., I drove down to the *Casket* newspaper to pick up my wife Jackie who was editor. At the Whidden corner at Hawthorne and Main streets I went to turn on a green traffic light with another green traffic light below it. I had never seen a light like that before–then I realized–I was seeing double!

I said nothing to Jackie, but the next morning I drove up to St. Martha's hospital to see the eye doctor–usually a nine-month waiting period. The receptionist–knowing full well the answer–snarked, "Do you have an appointment?"

"No–I have a problem."

I was in to see Dr. Hamilton in five minutes. He poked my eye, flashed lights, spun striped things around, and then pronounced "Now, don't get excited, but you have had a minor stroke affecting one of the three nerves that control the movement of your right eye. This is not a major stroke–or else I would be hiring six fellows to scrape you off my floor–but these minor strokes usually heal themselves in five or six weeks."

After some questions he prescribed the standard aspirin a day and told me to lay off lifting weights until further notice.

I was disappointed in this state of affairs because since last October 25th I had lost 50 pounds, and dropped my blood sugar from 11 to 5, and dropped my blood pressure to 130 over 80, the equivalent of a pup in high school! On my way out the doctor said very casually, "Oh, by the way, just to be safe and to see where the nerve acted up, I'd like to have you get a CAT scan at the Aberdeen hospital in New Glasgow [the neighboring town]. The problem could be in one of four places, and I'd like to see where."

After several weeks the Aberdeen phoned with an opening, and one of my colleagues drove me the 70 kilometers to the Aberdeen. They ran me through the CAT scan tube backwards and forwards twice and then told me to go home and wait for a call from Dr. Hamilton, my eye doctor.

I did.

I got his call a week later in the office on a Friday afternoon.

"How are you doing?"

Fine. Never felt better.

"How's the double vision?"

All gone after two days, I'm seeing fine.

"Well, the good news is that your eye is fine."

Then everything is okay?

"I didn't say that."

What the hell are you saying, John, I asked in a soft tone worthy of Brando's godfather.

"Well, totally unrelated to your right eye, which is fine, the CAT scan has revealed you have an arachnoid cyst on the left side of your brain."

What does that mean, John?

And then the double or triple talk began–it was on the outside of the brain, not in the interior, so it would be easy to get at, and there are three layers and it's in a good layer, and well, it was beyond him and the locals so they were recommending that I go to see the Grand Poobah of neurosurgeons 250 kilometers distant in Halifax.

The next weeks were stressful, but I remained very calm, having believed the literature I have taught about the human condition. Jackie was quietly asking our kids and our friends to say a little prayer for me. [Why little? I needed BIG prayers!]

Finally we both drove to see the big guy in Halifax at the Queen Elizabeth II Medical center: Dr. Holness–appropriate name, that. He asked my profession–English Prof at StFX University.

"Really? That's very interesting."

If it's not, I tell the students we may as well go home.

"No, no, I mean it's interesting in view of your condition–and you're right-handed. And you use a computer?"

Yes.

"Steady hands."

Graciously, he ended any suspense–"Get your wife in here."

When she entered he said to her, not to me, "Mrs. Walsh, your husband is fine. I'll show you his CAT scan and some models."

You may have already suspected. A major portion of the left front of my brain is missing! Empty, nada, nothing, zilch, zero, gone, never there! And the doctor explained–the normal site of my verbal and analytical skills! I have been empty-headed since birth!

It's a developmental birth defect. But at age 60, no sense worrying–I've adapted as necessary–obviously–although my colleagues have just about exhausted the jokes, e.g., "Pat's a couple French fries short of a Happy Meal," and other equally hairy old jokes about elevators not going to the top, etc. etc. etc.

Dr. Holness began to discuss how this might have happened–and all I can remember is that my mother who died at age 47 from heart trouble had her first heart attack carrying me. The birth was difficult, and my father was given a choice to save the baby or the wife–but being a Catholic college grad he said, "We will not make that choice. You will do your best to save both–and you will do whatever you have to do in the process."

We both survived and I have a younger sister and brother. We do remember that I did not speak until nearly four years old–my parents had me tested for deafness, but I could hear. [Typical comment made by almost 95% of friends who hear the story: "You've certainly made up for it!"] When I did begin to speak, I spoke in complete sentences! No baby talk.

Dr. Holness has referred me to a neuropsychologist at Dalhousie University who wants to run a few tests on me. [I have prints of my CAT scan and will attach them to this memoir for display, discussion, and distraction!]

I am now studying up on the brain and the mind and hope to become more enlightened about my own life.

The University is giving me a sabbatical and I am leaving next week for Calgary, Alberta, for a year.

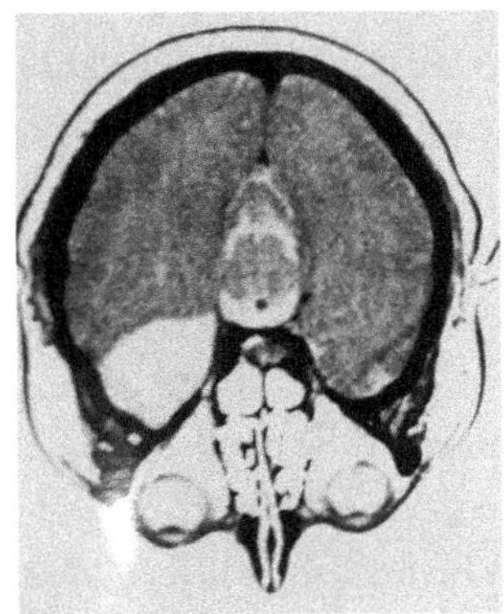

The blank spot over the left eye is the area of the missing left frontal lobe.

Pat Walsh 1997 Antigonish

PS: I never did get to that psychiatrist. So to hell with Warren Doolittle, I was fighting my way into becoming a reader with half a brain! And later I was informed by one of my classmates in the Nova Scotia Department of Health, that if my condition had been known in my early childhood, I would have been institutionalized. In Alberta I learned that if my condition had been known, under the laws here as recommended by the University of Alberta, I would have been sterilized! My five children and ten grandchildren are happy the governments did not find out my condition until I was 60. So am I.

PW 2014 Calgary

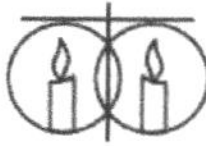

The advantage of moving away when retiring is that you get rewarded with praise before passing away.

The Russell Alcorn Memorial Award

Presented by Addy Doucette, Artistic Director, Theatre Antigonish

This award is presented annually by the board of directors to someone who has made an outstanding contribution to the activities of Theatre Antigonish, and whose contribution reflects the qualities of dedication, unselfish service, artistic integrity, and a generous spirit of support and cooperation.

This year for the first time, the Board has unanimously agreed to give the award to two people. Both of these people have made the type of contribution described by the creators of this award, albeit in completely different ways. And not just this year–but for the whole 25 years of the life of Theatre Antigonish. To make this year's presentation even more unique, the two people to whom the award is jointly presented happen to be married to each other.

I'm sure there's nobody in the Antigonish community who doesn't know this remarkable couple–they are Patrick and Jacqueline Walsh.

Jackie, of course, has been Managing Editor of *The Casket* for many years–for that alone she deserves a major award. Speaking as someone who occasionally drops in at the *Casket* office, I have always been amazed that so few can do so much, and do it week after week. But from the point of view of Theatre Antigonish, we are honoring her tonight for her staunch support of our activities over 25 years. She has seen to it that our productions have always been well publicized, gently reviewed, and frequently rewarded with glowing editorials. Her patience and generosity with those of us trying to get stories and photos to her every week has been nothing short of amazing. When we have had to beg for more time, special consideration, last-minute favors–with Jackie the answer is always "yes." The coverage we have had in *The Casket* has been one of the cornerstones of the theatre's success in the community. We owe Jackie and her colleagues at *The Casket* a debt of gratitude.

Pat Walsh. How can I possibly do justice to his many contributions without keeping you here until tomorrow morning? Well, he has been a playwright, a director, an actor, a brochure designer, a board member and board president, and adjudicator, a patron, a fund-raiser, an advisor, a writer of editorials, a settler of disputes, an advocate, and a true friend, for a start. He has seen the Organization, and the Board, and the University through all of Theatre Antigonish's ups and downs for twenty-five years. He is true lover of live theatre and who has dedicated much of his life to seeing, writing and teaching plays. He has supported whoever was running the theatre at "X" in thought, word, and deed. Even when we were wrong, and he knew we were wrong, he still gave his support, and that is the mark of a true friend. And he gave of his time and his energy with incredible generosity. I have been in one or two tricky situations over the years, and I can truly say that Pat has never let me down. A greater friend than Pat, Theatre Antigonish has never had. His generosity has been boundless.

When I came to StFX as a student in 1964, Pat was here, and when I came to be Theatre director in 1979, Pat was here–and tonight he is still here. It's hard to imagine the place without him, but as most of you know, sadly, Pat and Jackie are leaving Antigonish to move to Calgary at the end of the academic year. To say they will be missed is the understatement of the year. I think it's not an exaggeration to say that Antigonish will lose a piece of its heart.

And so, this award, in addition to honoring Pat and Jackie for their enormous contributions to Theatre Antigonish, is a very small way of saying: good luck, Godspeed, and please visit often. Dr. Pat and Jacqueline Walsh.

The tag team of Deagle & Walsh gets a chance to thank some people who have thanked us.

Thank You to the RK

1998 Annual Report of the Chair of the Board of Directors of the RK MacDonald Nursing Home Corporation

July 2, 1998

At this, our final Board meeting, I have been asked by the Chair to present his annual report, which is only fitting, for I have been putting words into his mouth for nearly thirty years.

Jim and I teamed up 35 years ago, as lectors at the Cathedral, then Chair and Secretary of the Town Planning Board, then requested by former Mayor John MacDougall to be Chair and Secretary of the Nursing Home Committee, and once the Corporation was formed, to serve as Chair and Secretary of the Corporation as representatives of the Sisters of St. Martha. We have never been able to say "no" to the Sisters, who have been our benefactors and dear friends for as long as we can remember. Thus, we joined the annals of such other duos as Batman and Robin, Laurel and Hardy, and Roy Rogers and Trigger.

Now, some 10,588 days later, we are leaving the RK Board, but not, we hope, the RK family. We have been very selfish all these years and we reluctantly surrender our positions to our successors. Why reluctantly? Because we have reaped so many benefits, so many personal blessings, from our association with the RK. We have truly enjoyed our duties. How have we loved them–let us count the ways:

We give thanks

For the privilege of representing the Sisters of St. Martha whose lives and dedicated service have been an inspiration to us. So close and for so long have we been associated with the good Sisters, that we often refer to ourselves in private as Sister Jim and Sister Pat.

We give thanks

For our association with the staff of the RK. Our part was easy. We formulated policy and the administration of the facility. But our admiration, and at times our awe, and always our deepest respect, was aroused by the tireless and dedicated workers who translated abstract policies into loving hands-on care of the citizens of the RK. And no one knows better than we, how deserving they are of a more just wage and wider recognition.

We give thanks

For the administrations we worked with: both administrators and accounting staff and department heads, who in the face of deadlines, byzantine government regulations, financial pressures, emotional and psychological stress, never measured their lives in punched clocks, but rose to every occasion to get the job done.

We give thanks

For the wardens and mayors and councillors and all our fellow Board members, who labored with us. We may have clashed on policies, but never on personal relationships. We never lost our respect for any of our elected colleagues and we believe we earned their trust, for we always debated any contentious questions openly and fully. As a result we leave the RK as the crown jewel in the relationship of our municipal units. Our elected officials never allowed the clash of Councils to interfere with making the RK a model of long-term care renowned throughout the province.

We give thanks

For the unstinting support of the good citizens of Antigonish, both town and county, who rose to the ramparts on any occasion the RK was in need. Such staunch public support gave both of us the courage to butt heads with governments at all levels. You may note the damage to both our heads and the ever-receding hairlines that resulted from those clashes. I leave it to you to judge which of us was the more effective head-butter.

We give thanks

For the many people who served on RK committees, and employed their expertise to make the RK second-to-none in the province. These generous souls don't get the headlines–they do the work that makes the headlines. The volunteers, the friends, the foundation–all people of goodwill, performing acts of kindness, acts of love, acts of inspiration.

We give thanks

To our wives, Mary and Jacqueline, who allowed us to share our lives in a worthy cause, never complaining about time lost with them, always supportive in times of stress and duress. Our staying power over the years was dependent on their cooperation–and for the RK they gave most generously of goodwill and understanding and encouragement.

We give thanks.

To the people in the beds. These most worthy builders of our community deserved our humble assistance, and they remained the focus of our efforts through the years. Our health and our vigor expended in service to them was a constant source of blessings and enrichment of our lives.

We give thanks

For our friendship. For thirty-five years, Jim and I have fought and disagreed over just about everything under the sun–except the RK. The RK has been the glue of our relationship. Our work at the RK took us out of ourselves and put us in the service of the most vulnerable in our society. Our differences melted away–for in matters that really count in life, we agreed. In our thirty-five years together, Jim and I have never parted in anger. We are as unlike as any two people can be, but we are absolutely unified in friendship, and that friendship is demonstrated in our service of the RK.

So, tonight we go. We hate to go. We hate to give up something that was a major portion of our adult lives. But, not to go would be selfish and self-serving. Someone else deserves a share of the blessings to be derived from serving the RK. We pass the blessings on to you tonight. May you have the joy and rich satisfaction we have had. Thank you all for allowing us to serve so long.

Patrick Walsh, Secretary [retiring] for James E. Deagle, Chair [retiring]

Chapter 11
The West Calls 1997–99

We were in our dream house for three years when we made a visit out to see our daughter Mary in Calgary. While there, I dropped in to see Dr. David Lawless, who had retired from the presidency of StFX to become President of a newly forming St. Mary's University in Calgary. They were preparing to offer a full slate of courses for the first time. Dr. Lawless wrote to StFX and requested that someone in the English Department design an English curriculum for St. Mary's, and the task fell to me. I sent the program to Dr. Lawless and since I was in Calgary I thought I would see how things were going. One thing that wasn't going was the search for an English professor. As we chatted I realized that I had a sabbatical coming up–wouldn't it be grand to spend it with my daughter and her family for a year.

Dr. Lawless was happy because, despite the fact we had had some clashes over policy at X, we had established a friendship. I would become St. Mary's "Pioneer" English Professor. That year went well, was exciting and exhilarating, and I made a whole new cadre of friends. When my year was up they wanted me to return. But my palace had hardly been broken in. I still had to go back to X for a least one year. Decisions, decisions.

But Mary and her husband put it to Jackie and me. "You folks are soon going to need care, and we can't give you care if you are 2,500 kilometers away. Besides, we want our children to have grandparents because all our grandparents died young. Mary went on, "Besides don't you remember the sign that you were destined to come here?"

And I did remember "the sign." When I had agreed to come to Calgary and St. Mary's, no one had any idea where the school would be located. Calgary is

25 miles north to south and 25 miles east to west–pick a spot! The car would stay with Jackie in Antigonish, who would still be editing *The Casket.* I would have to use public Light Rail Transit (LRT) and walk a lot. Walk a lot, is a sobering thought. But I walked in Nelson, but it was a small town and very walkable, although hilly. I bit the bullet and took the sabbatical–to be in on the birth of a new StFX would be worth it. When I arrived in Calgary, I asked Mary to take me to the new St. Mary's. I headed for the garage out back, she headed for the front door. I thought her car must be parked out front, but then I noticed she still had her slippers on–and she wouldn't go out in her slippers. We stepped out on the front stoop and she pointed up the street to the west, "See that white school with the playground two blocks away?"

"Come on, you've got to be kidding me?"

"No, that's not St. Mary's."

"Stop kidding around."

"I am *not* kidding around. St. Mary's is just across the street on the other side of that white school. You'll have to walk around the playground."

I was flabbergasted.

Mary smiled. "It's a sign," she said. "You can walk." And she turned around and went in the house.

It was the start of a great year. And as the year developed, so did the pressure to come west. Tom Norris, the Registrar, started the bandwagon. Fr. Dowling rang the bell. Dave Bershad became conductor. Stan Cichon became my PR agent and began introducing me to contacts in every sphere of Calgary life.

The "sign" must have been authentic. In 1999 I took early retirement; we set our wagon westward, and rode off into the sunset.

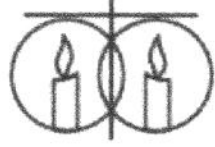

On our 1960 honeymoon in Deer Isle, Maine, all the beautiful scenery had us always looking west. Can't claim it was any kind of a sign, but the realization we ended up going west was still operative in the setting sun of our golden years in the approaching millennium.

*

looking west

on the Isle au Haut
when the truck got stuck
I opened the lunch
to munch a sandwich

you simmered suspecting
the steep climb of the time
ahead nothing you could do
being too many miles from anywhere

we made it to the cliff rocks
where we could see in the clear sea
the submerged trees swaying
displaying a flexible survival

dodging between the current
and the rattling bones of stones
bending to the push and pull of forces
like horses fighting through a storm

we sat hunched in silence save
the lapping waves against the caves
below immersed in our dreams
and beams of a smiling sun above

in our innocence we did not know
that at that moment we were so content
death was on the Isle au Haut stalking
us walking past our naïve reverie

on the mail boat home at end of day
no one told you or me could they see
the glow of the future in our faces
or traces of our recent pledges

back at Goose Cove Lodge for supper
the guests atwitter and shivering
couldn't wait to tell us about the killing
they found so thrilling that we missed

the next evening as we lay in the field
in Sunset at sunset we waved and gave
the old man and his dog a greeting–
and missed meeting Mr. Steinbeck

and Charley who were looking for America
we were searching for the part of the art
of being together in a marriage that would be
a carriage to a new world somewhere

we had faith that would allow us
to know each other and not to bother
with the distractions that swept by us
or crept like a killer past our dreams

on your birthday know that the oozy
woods have taught us to know that we go
wherever blessings flow destined to be
the three who got married thank God

for Jackie happy birthday darling
December 5, 1998

*

Having pursued my true love for 11 years since meeting her, I was determined to have a decent honeymoon: somewhere off the beaten path, private, with natural beauty. I spotted a little ad in the back pages of *The New Yorker* for a place called Goose Cove Lodge on Deer Isle, Maine, operated by a naturalist from the University of Pennsylvania named Ralph Waldron. There was a main lodge for meals but separate cabins scattered in the surrounding forest. Perfect!

I phoned Ralph to make a reservation, but was swiftly discouraged: the cost would be $300.00 per week for the three weeks I wanted. "Is that a problem?" Ralph inquired. I explained that I was a high school teacher making $3,200 a year. Ralph seemed sympathetic and continued questioning me until he got the drift of my epic quest for my bride. So Ralph said, "My wife and I live at the Main Lodge. Our home is a few miles away on the main road through Sunset, Maine. Why don't you stay at our home, and take your meals at the Lodge with us, and I'll let you have it for $300.00 for all three weeks?" I immediately felt that Ralph Waldron would be a fine man to know. And such he proved to be.

The accommodations and the food and the sloop to sail in were perfect, topped by nature tours conducted by Ralph. The evenings after supper were glorious. Right across the street from Ralph's home was an open field of green grass flowing down to the Atlantic with islands dotting the view to the horizon. The name of the town as Sunset was a no brainer, and in the evenings we would go out and lie in the grass and watch the spectacular sunsets, feeling, a couple years later like Natalie Wood and Warren Beatty in *Splendor in the Grass*.

For a couple days we had neighbors in the field: a kindly bearded old man in a camper truck, his lone companion a frisky poodle. We'd greet one another with a wave, but each of us sensed a desire for privacy and contemplative space, so we never got to meet. A couple years later I picked up a copy of John Steinbeck's *Travels with Charley* and as I read the description of the sunset from a field in Sunset on Deer Isle, Maine, I realized Jackie and I had shared the experience of one of America's great novelist's in his last visit across his beloved country. The closest Jackie and I ever came to a like trip was our drive across America when we moved from Nova Scotia to Calgary permanently.

Steinbeck made the trip because he was dying. I would love to see America, having outlived Steinbeck, but with all my preexisting medical problems, if I were hospitalized in the USA my pension would be wiped out in three and one half days, no matter how much insurance coverage I could buy–pre-existing conditions would be invoked. The word pictures of the people in this memoir are the closest I can come to seeing them again in the flesh. These words will remain, Skype visits will not.

Eulogy for My Brother February 13, 1999

The last picture I took of my brother, Fran.

Dear Sisters of St. Martha, benefactors and friends of the Walsh family,

Last Sunday morning in Adams, Massachusetts, my younger brother Francis passed peacefully into the hands of God, in his sleep next to his dear wife Nancy. The doctors assured her that he had suffered no pain, and his leaving was as simple as the clicking of a light switch. After 23 years of suffering through 10 major heart interventions, his body and organs could no longer carry on.

I am writing to thank all of you, and the many loving sisters of St. Martha who were there to welcome him into the presence of the Lord, for your many prayers over all these years. The doctors said that he lived much longer than they would have predicted, so his wife Nancy and his daughter Diana and all the Walsh family have many precious memories of Fran that we feel we owe to the Marthas and those who offered prayers for him during his long suffering.

Whenever Fran reached a critical situation, I would alert the Marthas to storm the gates of heaven, and we truly believe that the prayers and support you offered so generously over the years were a sustaining grace for all of us. We thank you. Please know that the Marthas are continuously in our prayers and are a deep and resonating part of our Walsh way of life.

I have enclosed the last photograph taken of my brother at a family wedding on Labor Day weekend this year. I took the photo of him and his wife Nancy, and it was the one used in his obituary in the newspaper.

We are often urged to celebrate instead of mourn at a funeral Mass. Seldom have I seen such celebration, but Fran's Mass was truly a celebration, despite the loss everyone present felt so deeply–for he was a truly loving and caring man.

After communion, the funeral director played over the sound system a song written a few years ago by Fran's friend, country singer Buddy Holland, who performed the song in Nashville. The song told of Fran's pitching skills and his devotion to coaching and his decency.

Fran's friend, Al Romano, a professional middleweight boxer asked Fran's widow if he could speak for one minute–and he did. [When Al found out that all the veins in Fran's body had been used up in all those operations, he offered his veins to the doctors!] Al said, "I knew Fran Walsh for 33 years. I am in a tough business, but in all those years I never heard Fran swear–which is incredible. Father, sometimes I would be angry and burst into the locker room swearing and cursing. Fran would sit there in silence, and I would turn on him, "What's the matter with you?" Fran would giggle his little giggle, and then smile that devastating smile of his, and peace would descend on me and my troubles would fade to insignificance. He had that effect on people. Maybe Fran didn't make the Baseball Hall of Fame, but if there is a humanity Hall of Fame, Fran is the best in it. I want you all to know that Fran Walsh was the finest and most decent human being I have ever known."

I followed Al and here is a copy of my remarks:

[Fr. Vincent Leggato, celebrant, a visiting Passionist priest, urged us in his homily to celebrate Fran's life. I said, "Friends, I want you all to know that Father and I did not consult one another on our talks. It is amazing, Father, that although you did not know Fran, you caught the spirit of his life from the wake last night and from the outpouring of sentiment from the people there."]

Text:

Friends, I am here today to celebrate my brother's life. Francis, who knew he would be leaving us early, did not want us to be sad today. If the liturgy had permitted, he would have had a jazz band here today.

[Fr. Vincent: "Yes, yes, you should have!" Me: "Father, we didn't know you were going to be here, or we would have!"' The old Polish pastor originally scheduled to officiate would not even allow *Bear Him Up On Eagle's Wings*!]

I remember the first time I saw my little brother: he was wrapped in a blanket and only his nose poked out. His nose was full adult size even then–and he was the ugliest baby we had ever seen. But Fran grew up around his nose–and became a strikingly handsome man. His beauty was not skin deep; his beauty was born in the glowing core of his heart.

My mother called Fran, who was so very dark, her "Black Diamond," and we did not know then the irony of "this nickname": diamonds are the most valuable of precious stones, so we treasure them because they sparkle with an inner light that dazzles our senses and our minds. But this beauty is won at a terrifying price–living plants are crushed under intense pressure over eons of time.

Our Francis was crushed under immense pressures throughout his life–and they made him a "Black Diamond," rare and beautiful.

A DIAMOND SPARKLES: Fran's sparkle was his sense of humor. He could see the irony in the ways of the world: the pretense behind the pompous, the foolishness behind the phony, the cowardice behind the bully. Through his humor he could fill us all with joy–AS JESUS WOULD.

A DIAMOND SHINES: Fran's smile, because it revealed his decency and caring, could light up any room. People responded to him because they knew intuitively that he cared for them–AS JESUS WOULD.

A DIAMOND IS HARD: Fran bore his afflictions stoically. Whenever we asked, he was "okay." Even when visiting the doctor because something else was failing, when the doctor asked, "How are you?", Fran was "Fine!"

I phoned him once from Canada when he was in the Deaconess Hospital in Boston. We chatted and I could hear some fuss in the background. "What's that?" I asked. "The doctors are working on me." "What's wrong?" "I think I better go now, Pat, I'm having an attack."

Fran strode though our lives with heroic vitality despite his pain, never uttering a word of complaint, suffering in silence–AS JESUS WOULD.

A DIAMOND STANDS FOR FIDELITY: Fran was faithful to his loving wife Nancy, who was his fortress and his strength, and his adoring daughter Diana, of whom he was so proud. He was faithful to his players and fellow coaches, and to his coworkers and friends, and to his family. And if a friend might let him down, he never turned on them. He continued to love them deeply–AS JESUS WOULD.

A DIAMOND IS RARE: When Fran was running a Submarine Sandwich Shop in Greenfield, the local inhabitants from the State Mental Hospital frequented his shop. They could have driven a lesser man to drink, but Fran–with infinite patience and tenderness–never ran them off. He treated them–AS JESUS WOULD.

Our Mass here today breaks the bonds of time and unites us to the passion and death of Jesus Christ–who also was crushed into a beauty surpassing understanding–a perfect act of love for each and every one of us here today. Jesus died for you and for me and for Francis. Jesus Christ set a perfect example of how to love–and Fran Walsh sought to live that example. Our Francis loved us all–AS JESUS WOULD.

*

Then Fran's daughter, Diana, delivered the most thoughtful and touching praise of her father and the wonderful love between her parents.

We proceeded to Southview Cemetery in the valley between the Hoosac and Taconic mountains and laid Francis to rest in the Walsh plot with his grandfather and grandmother Walsh, his father Francis, and beside his mother Carmen. The New England seasons roll eternal, from frosty white of winter, to the light green of spring, to the deep green of summer, to the blazing colors of autumn. The stars are bright in their diurnal rounds and the world unfolds in a solemn slide into eternity as the hills wear down. The promise of the peace of the Lord lies all around in quiet splendor. It will be a great place to gather when the trumpet blows!

Yours sincerely, Pat Walsh

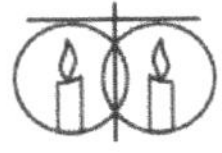

Patrick X Walsh

Remembering Father "JV"

In 1955, in my sophomore year at StFX, I roomed on the third floor of Xavier Hall over the Old Assembly Hall. The prefect for Xavier was Fr. John V. Campbell, known to all outside range of his hearing as JV. He was the bursar [now called the Comptroller] of the University, and his suite of sitting room, bedroom, and bathroom was at the top of the stairs on the second floor. We students could not enter or leave the building without passing by JV's room. We got our marks from mid-term quizzes from him, in a private and somewhat confessional session. Our habits of living would suddenly be seen to have consequences in our academic life. When leaving our quarters in the evening we had to sign out and sign in before the lights were extinguished at 11 p.m. Fr. JV was a prefect, a confessor, and *in loco parentis,* a parent figure.

Fr. JV was a *father,* and he took his paternal duties to his young charges very seriously. He was concerned about us. Imagine having the financial responsibilities of the entire university on his plate all day long, and then riding herd on some sixty young men, including the giant Xavier Dorm on the third floor. Thank the Lord that he had a keen and wry sense of humor, and a devilish propensity for the practical joke. Fr. John V. had served in the Air Force during World War II, after serving as President of the Students' Union in his student days. There was no trick or scheme of students of which he was not fully aware.

One Saturday afternoon, StFX won a grand gridiron victory and the denizens of the third floor were gathered in our room having a great celebration, singing and carrying on–without alcohol (even the possession of which was punishable by instant expulsion). In our joy, the not-fully-compulsory-but-extremely-highly-recommended time for chapel at 5:40 p.m. slipped by our revels.

Suddenly we became aware of a dark presence in the doorway–Fr. JV. A guilty silence descended on the room. "Oh," says Fr. JV, "I didn't know you wanted to have chapel in your room tonight." And with that he knelt down in the doorway, making it impossible for anyone to exit, fished out his rosary beads, and led us in the recitation of the Joyful Mysteries–and the Sorrowful Mysteries–AND the Glorious Mysteries, which he obviously knew by heart. We were getting hungry, but no one moved. Fr. JV went on! He intoned the Litany of the Blessed Virgin

Mary from memory! Our appetites were quelled in awe. What a performance. And he kept a straight face through the entire revival meeting.

That year I became a good friend of Fr. JV. My roommate, Jim Nicholson, and I would often talk late into the night with Fr. JV, and we were not surprised that sometimes he would begin to nod off. When I was away on a basketball trip, my job as manager was to call the score back to Fr. JV, who would then call CJFX and get the nearly always good news out to Antigonish.

Fr. JV was very devoted to the Sisters of St. Martha, because he was aware of the incredible work load they bore in providing for the priests and the boys–cooking, cleaning, laundry. If the priests were father figures, the Marthas were truly our mothers away from home. One Sister, who had charge of cleaning Fr. JV's room, would always rearrange his papers and desk and then put his wastebasket under the desk. Fr. JV wanted the wastebasket beside his easy chair, where he was comfortable and where he could lie back and relax, tossing away papers without the desk top being in the way. But the Sister was adamant that the proper place for a wastebasket is *under* the desk, so a prolonged struggle developed with the wastebasket as the medium of exchange. The war was finally concluded, victoriously for JV, the morning the good Sister came in and couldn't move the basket from beside the recliner–because it was nailed to the floor!

One successful practical joke stuck in Father's memory. When the evening grew quiet and the time to finish his breviary would arrive, he would flip on the half-globe light hanging in his sitting room and push back in his recliner. Eliciting the cooperation of the defeated Sister, I got into Father's room one morning and prepared a little surprise. That evening when he sat back to say his prayers, he found himself staring at–Satan! [I had cut out a piece of black paper in the shape of the devil and arranged it in the half-globe of the light to be smiling at him when he finally looked up.] He jumped up and knew immediately who had done the deed. We shared a chuckle over that incident for over 40 years.

In those days students were not allowed automobiles, so we were confined to walking distance of the campus. Fr. JV took pity on my roommate and me, and took us with him to his home in Inverness, Cape Breton, for a weekend with his family. What wonderful memories I have of that visit. We slept on straw mattresses in the room he and his brother, Joe D., had shared. We were treated to a veritable feast by his Mum, and surely we young blokes amused the "Guv'nor," his father, who displayed the twinkle of mischief we knew in his son, the priest.

We went for a drive up past Cheticamp 'til we hit the construction of the new Cabot Trail highway, which was getting underway. We stopped at the wharf to get fresh fish for supper. For a couple of Yanks from New England this was a great adventure.

The highlight of the weekend was to attend Mass Sunday morning, seated in the front pew of the church with Father's family. Fr. JV gave a touching and moving sermon [not yet "homilies" in those days] and the love and pride of his family was palpable. Over forty years later, he not only remembered the sermon and its prescient points, but he revealed how truly nervous he had been preaching to his family and friends. We youngsters had never suspected his nervousness, but we did feel the great love and affection and pride he had for his parents and his brothers and sisters. It was mutual. On the way home we stopped at a restaurant for a bite to eat. A lady came over to speak to him and he introduced us. They had a great chat.

When Fr. JV retired from StFX, he was assigned to the parish in Judique, which made him a very happy man. Judique was recognized as a plum, and for Fr. JV a veritable Garden of Eden. He was with his people and he was able to grow vegetables as "the Guv'nor" had done. On a visit, my wife and I enjoyed the vegetables at his table, and also the joy he so obviously felt in his life there.

When, in his closing years, Fr. JV returned to the campus to reside in Mockler Hall, he delighted in the companionship of his fellow priests. He always retained his mischievous sense of humor, and it was often on display at the post-lunch card game with Fathers Macdonnel, Bauer, and R. B. MacDonald.

When he began to ail and was no longer able to drive, it was my extreme pleasure to jump in my van and take him for a ride around the beautiful countryside of Antigonish. He so enjoyed the country and was filled with memories of the people he loved who were so close to the earth.

On one of these rides, Father JV recalled our restaurant stop on the way home from our Inverness weekend so long ago. He then informed me that his life might have been very different with the lady who came to our table to chat that day–if the War had not intervened. But he had become a priest and he devoted himself fully and unequivocally to his priestly calling. He was a man of prayer and deep faith who had given his all to his university, his church, and his people. And his beloved Marthas cared for him to the end.

I am composing these memories in the foothills of the Rockies where I now live. It is Saturday, and Fr. JV Campbell is being laid to rest in his beloved Judique. My heart and my mind are there. Last July, the day before I left for my new life in the West, I went to visit Fr. JV in his hospital room at St. Martha's. We shared an hour, most of it in silence, with sporadic lucid moments. I was honored to be in his presence. As we used to do when we had served Mass in our student days, when it came time to go, I knelt at his bedside and asked for his blessing. He laid his hand on my head, and said very clearly and distinctly, "We shall meet again, Pat, and we will be happy together again." I know what he meant, and I know he will be waiting to welcome me.

Patrick Walsh '58 Calgary

For Sheldon Currie

on the Occasion of his Honorary Degree from St. Thomas University:

At the StFX Convocation last week, Sheldon addressed the gathering, opening with the following statement: "As every Cape Bretoner knows, mockery is the highest form of flattery." And then [he] proceeded to roast the candidate for the Outstanding Teaching Award. But, because there is a just God, and the chickens come home to cackle, the candidate will now have his chance to get even.

Sheldon, tonight, I am the pigeon, and you are the statue, and I intend to drop the "highest form of flattery" on your recently laurelled pate.

Did you know that there is an historic cairn in Reserve, Cape Breton, in the front yard of the house Sheldon was born in? It's not for Sheldon. It's for the house–the first miner's co-op house built by Fr. Jimmy Tompkins! That Sheldon was born there is an accident of history, but nonetheless important, for Sheldon is from a mining family–and he escaped. Because he liked to read, Sheldon became family's designated escapee from the mines.

It would be Sheldon's intellect that would propel him to fame and fortune. He lived the adage passed on to every son: "If you keep your big mouth shut, people may think you are stupid. If you open your big mouth, they will know it." This may be the hidden wellspring of Sheldon's reputation as a bucolic seer.

Sheldon was a member of the first-ever class at Xavier Junior College in Sydney in 1954. His classmates, under the spell of either intoxicating beverages or a wry sense of precocious irony, elected Sheldon the First President of the Student Body.

Just as physicists predicate an anti-universe, Sheldon predicates an anti-administration. But more of his administrative skills in a moment.

Sheldon and Dawn Currie

Exiled to X after two years, he ended up in Fr. MacSween's first Creative Writing Class There he met his future wife, the lovely and beguiling Dawn Wolstenhome, of the Moncton Wolstenhomes, who obviously saw something worth saving in the tongue-tied lad, as well as my own not-so-humble American self–who was to become a flamboyant Costello to Sheldon's deadpan Abbott, a chatty Robin to Sheldon's laconic Batman, a departmental secretarial Bosworth to Sheldon's prudently-chairing Johnson. For as his colleague, Jim Taylor, toasted two weeks ago at the party celebrating–let me rephrase that, "commemorating"–Sheldon's retirement: "Who here has not been leveled by Sheldon's aggressive humility; made to feel an absolute acquisitive scoundrel; a self-centered unaltruistic lout? Sheldon is the master of the laissez-faire stratagem. He is truly creative, in the sense that from the seeming chaos that appears to surround his office–where his costly Pentium computer is used as a poster board for yellow sticky tabs–he produces fiction of world-class caliber."

Nonetheless, Sheldon's quiet humility and non-aggressive nature cannot blind us to disturbing forces buried deeply in his psyche. For instance, let me deconstruct the unveiled aggression in his first published work. In the pages of "X-Writes 1958," we find the first hint of the violent images that will reach full bloom in the bloody ending of "The Glace Bay Miners' Museum": Witness the Freudian frippery in his first published poem: "The Auto-maniac": "He seized by its wheel, his automobile, and threw it at mankind." As one of the students in my film course asked Sheldon, "Sir, are you obsessed with violence and dismemberment?"

Thus, we must ask, does this gentle man, this loving husband and father, this fictional force, have a "dark side"? The best story of Sheldon's laissez-faire philosophy I append here is from our colleague, Professor Jim Taylor, rendered in classical style:

"One of Sheldon's most successful strategies for life has been the laissez-faire philosophy. Usually, it works pretty well. But in some endeavors, it's just not right. One of these areas is bee keeping. The laissez-faire philosophy is just not compatible with the goal of bee keeping, which is to get honey, that is, to ROB the hive.

"When we started beekeeping, we wore masks to protect our faces, raincoats to avoid the stings, and heavy woolen socks with gum shoes. This was before modern beekeeping ziplock suits that offer nearly 100 percent protection, are lightweight, and actually make you look cooler than you are.

"When we set out to get the honey, we looked more like a pair of befuddled bank robbers than hive robbers. No doubt our appearance tipped off the bees. Furthermore, we didn't know at that time that wool is a substance that enrages bees; otherwise we would not have worn our hand-knitted loggers' socks, lovingly knitted for us by our respective great aunts. But it was a hot, muggy day and the bees were as nasty as John MacPherson during convocation week.

"When the bees eventually and inevitably found their way through his coat, Sheldon, looking like Colombo (not Effie's brother), pounded his chest in his futile efforts to kill the intruders, grabbed a two-by-four–anyone familiar with Sheldon's backyard knows that there's always a random two-by-four kicking around–just like Hubert's office–and began to swing it wildly and frantically:

"His roused vengeance sets new a work
And never did the Cyclops hammer fall

With less remorse than Sheldon's ugly stick
Then fell upon those bees.
"And he declared with uncharacteristic ardor and drive–
'I'll kill every fucking bee in the bloody goddam hive.'
"Ah, yes, the gentle apiarist!"

As with many famous authors, Sheldon may have been influenced by his military career, about which you may not have heard. Before he went to XJC, Sheldon was in the Air Force, but he never got airborne–because he was sartorially deprived. General MacArthur was the only cadet in the history of West Point without a single demerit for even dust on his shoes. Sheldon was the only cadet in the history of the Canadian Air Force who successfully ACQUIRED a demerit in every inspection. As a result, he was allowed to leave his military career behind, as the government recorded in his discharge papers: "for the betterment of the Service." He ended up working in the Frontier College, without changing his basic uniform, which was stylishly appropriate to his new environment.

After a BA and BEd from StFX, Sheldon finessed an MA from UNB, and trumped a PhD from the University of Alabama, where his laid-back style was in tune with Southern laissez-faire customs. The highlight of his PhD experience was that one day, as Sheldon came out of the library, he passed quarterback Willie Joe Namath heading to the football field for practice. That Sheldon tutored the future Broadway Joe is just simply not true. Neither is it true that Joe Willie hit on Dawn for a date.

As all wise observers of academia know in their hearts, a PhD is proof of absolutely nothing, except that the person acquiring one has the ability to gnaw like a rat. A PhD does not mean its proud possessor has "street smarts." As Jim Taylor recounted, Sheldon and George Sanderson, in Montreal recruiting students for StFX could not pass up the opportunity to practice their French on a man who said to them, à la Clouseau, *J'ai un pistol dans moi posh*. And Sheldon, master of the one-liner, has eternally regretted that he did not reply, *Moi aussi*. The gentleman with the "pistol" mugged the two innocent professors.

Back at StFX in the faculty lounge outside the Academic Vice President's office, the usual suspects, Bernie Liengme, the math prof coffee regulars, and Leo Gallant, were speculating as to why Sheldon and George were chosen as recruiters. Was it their mastery of French? Their business acumen? Their street smarts? Comments like, "They'll probably get mugged or bring back some muggers" were rife. The pay phone on the six-floor rings and it's Sheldon, who has to beg Bernie Liengme to get the Vice President to send them some money to get home. How this incident propelled Sheldon into the chairmanship of the English department on four separate occasions remains a mystery of the Byzantine machinations of the University.

One of the reasons for Sheldon's lack of pomposity is that his children could never take him seriously. When he finally completed his PhD, his children made sure he would not wring an ounce of inflated ego from the achievement by renaming, "Whimper," the giant, mangy, milquetoast family dog, "DOCTOR Whimper Currie."

Nonetheless, Sheldon has compiled an admirable record as an administrator, deftly using his public persona as a laissez-faire, laid-back, beekeeper, country-bumpkin, to achieve administrative triumphs. One notable Napoleonic administrator could not believe that Sheldon could shuck corn, let alone run a department of warring bibliophiles. But let me tell you, that four times over the thirty-five years of his career, Sheldon was appointed chair to bring peace to the Balkanized English department. And he was the only man who could have done so. And he did so.

On assuming his fourth chairmanship, Sheldon opened the meeting only to be barraged with a twenty-minute tirade of personal and professional vituperation by his predecessor. We all twitched in embarrassment and unease, while Sheldon sat in stone-like silence as the accusations and indictments washed over him like the cold Atlantic over the Titanic. When his attacker finally ran out of breath, Sheldon quietly looked up, and inquired as innocently as Monica Lewinsky to Barbara Walters, "Does anyone else have any comments?" We were all amazed that, after such a blast, the man could talk. Silence. "Fine," says Sheldon, "the next item on the agenda is a motion to change the calendar" [which would undo the changes forced on us by his predecessor]–and the motion passed immediately by an 11 to 1 vote. It was the most brilliant and self-effacing move I ever saw at the University, where insecure academics perpetuate conflict by rushing to self-defense as lemmings rush to the sea.

Let not Sheldon's casual ways deceive–he was recognized by his colleagues as one of the most sensible and fair-minded counselors in the school. He was elected to every significant committee of faculty and served with distinction on the committee that completely revised the University constitution and structure as we grew from a small school and faculty to a major university. And he has continued to the end of his career to be innovative. He went to Nicaragua two years ago and Jamaica this year with students as a leading force in Service Education. He has put in place a thrust for creative writing, which will revolutionize creative writing at StFX–and he did this in one year of his last term, despite the fact that he will not be at StFX to enjoy the benefits of the program. But, it's good for the students–and that was his motivation, as ever.

I personally appreciate that during Sheldon's tenures as chair, I was not just given the freedom to experiment and innovate, but encouraged to do so.

Sheldon is not merely a teacher, he is a great teacher, and unique in his approach to teaching. When my youngest daughter, Rebecca, who was the top English student at Antigonish Regional High School, entered StFX, she asked me whom should she take for English 100. I told her Sheldon. She did–and never talked to me about her class. She hated it. Then in her senior year, she took Sheldon's novel course, and finally talked to me about her experience. Rebecca realized at last why I had told her to take Sheldon's courses. In high school, a most popular teacher had taught her–and this teacher was an impeccable authority on all matters of English literature and writing–and the students were guided with precise instructions to perform with absolute accuracy and in a highly structured manner. In her senior year, Rebecca recognized that Sheldon's laid-back style and methods were designed to enable the students to explore their personal relationship with literature and writing, to enable them to be free and self-motivated, and to discover unique insights into their own lives without having every tittle and jot spelled out by an authority figure. Sheldon had freed Rebecca to be herself–and she understood the great gift Sheldon had given her. She is, today, a unique and effective English teacher herself–and she thanks Sheldon for his teaching–his wisdom, his caring, his encouragement, which [are] gifts he has given to all his students.

As a writer, Sheldon has honored his craft. The writer's life is singular and private and demands the utmost of motivation and perseverance. While carrying a full load of teaching and administration, Sheldon remained faithful to his drive to write the story of his people and his Cape Breton heritage. He wrote his stories believing, like a biblical Lot, that if only five people read his stories, they were worth writing.

We do not have time to recount all Sheldon's talents, but he has coached teams of young ladies in softball and handball, is bass player in the "Little Hope Parish Band" of Guysboro County, a student of the Gallic and–in light of his Service Learning–Spanish. He is a man of many parts, and all of them are in high gear beneath his placid exterior.

But all Sheldon's achievements find their wellspring in his character, his virtues as a human being. He is a caring man, a truly humble man, and a charitable man. His common sense, his simplicity, his sincerity, enable him to pierce the cant and pretense of phonies, of which there are many in academia. But Sheldon's startling and often enigmatic insights stop the pretentious in their haughty steps–for like Shakespeare's fools, he speaks the truth, often so contrary to the ways of the world.

Last week, Sheldon said, "I have known Pat for over thirty years, and never missed an opportunity to make fun of him." Well, it must be true that when you are having a good time, it passes quickly, for I have known Sheldon for over forty years. We have made fun of one another during these four decades, as Jim Taylor said, "Not only because that's what we would do to each other, or because we deserve it, or because we are easy targets, but most of all, because it is a way of showing how much we like each other." As I reflected upon our relationship that began 43 years ago, I can truly say that there has never been an angry word or moment of tension between us. What a personal blessing my relationship with Sheldon Currie has been. But, now that Sheldon has returned to his beginnings, he belongs not just to his family, to his friends, to his students, to his colleagues, but through his immortal characters, especially Margaret MacNeil, Sheldon now belongs to the world. And I wouldn't doubt that some day, real–instead of metaphorical–pigeons might do a job on a statue of him.

Chapter 12
Limping Home 1999–Present

This chapter is so titled because it is the chapter of retirement, and with the autumn of the years come the increasing number of eulogies, lost family and lost friends, and the inevitable battles within as life begins to take its physical toll and the spirit becomes more philosophical. More philosophical, but sometimes more fiery, as urge to call out is prodded by the approaching silence.

I began to face medical problems, starting gently with apnea, but beating that back with technology, by each night donning a Continuous Passive Air Pressure mask. Those youthful polyps, with their demand for constant checkups faithfully followed for a lifetime, finally launched their attack. An early resection of the colon vanquished colon cancer. The heart I had never trusted to get me to 50 finally had enough and decided to attack. You will find a more detailed account elsewhere, but when I underwent the first heart procedure, I was given two weeks to live–so back I went and in the next decade staved off the enemy with marvelous plumbing tunnels of stents. What saved me, the doctors said, was the rabid handball over the years at StFX. The heart developed multiple alternate arteries to see me through those vicious games. Being so huge, the drawback was that my knees were reduced to bare bone on bare bone–so I got a new titanium right knee. Unfortunately, it became infected and came within 24 hours of amputation. So I decided to not press my luck and get the left knee done. The one good thing is now that I have a straight right leg and a bowed left leg, I have the authentic cowboy sway of a John Wayne. And with my cowboy hat on, the only giveaway that I am not a true-born cowboy is that when I amble near a horse these days, they whinny and shy away.

My initial cardiologist recommended I have open-heart surgery about ten years ago. I wanted a second opinion and went to the surgeon who had masterminded my inner road works. He said, "You are 71 years old. I don't think it's worth it to crank you open and sew you up. You seem to know what you're doing on every front." (My wife has taken over every medical duty of mine and is determined to keep me running like the "wonderful one-hoss shay.") The surgeon, Dean Traboulsie added, "Keep doing what you are doing. Go home and live." So I did.

My wife got me a new cardiologist–hers–Dr. Stuart Hutchison, who took over recently and asked me to get an angiogram so he could see if my heart had changed since my decision not to go under the knife. I did, and he reported in the nine years since my last stenting, my heart had not changed. I could go any minute, but I am a walking medical marvel. I stay up-to-date on the latest medical aids for survival. Thus I have recently added further new parts: new eyes (cataract surgery) and new ears (hearing aids). As long as they keep supplying parts, I'll keep going. (By the way, our new cardiologist is the mountain-climbing doctor who had the sense to turn back 10 minutes from the top of Everest so he survived the storm that killed eight people. You might have seen him–really, the actor playing him–in the movie about Mount Everest.)

Here I shall make a small digression to demonstrate how to have a heart attack, Jackie-style. She has always tried to do everything well. Here's how: We were driving to Sunday Mass and nearing the Church at about 10 minutes to 9 a.m. We stopped for a traffic light, and Jackie said quietly, "I don't feel well." Coming from her, this quiet utterance was like the roar of a 747 taking off. I immediately hung a left onto Glenmore Trail, and before 9 o'clock dropped her off at the Rockyview General Hospital, plunked her in a wheelchair, and delivered her directly to the nurses and doctors. I ran out to park my car, and by the time I got back, the nurse told me she had had a heart attack, and as we were talking Jackie was on her way to the Cardiac Center at the Foothills Hospital. I took off, and by the time I got to the Foothills and parked, it was 10 o'clock. She was in the OR! Before 11 o'clock she was out, Fr. Jerry Dowling was attending her, and her stenting was done. Two hours, from attack to solution. Was this another miracle? Nope. Jackie had timed her heart attack perfectly. It was February 4th–Super Bowl Sunday! No traffic on the road, nobody in the waiting room, ambulances at the ready, Operator Room doctors relaxing. On duty, Dr. Stuart Hutchison. As they say, "It's all in the timing."

So here we are in what proves to be the last quarter of our lives, limping, but still running the race. We managed in this last quarter to delve ever more deeply into the Scriptures under the guidance of theology Professor Michael Duggan of St. Mary's University, Calgary. We look forward to each day, with joy and thanks, for it is the day the Lord has made, and we rejoice and are glad.

The new millennium begins with the retirements of the warriors of the last millennium. Asked to speak at the retirement of my friend, John "Packy" McFarland, I chose to make a pitch to those assembled to invest in a "movie" about our hero's life.

'Packy' Retires

Ladies and gentlemen, you have been invited here tonight to take advantage of a once-in-a-lifetime financial offer. We are going to give you the opportunity to invest in units of a new Canadian film, a real winner, a virtually guaranteed box-office smash. And the more units you invest in this exciting film project, the more tax savings you will make. It's a win-win, no-lose deal, folks. So, without further ado, here's my pitch for the next Canadian Genie-winning film.

The title is: *Packy McFarland and the X-Men Versus the Forces of the Dark Side*

Our hero, a man of few words, is relentless in his support of the Forces of Light. Facing wave after wave of adversity, he triumphs over every evil with the quiet demeanor of, say, Clint Eastwood. We intend to approach Clint for the lead role; he has the same unflappable look, the square jaw, the determined eye of a man who cannot be intimidated. Of course, we might have to get Clint to squat down a bit, but then a director can work miracles with camera angles. Our second choice is Robert Redford.

We need an action opening to hook the audience: we are in an airplane sailing through swirling snow. We see below an endless forest of stunted spruce trees, then a twisting and winding narrow road, with two cars pushing ahead against the storm. It is 1954, and the StFX basketball team is heading out the Old Post Road to the evil nest of vile beasts in Wolfville. Suddenly the lead car spins out of control, skids, and slides off the road into a drift up to its windows. The camera zooms in as the front window is rolled down, and slipping out of the car into the waist-deep snow is or hero, young Packy McFarland, from Portland's Cheverus High School. Clean-cut, blond, with the map of Ireland on his rugged good-looking face. Unfazed by the situation, young Packy hauls his teammates out of the window, organizes them to lift the car back onto the road. They pile in, and take off again into the jaws of the great Canadian cold weather. Americans will understand this film because everything bad about weather in America comes from Canada. Young Packy is determined to fulfill his destiny against the crazed Axemen [of Acadia University, Wolfville, Nova Scotia].

Note: the incident shows that our hero will never stop, never quit, never turn back in the face of a challenge. If duty calls, he will answer.

Of course, we are using subtle symbolism here: the road and the journey are a symbol of life. And the incidents that follow will be our hero's challenges.

Titles set against the X-Men, in symbolic blue for courage and white for purity, girding for battle in the foul lair of the blood-red-clad (obvious symbolism) Axemen.

Every hero needs a buddy, and our hero's buddy is another handsome young Irishman (please note–ALL Irishmen are handsome!), Packy's co-captain, Fran Shea of Boston, with an appropriate accent, for instance, pronouncing "car" as "ca"–an endearing character trait for audiences. Frannie–note, both heroes must have matching two-syllable names–we hope will be played by Paul Newman.

I know both these stars will be expensive, but they are box-office guarantees. Ah, but I hear you thinking, they are both a bit long in the tooth–but we have a great makeup artist, and we can get our director, Dannie Petrie, to use soft lenses to get rid of the crow's feet. The locker room shots will be discreet, of course, in keeping with the wholesome nature of our heroes, but today we can show enough skin to get the teenyboppers to start fan clubs. On the other hand, if you all purchase enough units, we are prepared to go after Keanu Reeves for Packy, and Brad Pitt for Frannie.

As the titles end, the team takes the floor to be met by rabid fans shouting obscenities–mind you, not the obscenities of today, like "you suck" and "screw you," and worse–but the obscenities reflecting the serious moral dimension of our hero's predicament. As Packy steps to the line, the partisan fans shout "Hail Mary," and "herring-choker," and other religious epithets, for the game in the fifties is a holy war! But there is never any choking for our hero–he coolly sinks his foul shots. Then the tandem of McFarland and Shea takes control of the game, masters of the pick and roll, unstoppable and setting a pattern that would come to fruition in the Salt Lake City duo of Stockton and Malone. Packy's deadly TWO-hand set shot–it should have been worth three points even then–is a precursor of Steve Kerr's. No jump shots–because our hero is a man with his two feet always solidly planted on the ground. Of course, the Xaverian warriors triumph–and win their 17th consecutive Maritime basketball championship! Ah, those were the days.

Can't you see it–Packy and Franny–Newman and Redford–now on the football field? McFarland a tiger in the trenches, Shea a sylph at end, leading scorer in the league. In the first year of Canadian football, our hero is a dominant force. It is the first year–and the Xaverians make the playoffs, young men facing a powerful military foe, the Shearwater Flyers on a home field covered the night before by a snowstorm. Picture the students shoveling snow off the field and sawdust on! Old Memorial field, the students going wild, the sun setting early, the dusky red of dying day lights up the mud-covered teams lined up at scrimmage. Their exhausted snorting, puffing into vaporous clouds like two lines of prehistoric monsters lining up for the last charge. Zoom in again, there is Packy, bloodied and battered by bigger foes, but undaunted and always in the middle of the action. Always ready, always willing, always dependable. And we have to let the audience know that this was before scholarships–these guys lived the game before the arrival of the almighty dollar and the glitz of TV. Close-ups will show–these guys actually LOVE the game. And if they don't win the required number of games, they won't get a letter, the X that is the mark of the victorious warrior.

We need a change of pace now, a quiet scene at the post-game snack. Well, snack is understatement. John's nickname "Packy" we are going to suggest is associated with his gargantuan gastronomic gorging. We are going to suggest Packy did not get his nickname from his Irish roots, but from his manner of eating–he could pack it away. (We shall take a bit of artistic license and shoot a scene showing Packy being picked on by kids for being a bit, shall we say discreetly, chubby. He will beat the bejabbers out them, and be named not after the actor "Spanky" McFarland of Our Gang fame in the thirties [the audience wouldn't believe he was a hero–imagine if he were referred to by us as "Spanky"]–no, we will have him named after the famous boxer "Packy" McFarland. Now, the truth is that he got his nickname from his brother who was called "Packy" when here at X, so when John arrived on campus the Scots typically referred to him in terms of his brother, and he became John "Packy" McFarland. Now, that's not as exciting as our movie version.) Anyway, the rumors of Packy's colossal consumption are half-believed, for he does have a voracious appetite. And we see the Sisters of St. Martha, mothers for the boys away from home, bringing more platters of sandwiches from the kitchen.

Flashback to how the rumors of Packy's appetite grew: In Halifax, the obviously naïve and inexperienced student manager, a geeky, gawky freshman from Massachusetts (C'est moi), enters a restaurant with Packy and Bob Moran and Dude MacDonald for a pre-game SNACK. Speeded up shots of waitresses bringing out not just pieces of toast, but whole loaves of bread and jars of jam and peanut butter, and mountains of eggs and heaps of bacon. Closing shot of student manager near tears because he has just fifty cents left for the post-game TEAM DINNER!

Next scene: the players with the metabolism of tyrannosaurus rexes are running the floor like gazelles and whomping Dalhousie when lesser gourmands would have tossed their cookies.

We follow with some scenes of our hero on campus–he doesn't think of himself as a hero. Despite his legendary feats on field and hardwood, he is pursuing an education, and he has to work for it. We see him making BLTs and shakes for red-eyed and weary students in the Co-op Canteen in Aquinas House on Confusion Square–a kind of non-alcoholic *Cheers* (get caught with booze = instant expulsion). Then everyone leaves, and we see our man washing dishes, wiping the counter, and cleaning the milkshake machine. No one is there to see that when duty is done, he whips out a book and studies. Never a wasted moment for our hero, always aware of the tasks and goals ahead. Never hanging out at the Brigadoon on the Main. Never an idler. The myths of his celebrating and feasting grew in inverse proportion to the reality of his work habits.

Scenes build–Packy gets his degree and returns for education, and another year of football. Now another perilous road trip, another slide off the road, but this time serious injury, and our hero's playing days are over. But as we zoom in to see him in hospital recovering, we see him fighting his way back to a full life. Therapy produces resolved attitude and maturity–for the dedication to duty and habits of his earlier years he realizes were preparation for the long battle of life that lies ahead. We see him leaving Antigonish and his beloved *alma mater*–going down the road to Maine to teach and coach. Is this the fate of our hero? Not on your life, for the President, Dr. Somers, calls him back and he comes to fulfill his destiny. Close-up of the salary negotiation to contrast the pittance of that day with the extravagances of today's salaries.

Now a series of battle scenes: fifteen years as head basketball coach, nine years as assistant and line coach under the legendary Don Loney in the golden era of StFX football. For the role of Loney, we are close to signing Jack Palance. The role of Bomber (his dog and closest companion) has not yet been cast. Whenever Packy coaches the line, X wins. The year Packy is on study leave at Springfield, X loses–suggesting Packy is an indispensable cog in the glorious era of Xaverian football. Don Loney and the players consider him thus.

But the hero must have many dimensions, so we follow with a series of domestic scenes: We see him teaching. We see a montage of family pictures, with one child, then two, then three, four, five, six, seven, eight. Is our hero driven to try by himself to maintain the college enrolment? Such a full life would be impossible without a supportive mate, and we see Packy and his lovely Irene at early morning Mass–no slack abed on weekends–too much life for them to live. The amazing thing about the family pictures is that the children grow older, but Packy never grows flabby and soft. The call to duty and the mouths to feed demand that he stays in shape. So we will need a montage of Packy in training: running up the steps of the Oland Center, running around the Oland oval in good weather, running around the gym in bad weather. See Packy run, run Packy, run. See Packy sweat. See Packy in his rubber suit (rumor has it he was an inspiration for the Michelin Man!), see Packy in the faculty sauna–lots of steam–we shall be discreet–run Packy, run.

The Great Handball Epiphany comes next, demonstrating our hero's mastery of strategy and stamina on the handball court. Ever the true sportsman, he always allows his opponent a let. And in the next shot we see him make a kill. A good sport, but a competitor nonpareil.

Now the Year of the Thumbs sequence: Packy's old sports wounds demand payment, as they will, of the aging. Both thumbs are operated on. The left thumb first–but he has to keep playing handball. His buddies accommodate and games are played using only the right hand. The left thumb heals, and there goes the right thumb–his natural hand–he'll have to give up the handball. Right? Not bloody likely. We see Packy and his buddies playing left-hand-only games. Everyone's skill level rises dramatically. Packy in his Jordanesque perseverance and commitment makes all his mates better. No quitting. A way must be found to carry on in every adversity.

But a hero's victories must be not only physical, but also mental. He must duplicate this kind of perseverance and commitment in his academic life. Despite a large family, despite his coaching and teaching and volunteer activities (we see him working as the founding father of Little League basketball in Antigonish), Packy continues his studies, for he faces that most heinous of monsters in the jungles of Academia: the two-headed beast known as the Publish or Perish Pachyderm, which has trampled so many to death. If he doesn't get a PhD and publish, he won't get promoted, and if he doesn't get promoted, he won't get the salary increases, and if he doesn't get the salary increases, the children will begin to whimper when they get hungry. So we see our hero climbing the stairs of Springfield College in summer schools, for who can afford a study leave, achieving a master's degree, and no stopping halfway, completing his PhD by combining his love for StFX and its sports heritage and publishing his books. Never waste a minute, never quit, never give up.

Key scene: Packy bound hands and feet and tossed into the swimming pool at Springfield College–we see him sink to the bottom, squat down, thrust up against the smothering water, break the surface, and sink again to the bottom, squat, thrust, gasp, sink, squat, thrust, gasp sink. If he can do this for twenty minutes, he can have his PhD and stay alive to boot!

In a series of tableaus, we see Packy inducted into the StFX Sports Hall of Fame, then on to the Nova Scotia Sports Hall of Fame, Chair of the AUAA Basketball, CIAU Top Ten Selection Committee and Wildcard Selection Committee, President of the Canadian Association of College Basketball Coaches. Then in his avocation, starting from the bottom up, he becomes President of the Nova Scotia Handball Association, Vice President then President of the Canadian Handball Association. His talents, his equanimity under fire, his indefatigable energy, his rugged good looks–strike that, the scriptwriter was getting carried away–his wise counsel, all propelled him into these positions of leadership. Despite these duties, he has been a member the Nova Scotia Sports Hall of Fame Selection Committee, and for the past twenty-two years a member of the StFX Alumni Board of Directors. And we shall make it clear in the film that his membership on all these bodies was not because they served tasty and bountiful lunches!

We shall show Packy's innate humility. We never see him seeking headlines. We see him prowling the sidelines, quietly observing and evaluating, in the Oland Center PR booth, keeping a keen eye on the referees, picking the MVP of each game, chatting with his buddy Doc John Howard, seeing who needed help and encouragement–and who needed to be introduced to something he knew so well: discipline! We see him as a teacher, that is, someone who wants to help someone else. Yes, that's our Packy–a true teacher, a true helper.

So as our hero grows a bit creaky in the joints, we will show him with his classmates, his colleagues, and his charges, bonding with them in friendship, loyalty, honor, and good hard work. But as the times change, the quiet man is not content to be silent when he witnesses the barbarities and stupidities of initiations gone berserk. See him in a faculty meeting, imploring his colleagues to assume leadership in maintaining decency and true bonding among the students. He is a Jimmy-Stewart-type hero, letting people know that love of *alma mater* and fellow Xaverians is not based on drunkenness and torture and the practices of bullies!

Having demonstrated his sterling qualities of body, mind, and soul–the whole man–we will use a real-life video clip of Packy serving as Honorary Atlantic Bowl Chairman–a Mr. Chips scene of appreciation for his lifetime of blue-collar ethic and devoted effort for *alma mater*. We linger on a close-up of this square: his rugged Irish face is square, his solid exercised body is square, his attitudes are, by today's standards, square. He is a foursquare stone in our midst. Upon such building blocks a caring university of excellence can be built. Let fads and jargon and pretensions swirl in the wind–when the storm has passed what remains are the building stones. Our film has shown the six decades in which Packy McFarland gave us a life to admire, to love and to emulate. He has been a rock, and we are all better for him and the gifts he has shared so generously with us.

The closing scene of the film will reverse the opening shot–great movies end where they began–and the camera will come gliding in from the west on the new Trans-Canada Highway, the old Post Road to the left where the car went into the snow, cross over Packy's beloved school, and glide right in the door to St. Ninian's Place, to this dinner, where all his friends will rise to their feet in tribute to our friend and colleague, John "Packy" McFarland. The end. Roll the credits.

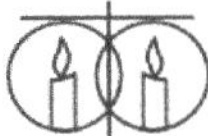

Remembering Jim

Remarks by Patrick Walsh at the reception following the liturgy celebrating the life of Jim Deagle–b. March 16, 1919, d. April 21, 2001.

Some people have thanked me for coming from Calgary to be here today. But there was no question of not coming–after all, Jim had to put up with me for forty years. But when I did get here, I realized I had put up with Jim for forty years. If a true friend is someone you can say anything to and never worry, then Jim and I were joined at the hip forty years ago. From the moment of our first handshake we never had an angry moment, even though we disagree about nearly everything in the encyclopedia of life–except for how to get the job done.

In his homily, Fr. Ray Huntley spoke about Jim as a man of faith. Fr. Ray had seen evidence of the great charity and compassion of both Jim and his wife Mary, who during Fr. Ray's first tour of duty in the parish, had always and ever opened the door of their home to Fr. Bernie Roddie MacDonald, providing him with a haven of rest and service whenever he needed it.

Over the years Jim and I logged many miles together, and our autos became mobile confessionals. We shared our lives fully without fear. Today I feel free to tell you some things about my friend that you may never have suspected.

In Inverness with its beautiful beach, Jim enjoyed a childhood as uninhibited as any sailor in the South Seas. But on a trip there one day with Donald Gillis, Jim kept waxing eloquent on the company house that he called home, because the screen door was still there. Yes, the highlight of our tour was the screen door–just the way he remembered it!

Young Jim fancied himself a fine dancer, which made him a ladies' man. Dances were banned in Inverness in Lent. However, the church authorities in Judique were either enlightened–or Satan's servants–and they had a dance. James got his father's permission to attend, which he did, with the one condition to be home by midnight. At the dance, Jim was in full flight and full delight, tripping the light fantastic, when a lookout shouted that Father B. from Inverness was approaching like a horseman of the Apocalypse. James, wrapped safely in his father's permission, continued to dance, while his fellow Invernessers exited via the nearest window. The priest came in and glared at young and innocent James–turned and stormed out. James was home by midnight, and dreamed the dream of the just. On Monday morning next, as James sat peacefully in his school seat, the door burst open, Father B. charged like a ruptured rhinoceros, and made a lunge for our dancer. James tried a head fake, but the Priest caught him by the cheek, and with a thumb jammed into our hero's cheek, hauled the lad out of class, out of school, and out of education. Those were the days when even a father's permission was futile against hierarchical authority. James's education had come to an abrupt end.

Later, a young lady from Mount Allison University established a class for such terminated students in the baggage room of the Inverness Railway Station. I was never there, but Jim's description of how the boys cleaned out the dust and grime, set up a stove in the middle of the room, and how this young woman, working for food and lodging, showed him how and why learning was worth it. The picture as Jim related it was so vivid and so heartfelt with gratitude and admiration that I remember the scene as if I saw it in an Academy Award film. I am sure this incident was a spark for Jim's commitment to his own teaching career.

Jim entered the workforce and toiled as a lineman for the Power Commission for eleven years. Jim loved traveling around Cape Breton, because at every town he could spruce up and go dancing with the local beauties. At one of these dances, our spit-and-polished hero met a fine young man who was a rotating manager for the Bank of Nova Scotia. They became buddies and Jim met him over the next decade of summers at various towns and hamlets. When the main electrical line was being built in Baddeck down along the swampy waterfront, the Bank Manager heard Jim was working there and went down to look for his dancing buddy. The Manager, spiffy in his banking suit, hollered down to the poor slob immersed in the mud and muck of the swamp, "Where can I find Jim Deagle?" The poor dirty slob up to his waist in the muck, said, "I'm Jim, Charley." Jim told me that the look in his friend's eyes haunted him for many years. That look of disbelief that the poor mucker was the elegant and polished dancer he had shared so much fun with drove Jim to think seriously about his future. Jim went to his lifelong friend and confidant, Father Malcolm MacLellan, and decided to go to college.

Jim was ten years older than the other students, and his life-long friend Bill Shaw claims that Jim singlehandedly raised the dress code several notches at StFX. In the forties, the campus was unpaved. Because of our wonderful Nova Scotia weather, and the mud it produced regularly, gumboots and T-shirts were standard dress. Jim took his young peers in hand and taught them how to tuck in a shirt properly. This demonstration takes Bill Shaw ten minutes. And to have shoes not shined was barbarity unspeakable. My children grew up as toddlers running to meet Mr. Jim so they could get down on their hands and knees to see their reflection in his shoes. I'm just happy that today my children don't kneel on the floor to comb their hair.

Jim loved his *alma mater*. To this day, I know a classroom where I can find a wooden lectern, with a cross, mounted on an M. I am the only one who knows it was built by Jim. In the Morrison Hall dining room, before its present re-incarnation, we dined like kings under the magnificent crest of St. Francis Xavier–built by Jim. The symbols of his love for StFX became our symbols too.

If we walk on Hillcrest Street, or Highland Drive, or College Street, we can see eleven houses, neat, tidy, solid, and inviting. Jim built them while working his way through college. Yesterday I met the son of the original owner of one who told me: "Jim built our family house in three months, with one helper, and we never saw him with a smudge of dirt." One house Jim built, he considered too small for the family destined to use it, so he added two feet to it, and never told the owners. [I can tell you now in 2019 that the house was that of Donald Gillis, who married Jim's sister, Evelyn. Jim thought his sister deserved a bigger house–and gave it to her, without ever letting his brother-in-law know that he was doing so.]

After being out of school for so long, Jim found his studies challenging. He thought about quitting–but a young student he deeply respected took him for a long walk and encouraged him to stick it out. So ever after Jim could tell how this fine young man had saved his academic life. That young man eventually became Chaplain at StFX, and in my sophomore year when I was ready to quit college, that same man gave me the strength and support to continue. So Jim and I shared a common bond with a common benefactor, who eventually became President, Fr. Greg MacKinnon.

Jim graduated–eventually. He established the first provincial Industrial Arts Program in Halifax. He met, wooed, and wed his wife, and with Mary Dorothy MacDonald Deagle built a home in Halifax. They eventually moved to Antigonish so he could establish the Industrial Arts program at the new St. Andrew's Rural School.

He felt pretty good that he got the hillside at the end of Cedar Terrace from Mr. Whidden, and put a house in the hillside–although some neighbors came over to warn him that the walls were crooked. They were wrong, of course.

Jim eventually decided to go on for an academic master's degree in biology and then taught at the Antigonish High School, now in the heart of the StFX campus. As Doctor Bill Foley told me last night, Jim, the challenged student entering StFX, ended up writing a thesis that was sought and read by scholars across the country. Jim's style has always been to start humbly and carefully and then to persevere to a successful conclusion. He did that all his life.

If you walk around town you will see twenty units of family housing, built by Jim—not alone, this time—but with contractors and architects and committees of many willing citizens. But now the products of his labors became larger—for Jim had the qualities of leadership that enabled people to share his vision, his work ethic, and his enduring sense of service. They were willing to follow him because he always delivered.

It's too far to walk, but next time you are on Dutch Village Road in Halifax, drive by the prizewinning Teachers' Union Building. Starting at the Antigonish local, Jim made a motion for a new union building in Halifax, followed that motion to Halifax as a Provincial Board Member of the Union, and then became President of the Nova Scotia Teachers' Union, built it, and came back to teaching in Antigonish. Mission accomplished.

There is Orchard Villa, and there is the J. J. Carroll House. And he expanded his capabilities by serving on the Town Planning Board and graduating to Town Council. Look over to Brown's Mountain, where the dam is—if Jim had not provided leadership, it would not be there.

Jim served for 17 years as a faithful member of the Casket Board of Directors—he didn't know a damn thing about printing—but he knew how to make things happen, and he knew how to build, and here is another example of his quiet, unsung, valuable service to his friends and neighbors.

Jim's true love was first, his faithful wife of 51 years, Mary—and then his second true love was some 429 other women. These women had come into his life in his youngest days as benefactors of his family in Inverness. They were to remain his benefactors to this very day—they are the Sisters of St. Martha—especially the beloved administrators of the RK and the movers and shakers, Sr. Irene Doyle and Sr. Gen MacArthur.

Jim could not say "no" to any request from the Marthas. And because of them his life was blessed. He started with that lectern and crest—and when he was through, he had, with the Hospital Board, overseen the building of a heating plant, the renovation of kitchen services, and the crown jewel of his career, the R. K. MacDonald Nursing Home Corporation—from the first home to the recent renovation, serving for 30 years, and when the government offered stipends for the board members, he said, "Not for me–thank you very much." And he served as an unpaid volunteer for all time.

Jim was a master builder–and a perfectionist–as was revealed by his impeccable attire and demeanor at all times. When the R. K. was under construction, Jim was feared by the contractor; for instance, on the day Jim got out his rule and found the toilets had all been mounted too low on the walls, they were all removed and remounted correctly. And the day he found the patio was too high to drain properly, it was completely torn up and the concrete re-poured.

We would like to dispel a rumor that has been circulating in town–the problem is, Jim started the rumor. When Jim was constructing his home, a neighbor inquired why he hadn't put hardwood in the living room. Jim replied, "I used up too much making my casket." Mary has asked me to make it known that the lovely wooden casket we laid Jim to rest in today was not made by Jim. If you hear this rumor again, please set people straight.

Jim, as a child of the Depression, was very careful with his money–and we used to joke about Jim going into the Bank of Nova Scotia twice every day to check the interest rates on his holdings. But his care with money was a blessing–town, county, and provincial governments respected and appreciated his care with public expenditures: Jim was a man of trust and impeccable honesty, devoid of any self-interest. His concern was for the people in need of his projects. They were his first argument in every budget debate.

Jim was careful–but this did not mean he was not generous. At his wake, one of his former students told me–because no one else in the world had known when Jim was alive–that as a high school student with good marks, the student had been encouraged by Jim to attend StFX. When informed that the family situation made attendance impossible, Jim had told the student, "You really should go to StFX, and if you do, I will pay for your tuition and books." This was the true Jim Deagle–who delighted in helping people–who gave away uncounted hours to help people in need; and how fortunate he had a wife who would share him with all the rest of us. Thank you, Mary–for the lives that Jim and you so generously helped.

If you walk a mile anywhere in this town, you will pass under the shade of Jim Deagle's influence–for Jim was the founder and driving force in the tree commission, and the program he initiated and developed provides the trees that make Antigonish so envied by visitors. Only God can make a tree, but Jim Deagle made sure He made them in Antigonish.

And I am sure that right at this moment, Jim is pointing out to St. Peter, that "that throne over there is not plumb–it should be straightened out–just let me get my level and I'll make it right, just get that big fella off the throne and let me get to work."

While we may tour the town and see Jim's legacy all about us–an accumulation of workmanlike accomplishments taken for granted and unrecognized by many recipients of his talents–I would humbly suggest that his true legacy is in the hearts and minds of the many, many, many people he touched so deeply, because he was a good listener, a tireless worker, a devoted teacher, and a faithful friend. When we look around us in this lovely valley, we are better because he passed this way–but when we look into our hearts, we are better because he was our friend.

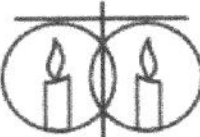

There were many deeds I performed in my life–but as this book takes shape, it becomes more and more obvious that the most important values of my life were formed by the extraordinary-ordinary people I established relations with. If a writer seeks to share his or her life through words that will live past that transformation into eternal life called "death," that spirit that will live on in the love of the creator of life and the love that lives on in our minds and souls. In the eternal triangle of love, these people who live on in me, are and will be forever.

Eulogy for the Funeral Mass of Angela Mullen

August 22, 1916–April 15, 2002

"This is the day the Lord has made, let us rejoice and be glad."

The family and I are grateful for the opportunity to personalize the great themes of Fr. O'Heir's homily.

My name is Pat Walsh. The oldest daughter of my Aunt Annie Cicchetti Cardillo, Angela Cardillo Mullen, was my first cousin, but being only six years younger than my mother, this remarkably warm and affectionate woman–in the minds of my sister Mary Ann, my little brother Fran and me–was known as "Aunt Angie."

Why I have been asked to reflect on Angie's life today goes to the heart of her life. Angie and her beloved Leo were best friends with my mother Carmen Cicchetti Walsh and my father "Duke" Walsh.

[I would like to point out a pattern developing here: vivacious and vibrant and strong-willed Italian girls, chose quiet, unassuming, and extremely patient Irishmen as husbands–Angie and Leo Mullen, Carmen and Duke Walsh, Angie's little sister Christina and Alfred Moran, my sister Mary Ann and Danny Rorke, and my cousin Carolyn Cicchetti, Uncle Tony's daughter, and Deacon Bob Moulton–alright, Bob is Scottish, but all the Scots came from Ireland–the point being that God provided for the fully balanced spectrum of skills and character to make these marriages work.)

Back to our Blessed Angela–so aptly named–for she demonstrated throughout her life the virtues of an angel, so aptly articulated by Fr. O'Heir. She was a "messenger of God," as an angel administering to those in need–for Angie was the quintessential nurse.

How appropriate that the family displayed at the funeral home, the Nurse's Prayer, for that was Angie's creed:

> As I care for my patient's today
> Be there with me, O Lord, I pray.
> Make my words kind–it means so much.
> And in my hands place your healing touch.
> Let your love shine through all that I do.
> So those in need may hear and feel you.

The only person not enamored that Angie was a nurse was her son, Jay: "Because I could never get out of going to school!" That creed was not mumbled by Angie; it was proclaimed to the world with the zeal of an apostle. She didn't just speak the words to her God; for all in her care, she lived them. Her care was manifest first in her love for her parents, Annie and Tony, and her talented and colorful siblings: Patsy, Peter, Frannie, and Christina. Her love for them was called forth so many times when they needed care, counsel, and support against attack from outside. In the ferocity of her love and loyalty to family, there are many people who are lucky she was not a member of the mafia. Those of us in the family could read her mind when she cocked her head slightly and gave us the eye–the stare–and we would know immediately that we had offended her innate dignity and innocence.

In her calling, as a nurse her patients became her family, her responsibility, her needy. And from all reports she was a tough perfectionist–quality of care meant not only feeling for her patients in the OR, but tubs-full of elbow grease and scrubbing and cleanliness. Woe be the rookie Florence Nightingale who slacked off on Angie's watch. She was demanding. She was entitled to be so, because her own standards were so high. Her work ethic was learned through the example of her mother, Annie, who was a laborer and provider of incredible strength and perseverance.

Then Angie lavished her care on her beloved Leo, and the only slight imperfection in that relationship was the duty she laid on Leo: to walk her little darling poodle, Renee, every night rain or shine–a task Leo sportingly and half-heartedly resisted, and unfailingly performed. Angie and Leo together devoted themselves to their two children, Ann Marie and Gerald.

Then failing hearts took their dear friends, first Duke and then Carmen, to a youthful and untimely reward, leaving my brother, sister, and me orphans. Offers of care came in to us from other relatives, but we three met, and in our anguish–and I might say, our wisdom–asked Angie and Leo to take over our care. When we went to them they were overjoyed, for my mother had asked them to take care of us if anything happened to her–not thinking it would happen so soon. Angie and Leo had been worrying about how to approach us, but were relieved when we approached them.

That's how Angie and Leo adopted the Walsh children. With less than two decades of our own dear parents, we experienced the care and prayers and support and love of Angie Mullen for the remaining 45 years of her life. Angie Mullen extended the love of our parents for three times as many years as we had known them. My brother Fran lived with Angie and Leo when my sister and I ventured off into our marriages. What a blessing Angie was for her second family. Thus, my duty and my privilege to speak our thanks today.

But Angie had more to give–and her family grew with the marriages of her children, and Peter and Carol entered her life and gave her beautiful grandchildren, with Peter supplying the granddaughters, Lisa and Kristin, and Carol the grandsons, Corey, Christopher, and Curtis. She became the veritable biblical matriarch of a double-barreled family.

Angie could be mildly critical of Peter's driving, noting in her journals of vacation trips, wry comments, such as, "We passed the red corner store three times before Peter admitted we were lost." Despite this drawback, she submitted to a two-day drive through the endless forests of New Brunswick and Nova Scotia, frightened the world might really be flat and she, Peter and Ann Marie would be driving off the edge of the world, to preside at the wedding of my firstborn daughter. In the photo of the clan, including some dozen Walsh "grandchildren," Angie reigns supreme, front and center, a woman of strength, dignity, and peaceful beauty, emanating an aura of love to everyone.

However, in the midst of all these joys, Angie suffered many sorrows: the loss of friends, family, siblings, and most challenging of all, the love of her life, Leo. And while a woman of strong faith, Angie experienced a dark night of the soul. I could show up at the house from Canada, from Ireland, from anywhere, at any time, and get a king's welcome. After updating each other, particularly noting any new arrivals to her bird-watching paradise, we would share laughs, tall tales of her golfing triumphs, our splendid children's accomplishments–Peter's PhD a special highlight–and finally her little aches and pains. Then we would sit at the table into the early hours of the morning talking about our deepest fears and longings, sharing our souls. For nearly ten years, Angie was angry with God–for one thing–for taking her Leo from her bosom to his own. Angie Mullen suffered a dark night of the soul–feeling confused, hurt, lonely, and betrayed.

For so long she had been the one all of us turned to for support in time of pain, need, and suffering–and she had ministered to us as Jesus himself would have. And now this gulf of darkness in her time of need. Yet, above all, Angie was a woman of deep and enduring faith. She never surprised us–she always demonstrated her faith, her fidelity, her fervor, her innate fairness and her devotion to family–no matter how badly any of us messed up. She was truly Christlike. And in time, with reflection and constant prayer and humility, she came to realize that God loved her with an infinite love that allowed her to share in the cross of his son. As Christ accepted his agony in the Garden of Olives, so Angie accepted hers.

Angie came to realize how the dark night of her soul united her with Jesus. This unity did not mean her life got easy. It meant no matter how difficult life got, in her suffering she was experiencing the suffering of Jesus–and learning that love is the answer to the brokenness of this tragic world around us.

Angie loved all of us. She gave us the opportunity to grow in love, and to her beloved children, especially Jay and Carol and Ann Marie and Peter and her faithful grandchildren, her suffering and her lingering life allowed them to give back to her the love she had given to them. The honoring of our fathers and mothers is a commandment–and Angie's children lived it. They demonstrated to all of us how to care–and thus they are passing on the deepest beauty and goodness of their mother. She taught them well, and they learned well. The ripples of love Angie passed out into the world around her will continue to widen in the living love of her children.

I am truly happy today, and I rejoice–sad for my loss, our loss–but joyful in the knowledge that Angie Mullen lived an extraordinary life of goodness, and that today, she is welcomed into the joy of heaven by a veritable symphony of relatives, patients, and friends–and the music and the singing will be great. No one I have ever known deserves the joy of heaven more. We can all thank God for the life she gave us.

Leo and Angie Mullen

Running the Gamut with Coach 'K'

from Silver to Gold: A Chronicle of Coach Steve Konchalski's 25th Year at StFX by Steve Konchalski, Bob Doherty & Pat Walsh, 2001

I hated Steve Konchalski's guts–when he was an undergraduate at Acadia University and kicking the bejabbers out of my beloved Xaverian basketball team. I used to see all the games in those early days of my teaching career as a young professor, because to make ends meet I needed the mileage for driving the team to away games.

I never saw a basketball until grade five when we moved back to my hometown of North Adams, Massachusetts, from New York State, where my father worked during WWII. The man who showed me my first basketball was a cousin of my mother: Coach Johnny Delnegro, THE reigning godfather of sport and coaching in western Massachusetts. Coach Delnegro was a sawed-off bald-headed Vince Lombardi, as beloved and driven and feared as the great one. He coached the Drury High School football, baseball and basketball teams after school hours and was in charge of phys-ed for the town grade school system during the school day.

I was new to Haskins school in the Italian section of town where Coach conducted a phys-ed class one day a week. When I showed up near the end of the year in 1947 and went to my first-ever gym class, Johnny Del divided the class into two lines. Each person had to shoot a foul shot, and keep shooting until making one, then follow with a layup. The first group to complete the shots was winner.

Johnny Del put me in one of the lines, after acknowledging me as the son of one of the finest athletes in North Adam's history, and a cousin of his. Remember, I had never seen a basketball or a basket. With my line ahead and headed to victory, I arrived at my turn and had no idea how to propel this immense sphere up into that basket. I failed at pushing, heaving, or under-handing the ball anywhere near the basket. As my team screamed in frenzy at my ineptness and the opposing team hooted in derision, I knew my days at Haskins School were destined to be a purgatory on earth.

And Johnny Del just stood there and bit on his cigar like a lion on the scruff of a hyena. He was no more happy than I at the complete failure of a relative. When I looked pleadingly like a prisoner headed for the gibbet, he just glowered and bit hard enough to crack a tooth. If I were not so humiliated I would have hated him.

As a result of this traumatic episode, I took up basketball in the neighborhood backyard and mastered a blind hook shot over the corner of Richie Davies' back-porch roof. I never became good enough to make a team until interclass basketball at StFX, but I became manager of the team at X and did the Public Address announcing until assuming the seat A1 in Section C at center court where I could harass the referees during time outs.

I can hear you thinking, what does this have to do with Steve Konchalski? Well, Johnny Del so fired up my determination to succeed in putting the ball in the basket that I kept on trying until I could. From adversity and humiliation to success, not Olympian, but success, nonetheless. When I graduated from college and returned to teach in my home town, I attended one of Johnny Del's last football games. His team, which had not been doing so well, won, I crossed the field and shook his hand and said, "Nice game, Coach. Congratulations."

I don't know exactly what I expected, but I got a bark and bite and a scowl: "Sure, when we win, you're ready to shake my hand–where were you when I was losing? You guys are all the same, here for a win, and gone for a loss." And he stomped off leaving me in the mud. I never saw him again, because I left to teach in Canada. But what he said stuck in my craw.

When Steve became StFX Coach I could no longer hate him. And remembering Johnny Del, during the early years of Steve Konchalski's days at StFX when had been reduced to spectator status, I made it a point to congratulate Steve after every game–win or loss. In those days Steve used to prowl up and down the corridor outside the dressing room, accepting congratulations and shaking hands after winning, venting and growling and utterly alone after losing. I became a lonely silent witness patrolling the corridor with Steve. My presence gave him a chance to explain the game to a sympathetic ear with the heat of the battle still pumping in his veins.

When Steve showed how much he cared for the students and put their studies first among his priorities I became a supporter. But then in 1985 in the late days of the regular season, his alma mater, Acadia, creamed StFX at the Oland Centre in front of the hometown crowd, by 34 points–the worst shellacking Acadia had ever inflicted on X, even worse than in Steve's day.

The search to find five fans who believed StFX was still in the running would be as futile as the search in Sodom and Gommorah. That night Antigonish fans wrote off the team. They believed the season was over, kaput, no way, no how, no matter, forget it.

In the hallway, Steve was vibrating with frustration. I said, "Hey, Coach, the guys seemed to be freelancing, they weren't in the game, don't blame yourself." And Steve turned on me in the most earnest rasping voice, "Listen, Pat, I'm telling you, this team CAN beat Acadia–IF they will follow the game plan and do what I tell them. I know they can, if they will only execute the game plan I give them. IF only they would believe in themselves, and believe that what I am telling them will work." From that moment on I knew how fortunate we were at StFX to have Steve as coach. In the darkest moment, Steve Konchalski would not write off his team. He believed in them, and in himself.

"You know," Steve continued, "maybe they need this humiliation to realize they need me, that they will have to work with me, in a united effort, to succeed as a team. I KNOW THEY CAN WIN." From that moment I considered myself a blood brother in basketball of Steve Knochalski. Adversity breeds opportunity.

In a prologue of the events in this book *[Back-to-back national championships, 2000-2001]*, when StFX beat Acadia to win the League Championship I knew then that Steve Konchalski was a great coach. And when he was carried around the O.C. on the shoulders of his team, I was the only fan he shook hands with.

I knew that whatever it was that would not allow him to quit, was the same driving force that Johnny Del had fired up in my boiler in that cruel foul-shooting contest–no quit.

Some days the effort produces a 'W' and some days an 'L'–but regardless–what's in the heart is an indomitable spirit that produces a life worth living. Steve achieved success–even before going from 'Silver to Gold'–it's just that the rest of the world now recognizes it.

With Coach K

[*Canada's Coach "K" is the winningest coach in Canadian University basketball history with over 905 victories to date. He is a member of multiple Halls of Fame: University, Provincial, National, with two decades of service with the Canadian National & Olympic team*s.]

Having started out in St. Anthony's school in Elboya, St. Mary's moved to the site of the Fr. Lacombe Home in Midnapore in the deep south of Calgary. The home, long closed, had become a boarded-up heritage site, which burned down in 1999, making the site available for St. Mary's College. The second president of St. Mary's, Dr. Terry Downey, was presented with the problem of relocating and establishing the College in its new site. He gave me a free hand as the oldest and most experienced faculty member, and involved me in many aspects of the college's life under his dynamic leadership. I wrote a historical fictional poem about the site for one of our Open House programs.

the phoenix site

In succeeding eras the phoenix bird
would be consumed by its own flames.
Nothing would be left of the bird but its own ashes.

Then the creature would be reborn, like the spark from a fire, and would become powerful and renewed.

The site of this University has been revitalized several times in its history.

i.

the men crouch in the high grass
humped and sweating under buffalo hides
backs to the mid-day sun squinting at the real buffaloes
bobbing to nuzzle and chaw the prairie grass

the west wind comes sliding down the crystal mountains
stealing across the foothills wending through the herd
fluttering the hair from the men's faces
as they leap to their feet
charging bounding like demented beasts
screaming yowling clacking sticks
whirling strips of hide

the buffalo raise heavy heads staring dumbly
bumping stumbling thumping those ahead
grunting snorting now bellowing
now stampeding south
creating a roar of thundering hooves

the women in the trees of the ridge across the ravine
watch the red-brown waterfall
of wailing carcasses tumble headlong
into a pile of twisted writhing bodies
on the bank of the creek
and when the waterfall of flesh ceases
they charge into the ravine
splashing across the shallow stream

delivering death blows to the wounded buffalo
trying to crawl away

it would be a good winter
fur clothing hides bone tools tent coverings
trophy horns for headdresses

under the river of stars above huddling together
against the ravenous dark they squat in a circle
aching muscles and gnawing hunger
warmed by the fire sleepy with full stomachs
after the pounding pulse of the day
chanting to the powers of the sun
and the moon and the wind and the hunt
in thanks for the gift of another season of life

ii.

a lone horseman squints toward the west
wrathful clouds floating from the mountains
promise rain or snow if the chill continues
realizing he will not make Fort Calgary by nightfall
he gently snaps the reins urging a trot
to make John Glen's Way Station at Fish Creek

hot food hot drink
a straw bed instead of a bedroll under the stars
best of all
the people sitting around the open hearth
kettle bubbling
human voices instead of the whistling wind
the rasping bark of coyotes
pacing in the dark edge
of a campfire's light

when the days are warm and sunny on the trail
under a big blue sky
a man can see his way ahead
the clump of trees along a stream
the dust of a threat approaching
but when cold and dark
and the unseen come creeping
a human huddle around a fire
is no dishonor to a man

iii.

Sister Mater Misericordia prays:

I kneel before you O Lord
because you have let me survive another day at the home
I ask forgiveness because I no longer can bear
to stand at the stove without wanting to sit down
I confess I want to get away from my duty at the stove
it is too hot lord
the boy who dropped his bowl of porridge
irritated me because
I can't bend to wipe up the floor
I'm sorry my back hurts lord
I'm sorry the new Sister irritates me
she peels the potatoes too thick too much waste
I'm sorry I was sullen when Father Albert
God rest his weary soul
asked me to help in the laundry this weekend
so I can't go to town with the supply wagon
to get the yard goods to sew the children's clothes
but forgive me Lord
I am sick of the smell of lye soap
I really wanted to go to get some pear soap

from the druggist
I'm sorry I did not want to come to this harsh place
when I climbed the hill to St. Joseph's Oratory
I thought I was climbing up to Calvary with you
O Lord
but like St. Peter you have put a rope around me
and taken me where I would rather not go
most of us here at the center have been roped like cattle
and led to our own personal abattoir
I am angry that I shall never again
see my parents and brothers and sisters
I shall not rest in the earth of Quebec with them
the price of serving here will be
a patch of wind-blown desert
on the edge of Fish Creek gulley
where no rock shall be rolled away
to greet the sunrise
flaming gold on the dome of the Oratory–
but not my will but yours be done O Lord
my heart and the hearts of my Sisters
and Father Albert
will wait beneath the stars for you to come to us
not with the pain of hell-fire
but the peace of eternal light with your mother
to gather us and our boys and girls
and the broken bodies of the men and women
we give our thought and work and love to
in your name in this home now
I lay me down to sleep
I pray you Lord my soul to keep
amen

Patrick X Walsh

iv.

Holy Thursday
the night of sweat and blood agony
in the Garden of Gethsemane
three crackheads He died for
ripped open the boards
the caretaker had nailed across the basement door
they snuck into the bowels
of the empty Lacombe Home
akin to the gophers burrowed into the field outside
the three needed warmth
needed to be wanted
needed to be free of the misery
they could see in each other's eyes
even when they shut their eyes
they were running from the dark and cold
and emptiness
trembling and twitching
huddling around the blowtorch
sucking in the sickening sweet smell
of the poison that would seduce them
out of this cold world
into the fiery pit of their own minds
their own private flashing hell

Calgary would never know they were there
but the world would see on TV
the billowing tower of smoke
the lickering flames
consuming the crumbling shell of the Lacombe Home
turning it into a rubble of ash and embers

V.

the heritage of succor and service
rendered on this site
erased from our sight

as after the buffalo jump
and the way station
and the home and renewal center
the embers in the ashes
are nourishing the heritage of the heart

the deep urge to gather in a circle
around a fire of love and learning
rises again on this site

a clan of truth-seekers
look up to the stars and beyond
look down into the soul
and huddle with the young and old
the lonely the needy the hungry
for knowledge and wisdom
and we strike a new flint
a new fire
an Easter-rising "dapple-dawn-drawn" sunrise
pledging our loyalty
to one another and our common goal
in this phoenix site

to all of you who gather with us
to make our vision a reality
we say thank you

patrick walsh may 7, 2001

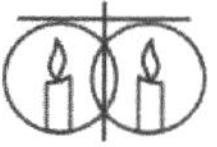

Traveling back and forth across the continent becomes more and more difficult as the years pass, physically and financially. Tapping into the new technology helps to keep the bonds of love alive through a video conveyed by my son, Francis. And when our time together physically is limited, we tend to delve deeply into the "heart" of the matter. Here is the text of the video.

The Golden Wedding Anniversary of Mary Ann and Dan

Mary Ann and Dan

Hearts–

Across the miles, and across the years, we have found a way through the miracle of modern technology to share what is in our hearts.

This evening I shall talk about the hearts of Mary Ann and Danny, their families, and their friends.

All of us present here in flesh and spirit know a lot about the human heart: that incredible pump of muscle sustaining every second of our life–keeping us going through soaring moments of joy and ecstasy, friendship and sharing–through crushing and wrenching sorrow and suffering, separation and loss.

Yes, we all know the mysterious fibrous tangle of tubes and valves that keeps each one of us alive to this moment–and we have known dear loving hearts no longer with us–those pumps that exploded violently, or wore out early, that were attacked by invading substances, or that simply slipped silently away in the dark of night.

The miracle of life we share tonight binds us to all those who came before us. Our human existence is the oldest story we know–we are all Adam. All life came from the atoms and molecules of the evolving universe. We all came from the earth–in Hebrew–A-daam-ah. We were molded into human form by a Creator/ Life Force who breathed life into the clay of the earth–we are all A-daam–from the earth–A-daam-ah–and when our heart's work is inevitably done, we return whence we came.

Why am I dwelling upon these sober and somber thoughts for this occasion of celebration? Because we believe that behind the physical atoms and molecules of our existence, lies a reality of deep and abiding relationship with the Creator/Life Force, and with each other. We believe that at the ultimate end of our physical existence, we are transformed into the deepest relationship of thought and reality–the ever-enduring triumph of love–the goal and reward of all our thoughts and actions, hopes and aspirations.

And now you see what we are celebrating here this evening: an amazing and glorious sharing of love between two extraordinary people: a woman and a man; a wife and husband; a mother and father; a sister and brother; a daughter and son; a grandmother and grandfather–friends and inspirers of us all.

We are gathered to celebrate, to give witness, to give thanks, for their love of one another, their love of us, their loving, healthy relationship with their Maker.

When we reflect, through modern science, upon the unfolding of the universe, we see that the pattern of existence is one of constant change and evolution, forces of creation and destruction. And thus it is, also, in each of our lives. We have plans and aspirations, hopes and goals, but–as in the unfolding universe–the dual forces of creation and destruction are constantly clashing and having their way with us. The key to survival is faith in the power of love–that desire to do good for the sake of another–to give ourselves in the service of others–as Jesus came not as an angry punishing God, or a powerful tyrant, but to wash the feet of those He loved. That act of caring turned the values of the world upside down. He taught us the truth about how to obtain happiness and love.

So, our lives never develop as we plan them–and the journey takes us where we might rather not go, through valleys and over mountains full of danger and peril, pain and suffering. But the journey teaches us that beyond the physical heart lies a great, mysterious, unfathomable aspect of life we come to understand as a spiritual "heart," keeping us alive, guiding us in goodness, buoying us up in sorrow, sustaining us in joy and commitment–and we call this "spiritual heart" LOVE–true love–beyond atoms and molecules, flesh and blood, matter and energy–and when we share it and commit to it, we are transformed into a higher state of existence beyond time where we will live forever.

Mary Ann and Danny: your lives and your love, your commitment to each other, to your family and friends and all you meet, to your Creator, are an inspiration to all of us. We thank you, we all thank you, for showing us the deepest, most powerful, transforming source of happiness and joy–the love that raises us to eternity.

God bless you both.

George and Gertrude Sanderson were a power couple in our StFX lives. They were a source of unending energy in the University and in the lives of the circle of friends around Father MacSween. Having left them behind in the east, when George died, we could be there for Gert only through traditional words in a traditional letter of condolence bridging the miles of separation in spirit.

For Gert

What thou lov'st well remains, the rest is dross
What thou lov'st well shall not be reft from thee
What thou lov'st well is thy true heritage
–*Ezra Pound*

George burst into our lives at StFX at the first meeting of the 1956 Student Government in the old auditorium on second-floor Xavier. The Senior leaders of the student body were recommending that StFX withdraw from CFCCS, a do-nothing, outdated, ineffective appendage of the Catholic Community: Canadian Federation of Catholic College Students, indeed. The packed hall was ready to turf membership and save a few dollars.

At the key moment, with impeccable timing, a new transfer student no one knew stood up in protest. By the time George finished talking, he had convinced StFX not to withdraw, but in the Xaverian tradition–which he became acquainted with only a couple weeks earlier–to ride to the rescue of this organization. So convincing was he, that the StFX student leaders not only rode to the rescue, but they put George on a white horse to Montreal to lead the charge–and they gave him an extra $200 to do something noble and heroic there!

He did not disappoint. He came home, not only the savior of CFCCS, but its new national president, with a program to revitalize the organization, transforming it into more than a coffee klatch–rather a hands-on ministry of service to the poor and dispossessed.

Unknown to us at the time, George met you, Gert. And this marriage under some mystery of heavenly serendipity would enrich all our lives and the lives of our beloved *alma mater*. In the last half of the twentieth century, StFX didn't need Batman and Robin, or Desi and Lucy, or John and Yoko–we had "George and Gert," as natural a combination as "love and marriage."

But, not to jump ahead, George organized a CFCCS project to visit the inmates of the Mental Hospital in Mulgrave, Nova Scotia, where people were confined in an old barracks left over from WWII, with no hope of treatment or eventual release, because no medical doctors were available. Young men and women of StFX went to Mulgrave to encounter absolute primitive conditions, with people condemned to Sunday dinners as dismal as dry corn flakes and a slice of raisin bread. The students talked to these people, held ceilidhs and danced with them, and even succeeded in getting one man who had not spoken a word in eight years to talk.

I go into these details, because, although a philosopher and imaginative thinker, George was firmly rooted in the practical world of helping those in need, the very neediest outcasts of society. This spirit provided a foundation for his teaching, and was much appreciated by his students.

We really got to know George as a classmate in the 1957 creative writing course by our beloved mentor, Fr. Rod MacSween. The students included George, Sheldon, Dawn, and myself–all destined to spend our lives in Antigonish and in the intimate circle of MacSweenites. You and George became the most devoted and faithful disciples of Father, and you were first in his heart.

Here is one of George's poems from the class, reflecting his geological background and work in the North:

Hills

I sat one night upon a hill
That long ago had reared high crags
To heaven's breast.
I thought while all the earth was still
That having seven ages seen, this mound
Should now be fit for quiet death.
But even as I listened, Lo:
Great savages at work beneath
Began their ageless task
Of lifting.

Father and the class rated the poem "very good," noting the poem's competence, its always good rhythm, but with some unnecessary inversions.

These first buds of creative writing flowered into an energetic competence and solid judgement that would enable George to carry on the editorship of *The Antigonish Review*, to Father's, and the Canada Council's, demanding standards.

Our Wednesday night "Discussion Club" meetings in Fr. MacSween's digs, surrounded by his invisible walls hidden by thousands of books, were a source of inspiration for us. Father opened our minds not just to worthy literature, but to every area of life that was waiting to be engaged: history, music, politics, art, drama, architecture, theology, psychology, archeology–the subjects were unlimited, and he pointed us to the challenges ahead. No one of us was more finely tuned and eager for the challenge than George.

One day, Father mentioned *The Lord of the Rings* had just been published, and that C. S. Lewis recommended Tolkien. Father relayed Lewis's praise of

Tolkien's creation of a veritable universe of palpable invention. George disappeared from sight for several days, and when he resurfaced he had devoured *The Hobbit*, and *The Lord of the Rings*, in a monstrous three-day-and-night buffet. In a similar burst of hunger, he devoured McLuhan, establishing insights and authority that would remain all his life as a member of the McLuhan Foundation Board of Directors.

George really hit his stride in Dr. Gillis' senior-level philosophy course. All of us, intimidated by the Deacon's imperious and condescending manner, were pretty docile. But, emboldened by "The Great Casket Controversy" between Fr. MacSween and Dr. Gillis (The two professors clashed over the Deacon's column in *The Casket*, with Fr. MacSween defending George.), George stood up to the Deacon, spoke up and gave the rest of us an example of intellectual backbone. Ever after George was an example for us, and for me particularly, of how to speak out with dignity and scholarly courage.

Our early days at StFX, when all of the young men Father had encouraged to return to teach at *alma mater* were becoming a merry band of MacSweenites, were exciting times. We were all carrying immense class loads due to the rapid expansion of enrolment, while at the same time starting families, establishing homes, and assiduously pursuing higher degrees. Those days were, for us, the "golden age" of StFX. Such a time of friendship, discussion, creativity, writing, editing, raising children, faculty get-togethers and academic battles–non-fatal.

In the midst of the academic confrontations, what could be more entertaining–and cleverly revealing–than George's witty and avuncular interjections. That sound we heard was the hissssss of hot air escaping an administrative balloon! And then Gert, you would stand up to inform the faculty, "What George meant to say, is . . . ," and then some more administrative hot air would heat up the room.

In the Great Student Strike of 1971, when tensions on campus were ready to burst into violence, strikers were physically preventing students from entering Nicholson Hall. An enduring memory for me was seeing George manfully confronting a number of towering students, wrestling to free a young woman who was crying, and rushing her safely through the crowd into the Nicholson foyer, where you embraced and comforted her. I remember the event as an example of strength in the face of violence, coupled with caring compassion–a translating of basic human and gospel values into a challenging, concrete, real-life situation.

But most of our days were full of fun and verbal wit, and our master was George. For sheer inventiveness and imagination he was supreme. Through all the years he continued to invent nicknames for me. The infinite variety of names that could be spun from "Pat" never ceased to amaze me–and every one was worth a laugh. If I said something mean, I became "Cad" Walsh; bought a new TV, "Fad" Walsh; if I walked slowly, "Pad" Walsh; got a Tilley, "Hat" Walsh; lost weight, "Gnat" Walsh; the list was never exhausted, much to Father's delight, and mine.

George and Father were always playing tricks on me. For instance, one day on a trip somewhere for *The Antigonish Review*, George started attacking me for treating Jackie like "an Italian truck-driver" would treat his wife. Father leaped to my defense. George persisted, and Father defended, but the more Father defended me the worse my case got and the more George developed the case against me. Finally, when I was nearly in despair, they relented and revealed that Father and George had cooked up the case and they were in cahoots. They were convincing enough however, that to this day, I suspected and feared they might have had more than a germ of truth in their sport.

One day in the beginning of the "hippy" era, Father MacSween confided to me that the Academic Vice President Monsignor Bauer, was concerned that George's hair was getting too long. Father MacSween said Father Bauer didn't want to embarrass George, so he was wondering, if maybe I, as George's friend, could somehow get George to get a haircut. Thus commissioned, I was set forth to get George shorn "as soon as possible."

I thought about the problem, and rapidly figured that if George were my friend, I should be able to tell him anything. So the very first time I saw George, I bluntly said, "George, Father Bauer is worried that your hair is getting too long, and you should get a haircut." George looked at me in surprise but said nothing. Later he and Father revealed that the two of them [not Father Bauer] had set up the situation to see how I would handle the problem. When I was so forthright the plot was thwarted. [That's the only time I can remember escaping one of their plots.]

As the decades passed and StFX grew, an early and pace-setting sign of intellectual life at the University was *The Antigonish Review*, known and appreciated farther afield than in Antigonish. George and you, Gert, were the key members of the team that sustained Father in his great dream. Your support was unstinting and unfailing, always timely and heartfelt, through challenge and triumph. It was seamless, natural, fitting and deserving that George succeeded Father as editor. And he kept the dream alive and the quality superior, and in doing so touched many lives.

Through all the years at X, when problems arose, I could drop up to George's office, and get advice and consolation. He understood the Byzantine machinations of University society, yet never dishonored his values by surrendering to venality or meanness or pomposity. George was a loyal and supportive friend in hard times and a generous friend in joyous times.

Your home at the harbor was so right for George. His mind was in the deep blue sky of philosophy, but his being was rooted in the land of the "real" world. Nothing was more enjoyable than to drive out to your home and chat about ideas of every magnitude: serious subjects, jokes and wit, memories of friendship and creative and ingenious projects for the future. Your harbor haven was a retreat from ugliness, a perfect island between earth and heaven. [Too flowery, some may say, but I for one–and I am not alone–found that after every visit to your home I felt somehow renewed and at peace.]

George was a decent man. Nothing in his talk or jokes was ever vulgar or mean. I never heard him utter an "ugly" word, no matter how provoked. Being an easy sufferer myself, seeking sympathy for even a hangnail, I am struck by the realization that George never revealed any hint of his own aches and pains and sufferings. He was of such even temperament and easygoing manner that he deflected any concerns from himself to his guest.

George did set a good example for an Italian truck driver in his attitude toward a wife. He knew that his choice of a wife was his salvation. There was no one whose advice and counsel he appreciated more than yours, Gert. Your relationship was so close and so deeply felt that your marriage became one in which the couple's names are breathed and uttered as one–and thought of by others as one–"George and Gert."

My last conversation with George was typical. He was full of fun and made light of his difficulties, despite the seriousness of his health. And then the shock.

Our thoughts and prayers go out to you and the boys. We do believe that love can transcend the miles and the days that separate us. You and George will remain an enrichment and consolation for us. The life we shared with you and

Father and our Xaverian colleagues continues to strengthen us in our journey. In love and appreciation and friendship,

Pat & Jackie

In our new life in Calgary, having left behind such a dynamic circle of friends, we soon found ourselves welcomed into a special group of people: Brenda Ann Taylor's Bible Study Group at St. Anthony's parish. Eventually when Brenda Ann left the parish for a new position with Suicide Prevention, I became the facilitator of the group, and Jacqueline managed the hospitality. Our parallel enrichment was to take the theology courses offered by Professor Michael Duggan at St. Mary's. Here in the west we found ourselves making another journey back into the origins of our inherited faith with a group of fascinating pilgrims who became a source of ever deeper understanding of scriptures and faith. Here is a poem that grew out of our Bible Study experience.

"God's Story of Job" - Bible Study 2002

i.

Job was not a living person
did not see his children die
his crops did not rot in the fields
nor cattle turn to bleached skeletons

his tormentors were merely actors
in a story around a campfire's huddle
spun to life in a storyteller's web
as evanescent as the falling dusk

ii

on Broadway Raymond Massey as “Mr Zuss”
and Christopher Plummer as cynical “Nickles”
behaved like Beckett clowns waiting for Godot
as darkness descended like leaves from trees

the stage a circus ring a gray tent of heaven
the spotlight probing JB’s stubborn pride
the wide-bottomed audience so comfortably ensconced
vicariously thrilled to witness the unfolding tragedy

saunters from the theatre to go for drinks
air-kiss cheeks hail a cab and trundle home
to linger over one last nightcap a hot shower
check the children tumble into bed and dark oblivion

JB is just Pat Hingle pretending pain and suffering
his lines the sound of consonants and vowels in the air
his world just props and costumes scrims and gels
his boils greasepaint dissolving into cold cream

is everything we see an imaginary dung heap
how can what never was be the stinging truth
the sibilant whisper of the wind of Holy Spirit
the thunderous tornado of a whirlwind Yahweh

iv

Eliphaz and Zophar and Bildad and Elihu
are alive and well and living in Calgary
sitting on mall benches at Chinook Center
in our pews rinks parks and busses coffee shops

we look around and see the psychic wounded
gumming sandwiches in our soup kitchens
wanderers stumbling into the Inn from the Cold
walkers wheelchairs tubes and beeping boxes

we come home to silent rooms and half-empty beds
we know the fading light of crumbling macula
the insidious accumulation of arterial plaque
polished ridge of scar witness to the surgeon's knife

the empty stare of a friend's once sparkling eye
the swollen feet the migraine the nagging suspicion
that the viral dunghill waits around the corner
beckoning our "long day's journey into night"

v

when a smiling four-year-old boy is blown away
by the unfathomable violence of his own father
we feel it in our gut we cannot help but cry the cry of Job
Yahweh can this be true we are not fiction we are real

the mystery of innocence iniquity suffering and death
lies too deep in earth sea time or mind for us to plumb
microscope and Hubble cannot reveal the edge of the universe
the reclining creator gazing unmoved at what God wrought

vi

facing one another around the biblical table at St Anthony's
we have no answers we mumble stumble hem and haw
we share our questions leave others gnawing in the throat
sense an inarticulate moan of unspoken empathy with Job

the dung heap of the world is a living reality not a fiction
Job haunts our dreams alive in us as surely as the sun rises
in each other's eyes the only truth we see in the dawning light
is the human heart's unreal tale of eons past telling the truth

the story of Job we share is for each of us our own story
faceless God hears our solitary sobbing and our public crying
knows our interludes of laughing and our raucous singing
and we have faith we matter truly matter in God's story

December 11, 2002

Explication of "Job" poem

Jackie and I studied the *Book of Job* and this poem is a reflection on the experience written for the group.

1. This stanza refers to the fact that Job was not a living person, but a compilation of a story known to the Mesopotamians and Egyptians–an oral story passed on from generation to generation of peoples in the Middle East and finally recorded in Jewish scriptures.
2. This stanza refers to the 1959 Broadway New York drama, *JB* based on the Book of Job and written by Archibald MacLeish, national librarian of

the USA. The play won the Pulitzer Prize that year. I saw the play while chaperoning a high school class to New York. It impressed me deeply. Raymond Massey played "Mr Zuss" [Mr. Zeus] a figure who represented the voice of God, and Christopher Plummer was "Nickles" [Old Nick–euphemism for Satan] representing the voice of Satan–not the later Satan of evil, but the angel in the heavenly cabinet who was an advocate who questioned the justice of things in the heavenly council. In the play, these two characters are circus people, Mr Zuss, a kind of impresario, and Nickles, a balloon seller. They comment on the action on the stage which was like the center ring under the tent of a large circus where the scenes of Job's life are acted out. [A metaphor for life as a "circus": we human beings are a ridiculous show controlled by higher forces.] The spectators who go home don't realize the play is really about themselves!

(The reference is to Samuel Beckett's play *Waiting for Godot* in which two tramps [like Zuss and Nickles] are puzzling over the meaning of life and suffering.)

3. Pat Hingle was the actor who played Job. It makes the point that our lives are not seen for what they really are, they are just like the illusions of the theater or the circus–the second stanza questions how such a story or show can tell us any truth about God or the realm of the spirit.

4. These characters are the three "friends" of Job [and Elihu, a young know-it-all] who chastise Job for claiming to be innocent and for questioning why God should send him all his suffering. The images pile up expressing how such people are all around us, and suffering in oblivion of God's way as they head inexorably toward death.
   Chinook Center is a mall in Calgary. The "Inn from the Cold" is a program in which our parish and others take in street people overnight, feed, and sleep them.
   Long Day's Journey into Night is the Pulitzer Prize winning play by America's greatest playwright, Eugene O'Neill, about the Tyrone family who are all headed to death [i.e., the "journey into night."].

5. The opening lines refer to a horrific murder in Calgary: a father estranged from his wife for beating her, was given visitation rights for his four-year-old son and took him out into the countryside, shot the son and

then himself. This incredible crime causes the cries to God–that we are not "stories" like Job, we are "real" people and it asks why such evil is permitted in the world.
The view of the microscope takes us inside ourselves and down into atoms and molecules, and the Hubble telescope takes us to the edges of the universe–but in either direction–only more questions are raised–there are no definitive answers to the basic questions of why we suffer, die, and why evil exists.

6. In the last stanza, the idea is that our bible study group struggled together to deal with these unanswerable questions–and in the process we shared a search of our own lives and sufferings–and all we can conclude after all, is that a God exists and we have "faith" that that God loves us and cares for us. Therefore, there is no definitive story giving us answers, just an endurance through faith.

These ideas are so hard to put into words–which seem inadequate, so a poem just tries to present word pictures to convey the "feelings" we experience when dealing with these mysteries of life. The poem sounds better and feels better than all this explication! Because the mystery remains! Yet, despite the mystery, we have faith that we matter to God!

Hope this helps.
Pat

In Bible Study, the Far East occasionally met the West. Here St. Paul meets Calgary:

Patrick X Walsh

Paul and the Romans

Paul didn't know the Romans
and he sure didn't know any Calgarians
but that didn't stop him
from writing all of us a letter

he usta be a pretty tough hombre
burning with zeal
to send us Christians ass over teakettle
to the oblivion of the hereafter
until Jesus knocked him off his high horse
how did it feel big shot
to land on your arse
and not be able to see who whacked ya

we were kinda leery about some of his earlier letters
we who trembled at the thought of him
we who shuddered at his command
to be subject to our husbands
like faithful dogs
or dull-eyed cows to be milked
and expectin' men to love their wives like themselves
real men on the range
lovin'
c'mon Paul get serious

once he saw the lightning
that seared a new brand on his hide
he sang a different tune
around his campfires
thank you Jesus

so in his letter to us all
he insisted the gentile Christians
akin to the post-Vatican II Catholics

lookin to the new millennium
and the Jewish Christians
akin to the Latin Catholics
lookin back to the old millennium
should sit around the same campfire
and eat from the same pot o' beans
under St. Anthony's roof

he put the words down straight
we gotta love not hate everybody
hell friends is easy
but others is hard
but the Spirit will help us
'cause the Spirit is in all of us
and if we ain't gettin along
we aren't gonna be happy
in that last great roundup

ain't it funny kinda funny sad
that we been sittin in the pews
sunday after sunday after sunday
hearin' bits and pieces of his letters
and wonderin what in hell
any of it had to do with real life

but Paul got the skinny
right from Jesus himself
followin the law don't make anybody a saint
ya gotta love God
and prove ya love him
by lovin those pesky and irritatin neighbors
no 613 rules and regulations for Paul
just 2
love God
love yer neighbor
that's it

and you ain't a good guy
if all ya do is like they do in the movies
ya smash and stomp the "bad guys"
and then kiss yer horse
no sirree
ya can't smash nobody
and ya gotta be careful who ya kiss

I think we're kinda lucky
or better to say blessed
cause we sat around the little flame
at St. Anthony's
and shared our lives with each other
countin on Paul
to explain God, and his plans,
and Jesus and his dyin
and most important
his risin from the dead
kickin that old stone away down the gulch
and sendin the Spirit
to help us
so's he could go home to his Da

so what did we find out
that every darn one of us
has got the Spirit in us
workin away like Jesus never left

well old Paul
might not know much about Calgarians
or maybe even about stayin on his horse
but he sure as hell
knew the important things
to write to us about Jesus
and his Da
and the Spirit

who is still hauntin some of us
in his youthful self as a Ghost

so thanks Paul
for showin us how to ride off into the sunset
your trail was never easy
you had a lotta tight squeaks
but you knew
that you was closest to Jesus
when the ole aches and pains
and sufferin was worst

and every night
here in the foothills
we can watch the sun set on the Rockies
and be reminded
where we gotta be goin

thanks pardner
May 16, 2005

One of the great pleasures in life is to meet someone and realize that you don't have to build a relationship–you have instant compatibility–for life.

*

Lunches with Fr. Jerry: A Personal Reminiscence

Fr. Jerome Dowling OMI

Fifteen years ago, as I taught the first-ever English class at St. Mary's College in the classroom two blocks north of here in what used to be St. Anthony's Grammar School, my class was making a lot of noise–laughing and dialoguing vociferously. With just 27 students [the College's total enrolment] and no other classes being held at that time because all the students were in the classroom at one time, the classroom door was open. Suddenly, framed in the doorway standing outside in the hallway, unseen by the students, I first saw Jerry Dowling. He was curious to know what caused the ruckus that bounced down the hall to his classroom. It was my first glimpse of a man who would become a dear friend and counselor who would deeply influence my life and convince me to move permanently to the West.

It was evident immediately that Fr. Jerry Dowling was a wise guy. He continued to stand out of sight in the hallway, and began shaking his head and making faces at what I was professing to the students about English literature. After class as the students filed out, I confronted the wise guy–and when we shook hands we sensed we were kindred souls. He had been attracted to the sounds of a classroom where the students were obviously enjoying themselves. He invited me to go for lunch–and for the next 15 years we went to lunch nearly every Monday at 11:30 a.m.

Monday was a good day for our lunches, particularly in the last decade or so when Fr. Jerry was chaplain on call all weekend for all the hospitals in the city. Many are the days he came to lunch after being on duty with the dying and their families since the middle of the night. Monday was good for me because it was my wife's cleaning day, and my absence meant she didn't have to clean around me or prepare a meal.

At these lunches we got to know each other and share our lives and our ideas. He *was* truly a wise guy, ready with a quip to puncture any signs of pomposity, of which I gave him many opportunities. I had to defend myself by returning fire, so our relationship became a weekly shootout by two academic cowboys quick-drawing–if the bullets had been lead instead of wit, three weeks out of four every month, I would have been interred in Boot Hill.

We were truly an odd couple: he Canadian, me Yank; he a Western conservative, me an Eastern liberal; he anti-CBC, me pro-CBC; he plain bland food, me spicy Italo-Mex; he thin, me fat. Thus our lunches were always occasion for brisk and provocative conversations. After the first few times I gushed over the latest sports triumph of the Red Sox, Celtics, or Stampeders, I realized I had to stop reliving games. He was not the least interested in sports–they turned him off and drove him to light up another fag [He would have said "cigarette"]. On the other hand, the use of the comma could be debated through dessert. In matters of grammar and usage he was a strict traditionalist, resisting modern barbarisms, while I was all for embracing the heady development of living language. When we reached an impasse over grammatical procedures, we would turn to my wife Jackie, a newspaper editor for 25 years, and accept her judgments as peace treaties of sorts. We both agreed that she was probably the only person in our lives who knew how to use a comma correctly–and to whom we could defer to save face.

In the fun of those shoot-outs, I found out that Fr. Jerry Dowling really was 'wise' in a much deeper sense: behind his cavalier manner he was a man of deep wisdom. His seemingly casual conversations were employed to enable people to see themselves and their situations more clearly. He didn't ever preach; he led people to make their own decisions and with his help they came to see themselves as they really were.

Over the years I became aware of the incredible range of people who turned to Fr. Jerry for help and counseling. Not just students, or parishioners, or friends or acquaintances, but people of other faiths and denominations, or of no denominations. A singular moment of compassionate communion with someone suffering, or troubled, or searching, often led to a continuing relationship in which Fr. Jerry continued to give of himself and his wisdom in his unique and engaging manner.

Fr. Jerry entered into the lives of the Walshes and our children and grandchildren. He loved young people and delighted in their spontaneity and exuberance. Along the way he was ever just a phone call away from instantaneous response in medical and personal emergencies. In one case he arrived at the hospital before my wife arrived at the ER. In personal family matters he could lead us to solid decision-making by asking leading questions until the right course was as obvious as a giant billboard. And then he would personally take the steps to arrange for the solution to be realized. He beat Bush 43 all to hell as an "enabler."

Whenever we moved to new quarters, Fr. Jerry the designer bubbled with enthusiasm while helping us: with new furniture selection, color selections, where and how to hang our art work, and especially how to arrange the furniture–he was a veritable potentate of feng shui. He really let me down on the placing of my big sports TV, the placement of which Jacqueline and I disagreed on: he voted with her! Come to think of it, he was wise enough never to vote against her. Obviously, the man just loved chocolate cake. He even bought us a new chair for our living room set (The deal was buy one chair and get the second for a dollar, and he just reached into his pocket and flipped me a loonie [A Canadian dollar]).

In his liturgies, homilies, and parish activities, Fr. Jerry was a pre-eminent designer. His goal was always to involve people in a meaningful way. His style of presenting a homily with no notes while roving the aisles was designed to make contact with the congregation not just through sound and inflections, but through all the methods of engagement: eye-contact, gestures, pauses and glances, facial expressions, body language–all the while presenting the underlying spiritual concepts in a most inviting, accessible and effective manner. He never, ever gave a long homily–knowing that the attention of the congregation would wane if they became numb in the bum.

As an example, one of his characteristic events was his officiating at our 50th wedding anniversary here at this very altar at St. Anthony's. Our family and our invited guests, many of whom were non-Catholics, were at the regular Saturday evening Eucharistic celebration conducted by our parish priest. Following Mass, Fr. Jerry, in his deft and accomplished manner, quietly gathered everyone out of the pews and arranged them in a circle flowing down the steps and around the altar. When we renewed our vows he engaged everyone present in the affair and the blessing. I was so thrilled to have survived to a 50th anniversary I stood there with a grin as wide as a Cheshire cat's, until Fr. Jerry interrupted my reverie–"She's waiting for a kiss–did you forget how?"

Many of the non-Catholics told me afterwards how touched they were to be included in the ceremony in such a personal way. The Spirit seemed alive in all present that evening.

This magnificent gift of making the Spirit present was Fr. Jerry's special charism. He related to his fellow priests–especially the retired priests entrusted to his care–religious, his parish staff, his students, patients, concerned families, and especially the caregivers, the hospital staff and workers on the frontline of all the daily tasks of doctoring, cleaning, nursing, attending, washing and dressing the sick–for all of these myriad suffering and working souls, he enthusiastically gave of his substance, skill, and love. The servants of the servants of the Lord were the focus of his life and his energy. And in the challenging environment of the suffering and ill, they all loved him back for his faith and vibrant joy in living and working.

Very few were aware of how hard he worked–he always seemed on the fly. But his wisdom and counseling skills were much in demand by the Diocesan Tribunal for his assessment in cases before it. One such report involved the Toronto Archdiocese, and before you could order dessert, he was engaged in doing assessments for Toronto, too.

One of the things that made him able to multitask at a prodigious rate was his enthusiasm for the new technologies. I thought at first he was addicted to his gadgets–but I soon came to realize that he kept on the cutting edge of computers and stuff so as to be more efficient, especially across the miles and distances that separated him from those in need. He was the first to try the new and to conquer the techniques necessary to use them wisely. I must confess that I personally benefited from his castoff phones and monitors, as well as from house calls when managing these arcane devices stumped me. Whenever my son Greg, a computer expert, visited from the East, the conversation at lunch would leave me in the dust picking up an occasional word among the "bits," "mega-pixels," "defragging," "gigaflops," "spooling," and "Tetra-hertz."

So, over the years together, Fr. Jerry and I broke bread together many times. And it is no accident that our friendship grew deeply, for what better way for opposites, for "others," to come to know one another than through sharing a meal. It is the basic interaction of human relationships dating back to the Hebrew tradition, the source of our Christian Eucharistic tradition, and in basic human psychology, an unfailing way to encounter another soul on the road to Emmaus and to our destiny in the New World of the Christ. Hence his pleasure in food.

I am so grateful that the paths that Fr. Jerry and I took came together for these past years. Over our lunches our past worlds interacted: he introduced me to Peter's Drive-In for burgers and shakes, as well as Your Favorite Best Ice Cream Shop. Before he was on call for the hospitals, we used to explore the hinterlands of Calgary, venturing as far as the Station in Strathmore. We took advantage of the deals at Casinos, which Father especially favored because he could smoke there. The anti-smoking law changed our venues considerably, until he was able to manage his habit postprandially. So we waltzed together from the Friars' Pub at Glenmore Landing, to the Red Carpet Inn, to Boston Pizzas, to Ricky's, to Moxies, to Chinese Home Inn, to CocoBrook's, Smugglers' Inn, and numerous other eateries searching for the elusive perfect burger.

Our last lunches were shared in his apartment during his final illness—I knew what he liked and would bring it to him, along with my wife's chocolate cake, and he confessed that he had eaten every piece of the last cake she had sent him.

In Southwood Hospice, our very last sharing, which could not be called a meal, was just days before he passed away, when, unable to swallow, all he could handle was a small chip of ice. Our last days, facing the unfathomable mystery of the creative and destructive forces of existence, are impossible for us to understand. But in our faith, that is, our loving relationships with others and with our God, we look forward to leaving our pains and sorrows and losses behind, and entering into the fullness of life with Eternal Love.

Fr. Jerry would not want to leave us on a morose note, and being as full of wisdom as he was, he would, nevertheless, appreciate a joke however politically incorrect, so here it is. In the gross imagery of our limited human ability to picture the infinite realm, I think I can see Fr. Jerry up there in the great beyond, puffing away gloriously, creating his own private cloud and sprouting wings.

Pat Walsh, Calgary, July 25, 2012

The following poem was written for a memorial service on the first anniversary of 911.

the tent

i.

in the desert night
the stars dance on the nerve ends
of a frontal lobe

flittering star light
whispering of what transcends
the bonds of our globe

makes us huddle in fright
the body trembles and bends
at stars piercing probe

linked to big-bang's site
fear clutches the heart and sends
thought to seek safe abode

ii.

the desert's night-cold stone
yearns for warmth of morning sun
the balm of water

but dawn lets loose moan
brothers crumpled by the gun
a weeping father

hate drying the bone
has waterless darkness won
killed mother daughter

do all crawl alone
raving fools what have we done
to cause this slaughter

iii.

each alone is doomed
for life cries out for union
with someone other

nothing ever bloomed
without opposite communion
we need our brother

envoi

we gather here to accept a call
on line 911
to hear the inner voices

of Adonai Allah God
and
Abraham Jesus Mohammad

who lived under the same desert stars
who knew the dark night
of the lonely soul
who knew the weariness of bone
who lived the mystery of suffering

the difference is
they heard the music of the spheres
saw the infinite light
revealed in the stars
through the tatters of the tent of night

we are all brothers and sisters
in our mutual desert
huddling under the one tent
of the infinite sky

September 11, 2002

The Breath of Life

From: Peter Cardillo
To: Pat and Jackie Walsh
Sent: Tuesday, April 08, 2003 5:10 PM
Subject: Re: Emailing: index

Dear Pat,

This is Pete's oldest daughter Paula. How are you? I'm here with my two kids visiting on spring break. Dad lets me know when he hears from you. Your email mentioned a breathing machine. Are you having respiratory problems? We all care and want to know.

Take Care
Paula

From: "Pat and Jackie Walsh"
To: "Peter Cardillo"
Date: Thursday, April 10, 2003 3:17 PM

Hi Paula and Cardillos *et al*;

Thanks for your concern–but the problem in question was solved. Here's how:

I was a terrible snorer. [Sound strange? Not bloody likely in our clan!] About eight years ago I built a perfect retirement house for Jackie [to handle her allergies] in Antigonish–filtered air, hardwood throughout, special windows, heat from the ground, maintenance free, etc. etc.

I was having a hard time sleeping–would toss and turn, wake up sweaty and tired, the sheets twisted and wet. I was working like a dog, driving myself, but coming home I often sat in the car for twenty minutes before being able to go into the house. I built a small bedroom on the top floor across the hallway from the master bedroom and near the big master bathroom. We referred to it as the Snoring Room–even labeled thus by the architect. When Jackie would kick me I would waddle across to the Snoring Room' and toss and turn all night. To dull the sound I put extra insulation for sound in the wall of the master bedroom, in the wall of the doorway to the master bathroom, and in the wall of the Snoring Room–that's three walls of extra insulation.

I was teaching out of town and had to take students with me because I was falling asleep at the wheel. Jackie started taking my courses out of town so she could ride with me and keep me awake.

I did a summer school film course—and when I would go to show a movie in class I would sit in the front row once the lights were out. Now, I had a reputation as a dynamic and energetic teacher—bouncing all over the classroom like a cross between Ben Blue and Jerry Lewis—but lately I was taking to sitting down at a desk during class. And the inevitable happened—one morning I FELL ASLEEP. A student from out of province who didn't know me cried out when I started snoring: "J—s C—t, this guy can't even keep himself awake!" That moment was the nadir of my teaching career.

That fall we went to Quebec for my son Fran's wedding. At the reception Jackie was telling Mary's husband, Neil, a doctor, about the strange noises I would make when sleeping—how I would go silent and then burst out with a gasping explosion of breath, creating a noise like a jumbo-jet sucking wind, and wake myself up. Neil came running to talk to me and told me to see my family doctor the minute I got home to Antigonish—he suspected I had sleep apnea. I did.

I was sent off to Halifax, Nova Scotia's capital, where I went to a motel—[the sleep clinic was fully booked—but they considered me an urgent case]—where a beautiful 6'4" blond came to put me to bed. I recognized her from somewhere—[Yeah, yeah, in my dreams, you say?] and I did, because she used to play basketball for Dalhousie University when I was doing the p.a. for the StFX games. She hooked me up to a machine to read how well I utilized oxygen—I had to wear a mask over my nose and had a wire clipped to a finger. She had to leave the room so I could fall asleep—[I'm just an old-fashioned guy] and then sneak back in later to make sure everything was operating alright. It was.

I was waking up some 800 times a night—getting no deep REM sleep—and utilizing about 57% of my oxygen. When I would stop breathing the pressure would build up on my heart—not getting enough oxygen for the blood—and I was in danger of having a heart attack. Snoring was no laughing matter.

They gave me a CPAP machine–Continuous Passive Air Pressure–and taught me how to operate it. A mask hooked over the nose, the machine would give me 5 minutes to get to sleep at a low pressure–about 5 mm–[enough to push a column of mercury up 5 mm–like a blood pressure machine]. Then it would automatically go up to 18 mm of pressure [the max of the machine was 20 mm]. Whenever I go to sleep I hook up to my machine. I have to take it wherever I go and it has become such a part of my life I don't even think twice about it now. I am on my third machine–the newest one covers my mouth and nose [I had to wear a chin strap on the early model to keep my mouth closed–yeah, I know, a lifelong problem a lot of people wanted to solve for me–ha, ha!] and is self-adjusting so it automatically gives me just the right amount of air I need. It has a humidifier attached now because Calgary is high desert and very dry.

After I got my machine, my oxygen utilization shot up to 97/98%, no more snoring, and two days later I drove all the way to Halifax and back with no drowsiness–300 miles! How's that for turning a life around? No more Snoring Room exile for me–I've been sleeping with this great brunette ever since!

In the ensuing years I have spoken to my classes about sleep apnea, and there are many guys out there falling asleep in front of their TVs and sawing cords of forests who are at great risk and don't realize it. And it's an easy thing to diagnose, once you realize what the symptoms are.

So the machine is my friend–and the new model is compact–like a little boom-box or tape recorder with its own case which I take as carry-on wherever I go. I have converter plugs for use in Ireland, etc. So that's the story on my machine. If you know anybody with a snoring problem–get it diagnosed pronto–a life may be a stake.

Needless to say, Neil, is a fine son-in-law!

As the old Irish storytellers would say, "That's my tale."

So good to hear from you.

Love to all,

Pat and the Brunette!

The Man in the Corner

The printer is the friend of intelligence, of thought: he is the friend of liberty, of freedom, of law; indeed, the printer is the friend of every man who is the friend of order–the friend of every man who can read. Of all the inventions, of all the discoveries in science or art, of all the great results in the wonderful progress of mechanical energy and skill, the printer is the only product of civilization necessary to the existence of free man. Charles Dickens

Donald Leonard Gillis

If ever you passed 88 College Street late at night, or even on weekends, there was often a light on in the corner office. Donald Leonard Gillis was always the man in the corner. If you were ushered into his Publisher's office at the Casket Printing and Publishing Company, Ltd. Donald's desk was kitty-corner, putting him in a corner, with his back to the wall and the world facing him.

There are many ways for a man to be in a corner:

1. For public causes and people's needs, he could "be in your corner.'
2. A man can "corner" a market or a commodity.
3. In a tight spot, threatened and challenged, a man can be 'cornered' by converging walls or ideas.
4. A "corner" is where a contestant rests between rounds.
5. And finally, he can be a 'corner'stone.

1.The Public Man in 'our corner'

Donald Gillis was always THE man in our corner. For a publisher of a newspaper, he was the most adroit avoider of a photographer. He shrank from the public spotlight and made certain that all the other people involved in any project were front and center.

And no one person in Antigonish was ever in more "corners" for more worthy causes than Donald Gillis. He did not just cover the stories of worthy causes–the ideas many of the projects originated in his office. The secret was that Donald tapped the people in the community best able to accomplish the goals, and then supported them, not only publicly, but privately–never seeking any credit for himself.

He welcomed ideas from all quarters, and enabled people's dreams to become realities. Donald loved the horses [more on that later], but he never jumped on a white charger and rushed off to war. His friend, Ray MacLean, in his history of The Casket Company, described watching Donald Gillis make a decision, to be like "watching a mud puddle dry up." Ray's wry observation was apt. Donald was never one to rush precipitously into a perilous situation. He would muse in his corner, into the wee hours of the night, and consider all possible results, repercussions, political angles, practical problems, personalities involved, hidden road blocks. Then he would quietly and effectively touch those souls capable of realizing dreams, and enable them.

For more than a half-century Donald Gillis exercised his power, judgment, and commitment: on the national scene as Senior Director for Teleglobe Canada; on the Maritime scene: for the Canadian Community Newspaper Association [Gold Quill Award], The Atlantic Provinces Graphic Arts Association, North

Shore Drug Dependency Association, Nova Scotia Weekly Newspaper Association; on the local scene: for St. Martha's Hospital, The R.K. MacDonald Nursing Home, L'Arche, Canadian Association for Community Living, Public Housing, The Building for Youth Arena, the Parish Hall, his beloved Legion and the international championship Legion Pipe Band, The Highland Society, the Red Cross, Theatre and Festival Antigonish, and his *alma mater*, St. Francis Xavier University–who recognized his contributions to town, college, province and country with an honorary degree in 1992. Of course all these marvelous accomplishments were the work of many, many people–but Donald's finger, often pointing a way, was in every pie. And when he stuck in his thumb, he often pulled out a plum!

2. The Newspaper Man who 'cornered' the market.

At the mid-point of the twentieth century, The Casket Company tapped Donald Gillis to become general manager. The enterprise was practically bankrupt–there was no working capital, equipment was outmoded, and radio was gobbling up the major share of advertising dollars. In the face of desperate challenge, Donald introduced the first of three revolutions: 1st, in the sixties he switched production from the antiquated hot-lead printing to offset printing; 2nd, in the seventies he aggressively obtained government assistance through DREE and Manpower to expand services and training, thus increasing revenues; 3rd, in the eighties and nineties he personally led the entire staff through the computerization of the company.

In his sixties he abandoned his beloved typewriter and learned Word Perfect, and inspired his staff to accompany him on a crusade to modernity. This was no mean feat, for Donald, inspired by the social justice teachings of Doc Dan MacCormack in his St. F.X. classes, did not fire mature staff and replace them with younger and less expensive newcomers–he encouraged them by example to embrace the new, and kept them in 'the Casket Family.' Some of his peers in the industry have noted that the Casket is the only newspaper the Maritimes that did not disappear or change ownership during these challenging years. Times were often hard for everyone at the Casket, but Donald was committed to each dedicated and loyal employee–a rare feat indeed.

The Casket not only survived, but flourished under the guidance of Donald Gillis, remaining the oldest continuously-published newspaper in Canada, despite takeover attempts from the Thompson chain and challenges from competitors. The Casket remains solidly in the corner and in the hearts of Antigonishers.

3. The Man who was 'cornered' where ideas clash.

In the corner behind the desk of the Publisher is where ideas clashed for over half-a-century of Donald Gillis's life. Not many people have to satisfy so many bosses with so many differing ideas. Most of us have to satisfy one boss to survive. But a publisher is subject to many pressures: he must satisfy a Board of Directors representing his owners, but if he doesn't satisfy his readers and advertisers, the ship will sink.

The Casket is unique: a public community newspaper, with a religious component of interest to its principle shareholder. It was no mean feat for Donald Gillis to be at the wheel and steer this ship between the Scylla of the secular community and the Charybdis of his religious faith. In the first lay his worldly salvation through revenues, in the second his eternal salvation through the values of his faith. Many a day, or week, or month, Donald wisely waited for many 'mud puddles' to reveal whether or not they hid a disastrous pothole!

Every day values clashed: Town vs. Gown, Town vs. County, Antigonish vs. the Outside World, Conservatives vs. Liberals. Donald was answerable to all. He had to be seen to be even-handed to all–and even more important, actually even-handed to all. He was always in a corner and always being judged–week-in and week-out, year-in and year-out, for decade after decade–challenged to maintain and preserve tradition and to embrace the new and innovative. And thousands of readers were always ready to pounce. Few of us face such public pressure.

The miracle was that Donald was able to weather any gale, keep a steady hand on the tiller, and reach a port in any storm. His quiet and gentlemanly demeanor instilled confidence. Both staff and public and owners were assured by his calmness and confidence. His advice was never glib or dismissive. You knew that he thought deeply and sincerely, and cared.

As publisher Donald dealt with the powerful people, especially government officials at all levels: local, provincial, federal. His skills of thought and communication, his character of trustworthiness, and his indefatigable work ethic, tempted him to leap from Antigonish to the corridors of power in Ottawa. But Donald knew only too well, the temptations of power and wealth. He had seen marriages founder, dreams dissolve, high-mindedness laid low. His little corner in Antgonish was what he could handle, was where he could overcome his personal demons, where he could be nurtured and sustained by his family and friends and colleagues. He resisted the siren song of public power and settled into a life that concluded with his values intact, his accomplishments unsullied, his faith rewarded.

4. The 'Corner' is where a fighter rests between rounds.

The beginning rounds of Donald Gillis were in his home town of Inverness, mining town of western Cape Breton. The cliché is that you could take the boy out of the town, but you couldn't take the town out of the boy. For Donald this statement was not a cliché, it was a living reality. Inverness was always with him: it was his biological birthplace, his psychological birthplace in a family and environ of strong faith, it was his intellectual birthplace where he witnessed the grit and honor of hard labor and quest for social justice, it was the birthplace of his adult sense of commitment to family, friends and neighbors.

Inverness ignited a pilot light in Donald that never flickered out. The sheer beauty of Cape Breton, the sunsets, the nearly idyllic beach, the rhythm of close-knit families, the spirit of independence of mind–all found a fertile ground in the young man. 206 MacKenzie Avenue in the Red Rows was his potting shed, but the flower of his life he found next door in 208 MacKenzie was Evelyn Deagle. Near the end of his life Donald wrote of her, she "was endowed with Mother Nature's most elegant and elaborate attributes....unbending determination and an uncanny discipline to the job at hand, she persevered and became a clever student, a compassionate nurse and a consummate wife and mother. She was the class of the Red Rows." So naturally, he married her, and obviously enamored of such perfection, fathered five replicas of such a remarkable woman.

I personally recall a trip to Inverness with Donald and Jim Deagle, Evelyn's brother, on some task for the Casket Company. The two Invernessers decided to show their young American-born friend the incredible benefits of Inverness. We drove up and down the Red Rows, the two locals recounting in a blazing hale of memories, just about every misadventure that ever took place in their youth. The two things they waxed on about that are embedded in my memory are the 'screen door' that was still valiantly hanging on 210 after a half-century of wear, and the marvelous railing on Allan J's porch, an architectural feature I was forced to equate with the gold dome of the State House my home Commonwealth of Massachusetts. Those boys loved their roots.

What a shock the early rounds of life must have been for young Donald, still in his teens, to go off to the Big One, WWII, leaving the beach at Inverness to end up on the beaches of Normandy. Raconteur that he was, Donald would never talk about the trials and pains of the war, but rather about the ironies and foibles of those mates who shared the experience of foreign war.

Years later, we used to tease him about his most memorable exploit: "walking barefoot in Belgium." Donald got a pair of fine leather shoes from his mother in Inverness. He knew the expense and the sacrifices that had been made to send him those shoes. He appreciated the recognition that those shoes would enable him to kick off the mud of the battlefield and dance a mighty fine dance in a church hall in a liberated little corner of Europe. So he did. But after the dance, the weather had turned, the snow was flying and the slush was ready to destroy his incredibly magnificent shoes from Main Street, Inverness. So Donald took off those shoes, tied them around his neck, and trudged through the muck and mud four miles back to camp. The lad could see that those shoes were more than shoes, they were an act of love and sacrifice and caring across an ocean from his loving corner to the center of the ring of a violent, world-wide contest.

When my film class at St. F.X. studied "Saving Private Ryan" I invited Donald to come to the class to see the movie. He was deeply moved by the opening sequence of the film when the troops stormed the beaches at Normandy. Surprisingly he ascribed the realism of the movie not primarily to the visual aspects of the scene, but to the sound track of bullets ricocheting off steel, and thumping into rocks and flesh. The film moved him deeply to memories he still found difficult to verbalize.

After the war, Donald married his sweetheart, and found himself challenged in another corner, at St. F.X. in Antigonish. The world-famous University tapped Donald's altruistic nature: a veteran who had seen and survived the brutality of war, and who had imbibed the Inverness, Cape Breton, coal-mining community mentality, knew that when times were tough, you stuck it out, and picked up the pieces and made it better. With these attitudes, and the values of his *alma mater*, Donald honed his business acumen and charged into the middle rounds of his life in the newspaper business, and the family-making business, along the way making his adopted home of Antigonish a better place to be.

Having survived war and the necessities of family life, Donald settled into the contest of fighting the good fight, day by day, deadline by deadline, year after year, for a lifetime.

5. And finally, the Man can be a 'corner-stone.'

For Donald Gillis, 'family' was the theme of his most cherished values. And his most deeply felt commitments and responsibilities were centered in his concept of 'family.' His families were many: his personal family, his "Casket family" [so characterized in his own thought and in the thoughts of his staff], his community family of Antigonish [including both "The Heart of the Highlands" and "Little Rome"], and a veritable family of friends.

In facing all these family responsibilities, Donald developed a paternal management style. 'Paternalism' became a negative term for academic and worldly business types, but Donald Gillis felt strongly the duty of a father with the gift of education and the insight of experience to nurture and care for his 'family.' That Donald's various 'families' thought of him in the same positive manner as 'Dad', expresses a mutual respect and appreciation both rare and deep. Such a 'Dad' is not perfect, he can make mistakes, but his family understands his love and concern and desire to help them at all times, to become a living testament to the things in life that really matter. We can learn from our mistakes, and correcting them, strengthen the bonds of love and friendship.

Donald's 'mud puddle' decision-making process enabled him to solve many problems for all his various families–so many went to him for advice and counsel–both outstanding public figures and unknown clerks and workers. Not being quick to embrace the new, he was the perfect advisor to assess problems family members fell into, or rushed into, or stumbled into. When the pieces were picked up, and a plan layed out, he could help us to go on, to face the future. In his own life, he had picked up pieces, and gone on to better things. One example, is his giving up smoking after 'dying on the slab at St. Martha's' after his heart attack in 1961. What a blessing we shared in the years we were granted by his reform–another two decades for family, children, grand-children, great grand-children and friends.

Donald's Casket family was unique in the annals of business. His staff loved him. Oh, yes, sometimes some could grouse about his 'mud puddling,' but they knew in their hearts, as was proven time and again, the Man would go to any length to help them. As a child knows, later if not sooner, when a father chastises, it's for the child's own good. I believe Donald knew not just the situation of his personal family, but the situation of the family of each of his staff–and many of those wee hours in the corner of his office, he agonized over how to help the family that was his staff. [I speak here from personal experience a number of times.]

The Casket 'family' had a magnificent cast of characters, with an amazing variety of skills and talents, and Donald was the manager of this motley crew of fighters: to mention just a few–the families within the Casket family: master printer, John MacDougall and his daughter, the finest sports writer in the Maritimes, Gail MacDougall; and the queen bee of the bindery, Mary Snook and her family line of worker bees; then the memorable individuals: the indomitable bundle of energy, Eileen Cameron Henry; the cantankerous codger who could tickle our funny-bones and melt our souls, Brian O'Connell; the distinguished and eloquent sportsman Dr. Cecil MacLean; the forthright and literate Zita O'Hearn Cameron; the heroic and compassionate Kingsley Brown, Sr.; the innovative and indefatigable problem-solver, Jack MacMillan; the steady and reliable Huntley MacIsaac; the quickest wit in town, Blaise Cameron; and the imperial and stately C.R. Chadwick, our Chad, who just had to follow Donald to the great Senate meeting in the sky. And I would be remiss not to mention a trio of graces in Donald's life: three calm, indefatigable and talented women who never ever missed a deadline or a comma: Kaye MacGillivray, Jackie Walsh, and Dawn Currie.

Which brings us to Donald's friends, too many to mention all. A few examples will have to suffice: in government, former Casket staffers, Senator Lowell Murray, Senator Al Graham, as well as the nonpareil Allan J. MacEachen, fellow Invernesser.

The local Senate, the ironically named Saturday morning gathering of Donald's friends at Farmer Brown's, and later Tim Horton's, was a great source of respite and relief for the man in the corner. It was a gathering of diverse characters who could chew over any problem of local, provincial, national or international import–and come up with a solution. Ah, if only the world had listened!

Chief among the Senators were the brothers-in-law: Hughie MacFarlane, Ralph Schurman, and James Deagle, and fellow horse enthusiast, Doc 'Cec'; 'Chad"; Archie MacLean; your humble scribe; and youngest Senator, son-in-law Dave Moeller and in recent years Dave's progeny. Among close neighbors representative were the families of John Broderick, Ray MacLean, Jack 'D. Roy' MacDonald, and Stillman Smith.

Donald was not above a bit of chicanery. On one occasion, your humble scribe was going off to Hollywood to research a film, so Donald arranged for Joe Stewart to arrive at Senate to present a check to me from ACOA for my "expenses," much to the consternation of Ralph Schurman, who was the only Senator not in on the ruse that the envelope was empty. An official photograph of the presentation by Casket photographer Archie MacLellan was the clincher for Ralph. Before the day was over, fearing Ralph's vigorous public opposition, Donald had to reveal his ploy. Ralph took a bit of convincing, but eventually backed off from public protest.

But Donald's true escape from his burdensome corner was in Truro, at the Truro Raceway. Raised in the Inverness with its racetrack, he did once own a horse, but his life and duties prohibited the pleasure. He admitted to me on my last visit to Antigonish, that he would still love to own a horse again and train it. The Sport of Kings was Donald's primary outlet for relaxation. The betting was controlled and he had encountered the world of chance and challenge in racing, and mastered it. He budgeted for the entertainment as he would to go to the movies, so no catastrophe of gambling could befall him. The attraction was the sport, and especially the camaraderie of his mates. The drive was out of town, out of his corner, but not too far. He took me to the races a couple of times, and he would go off to study the horses, make his observations, and lay his bets–into the game–into the diversion from duty and care–playing his chess match with the numbers and odds–his keenness for accounting standing him in good stead. The rides back and forth were full of fun and stories. The joy of his youth was evident.

Donald's last round in the contest of life, ended where he had begun; in his beloved Inverness. Relieved of his lifetime of duty he produced with Ned

MacDonald, the book, "Inverness: History, Anecdotes, Memoirs; Centennial 1904-2004." Donald had always fostered local writers and local publications: for poets, artists, cartoonists, historians, novelists, pundits, and The Antigonish Review of literary fame.

For all his years, Donald had written anonymously in editorials, or through his staff writers. Now he could write in his own name, in his own style, in his own witty and charming manner, a gift to his beloved Inverness–and to his many families and friends. This book reveals at last the deep interior joy and intense feelings hidden in his placid demeanor. And in the stories he tells, he gets away with murder! The stories of the people of his youth are entertaining and engaging even to one who wouldn't be able to find Inverness without a GPS.

I know because many of my friends in Calgary found the book and the people and the author absolutely interesting–and he got away with describing and "rating" their stories because the love for them shows through. The stories of Inverness Donald has shared with us can be appreciated anywhere in the world. So, in the end, Donald gave back to his roots and his people the blessings and humanity that drove his life–the cornerstone of a life well-lived.

The light in the corner office of Donald Leonard Gillis is now dark. We are all deprived, but the memories of this lovely man will continue to lighten our memories. He touched us all, and we are all better for that.

Patrick Walsh
Calgary, Alberta

One of the projects that grew out of our Bible Study program was Brenda Ann Taylor's brilliant creation she named "Soup and Silence." During Lent each Monday evening the parish hall was set up with long tables such as would be found in a monastery. At 5 p.m. the doors would be opened for any and all to enter in silence. Gregorian chant would create an atmosphere for contemplation. At exactly 5:30 p.m. the ladies of the group would serve sandwiches and soup and I would present an eclectic widely-researched interpretation of the preceding Sunday Gospel. At precisely 6 p.m. as the Angelus was ringing the group would recite vespers, the evening prayer of the Church for that day.

Inspired by doing this for the Lenten season, on the last session of each year I wrote a dramatic monologue a la Robert Browning's *My Last Duchess*, but with appropriate scriptural themes.

Brenda Ann Taylor

Here is a dramatic monologue from our "Soup & Silence" program:

The Statement of Centurion Marcus Lucius

[based on the Gospel Passion of Matthew]

In Jerusalem at the private quarters of Centurion Marcus Lucius, as dawn approaches on the first day of the week following the Passover Festival. Centurion Lucius is asleep on his bunk. A knock on the door awakens him.

Yes, yes. Still dark. Can it be dawn? Who's there?

Enter Benevenuto and Antonius.

Ah, my dear Benevenuto. What brings
you to my cell in the middle of night?
Dawn cannot be breaking, the sky is pitch–
did yesterday's darkness murder the sun?
Though you may have suspected otherwise,
believe it or not, my friends, I slept well.
Why not? No Centurion ever had
a better, loyal second-in-command–

now you are first-in-command—my good keeper.
I am quite ready to make my statement.

No breakfast—a cup of water. Thank you.

Welcome friend Antonius, most noble scribe,
I have complete faith in your transcriptions,

Then, for the record: Marcus Lucius,
a Centurion of the Xth Cohort,
of VIth Ferrata Legion of Italy,
under Legatus Iulius Valens,
and Procurator Pontius Pilate,
for Tiberius, Emperor of Rome.

Must I, Benevenuto? The record?
You remember better than I, my friend.
Ah, when we were callow youth, cavorting
in the comforting hills of Tuscany.
That fateful day when the gods—yes the gods—
we both credited the gods for our fate.
We saw the shepherd slave fighting off wolves,
he fell, we ran to his rescue, beating
ravening beasts from his bleeding body,
carrying him back to his master,
realizing we, too, had wounds only when
Iulius Valens, Centurion,
Primus Pilus, First Spear, VIth Ferrata
Legion, pointed them out to us. That day
cast our lot in the Imperial army.
His patronage enabled us to rise
quickly through the ranks. We have seen the world.
And better parts than this dry, strange country,
where Emperor god sees not his subjects.

You know my friend, we never sought honors:
side by side we fought well and slept soundly.
Yet, those honors may stand me in good stead.

I shall list them, with your help, my good friends:
three torque necklaces; one armband; two discs;
and silver crown, corona civica.
Yes, won in the ranks. As Centurion,
a golden crown, corona aurea;
a corona vallaris–first over
the ramparts, at the Battle of Minden;
a corona muralis–first over
the wall, I remember, along the Rhine.
And–let me see, one more, now let me think–
Peace, Benevenuto, I am jesting,
well I know the award I cherish most–
the corona civicae aurea–
gold oak leaves–for saving your sorry hide
in the Battle of the Weser River!

You are correct, facing charges, I should
be serious, but I am not the man
you knew a week ago–and you knew me,
and my heart–best of any man alive.

I'm afraid I don't know how to explain.
I shall attempt to tell you, as bluntly
and straightly and swiftly as the arrow
that pierced my own faltering heart and mind.

Before testifying on my mission
this week, I want to get on the record
the state of my mind and heart these past years.
Together we swore oath to Tiberius,
fought honorably for kin and country,
observed the festivals of our gods,
national and domestic, and refrained
from graft, bribes, and barbaric violence,
despite what we saw others do in stealth
under cover of battle or darkness.

We were ambitious, but not for riches
or spoils of war, but for honor, in our
own hearts, even if unknown by others.
Religion was more important for us
in our hearths, rather than in pomp of state.
We did often laugh at our gods' foolish
deeds and arbitrary granting of favors.

Scribe, I think Benevenuto would like
you to be discrete–don't record my view
of his thoughts and deeds, just my acts and views.
You must not fear for me, my friends, I know
what I am doing. I must speak the truth,
for I have seen portents, wonders and signs
of a new world and a new way of life.
I am fond of the past life we have shared–
but what lies before me I never guessed.

Let me tell you how it began. First day
this week, I was in a festival mood,
the streets teeming with people of all stripes.
A great tumult arose, frenzied people,
waving palms and shouting wild 'Hosannas,'
were laying down their best cloaks for a man
seated, not astride, an ass. What a fuss
over a commoner. And then I found out
that this was Jesus, the healer. The crowd
hailed him "Messiah!" I smelled trouble.
Procurator Pilate would not be pleased.
I was glad I was not in uniform.
I thought, were there enough troops on duty?
Would my cohort be called up? The wind
carried the crowds' cries, but not rebellion.
Then I looked closely at this man Jesus.
He didn't look like a King, or a rebel–
on the little ass, he looked like a clown.

We've seen an Emperor enter a city:
Chariots, Legions, conquered foreigners,
Dancers, Music, weapons, robes, stomping troops.

This quiet Jesus was a parody,
mockery of a king, surely a joke–
the crowd seemed drunk or foolishly happy–
those celebrating did not look like Zealots–
if this was rebellion in the making
it could be crushed by ten of my good men.
Jesus rode by, but he did not seem happy,
more like he was going to a funeral.
I did not realize it then, but my thoughts
presaged the future–little did I think
my life would be involved with this Jesus.

Then four days ago, Pilate summoned me.
I had often served as his liaison
to the Chief Priests and Levites, overseeing
our relations with these Temple rulers,
who were not pleased, in fact, downright angry
with this Jesus. Fearing he might cause trouble
for our Roman administration, Pilate told
me to prepare a squad as support for
the Chief Priests and Elders, who were going
to arrest Jesus, who would be betrayed
by one of his very own disciples.

The bickering between Jewish factions
left me cold. Some wanted Jesus as King;
a handful of leaders wanted him dead.
I couldn't see him as a threat, but maybe
followers were setting up a front man.
Orders are orders, and my squad and I
became back-up for Temple officials.

That night we spied Jesus and his twelve men
at Gethsemane on the Mount of Olives.
Jesus calmly welcomed the betrayer
guiding our party, who embraced and kissed
Jesus–my throat clenched to restrain a reflex
to throw up–you know, Benevenuto,
our sacred loyal oath to our leader.
Never had I seen such blatant betrayal–
yet Jesus calmly returned his embrace!
At this sign the Temple gang sprang forward
grabbing Jesus, who meekly surrendered.
What kind of leader was this strange fellow?
Resistance? Physical reaction? None.
Thinking the mission over, I relaxed.
Mistake. Before anyone could react,
a heavy-set, wild-eyed man with Jesus
struck out with his sword, cutting off the ear
of High Priest's slave. As I moved toward him
Jesus restrained the attacker and said,
"Put your sword back into its place. Do you
think I cannot appeal to my Father,
and he will send me more than twelve legions
of angels?" Turning, he addressed the crowd:
"Have you come with swords and clubs
to arrest me as though I were a bandit?
Day after day I sat in the Temple
teaching, and you did not arrest me."
He then claimed that all this had happened
To fulfill the scriptures of their prophets.

I froze in my steps as this Jesus spoke.
The crowd, too, was suddenly quieted.
The only noise--the clatter of sandals
of his followers fleeing in the night.
The Temple authorities had control,

and marched a subdued and sedate Jesus
to the house of the High Priest Caiphas.
My squad and I returned to our quarters.

Walking back my mind was restless, confused.
I could not understand this man Jesus.
He stopped his men fighting or resisting.
My whole life has been to fight, to control
actions of others, follow my leader.
The ultimate failure of soldiers would be
to desert in the face of enemy attack–
What traitorous followers Jesus chose!
Yet, *he* did not run, and *he* did not plead–
he stood his ground, and declared his belief
That the sword is not the answer to life.

Leave the field of battle with breath in them?
He embraced his betrayer! Now, you know,
Benevenuto, that our greatest test
is to lay down our lives for our comrades.
I know and believe you would die for me.
And you know, truly, I would die for you.
But this Jesus put his life on the line
for wimps who betrayed and deserted him.
What manner of man, of king, could this be?
His Empire is not our Empire. And who
is his Father? To send angel legions?
Troops as fanciful as our unseen gods.
We live by the sword in an ugly world–
If Jesus lives without the sword, he lives
in a world beyond the ken of men.
Yet, I could not sleep that night. Despite
his apparent cowardice this Jesus
was a man so utterly unafraid,
so in control–calmness I never saw
in a foe–or prisoner–or leader.

I could have used some sleep. In the morning
the Legate said "Report to Pontius Pilate."

My squad and I entered the hall in full gear.
Standing there before Pilate was Jesus.
The Chief Priests and the Elders had found him
Guilty of claiming to be the Messiah,
the one who would come from Abraham's God,
at the end time, and restore their kingdom.
A guilty blasphemer, they wanted Rome,
through Pilate, to issue a death sentence.
The Governor asked Jesus, "Are you
the King of the Jews?" The prisoner said,
"You say so." The Chief Priests and Sanhedrin
began shouting, "He said he could destroy
the Temple, and rebuild it in three days!"
Jesus ignored them, refused to answer.
Pilate asked him, "Do you not hear them?
How do you answer these accusations?"
Jesus remained silent–not speaking a word–
Pilate was amazed, and I was also–
the man would not answer a single charge,
I could see Pilate becoming frustrated,
not a good situation for the mute King.
To refuse to respond to the Chief Priests
was one thing; to refuse to answer Pilate
was to challenge the might of the Empire.
Yet the man stood tall, serene, and composed:
he seemed in charge of unfolding events.
What an army of ONE, against the world!
Here was a man of uncommon mettle–
worthy to be followed, not abandoned.
I would have stayed by *his* side in the Garden.
I could not help comparing his manner
with the character of Pontius Pilate.

No, Benevenuto, I must speak out.
Know what I speak was in my heart before,
but I buried the thoughts, not even thoughts,
mere feelings, unacknowledged suspicions.
Then I met this Jesus—who spoke his mind
without guile, without manipulation,
without desire for power or control.
Recall when Pilate arrived in Judea,
he displayed gold shields in Herod's temple—
not to honor Tiberius, but rather
to annoy and provoke the Jews, who begged
him to not violate sacred customs.
Pilate revealed he was inflexible
and cruel when he obstinately refused.
We were not proud to be in his service.
Nonetheless, we stood ready to deal death
when the Jews predicted revolt and war
would result from his headstrong policy.
But then, when they threatened to petition
Tiberius, he hastily backed down—
we knew, though we did not talk openly,
Pilate was afraid that their embassy
might reveal his thefts and venality,
executions of untried prisoners,
abusiveness, savage ferocity.

Benevenuto, as I watched Pilate
and Jesus face to face, I suddenly
realized which one was the better man.
Protest not, Antonius, the die is cast—
my fate beyond the reach of mortal men.
Record just what I say, my hour is past.

What happened next affirmed my hidden thoughts:
seeking to weasel from his dilemma,
Pilate offered to free either bandit

Barabbas, or Jesus of Nazareth.
How many times in the past had I seen
such choices serve a politician's will?
Barabbas, monster of depravity,
or a man who had only helped people,
cured the sick, made the halt and lame to walk,
a man preaching peace, eschewing power.
This was no choice for a man of honor–
but Pilate placated the frothing mob.
My heart sank, realizing that decision
would make me face impossible choices,
when Pilate ordered me to execute
his will–yes, judge not lest ye be judged:
I became the arm of Pontius Pilate–
the might of the Empire in my muscles,
my duty to crucify this just man–
My silent disapproval was revealed
for its true nature: fawning cowardice.

As my failure of will felled my false pride,
Pilate's wife, spoke to him, and I was close
enough to overhear her: "Have nothing
to do with that innocent man." And she
intervened on behalf of Jesus, who,
betrayed by a speechless Centurion,
was defended by a mere weak woman!
I, who had disparaged his disciples,
understood myself lower than a snake–
they abandoned him, but I would do him harm–
sin of commission, more vile than omission.

Pilate, understanding his game was lost,
washed his hands before the crowd, pronouncing
loudly, "I am innocent of this man's blood."
Then he handed Barabbas to the crowd,
Jesus to me, to flog and crucify.

Yes, my friends, I carried out my duty,
but sympathy for the innocent man
caused me to turn away. I stepped into
the outer hall, let the flogging proceed.
The whole cohort witnessed the punishment,
and their noise summoned me back to my post:
What had I done? They had stripped and scourged him,
flung a scarlet robe over his torn back,
crushed a crown of thorns on his bloody brow.
The most brutal, barbaric of my troop
spat on him, knelt in false homage, struck him
with reeds, mocking him, "Hail, King of the Jews."
Five days ago this man entered the city
acclaimed by the masses with those same words–
yet, if his own people were so fickle,
by what right could I question their actions?
I gave his tormenters orders to cease
and give him his own robe. As Jesus turned
he looked me in the eye–there was no hate,
but sorrow, as if he mourned a comrade–
as if *I* were that comrade, as if *I*
were the man he hugged that night the garden.
I spun from his gaze and barked the command
"Squad, to Golgotha, the Place of the Skull."

The crowd was rabid as a pack of wolves.
Jesus, tortured and weak, nearly buckled
under the weight of the cross on his back.
Afraid he would not make it to Golgotha,
Scanning for any trace of sympathy,
I spotted a big man with neutral gaze,
obviously foreign, a Cyrenean,
and roughly I pressed him into service.
I understood later that my roughness
was unnecessary, I was really

punishing him for my traitorous self–
if I were true to my heart I should have
Stepped forward and carried his cross myself.
Duty. Valor. Honor. Service. Truth. Love.
All I professed to be, turning to dust
on this guilt-ridden road to Calvary.
I saw myself face down in the dirt road,
but knew people saw my noble bearing–
but the true noble man fell in the dust.
It came clearly to me that the world saw
events opposite to their true nature–
I alone, my friends, could see my true self.

We reached the spot where passersby could see
Jesus flanked by two convicted bandits.
I turned from the proceedings, for my men,
experienced, knew the steps. I did not want
to see the travesty unfold, but sounds
of the hammer and the thump of the beam
painted the scene more vividly than sight
in my mind's eye. I spied at a distance
some of his disciples including women.
Would that I could be that far from the scene,
spectator, not actor in the tragedy.

My next duty was charged with irony:
by order of the Governor himself,
I must mount a ladder and nail a sign,
over his bloody, thorn-crowned head: the charge
read, "This is Jesus, King of the Jews."
I made them prop the ladder from behind–
I could not bear to have him look on me,
two-faced enemy avoiding his gaze,
my head over his, higher than the King–
another sign for the crowd to misread.

I was happy not to fall off the ladder.
Then the shallowness of my self-concern
made me ashamed: to fall off a ladder
did not equate with the ignominy
of the Empire's despised execution:
crucified as a common criminal.

Five days ago, Benevenuto,
I was a respected and honorable
Centurion, loyal and trustworthy–
today I am dishonored by the world,
but, Jesus taught me to see my true self.

Three groups mocked him as he hung on the cross:
casual passersby, echoing false charges
of the trial before the Sanhedrin,
laughed at his claim to destroy the Temple
and then rebuild it in only three days.
The Chief Priests, Scribes and Elders, taunted him
to come down from the cross and save himself,
if, as he claimed, he was "The Son of God."
Even the bandits could not resist mocking,
calling out for Jesus to save them, too.
Revealing challenges–for if Jesus
did come down from the cross, would they believe?
This manly man had never wavered
in the face of his suffering and death
buoyed by some strange unfathomable force.
My hope was that this man was what he claimed.

As the crowd thinned and passersby dwindled
the squad relaxed, casting lots for his clothes.
I was drowsy, believing against doubt,
this crucifixion would follow routine–
but at noon darkness came over the land
and grew ever more eerily darker.

We know, Benevenuto, darkness
of daylight heaven portends evil deeds,
as witnessed in the murder of Caesar,
and other cases recognized as crimes
calling out to the heavens for vengeance.
My fear deepened, not only for myself,
but for the sad lot of humanity.
The pillars of the cosmos could crumble
if the claim of this hanging man was true.
Then startling and swift as a lightning bolt,
Jesus cried out in loud unearthly voice,
"Eli, Eli, lama sabachthani?"
"My God, my God, why have you forsaken me?"
I'd heard men cry out at crucifixions;
but never was my heart pierced by such a cry:
this was not rage, but an agonized prayer–
Jesus had suffered all torment in silence–
this was one last plea, no longer filial,
not to his Father, but to his mute God.
This was a spasm of impending death,
I knew, for once, I was screaming in pain,
wailing for help in a bloody battle,
duty heaving me forward like a spear
To breach a wall of enemy archers–
deep-seated will would accept whatever
fate I might embrace–victory–or death.
Not thought, but some visceral habit of life,
or whatever it is that makes a man,
burst out of my lungs–it was either
the breath of life or the last gasp of death.
In such a moment a man feels alone,
utterly abandoned–our gods–his God!
If we accept the challenge, our prayer
can be answered. I won the gold oak leaves!
Would Jesus thwart the darkness crushing him?

A soldier lifted a stick with a sponge
soaked with sour wine, but Jesus refused it.
The echoes of his first prayer were drowned
by a second wail of supplication–
And he breathed his last. Innocence was dead.

At this sight the mute God, his Father, spoke
through His creation: the earth quaked and shook,
rocks burst asunder–hell was breaking loose.
Tombs cracked open and saints walked again.
Heaven had answered his prayer, beginning
in darkness of sky, dropping down upon
a trembling earth, invading underworld.
I knew, Benevenuto, in my heart
I believed, "Truly this man was God's Son!"

* * *

Yes, Jesus, had died. But we know too well
leaders may die, but they can win battles.
At that hour, I believed and understood
that the world of Jesus, the Christ, was what
our broken, war-torn world needed to know:
I can't explain my heart and mind to you,
But I believe that Jesus knows my heart.

When I reported his death to Pilate
He had heard what I said. He was not pleased–
But I did not care. I had a duty
to a new master, new world, and new life.

That is my happy tale, Antonius,
It's the *truth* as well as I can tell it–
Pilate can figure out *truth* for himself.
Benevenuto, may I eat now?
I am quite ready to be bound over
for passage to Rome for my court martial.

Please do not grieve for me my dearest friends;
I have lost my Imperial commission,
But, no longer slave, I have a free mind
and a free heart. What more can a man ask?

Patrick F. Walsh, Soup n' Silence, March 17, 2008

[*I thank my friend, Jim Schmit, professor of Latin and Classics at St. Mary's University for the background information to profile my imaginary Centurion.*]

Charter Day at St. Mary's University College

September 18, 2006 [September 18, 1986]

A reading from the First Book of Kings: 3:5-15

At Gibeon the Lord appeared to Solomon in a dream by night; and God said, "Ask what I should give you." And Solomon said, . . . "O Lord my God, you have made your servant king in place of my father David, although I am only a . . . child; I do not know how to go out or come in . . . Give your servant therefore an understanding mind to govern your people, able to discern between good and evil; for who can govern this your great people?"

It pleased the Lord that Solomon had asked this. God said to him, "Because you have asked this, and have not asked for yourself long life or riches, or for the life of your enemies, but have asked for yourself understanding to discern what is right, I now do according to your word. Indeed I give you a wise and discerning mind . . . I give you also what you have not asked, both riches and honor all your life . . . If you will walk in my ways, keeping my statutes and my commandments, as your father David walked, then I will lengthen your life."

Then Solomon awoke; it had been a dream. He came to Jerusalem, where he stood before the ark of the covenant of the Lord. He offered up burnt-offerings and offerings of well-being, and provided a feast for all his servants.

Dear friends and members of St. Mary's University College family, this isn't exactly a feast, and there are no burnt offerings of Alberta beef. But this IS a gathering of dreamers–many, many dreamers. And this is a day for dreaming–As the Bible tells us: In the future the young will see visions, and the old will dream dreams. I guess I am here today to remind you how we old guys had visions in our youth, and now we are entitled to our dreams.

In our text from Kings. Solomon is a dreamer. I believe in the biological theory of dreams, expressed by J. A. Hadfield, who said all dreams are an attempt to solve problems. Solomon has a problem, he is thrust into the kingship at a young age and he doesn't feel prepared. I suggest that Solomon's fears must have struck the hearts of many people in this room–who faced the responsibility to make a Catholic College a reality in Southern Alberta.

The dreams of various people reported in the Bible represent a way God communicated with his people. Note they all had problems. In the First Testament: Jacob wrestling the angel at the gate of heaven; Abraham with the command to slay his son, Joseph coping with his brothers and then the Pharaoh; Daniel coping with Nebuchadnezzar; Job with his nightmares. In the Second Testament: Joseph pondering his wife's pregnancy; and Herod's murderous wrath; Paul four times directed by the Lord. You dreamers here present are in good company. And I humbly suggest that without divine guidance, you might not have survived your role in the problem and challenge of St. Mary's University College.

I suggest to you that the problems that we faced in bringing St. Mary's to this historic milestone were reflected in our dreams. Both the biblical dreams, and our dreams post-Freud, are understandable in the minds of people striving to do as Solomon wanted to do, to be good for the people he was (and we are) responsible for. The Bible tells dreams in the forms of stories intelligible in those historic days. We understand our dreams intelligible in light of our own day.

So many here present were visionaries, that is, people with the imaginative insight to formulate a mental picture of a Catholic College for Southern Alberta. The dream of a Catholic College was a dream of the Oblates in 1903. The dream proved a nightmare for the Benedictines in 1913 and lay dormant until the 1960s until the dream of Calgarians conceived the University of Calgary. The Basilian Fathers anticipated a Catholic College affiliated with the UC in 1964, and the grassroots people of the Diocese began to see the possibility of making the dream a reality. In the 1970s the Diocese dreamed of an ecumenical Christian College with the Anglicans, Lutherans, and United Church, but the dream was dashed, but not dead.

The dream came true on September 18, 1986, when the St. Mary's College Act was given Royal assent. But, as for our biblical dreamers, many valleys and sloughs of despond lay ahead. The dreaming part is easy, the making it happen part is harder than hell–and I say that because many good souls in the course of the struggle felt they were being dragged through Hell.

In the 1980s, when the dream of affiliation with UC bogged down, our Catholic leaders refused to let the dream die. In the 1990s, in the face of continuing opposition and seemingly insurmountable obstacles, some true visionaries mounted their chargers–and vowed to go where no Catholics had gone before. Their dream, in its darkest moment, was transformed into an enlightened vision: *in lumine tuo videbimus lumen:* in your light we shall see light! [Psalm 36:9]

Catholics have a wonderful ritual called "Retreat" in which they withdraw from the world and pray and reflect about their problems and ask for divine guidance to help them out. In 1994, the Board of Governors went on retreat and made several bold and daring and inspired moves:

1. Stuff the affiliation, we'll go it alone as a free-standing private college;
2. We will start modestly with a two-year transfer program, but our ultimate goal is degree-granting status;
3. We shall be a Catholic college, but a Catholic college open to all, and committed to a synthesis of faith and reason, through liberal arts and sciences;
4. We need the support of the Diocese, the Bishop, and the religious, but we laypeople will be "masters of our own destiny"–the first Catholic college NOT founded by a religious congregation or a Diocese.

What a bold vision, worthy of an Ignatius or a Theresa of Avila!

The rest, dear friends, is recent history. We have gone from 27 students in our first full-time year to over 750 today; from 6 professors to 52. From transfer courses to degree-granting status. From a visionary dream of a handful of pioneers and a non-entity to a University now in the company and practices of the oldest and largest universities in the country.

All of you who are here today are dreamers, some of you visionaries, but all of you, blessed and honored because you have made this unique and challenging dream into a living, breathing reality. All of you have played a role in serving the people of our scholarly community, our city, our province, and increasingly, our nation, in a noble and sacred undertaking for the betterment of all.

Let us return to our text about Solomon. When the Lord, in a dream, asks Solomon what he wants, Solomon doesn't ask for power or wealth–he asks for wisdom, for understanding, for ability to discern between good and evil, for the skill to govern rightly. I do believe that you wonderful people have made such wisdom and understanding a reality here at St. Mary's. No one will ever know the painful decisions, the struggling steps, the amount of energy, time and money–with some incredible financial support from people of faith in us–that went in to making this silver anniversary possible. But know this, my friends: of all the difficult tasks and dreams and visions of what can be done to make this a better world–it doesn't get any better than this.

So, God bless you all, as we are about to enter the fullness of adulthood in our 25th year of existence. I am proud to have been a modest part of such a dream.

Amazon.ca review of *The Calcium Bomb* Format: Hardcover

Living with *The Calcium Bomb*

By Patrick F. Walsh on March 19, 2005

I am living with "**the calcium bomb**" in my body. My family did not live with it. My father had his first heart attack at 45, died at 51. My mother had her first heart attack at 30, died at 47. My kid brother, a superb athlete in the Red Sox farm system, had his first heart attack at 29 and died seven years ago at 54. I am 68 years old and in February of 2000 an angiogram revealed a 98% blockage in the main artery in the front of my heart, and an 85% blockage in the main artery in the back of my heart. The doctor gave me 2 weeks max to face a massive heart attack and irreparable damage to my heart.

I am not a disinterested or merely curious reader of *The Calcium Bomb*, because I find its story to be a macrocosm of the microcosm of my own heart story. Too late for my parents, but not quite so late for my brother, I investigated chelation therapy. Dr. Robert Willix, who had abandoned his heart surgery practice in favor of chelation, introduced me to chelation. After ten major heart interventions the surgeons of world-renowned heart hospitals of Boston felt my brother was too far gone to put on a heart donor list. They sent him home to die. With chelation therapy his life was extended for another five years–with quality: he coached his college baseball team to the NCAA division III championship game before dying peacefully in his sleep.

When I got tightness in my chest while exercising in November of 1999, because of my family history, I knew where I was headed. While waiting for my angiogram, I started 10 sessions of intravenous chelation therapy treatment. After a successful implant of 2 stents on February 8, 2000, I continued with 30 treatments of chelation therapy followed by a once monthly maintenance program. My cardiologist was enraged that I was doing chelation therapy. He called me, "a damn fool," who was "throwing his money away" on an "unproven, untested method of treatment," a "snake oil operation." I told him I was following all his directions of medication, vitamins and anti-oxidants, diet, meditation, exercise, and lifestyle reform. Following implant of my stents, my cardiologist said, "You're cured." I took exception: "My blocked arteries are open, but what have we done to prevent the systemic calcification that is causing the blockage?" We agreed to talk about everything except chelation therapy, which I would pursue with my alternative family doctor, who is both a "standard medicine practitioner" and a "preventive medicine specialist."

When the NanobacTX protocol, as described in the book, became available, my "alternative" doctor suggested we try it. I have been on the NanobacTX protocol for over two years, and three CT scans of my heart have revealed, in independent evaluations, a 40% reduction of calcification in my heart. I am biking 10 miles a day and leading a full life in retirement.

This lengthy background will explain why I am so enthusiastic about *The Calcium Bomb*. The struggle against the "standard medicine" establishment that I have lived through has been vindicated. This book presents an assessment of the "calcification" problem by two highly qualified independent journalists. Their investigations have revealed an overview of the struggle to establish the validity of Chelation therapy. They set the calcification problem in its historical perspective. They are scrupulous to present a full discussion of the clashes in the development of this therapy, both between "standard" and "alternative" medicine, and within the chelation research community.

The Calcium Bomb shows that more and more, the standard medical world is beginning not only to take chelation therapy seriously, but better yet, is beginning to conduct the research and produce the studies and statistics that will bring this therapy into the mainstream. Untold numbers of suffering heart and cancer and diabetic patients could benefit. And health care costs could be cut beyond our wildest dreams. More and more mainstream practitioners are turning to chelation therapy as a safer, long-term, less intrusive treatment than angioplasties and surgical bypass. Of course, acute care is necessary in critical cases. I would not have been able to reduce my blockages in two weeks! For that I thank my cardiologist.

Would that this even-handed, comprehensive and accessible book had come along sooner for my family. With another CT scan in July, I hope to see further progress.

That this book has come in time for me causes me to give it to my children, my family and my friends. I am deactivating the "calcium bomb" in my body. I cannot recommend this book highly enough. The story it tells is for me "a matter of life and death." I can't help but believe this book will help so many others. See for yourself.

14 people found this helpful

[And at 82 years old, I am still here scribbling away!]

Following the fateful Salzburg Conference of 1973, Jackie and I made a trip to Italy to pay respects to my Italian heritage. One of our stops was in Capri, where we decided to take a boat trip to visit the Blue Grotto, the summer playground of the Roman Emperor Tiberius. The part of the trip most memorable for me, was how Jacqueline probably saved my life. The incident didn't seem like much at the time, but with my fear of water, it grew in my mind into a life-saving incident, and in my memory over the years inspired this poem some 36 years later.

The Blue Grotto

from the cliff top of Capri
the Emperor of all the world
could drop his gaze
from the infinite canopy of an azure sky
to the diamond sparkle on the blue sea far below
carpeting his realm to the hazy horizon
like the god he thought himself to be
he descended into the very earth
down the stairs of his tunnel to his pleasure dome
the Blue Grotto

two millennia later if the Emperor still reigned
he would have seen a pod of tourist Yanks–
among them an illiterate Fascist peasant's grandson–
on the Mediterranean Sea below
bobbing along in a boat
piloted by a bare-chested young sailor
as cocky as Antony at Actium

the grandson was seeking entry
into the womb of imperial fantasy–
the Blue Grotto–
like an insect at the nexus of earth and heaven

in the manner of invading troops
I had to debark from tour boat to landing boat

into a rowboat
and with precarious timing
on the ebb of swelling wave lapping the shore
duck down into the boat
to be drawn by the boatman tugging on a chain
through the mouse-hole entry
into the dome of the Blue Grotto
I plunked myself in the stern of the rowboat
ready for a taste of an Emperor's fantasy–
an Icelander leaped into the boat
awkwardly floundering to sit beside me
the ancient Italian rower barked incoherently
the Icelander stared quizzically
and all the tribal tongues of the Empire
could not avert the imminent disaster

panic froze me
the childhood fear of water
closing over my head
into my mouth nose ears lungs
I knew I would make
a thrashing descent into the mud of sea bottom
to settle my bones into the chalk of eons past
cold spasm paralyzed my back
as sea water began to suck me down
at the very gate of joy
at the moment of expected ecstasy–
how presumptuous and vain for a peasant
to seek to know the secret pleasures of Emperor-gods
in the Blue Grotto

then you were there by my side
needing no translator
your small fist
grabbing a handful of the lanky Icelander's shirt
jerking him from beside me

tossing him like a bag of laundry
to the prow of the rowboat
which righted itself
rebalanced to the horizontal sea

for forty-seven years
you have arrived by my side
in any crisis
bringing balance to my life
so often offsetting
my tendency to self-destruct
my penchant to leap from cliffs
my urge to mount white steeds and gallop off
you have tempered my language
translated my fears to peace
remained by me in my folly
and in my excesses
so that every dark and hidden grotto of my mind
became a sparkling dome of phosphorescence
a Blue Grotto of the soul and mind
where—could an Emperor-god himself have done so—
we have experienced together
the mysteries of both dust and starlight
time and eternity

words and language can only hint
of such love that we have shared
but every day
as you did at the Blue Grotto
you are still reaching out to me
my salvation and my joy

thank you, Jacqueline
August 20, 2007

The following poem seems to be crystalizing a new cosmic element and direction in the theology of the new millennium. I believe this cosmic element will continue to flower as the years roll on.

Christmas 2004

at the flowering forth of universe
our protons and electrons
became potential seeds of life
although each consciousness
would take fifteen billion years to blossom

over half a century ago
our atomic particles collided
unable to pass through each other
opting for fusion
through some primordial mystery
of the universe's forces of attraction

we met in a micro-universe
bound east and west and north and south
by gentle weary mountains
robed in technicolor
where the souls who twined our DNA
sleep beneath the watchful stars
of the instant of the flowering forth
the collision of our beings
was not by accident

rather the tuning forks
of a common faith
and sympathetic vibrations

of the music of the spheres
created a harmony
we could sense
but could not see

we shared a common Christmas
a common God
a common heritage of loving parents
a common cocoon of school and catechism
a common faith
that beyond the mountains
we could fill our world
with overflowing love

we could not foresee
how turbulent the forces of the universe
would toss us about
flipping us from chosen vocations
to unsuspected occupations

we did not understand the patterns
of creation in our children
or how the universe would take their lives
out of our hands
as our trajectory had bounced us
from continent to continent
from sea shores to majestic mountains
like a stone skipping on a lake

creative forces built our love
with sturdy beams and broken bricks
with meadows and swamps
and bright towers and dark cellars
sunsets over water
ice-caked windshields

and as the universe bumped along its eons
we bumped along our decades
not noticing the entropy stalking at our backs

today we are aware of the pattern
the creative forces include our destruction
because sludge damming arteries
blood blistering in lungs
unsuspected gnawing in the gut
clouds fogging the lenses of our eyes
have jolted us to the patterns of the finite

yet we are setting sail together
to galaxies unknown to our childhood
to stories and images
beyond Bethlehem
beyond Hiroshima
beyond the Hubble's mechanical gaze
beyond the Trinity of our youth
to the mysteries of the flowering forth
to our union with the instant of creation
beyond destruction
to the heart of love
human and infinite

as that seed moment of creation
is active in every being in existence
as it was active in our coming into being
it is active in our lives' union
and that spirit will be active in our future being
a consciousness in love
shared forever

to be with you
is a blessing for me
and my gift to you
this Christmas

your patrick

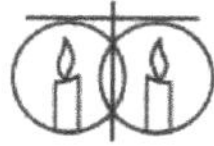

In our Bible Study group, the ladies especially began to open up about the role of women in the Church. They began to be disappointed and sometimes angry about their exclusion from the hierarchy and, thus, the fullness of participation more and more of them desired. They asked me what could I do about their increasing frustration concerning the direction of the Church. I suggested a first step could be letting the Bishops of Canada know how they felt. The group then embarked on a mission to seek a dialogue with the Bishops about what our group saw as problems in the Church. The exercise of this collaboration is contained in the documents below which have not been edited or changed in any way, except for the omission of phone numbers.

Canadian Conference of Catholic Bishops Correspondence

[COVER LETTER]

The Most Reverend Richard Smith, Archbishop of Edmonton
President, the Canadian Conference of Catholic Bishops
2500 Don Reid Drive
Ottawa, Ontario
K1H 2J2

January 24, 2012

Dear Archbishop Smith:

We are a group of lifelong, practicing Roman Catholic laypeople enrolled in ongoing study of the Scriptures. Our current focus is the Acts of the Apostles, and we find the tensions of the early Christian communities similar to the tensions of our parish communities in the twenty-first century.

OUR CHURCH IS IN CRISIS

We believe Vatican II provides a blueprint for the future of our Church. We understand ourselves to be *"the People of God"* (*Lumen Gentium II*). As such, we take seriously our responsibilities to participate as baptized Christians in the ongoing mission of Christ in the fullness of our baptismal roles, both *"priestly and prophetic"* (*Lumen Gentium II*). When we *"read the signs of the times"* (John XXIII), we are prompted to express our concerns, particularly in four key areas:

1. the absence of meaningful *dialogue* between hierarchy and laity;
2. the role of *women* in the Church;
3. the problem of *clericalism*;
4. the need for a *living tradition.*

We see an ever-widening breach opening between the hierarchy and the laity. The Church–hierarchy, religious and laity integrally related in our baptismal duties–is suffering because we have neither a structural mechanism nor a process for meaningful DIALOGUE among the three functional groups that are the living Body of Christ.

OUR REQUEST

Our group requests the cooperation of the Canadian hierarchy in the formation of a Synod of the Laity [see accompanying text]. Such a Synod would provide a structure for the laity to participate actively in the mission of the Canadian Church.

We shall continue to pray for a forward-looking reform within our Church.

We remain, yours faithfully,

A Bible Study Group in Calgary, Alberta, Canada.

Anna Glynn, Catherine Kennedy, Dorothy Loucks, Elaine Stoiciou, Jack Scissons, Joanne Campbell, Carole O'Flaherty, Lea Cornelesen, Liz Bergman, Marie Cameron, Yvonne VanHelden, Jacqueline Walsh,

Patrick Walsh, Facilitator cc. Most Rev. Frederick B. Henry, Bishop of Calgary cc. Msgr Patrick Powers, P.H., General Secretary CCCB

[OUR REQUEST]

Request for Action by the Hierarchy of the Canadian Church

STRUCTURAL WEAKNESS PREVENTING DIALOGUE

We agree with Jose Antonio Pagola of Spain: *"The most serious temptation of the present Church is to strengthen the institution, tighten discipline, rigidly preserve tradition, raise barriers . . . It's difficult for me to see in all this the spirit of Jesus who continues to invite us to put 'new wine in new wineskins. 'Restorationism' can lead us to make religion a thing of the past, increasingly anachronistic, and less relevant to modern men and women."*

We can look to the future of the Church with hope, only if, as Pagola says, *["We] . . . promote creativity in experimenting with new forms and language of evangelization, new proposals for dialogue with people who have left us, creating new spaces for women's responsibility, worship based on sensitivity to the Gospels . . . I believe we have to devote more time, prayer, listening to the Gospel and energies to discover new vocations and charisms to communicate the experience of Jesus."*

We read in Ephesians 4:11-17: *"The* ***gifts*** *he gave us were that some would be apostles, some prophets, some evangelists, some pastors and teachers, to* **equip the saints for the work of ministry**, *for building up the body of Christ, until* **all of us** *come to the unity of the faith and the knowledge of the Son of God, to maturity, to the measure of the full stature of Christ.* **We must no longer be children**, *tossed to and fro and blown about by every wind of doctrine, by people's trickery, by their craftiness in deceitful scheming. But* **speaking the truth in love,** *we must grow up in every way into him who is the head, into Christ, from whom the whole body, joined and knitted together by every ligament with which it is equipped, as* **each part is working properly**, *promotes the body's growth in building itself up in love."* [Our emphasis] These lines clearly define the roles that must be fulfilled by ***all the members*** of the Christian community.

Common sense tells us no one person, Pope or bishop, can be all to all. A healthy relationship among all the members of the Church will enable us to grow in love.

Dialogue is absolutely necessary. Laypeople should be able to communicate their life experience of the Spirit to an open-minded hierarchy who will listen to learn about the faith of God's people. Without such dialogue, the work of the Spirit in bringing humanity to Christ will continue to be severely crippled. In the *sensus fidelium*–that is, what the Christian people believe, accept, and reject–resides the promise of Christ to protect us from error with the guidance of the Spirit. For the faithful to believe with blind adherence is the death of personal responsibility, conscience, and free will. We hold with Cardinal Newman that when the Church, through the hierarchy, "*. . . cuts off the faithful from the study of her divine doctrines and the sympathy of her divine contemplations, and requires from them a fides implicta in her word, . . . the educated classes will terminate in indifference, and . . . the poorer in superstition.*"

WOMEN IN THE CHURCH

Our scripture studies have made it very clear that over the centuries women played a role equal to men in the early life of Christianity. Why has the role of women gradually diminished? When a Pope stops discussion of full consecrational ministry for women, the sense of the faithful is quite frankly, not only disappointed, but offended. Common sense shouts out loud that such a command denies more than half the faithful full participation in the consecrated ministry of the Church. How can those entrusted to teach the position of the magisterium possibly do so without discussing the subject? . . . 2

Equally obvious is the undeniable fact that our parish communities' ability to minister to those in need would be impossible without women. We believe such exclusion is a glaring example of hierarchical blindness to the realities of Christian life in our enlightened age. And many, many women feel this injustice, yet remain faithful to our Church, and continue to serve–a truly Christ-like devotion to duty.

CLERICALISM

We define "*clericalism*" in the sense expressed by Charles Taylor: "*...the reduction of the laity to passive bystanders where they should be active participants . . .*"

WE NEED A "LIVING" TRADITION

As Catholics, we can neither accept nor defend negative actions of the institutional church based on an "unchanging tradition." Our scriptural studies have shown us how, from the earliest encounters of human beings with the mystery that is God, our faith has evolved and developed in succeeding generations, through an ever-deepening understanding of human history and the development of modern knowledge. A "living" tradition must embody the eternal truths of Jesus as revealed through his life, death and resurrection, and the coming of his Spirit. Nonetheless, as our understanding of these truths continues to deepen in succeeding ages, such knowledge demands we refine our relationships with each other and our God. We hope to do so, in freedom and good conscience, in the spirit of Vatican II; just as a tree must continue to grow with new branches, leaves, and deeper roots to remain alive. To stop growing is to rot and die.

OUR REQUEST

Energized by our baptismal calling, we believe our duty is to speak out with freedom and devotion. We trust the inspiration of the Spirit as we have perceived that mystery of love in our scriptural studies. We are asking for an active lay voice so as not to be passive bystanders in the mission of Christ.

We strongly request that the leaders of the institutional Church find a way to open a dialogue so as to listen, not direct, but listen, to the voice of the People of God and how the Spirit animates our lives in Christ's mission. We believe that the Church must create a structure to enable the laity of Canada to raise our concerns in the Canadian Church.

Such ***a forum for discussion and dialogue [A Synod of the Laity, perhaps?] must be organized and conducted with active participation of the laity.*** We would hope to foster such a forum in cooperation with the hierarchy–a dynamic sharing to join in fruitful dialogue toward a unified mission utilizing all the skills and knowledge today's laypeople have to offer to our Church. May we have a *commitment* from you, animated by the Spirit of Vatican II, to participate in the formation of such a communion of faithful Christians?

We shall continue to pray for a forward-looking reform within our Church.

We remain, yours faithfully,

A Bible Study Group in Calgary, Alberta, Canada.

Scripture Study Facilitator, Patrick Walsh

*

[RESPONSE OF CCCB]

CONFERENCE DES EVEQUES CATHOLIQUES DU CANADA/ CANADIAN CONFERENCE OF CATHOLIC BISHOPS

February 6, 2012

Mr. Patrick Walsh
Facilitator
435 48th Avenue SW
Calgary, AB
T2S IE3

Dear Mr. Walsh and members of the Bible study group,

Thank you for your letter of January 24, 2012, outlining your concerns about the state of the Church in Canada today. Our President, the Most Reverend Richard Smith, has asked me to respond on his behalf. I wish to begin by affirming that indeed, as Christians, we must always be seeking new paths of conversion and renewal. In your letter, you grouped your concerns into four categories, so I will try to respond to each.

1. "Structural Weakness Preventing Dialogue"

There is certainly always room for improvement in the communications of the Church, including between clergy and laity as well as for that matter even among laity. In general, collaboration between clergy and laity happens best at the local level, in keeping with the Catholic principle of subsidiarity. Bishops and priests have the task of getting to know the laity of their respective dioceses so they can serve them better. Of course, as the Second Vatican Council teaches us, the common priesthood of the faithful and the ministerial (ordained) priesthood remain essentially different, even though they are directed towards the same goal (Lumen Gentium 10). We are one body, but different parts playing different roles (cf. 1 Cor. 12:12-31), and the role of authoritative teaching belongs to the Bishops (Lumen Gentium 25). None of this precludes consultation with the faithful, as suggested by Blessed John Henry Newman in his essay "On Consulting the Faithful in Matters of Doctrine." Nonetheless, as the Blessed John Henry was keenly aware, it is never a simple matter of taking a democratic poll of registered Catholics in order to determine Church teaching. The "sensus fidelium" refers to the experience or understanding not simply of "the laity," but all the faithful. Newman's point is that the faithful are witnesses to the apostolic tradition. This is absolutely correct. However, we must tread carefully here since in Western Europe and North America certain philosophical errors have led to ways of thinking that induce people–even Catholics–to have difficulty accepting important elements of that apostolic tradition. Thus, in our Western culture, we sometimes have "blind spots" which inhibit us from seeing things that seem obvious to Catholics elsewhere in the world. This brings us to the next point.

2. "Women in the Church"

While personal study of the Scriptures is always laudable, and necessary for growth in one's relationship with Christ, caution is called for when drawing conclusions on historical questions not directly discussed in the New Testament. On the question, for example, of the ordination of women, expert scholarship and the writings of the early Church Fathers clearly show that while women exercised a vital and irreplaceable role in the early Church, they were never ordained to the ministerial priesthood or episcopacy. This decision by the Church stems from the decision of Our Lord himself in his choice of the Twelve. It is a decision that by no means "excludes" half of the faithful from serving God or having an important role; rather, according to Vatican II, the laity have a specific mission: they, "by their very vocation, seek the kingdom of God by engaging in temporal affairs and by ordering them according to the plan of God" *(Lumen Gentium* 31). With respect to the liturgy, *all* are called to a "fully conscious, and active participation in liturgical celebrations" *(Sacrosanctum Concilium* 14). For the laity, this is normally "by means of acclamations, responses, psalmody, antiphons, and songs, as well as by actions, gestures, and bodily attitudes" *(Sacrosanctum Concilium* 30). It is not necessary for everyone to be ordained in order to be equal. In the very act of their creation, "God gives man and woman an equal personal dignity" *(Catechism of the Catholic Church* 2334, citing *Familiaris Consortio* 22). Christ calls us to play different parts in his Body, yet no part is greater than the others.

3. "Clericalism"

Clericalism–that is, any arrogant attitude of superiority on the part of clergy–ought to be eradicated. In the recent words of the Holy Father, "Authority, for human beings, often means possession, power, dominion and success. Instead for God authority means service, humility and love; it means entering into the logic of Jesus who stoops to wash his disciples' feet, who seeks man's true good, who heals wounds, who is capable of a love so great that he gives his life, because he is Love" (Angelus Message, January 31, 2012).

Of course, to eliminate clericalism does not mean to treat clergy as if they were laity, or vice-versa; it means rather recognizing our equality before Christ, as well as the unique roles he has given us in together building up his Kingdom. "As all the members of the human body, though they are many, form one body, so also are the faithful in Christ. Also, in the building up of Christ's Body various members and functions have their part to play. There is only one Spirit who, according to his own richness and the needs of the ministries, gives his different gifts for the welfare of the Church. What has a special place among these gifts is the grace of the apostles to whose authority the Spirit himself subjected even those who were endowed with charisms" *(Lumen Gentium* 7 §3).

4. "We Need a 'Living' Tradition"

You are correct to point out that the Church's Tradition is not dead but living. As such, it develops (cf. *Dei Verbum* 8). However, all true doctrinal development is organic. An oak tree may grow a new branch from an old one, but it cannot suddenly produce a pinecone. This would be against its nature. For this reason, all Christians must constantly scrutinize their own ideas, weighing them against the Church's Tradition, in order to verify whether these new ideas are really compatible with what we have received from the Lord. The task of doing this verification in an authoritative way, of course, belongs to the Bishops, in communion with the Holy Father:

> But the task of authentically interpreting the word of God, whether written or handed on, has been entrusted exclusively to the living teaching office of the Church, whose authority is exercised in the name of Jesus Christ . . . It is clear, therefore, that sacred tradition, Sacred Scripture and the teaching authority of the Church, in accord with God's most wise design, are so linked and joined together that one cannot stand without the others. *(Dei Verbum* 10)

We all need to pray that Bishops and laity–different yet essential parts of the Body of Christ–will hold fast "to the Head, from whom the whole body, nourished and knit together through its joints and ligaments, grows with a growth that is from God" (Col 2.19).

You conclude your letter by suggesting a "forum for discussion and dialogue . . . organized and conducted with active participation of the laity." For your information, the Bishops of Canada shortly after Vatican II had attempted to establish a national pastoral council. By 1970, it was evident the idea was too premature at the time for the laity who were participating in this endeavor. In 1986, when 150 lay representatives from every diocese across Canada met with Bishops in preparation for the 1987 Synod of Bishops on the Laity, there was no desire among the laity present to try again to form a national pastoral council (see Bernard Daly, *Remembering for Tomorrow,* pp. 91-98). In 1983, the Bishops of Canada encouraged and helped sponsor the Canadian Conference of Catholic Lay Associations (CCCLA), which was "committed to promoting the unique vocation of the lay faithful, thus reaffirming their participation in the priestly mission of Jesus Christ in the Church and society" (CCCLA mission statement). However, the CCCLA was unable to find sufficient backing from the laity and lay organizations, and so disbanded in the mid-1990s. Since that time, the CCCB has instead sponsored what is now a biennial forum for national movements and associations, to help encourage an exchange of information and views among the laity themselves and with the Bishops.

It seems to me several conclusions can be drawn from all this. First, it is already clear in Canon 299 § 1[,] that "The Christian faithful are free, by means of a private agreement among themselves, to establish associations . . ." Secondly, if there is to be "a structure to enable the laity," to use your own words, then laity themselves need to take on the responsibilities involved. Thirdly, the basic underlying structure of the Church is diocesan. This means that any regional or national ecclesial structures must be built on the realities, needs, and capacities of the dioceses. For this reason, I would recommend that if you are convinced there is need for a forum for discussion and dialogue involving laity, then your initiative necessarily will involve discussion and dialogue with your own Bishop, together with a concerted effort and commitment from the laity of your diocese.

With every good and prayerful wish, I remain,

Sincerely yours in Christ Our Lord,

(Rev.) Msgr. Patrick Powers, P.H. General Secretary

c.c. The Most Reverend Richard Smith, President of the CCCB

The Most Reverend Fred Henry, Bishop of Calgary

*

[OUR REPLY]

The Most Reverend Richard Smith, Archbishop of Edmonton

President, the Canadian Conference of Catholic Bishops
2500 promenade Don Reid Drive
Ottawa, Ontario K1H 2J2

March 8, 2012

Dear Archbishop Smith,

Thank you for the letter of February 6, 2012, from Monsignor Powers, in response to our request for support of the Canadian hierarchy in our seeking to establish a method of dialogue between laity and hierarchy.

We appreciated the comprehensive response to our major points and the review of the history of the Canadian church's very limited success in establishing a structure for such dialogue following Vatican II. [More about that below.]

We concur with the suggestion that we first proceed to dialogue with our own Bishop in Calgary. That was always our intention, and, as facilitator of our group I met with Bishop Henry to present him with our request before mailing it to the CCCB. Bishop Henry graciously received our request and deemed it worthy to be taken to his Council of Priests for their consideration. We are now awaiting word from the Bishop and priests in order to move to the next step in establishing a meaningful dialogue.

Having expressed our appreciation for your earnest response, we believe that our first step towards honest and open dialogue requires us to express our sincere thoughts about Monsignor Power's and your letter. We all were disappointed, and hurt, that your letter dove headlong into a point by point expression of standard hierarchical pronouncements we have heard over and over again. We felt that your response was strong on the teaching authority of the hierarchy and weak on any compassion for our concerns.

Frankly, we found the response to our request, particularly in regard to the role of women in the Church, condescending. Recent biblical and archeological scholarship indicates that there are many aspects of the role of women in the early church and today's church that are begging for discussion. For example, if women were never ordained, what shall we make of Phoebe, one of only two deacons in the New Testament whom we know by name (Rom 16:1-2)? In this matter, as in many others, we find room for fruitful examination of a "living" tradition.

Your caution of a "blind spot" in our North American psyche, might equally reflect a "log" in the eye of the hierarchy regarding the inclusive thrust of the spirit of Vatican II which of course, was nurtured by North American theologians, among others.

Furthermore, we feel that the failure of the efforts to establish a structure of dialogue after Vatican II may very well have been the primary fault of the laity. However, we are now fifty years on, not only in the synergies of Vatican II but also in biblical scholarship, as well as a whole new world of social communication. We would hope that, as we begin again to develop structures for meaningful dialogue between laity and hierarchy, we can get up again and carry on, as Jesus did after falling several times. We intend to give this request our best efforts.

A main point in your letter regarding our interpretation, or understanding, or lack of understanding, of the *sensus fidelium,* seems to be matter for serious dialogue. The teaching authority of the hierarchy seems more and more to rely upon authority, and to be growing more and more distant from the experience of a majority of ordinary Christians. We are not calling for a simplistic system of voting on doctrine. However, when a majority of people do not recognize or choose to follow or believe pronouncements, especially those contradicting their input even when they are consulted, means that only honest and open dialogue can resolve the matter. In our living tradition, laity are no longer sheep, as in *Vehementer Nos*, Pius X wrote: " . . . the one duty of the multitude is to allow themselves to be led and, like a docile flock, to follow their pastors . . ."

We do recognize that our request is a work-in-progress. As we feel our way forward, seeking collaboration and support of the hierarchy, we are beginning to recognize certain underlying principles of our efforts:

1. We are guided by our understanding of our duty as baptized Christians to share in the mission of Christ.

2. Our basic purpose is to validate the experience of the Spirit working in laypersons, by bringing stories of our experiences to the hierarchy.

3. The essential "voice" we are asking the hierarchy to hear is "the cry of the poor," that is, ordinary Christians guided by the Spirit in their consciences, living in a challenging and suffering world.

We do hope that one day our efforts on the diocesan level will arrive at the doorstep of the CCCB.

We shall continue to pray for the guidance of the Spirit in our efforts, and in the work of our Canadian bishops. We hope to be in dialogue with them when the time is ripe.

Yours sincerely,
Professor Patrick F. Walsh, AB, MA, PhD.
Facilitator for the Calgary Bible Study Group

Anna Glynn, Carole O'Flaherty, Catherine Kennedy, Jacqueline Walsh, Joanne Campbell, Lea Cornelesen, Dorothy Loucks, Elaine Stoiciou, Liz Bergman, Marie Cameron, Yvonne Van Helden, Jack Scissons,

Facilitator: Patrick Walsh, 435 48th Avenue SW, Calgary, AB T2S 1E3

cc. Most Rev. Frederick B. Henry, Bishop of Calgary

cc. Msgr Patrick Powers, P.H., General Secretary CCCB

Added Signatories:

John Currie, Brian MacDonald, The Sisters of St. Martha of Martha Centre Lethbridge, Colin MacIsaac, Helen MacIsaac, Yolande Gagnon, Michael Carten, Paulette Carten, Frank Firkola,

*

This effort for dialogue died in the Council of Priests of the Diocese of Calgary. In one sense, we are blessed for we have priests to serve our parishes–but some 2/3 of priests are from foreign countries. At one stage, we had as many ordained local deacons as imported priests. These observations are in no way intended to criticize what foreign priests bring to us–especially since they have the fullness of ability to consecrate and forgive sin. But the Bishops should know that the cultural background of some of the foreign priests, only some, of the foreign priests are not reflective of the views of most of their parishioners.

We are struck that the areas of our concerns are amazingly close to the concerns of Pope Francis. And we are also struck that the Bishops of North America are even today not rushing to support the Pope's desire to deal with these problems. Many Catholics, with no way to feed their views up to the hierarchy, are speaking with their feet, that is, walking. Our group is not walking, but we are aging, and the ability to engage in dialogue with an "uncircumcised of eye and ear" hierarchy is fading fast.

Since we wrote our letters the world-wide scandal of abuse has subsumed all other problems in our Church. We perceive a continuing reluctance of too many members of the hierarchy world-wide to hear the cry of the people who wish to follow the way of Christ, rather than the broken rules of a failing institution.

You have met some of the great teachers who influenced me greatly in my youth and middle age. When we came west Jackie and I met a remarkable teacher who has touched us deeply in our golden years. I first heard Michael W. Duggan give a talk at St. Mary's in 1998 and I can remember the core of that talk to this day: the Catholic Church is a vertical church, and it is in the process, and needs to be, a horizontal Church. Our experience affirms this insight. So Jackie and I began taking Michael's theology courses at St. Mary's. What a joy. Michael was educated at the Gregorian University in Rome, and in his classroom his students are introduced into the Hebrew Scriptures of the First Testament (Old) and the Second Testament (New). As we made an intellectual and spiritual journey through the Scriptures we realized that we were on the downward slope of our lives, but the journey was more exciting than any cruise or vacation trip. We gained insight into the sublime mysteries of the path of humanity in the footsteps of Jesus. Our most exciting exercise was to serve Michael as editorial assistants in the revision of his master work, *The Consuming Fire: A Christian Guide to the Old Testament*. He remains a friend, a prophetic guide, and an inspiration, for he walks the walk of a true Christian and is a leader in the ecumenical movement seeking to unite all souls of good will.

Professor Michael W. Duggan

Here is a generous and entertaining summary of the mythic Pat Walsh's career by a colleague and friend. It leans a bit toward hyperbole and fiction, but that has been my style, too. Put a little salt on this tale.

Pat Walsh of Massachusetts, Antigonish, and Calgary

by Phil Milner August 20, 2010

August 20, 2010 When people ask about my life in as an Antigonish professor, I sometimes say, "Antigonish is a one factory town, and I work at the factory." If they want to know about the university I often get around to saying this. "When the history of StFX is written, I'll be a footnote to what will be called the Age of Pat Walsh."

"All I know is what I read in the newspaper," Will Rogers famously said. That truism (not true in the digital age) was certainly true from 1975 when Marilyn and I showed up, until the mid-1990s when Patrick took early retirement and moved to Calgary. Our newspaper, *The Casket* featured stories about town councilors, about the actions of the chairman of the school board, about the paintings of our artists, the achievements of our professors, about books written by our authors, as well as the pronouncements and actions of our religious leaders. Pat Walsh was all these things, and more. He served on town council, ran the school board, wrote a half dozen books on everything from Antigonish history to how to play championship hockey.

During my first 25 years in the 'Nish, when anyone needed a conversation topic, Pat's latest, triumph, defeat, or outrage was a primary topic for analysis.

Pat said he'd never get a PhD, but times change. By the early 1970s, an English professor had a PhD or he walked. Patrick broke the all-time speed record for PhDs at the University of Dublin, and, while there, he designed and marketed a cool chess set: Irish marble bases, Druidic sterling silver figures on top. Patrick, who always possessed a commercial sense, sold several for $500 a set. Last I looked, Patrick's Irish chess set held a place of honor in the StFX library. You can read about it in *The Casket*, edited by Jackie Walsh. Patrick also completed a novel, *The Cave*, which sold in Antigonish bookstores, and several short stories which appeared in early editions of the *Antigonish Review*.

As an American who came to Nova Scotia knowing almost nothing about hockey, I learned my hockey from Pat Walsh and Giles Léger's *Championship Hockey*. The book (the reader may marvel at Pat's indifference to the ridicule of his envious townspeople) had a bull on its cover, in honor of Gilles Leger's post- StFX team, the Birmingham Bulls. The most fun thing I learned is that the penalty box in hockey is sometimes called the "sin bin."

In my second year as a professor–partly in order to advance my skills as a lecturer and classroom presence, I volunteered to be in a play, Shakespeare's *Taming of the Shrew*, staged by Theatre Antigonish. After six weeks of rehearsals, I'd developed a character that, while not memorable, would get me through the experience without humiliating myself. Three days before opening night, an actor playing an important role quit the play.

Patrick was pressed into service. He became Christopher Sly, a drunk beggar, with the exuberance and flair he brought to lots of tasks. He stole the show.

A year later, he wrote a play, *Mad Shelley*, that played in Antigonish, then represented Nova Scotia in the national Dominion Drama festival where it swept the awards. .

Here is a totally true story that sounds like a fib even as I write it. Pat told me once that he was a bit of a gourmand, that there was a quality restaurant in PEI that featured his food. I only half believed him. In five years of friendship, Patrick had not shown any particular interest in preparing food. But Marilyn and our kids and I made a camping trip to the Island to see *Anne of Green Gables*. On the way home, we stopped at a restaurant on the highway. I opened the menu, and there, the feature item, was Spaghetti Julius Caesar a la Pat Walsh. Patrick may stretch things some, but he doesn't fib (of course Jackie was the source of this delightful dish).

I have not watched a Super Bowl with joy since Patrick left town. Patrick had the first big-screen plasma TV in Antigonish, and on Super Bowl Sunday, Pat and his gathered. We'd ogle the cheerleaders, laugh at the goofy Super Bowl TV commercials, and pay intermittent attention to the football game. I and others drank beer; Pat sipped soft drinks. Jackie would pop in, refill the bowls, and retreat to some part of their house where the super bowl could not be seen.

I came to X as an American with a lot of enthusiasm, and some knowledge of movies. I ran the StFX movie series until my fifth year–the year they gave me tenure, at which point I told the English Department chair, quoting *Bartleby, the Scrivener*, a story Pat and I both loved, "I would prefer not to." Pat took over my movie series, and took it to the next level, and then to the next level after that. Then, he achieved something I'd been trying my five years to do. The English Department chair was Derek Wood, and anytime the two of them got in the same room with learning or literature or power on the table, there was going to be something great to watch. We all could laugh or cry at the outcome at the hours and years of happy entertainment Pat and Derek gave us by-standers. Pat stick-handled the movies course past Derek and through a byzantine administrative structure, onto the university calendar. He quickly established the movie course as–depending where you stood–the most original and exciting elective course StFX had, or the final triumphant assault as the barbarians took over the University. Lest the reader not know where I stood on the issue, I am proud to say that one of his last acts on the way to Calgary was to turn over that splendid course to me.

Sometime during the 1980s, Patrick gave up writing, and become a painter. In six months he created almost a hundred abstract paintings. He filled the walls of the huge Student Council Chambers of the Bloomfield Centre with his pictures. He sold more than half of them. Twenty-five years later, you still cannot go far in this town without coming upon an original abstract painting by Pat Walsh from that era. The Sisters at Bethany have them dominating their walls. Last year, I was given a new office in Camden Hall. I went next door to chat up the woman in the next office. There, on my colleague's wall, was a Pat Walsh abstract painting. I have also seen them on walls at St. Martha's hospital, in the student center, in our MLA's downtown office, and at the bank.

On his way out of town, Pat put together two books that no one else could have done, and that continue to enrich the lives of all who peruse them.

Ah, Patrick's *History of Antigonish*. Pat did it, and I never go into a book with more expectant curiosity than I go into this one. The book is an epic. It begins with what is now Nova Scotia breaking off in the Atlantic from the coast of what is now Africa. It shows how Micmac trails leading away from the landing became Main Street and Church Street. Who else would have had the courage to come from North Adams, Massachusetts, and tell this Maritime town about its Scots, its French, its politics, its hockey, its Catholics and Protestants and Muslims? The verdict on that book will never be in. Throw an egg off a truck in Antigonish, and you will hit someone with a passionate opinion on Pat's History.

His other late book, The StFX Prayer Book, might be my favorite book in the whole world. There are several copies in each pew at the chapel. I spend five to forty minutes at each mass (depending on what is happening at the front of the church) paging through it every time I go to mass there. It is the prayer book I myself would create if I possessed Patrick's skills as an artist, if I had his gifts for layout and design, and, if I loved humankind more, if I felt in my blood a Roman Catholicism that derives from Jesus and St. Peter. Pat saw the way a university prayer book could reach out to Muslims, African tribespeople, and Jews, homosexuals, the divorced, unbelievers, and all the other diverse peoples that our Church leadership ties itself in knots trying to extend our Savior's embrace to. If bishops and popes understood our faith the way Patrick's prayer book reveals it, we Antigonish Catholics would not be despairing over the horrible actions and various forms of bankruptcy our Church is experiencing.

The StFX Prayer Book is the Patrick Walsh of prayer books–huge, accepting, embracing all people, all faiths, generous in letter and spirit. I bought ten copies at the launch, and deepened a bond with each of the ten people I gave it to. And, Dear Reader, miracle on top of miracle, Pat did the work, but his name is not on the cover or anywhere else in that book.

It was Patrick, not Jackie, I got to rub elbows with most every day for 25 years. While Pat was cracking heads at the university and in the town, Jackie led a quieter life–making sure five kids turned out wonderfully and running *The Casket* newspaper. In short, she was serving StFX, the Church, and our town in the self-effacing way that the university, media, and town wanted women of her generation to serve during those transitional years.

Postscripts September 19, 2017

Postscript 1: I, with Marilyn standing behind my shoulder suggesting paragraphs and correcting my hyperbole, wrote the above in the hours before attending the mass at the StFX chapel in which Pat and Jackie renewed their marriage vows.

It was epic Pat Walsh from the get-go. What the Walsh family produced was not so much a renewal of vows, as it was a redoing of the original marriage ceremony 50 years after the fact. The Walshes gave us something more splendid than any wife could dream of after a half century. It was a total re-enactment of the marriage that took place in North Adams, USA, fifty years ago. The original bridesmaids, ushers, best men, perhaps even flower girls were there if they were around and alive. If they weren't, the talented Walsh children and grandchildren stepped up to do readings, play the organ, and sing solos.

Coming out of the Church, the first thing I whispered to Marilyn was, "Don't get your hopes up. You aren't getting one of these."

Life as a footnote has an immense up-side.

After the ceremony, we well-wishers and family took over the Morrison Hall Dining Room for a 50th Anniversary Wedding Reception. We have a tradition in the 'Nish of great wedding receptions. This one, 50 years after the fact, was as splendid and evocative as most. There were good speeches by Pat's children, by Pat himself. Pat, imposing as ever standing there with two canes, his rich voice, containing, still, an unmistakable trace of Massachusetts, filled the hall. Patrick acknowledged of our presence, thanked his family, and ended with an emotional climax. A cherished former student, now professing at St. Thomas, read a poem about Pat's old house on Sunset Terrace.

Then it was Jackie's turn. My favorite speeches are by people who don't know how to make speeches, and who try to get by with telling the simple truth as they understand it. We professors, who give speeches nine times a week, know too well what works in front of a crowd. Jackie stood at the podium as though she had been nudged up there against her will. She spoke softly. She acknowledged her immense love of Patrick, her joy in the grandchildren and adult children who surrounded her and Patrick on this day. She spoke touchingly of her Casket colleagues. She was pleased to have known them, and pleased to have accomplished what she accomplished with the people she knew and worked with there on College Street.

Jackie and Patrick did fine things, together and separately, and we friends were privileged to be witnesses to much of it. The greatest thing they did, in spite of the accomplishments I list above, was producing that fine and accomplished family who chose to honor the two of them in this unique and splendid way.

Phil and Marilyn Milner

Postscript 2: It is September 19, 2017, and I just got back from Calgary. Pat's enormous energy, enthusiasm for the people and places he loves, and for life itself, are undiminished. He has switched his allegiance from Antigonish and StFX to Calgary and St. Mary's University. When he tells stories of accomplishment and triumph now, they are set in Calgary, and peopled with characters I do not know. But he knows them, loves them, and is proud to tell who they are, and what they have accomplished.

His body is letting him down, though. He operates from a wheelchair and a walker, and operates extremely well. With a wheelchair, a walker, and a car adapted to his needs, he moves as quickly and with as much energy as ever.

He took us to mass at St. Mary's University, and it was lovely. The Bishop of Calgary celebrated the mass. The altar was a table. We congregants sat on folding chairs, and knelt as best we could. Want to reach young people? Consider starting with folding chairs and no statues.

--end--

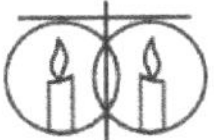

An ecumenical memorial service of the Shoah [Holocaust] was held at St. Anthony's parish. I was asked to speak for our congregation.

Memorial Service, Calgary – May 25, 2011

William Wordsworth, the great English Romantic poet, wrote:

My heart leaps up when I behold
A rainbow in the sky:
So was it when my life began,
So is it now I am a man,
So be it when I shall grow old
Or let me die!

The poet knows that when we see beauty, endorphins fill our minds with pleasant sensations. But, much more deeply from the earliest days of human existence, as we find in the Book of Genesis, the rainbow is a symbol of Adonai/ God's covenant with Noah and with us: "Here is the sign of the Covenant I make between myself and you and every living creature with you for all generations: I set my rainbow in the clouds and it shall be a sign of the Covenant between me and the earth."

That Covenant is with "every living creature" and "all generations."

That's you–and me–all of us–brothers and sisters–now and in all ages.

But in the time of the Shoah, an anti-rainbow of the forces of darkness hovered over our world. It was not red, orange, yellow, green, blue, indigo, and violet, but Green, Red, Black, Pink, and Yellow. These were the colors of the armbands of prisoners in the Nazi death camps. The Six Penal categories were Green for ordinary criminals,

Red for political prisoners,

Black for asocials [slackers, prostitutes, procurers, etc.],

Pink for homosexuals, and

Yellow for Jewish people.

The Nazi extermination program has been likened to a large fishing net sweeping across the world, snaring people of many backgrounds.

We know that the Jewish People were the single most persecuted group by the Nazis. But other groups based on kinship, religion, nation, or other identity, were also persecuted by the Nazis.

These forgotten millions included Communists, Czechs, Greeks, Gypsies, Homosexuals, Jehovah Witnesses, Mentally and physically handicapped, Poles, Resistance fighters, Russians, Serbs, Socialists, Spanish Republicans, Trade unionists, Ukrainians, Yugoslavians, Prisoners of War of many nations, and still others whose identity may never be recognized.

Our common "otherness"–the fact that we differed from the perverse Aryan ideal–is what called for annihilation.

The common denominator for all the victims was DEATH–and they were all brothers and sisters–as we are today–in that common destiny.

One noble brother and friend of all was Maxmillian Kolbe, born in Poland in 1894. In 1907 Kolbe joined the Conventual Franciscans and went to Rome where he obtained doctorates in both philosophy and theology and was ordained to the priesthood. In 1927, he founded a monastery near Warsaw, where during World War II he sheltered 2000 Jewish refugees–because "all men are our brothers."

On February 17, 1941, Kolbe was arrested by the Gestapo, and on May 28, ended up at Auschwitz as prisoner #16670.

When three prisoners disappeared from the camp, Camp Commander SS-Hauptsturmfuhrer Karl Fritzsch, picked ten men to be starved to death in an underground bunker to deter further escape attempts. When one man, Francis Gajowniczek, cried out, "My wife! My children!" Kolbe volunteered to take his place.

In the bunker, Kolbe led the men in song and prayer and encouraged them, telling them they would soon be in heaven.

After two weeks of dehydration and starvation, only Kolbe remained alive. The guards wanted the bunker emptied, so Kolbe raised his arm and calmly waited for the lethal injection of carbolic acid–becoming a man who laid down his life for his friend, his brother under Adonai/God.

On October 10, 1982, Fr. Maximilian Kolbe was canonized a martyr by Pope John Paul II.

In the words of Rabbi Avrohom Resnicoff:

Let us pray that if the day has not yet dawned when we can see the face of God in others, then we see, at least, a face as human as our own. Lord, help us keep faith the day will dawn when justice flows–for ALL–like mighty waters, when liberty will be proclaimed throughout the land, when

every man or woman can stand tall, and none shall be afraid. And may we say, Amen.

May the rainbow of Noah shelter us again.

Patrick F. Walsh May 25, 2011

*

As I reach the close of this exercise, this talk seems prescient, for the unthinkable is returning to haunt my native land. The massacre of the Tree of Life Synagogue in Pittsburgh has just happened. There is no closure in sight for the suffering of humanity which began in the Garden. And the only things that will save us all are the healthy relationships between us and our neighbors and our Maker. Even the "rainbow" symbol is being persecuted as it was under the Nazis.

Here in 2019 in my home diocese of Calgary, Father Jerome Lavigne, Vicar of Catholic Education in Calgary, preached that the #LGBTQ rainbow flag is "a sacrilege of unfathomable proportions ... nothing short of spitting and laughing in God's face." To me, the sacrilege is Fr. Lavigne's preaching, which seriously flies in the face of modern biblical scholarship regarding the ancient scriptures and their historical context. Further my life experience with LGBTQ persons belies Fr. Lavigne's statement; I knew, even growing up, for example, that all Italians are not mafia members and all Irish people are not terrorists. [As we go to print, Father Lavigne has been removed as Vicar of Catholic education.]

This final chapter is called "Limping Home." The term applies to both our physical pilgrimage and our spiritual journey to the Promised Land.

*

At 8 a.m. on the Sunday morning of May 17, 2015, I was just beginning to get dressed, and both legs gave out on me at the same time. I crashed to the floor like a bull receiving the coup de grace. EMS had to be called, but by the time they got me up I was feeling okay and refused to go to the hospital. I went for some physio that week, but after four weeks I was losing strength and feeling weak and getting scared.

I had known for some time that to get around in public I would need a power wheelchair, so I had ordered one and it had arrived on May 16th! Perfect timing– trying to keep up with my wife. But when, after four weeks of physio and going downhill like a soap-box derby, it took a full hour for Jackie to transfer me from the wheelchair into bed, she was scared, and I was scared. The next morning we went to our family Doctor Brad Davies, who we put into stitches laughing at the twists and gyrations, ropes and pillows and tugging and pulling necessary to get me into bed. He said, "I'm going to give both of you A for effort, but an F for stupidity! You have a torn ACL, and you'll both die if you keep going. It's over. ER immediately." I ended up at ER having to be put into bed by ceiling hoist. I could not even stand anymore. ER started physio, but were frantically searching for a rehab facility to send me to. About a week later, they shipped me to Carewest Sarcee with a great rehab department, and after 12 weeks I was much better than before I fell. I was very grateful for the care.

But the caring that sustains me every day in every way is lavished upon me by my wife, Jacqueline.

listening

God speaks to me each day
I hear him in your voice
God daily soothes my ache
your hands apply balms choice

God feeds my soul rich thoughts
to match your healthy meals
God sends me lessons taught
by your sweet grace that heals

the mystery of love
beyond what we can see
you translate from above
into the care of me

when I am by your side
such joy wells up in me
that darkness flees to hide
from love that glows in thee

and when I am apart
the gap is only borne
by knowing in my heart
that in your heart I'm worn

your deep love will survive
memory time and space
and bring us both alive
to rest in God's good grace

thank you my darling you are my inspiration and my salvation
your loving Patrick
Christmas 2014

We all need "caring" in the inevitable battles that conclude our "long day's journey." This poem was written for my sister, Mary Ann, who is courageously battling cancer in Plaistow, New Hampshire.

armies of the night

in the dead of the night when all is still
the bugles blare
the body politic turns sour with gastric juices
inflaming the tunnels of digestion
platelets scurry in the darkness
bumping into twisting and coiling walls
whining and complaining unable to form ranks

the civilian stages snore on
but the military brass who rule the night
rush to muster points reeling and boiling
in the nooks and crannies
of the body's weak and worn joints
heating up the dogs of war

in the subterranean vaults of the heart
the platelets scurry from stent to stent
unable to form organized ranks
they keep winding along
bilge pumps pushing through
the sewer lines the gas lines the water lines
the schedule of night trains and subways
carrying platelets to their work stations
to demolish the barriers designed to keep the peace
until our sun arises
another day the lord has made bringing joy
to the consciousness of wakefulness
and the platoons of the armies of the night
retire to R & R in the wakefulness
of the body's consciousness
answering reveille standing forth
to resist for another day the encroaching
never ending advance of the armies of the night

there are scenes of triumph in the body politic:
a Troy of cancer never reoccupied after victory
infrastructure of stents periodically renewed
slowly clogging but fended off
in daily ops of chelation militias
despite the scorn of standard military defense forces

recent defenses include Distant Early Warnings via hearing aids
improved surveillance of horizons by replacing lenses
impervious to invading cataracts

yet despite these valiant efforts the mind of the brain knows
inevitably the clockwork of time will break down
and in the final darkness defeat will send us
immigrant to an unknown land beyond the edge of time
either to a blank vale of nothingness or
a universal singularity of light and everlasting joy
where we shall be united with those who left us young
with bags packed or unpacked
body shall go alone in a final skirmish

but in the end hope says all those fleeing in that dark night
will be transformed in a blazing glorified "singularity"
called "love" in eternal timelessness

4:44 a.m. to 5:31 a.m. February 22, 2018 Calgary

from the other side of the continent
I shall be reunited with Mary Ann my sister
in whose final skirmish she fights the good fight
with golden bullets and with her inborn grace and beauty
rising above the messy battlefield

your loving brother, Pat

Oh, how much more deeply I understand the concept of "caring" 44 years after I originally gave this talk. "Caring" is the central force in all healthy human and spiritual relationships, I know now, having examined my life into my ninth decade.

"Caring and Curing": Concepts Intrinsically Linked

From The Casket in 1975

(*Editor's note: Following is the text of the address delivered by Dr. Patrick Walsh to the Personal Care Workers graduating at the R. K. MacDonald Nursing Home and Guest House last Friday. Dr. Walsh is the secretary of the Nursing Home Corporation.*)

I want to share some thoughts with you today on the call to "curing and caring." The thoughts I have gathered come from two gentlemen I first encountered upon my arrival in Antigonish some 36 years ago. The first, whom I met in person, was my professor and mentor, Father Roderick J. MacSween, poet, professor, and priest. He inspired me to devote my life to the study and teaching of writing and literature, and in his Wednesday night Discussion Club he introduced me to Daniel J. Callahan, a writer for Commonweal Magazine, whom I have never met, except through the magic of the written word. These two men continue to influence the way I try to cope with the problems of living a useful life.

First let us turn to Fr. MacSween, the retired editor of *The Antigonish Review*, who continues to share his piercing insights into the human condition in both the Review and our own *Casket* newspaper. Father MacSween's latest poem, in the 79th issue of *The Antigonish Review*, examines our relation to heroes–you know, people of distinguished courage or ability, admired for brave deeds and noble qualities. To see what we have to do with heroes like the noble knight Lancelot, or Alexander the Great, or St. Paul, or King Henry V, let us turn to Fr. MacSween 's poem:

THE CALL

in the fading light
we are all surprised

by a challenge certainly known
but not comprehended
we stare at the sudden ghost
as though it were a mistake

from youth we have been trained
to struggle with the ordinary
until our time is done
not for us the heroisms
in our books and movies
we stood on the sidelines
while others battered opponents
with strength and skill
we showed our skill
in evasion in delay
in turning away
from the barren shores
and the pale cliffs

we openly admired
those who design the world
those who build the world
those who die for the world
some are born in lucky centuries
when the walls fall down
some are born in stringent times
when breath itself is precious
but their names slowly rise
from a stubborn root
and flourish

while we praise
we ourselves are asked to be heroes
to be Paul to be Lancelot
to be Alexander to be Harry
we who have been spectators

at the martyrs' fall
we who have accepted to be
of the herd and the flock
we who have resigned ourselves
to mediocrity
we are called to greatness

not one of us shall escape the call
not one of us but will face
the center of force
the fire at the burning core
we are all called to die
no greater test could God give
to the glory-haunted soul of man

What a magnificent insight into the moment each of our patients face, and into the moment each of us shall face. For further insight into our role as people concerned with personal care, let us turn from the spiritual to the physical, from soul to its home–the body. Here are the thoughts of Daniel J. Callahan, PhD, now director of the Hastings Center in Briarcliff Manor, New York. He distinguishes between curing and caring. Curing is ultimately impossible, and caring is always possible. Let us examine the difference a vowel makes.

Curing is never certain, for victories over sickness and death are always temporary. On the other hand, in the face of sickness and death peoples' need for support and caring is permanent.

The point of medical research and practice is to find cures, but our ability to find cures is limited, especially today by economic pressures, and the emphasis on cures, can all too often lead to impersonal medicine, with attention to goals rather than people. We all want to be assured that we will be cared for, regardless of the likelihood of being cured. The thrust and drive of our health delivery system is to know how to prevent disease and to cure disease if contracted. The fight against disease is glamorous: witness the telethons and campaigns on TV, etc.; the dramatically presented war to find cures. But, behind the hoopla and glitz and the PR, we are called to a different kind of heroism; to support and minister to sick people, to care.

The individual need for cure is infinite in its possibilities; the need for care is finite: we are called to do something for each other. When we examine the possibilities, much more can be done for people by caring than curing, that's why the absence of caring for others is inexcusable.

Sickness alienates us from the familiar, from the comfortable, from the healthy body or mind. Such alienation spreads insidiously, creating a sense of alienation from others, a sense of being alone and abandoned. When we become so alienated, and the illness goes on or is severe enough, we feel we will lose the love and respect of our family, friends, and associates. The problem is not just the pain of the illness, but the suffering that oppresses, that creates fears about the future, the feeling of loss, the anxiety that control and self-direction are or may be lost. Caring administers to these fears.

In today's impersonal health delivery systems, you are "Personal Care" Workers. The patient is a "person," and you are a "person," and the bond between you both is love, that is, patient fidelity to another person's anxiety about separation from other human beings. To be a "Personal Care" Worker, you need skill, you need insight, you need commitment.

Today we are here to recognize your completion of a course of training, a curriculum of theory and ideas and practice. We are proud of you. But all this is tinkling cymbals and sounding brass, because scientific knowledge and technical skills are nothing, if the point and purpose of what you do is not based on caring.

Patients in our home and others where you may administer, homes of brick and mortar, buildings, equipment, supplies, theories, structure of management and chains of command, are for naught, unless the possibilities of caring are realized, for curing is ultimately impossible. No one can be cured forever.

Caring, therefore, is the foundation stone of respect for human dignity and worth. The presence of caring can be steady and faithful in the absence of curing. In caring we respect the claims and calls of people in need; in caring we show our true solidarity with each other. Even if everything else in our fallible society fails, if we give priority to caring for each other, we are worthy of praise.

Sixty years ago, we were called to be caring Sisters, Councillors, Nurses, Personal Care workers, Staff, Administrators, Volunteers, a Foundation, Governments.

Today, *we* are called, *all of us here*, "Personal Care" Workers, to be present at that heroic moment Father MacSween so brilliantly evoked in his poem, the heroic moment for the hidden heroes of humanity: the Lucys, Theresas, Sallys; the Colins, Williams, and Jameses of Antigonish, or Canso, or Port Hawkesbury. When you are there for them in their heroic moment of need, you are no longer "evading," "turning away," or "standing on the sidelines." You are caring. You are in the ranks with Paul, and Lancelot, and Alexander, and Harry and . . . Jesus! God Bless you all.

*

Addendum:

In October 2018, at the 60th Anniversary Celebration of the establishment of the R. K. MacDonald Nursing Home Corporation, I gave this speech again, with the addition of a sentence at the beginning of the last paragraph above, in italics. For the gathering included all those who to this day are carrying on the work of caring for the citizens of the R.K.

Back in 1958, Fr. J. V. Campbell burst into the room of Pat Walsh and Jim Nicholson and said, "I need two altar boys, immediately. Let's go." And Jim and I were off to the Chapel of the R. K. MacDonald Guest House for the grand opening where we would be altar servers for the Bishop presiding. Little did I realize then, that I would be tied to the "RK" for the rest of my life.

At our 50th Wedding Anniversary on August 20, 2010, in Morrison Hall with some 300 relatives and friends present, Stewart Donovan read his poem divining the spirit of our life together.

Patrick X Walsh

Evenings at Sunset Terrace

for Jackie and Pat

In a time of elegy you give the gift of a marriage hymn
golden, but no epithalamion for professors, late-
night edition for editors. Lectures and stories done, the
kids asleep and a town at your feet. Nova Scotian
winters worthy of *la Ville de Quebec* and Jacqueline
Duguay leaves the comfort of old New England
to journey north from North Adams into dreams her
grand-pere made and the pleadings of an Irish
Italian boy, all bluster and brush-cut, boasting how he
stormed Camelot by not voting Irish-Catholic
Wexford be damned his dad knew Honey Fitzgerald.
Chere Jacqueline all those young Novices
you prayed for believed they'd met Mario Lanza,
but you had Caruso in your heart and knew
how to mold this rough hewn dolmen with the
Pagliacci pose shouting Shelley to all who'd listen.
You both knew beginning with poetry would bring days
and days of working prose, but what did you say
that day in May when he proposed an Irish sojourn with
Dublin digs–five little ones in tow? *Slainte* or
Slan leat, cheers or goodbye. Not even *Ulysses* took the
kids. But perhaps the Walshes were Two-boaters
after all, so the journey east brought them west and west
again. And like some Alberta Clipper they now
bring warm Chinook winds to the plains and prairies of
hope where their children leave a footprint of
moderation in praise of maritime promise, its endless
waves of prayer. And now as the tents begin to be
folded, it is not Ezekiel you share over oatmeal mornings
and grandchildren afternoons, but a Song of Solomon.
And together, like two hermetic rabbis, you build a golden

carapace reflecting a light not seen since catechism
days, its click in the leaves sound out the lullabies of Mourning
doves, counter-pointing the typewriter tick of those
pileated wood-peckers, who mated for life so long ago, but now
still flare for us the color of their hearts, red and laughing
in the still dark mystery of these unending eastern skies.

Stewart Donovan August, 2010

So to get to the core of this odyssey with my true love, here is a poem celebrating the one who made my joyous life possible.

Travels with Jackie

in SPACE

from Kemp Avenue via Notre Dame
from Bracewell Ave via St. Joseph's School
from two spaces two worlds hardly the same
two elements alone one hot one cool

yet when we bonded as one we saw the world
from Worcester Paxton Putnam Roslindale
Antigonish to Ireland our lives unfurled
in Rome and gay Paree quaffed Salzburg ale

at the White Swan we sat in Wordsworth's chair
stood in the shadow of the Stonehenge Key
survived our Channel crossing's salty air
nearly capsized in Blue Grotto's Capri

we never suspected we would trade Monk's Head
for a man-made duck pond in Fish Creek Park
or the flaming sunsets of Arisaig
for Rockies sparkling under Chinook arch

yet here we are bound to earth with clipped wings
the dreams of distant venues fading fast
yet floating in our minds such happy things
we cherished through our travels in the past

in TIME

time is still alive of moments glowing bright
the glance I cast across the old school hall
possible rejection freezing me in fright
emotions turbulent as nature's squall

that fatal prom-night kiss lives on in me
a promise long sustained through joy and pain
and just tonight unbidden loving free
you silently appeared and kissed again

half-a-century plus we have shared time
our rhythms of heart and mind are tuned
we breath and dream harmonious as rhyme
despite some painful moments and the wound

withstanding peaks and valleys of the hours
knowing each second binds us in the core
of our inmost hearts and our deepest powers–
our spirits will be one for evermore

inexperienced children we started out
trusting and ignorant as we surely were
we sallied forth through age's darkening doubt
to dock in Time's haven where souls concur

in FAITH

spouting the frozen answers of our faith
we memorized the catechism's answers
put on a Catholic's triumphant face
knowing we were safe from worldly cancers

we did know love in parent's sweet embraces
noble priests' and sisters' kindly advice
we flourished in timely bestowed graces
practicing rites and norms in rules precise

agonizing changes from Vatican Two
shattered our cozy Catholic cocoon
new worlds and other faiths hove into view
and swept us from our deck like a typhoon

through the stormy days we had each other
lashed by the ropes of inherited rites
the Mass our strength and comforting mother
helping us to reach ever higher heights

bible study leads us to see the past
to see within the burning bush and cloud
to sense the ambiguous word at last
and know that we have lived what we have vowed

envoi
dearest Jacqueline I travel with you
in deepest joy through space and time and faith
that you are with me in all I live through
is source of all my happiness and grace

Happy birthday, my darling
December 5, 2006

[At our Golden Wedding Anniversary we had a huge gathering of friends to recreate the event and I was given three minutes to speak. A seemingly impossible feat for a voluble professor who earned a living filling silence with sound and passionate fury. Here's the effort. You can time it.]

A psalm of thanksgiving for the gift of friendship

O Lord I thank you for the gift we could not choose–
our families who gave us life and nurtured our faith
those dearly departed and those here present
may they all be secure in your arms O Lord
we appreciate their deep spirit of caring
and how lovingly they share their lives with us

O Lord I thank you for the gift of loyal friends
of Antigonish town and StFX University
enduring friendships–started with a spark
and tendered over the years through sharing
works and joys pain and suffering–
flames still burning brightly in our memory

O Lord I thank you especially for the gift
of loyal priests and sisters who inspired us–
sisters of St. Anne Joseph CND and Marthas–
who brought so many blessings to the Walshes
they brought us ever closer to you O Lord
for they are always walking in your way.

O Lord I thank you for the gift of closest friends
who stepped into the stream of our lives
those friends with ready ears to listen
with hearts to encourage and support us
with open doors at any hour of day or night
who welcomed us in hours days or months of need

O Lord I thank you for the gift of spouses for our children
who became another daughter and three sons
they bring such happiness and hope to our children
when we gather around our festive tables we know
true sharing and bonds foretelling a fine future
of love and caring and strength and faithfulness

O Lord I thank your gift of sharing the creation
of our children–and for allowing us see their maturity
we see they have surpassed their inherited weaknesses
and we admire their superior sensitivity and goodness
their devotion to family and friends their care of us
and especially that their lives are intertwined in joy

but most of all O Lord I thank you for your gift of Jacqueline
I have no memory that she does not live and dwell in
in my every joy she is the loving warming flame
to any suffering I have she always bestows relief–
there is no act of caring and service she does not perform
the unmerited love she gives me draws me closer to you

O Lord I am truly a blessed man and I thank you
for letting me reach this milestone in her company.

Patrick Walsh
on the occasion of our 50th wedding anniversary
celebration at StFX in Antigonish

Pat and Jackie 2019

Epilogue

Gentle reader, in your journey through this smattering of documents and comments you have encountered a man's happy but far from perfect life. TRUTH is in these words; both facts and imperfect memories, sometimes buried in FICTION. Any intentional LIES are intending to do good. LIES of evil intent have been avoided, hopefully successfully, and LIES of entertaining and moralizing value should be readily recognized. [As my sister's passing approaches, I am inspired to settle my own scores before passing: I picked up the telephone and called my estranged best friend, Jordan Mastroianni, in California. He had been agonizing over such a call himself. We are reconciled and shall not let the ugly politics of our time ruin our life-long happy relationship.]

In the "field hospital after battle" [Pope Francis' term] in this "messy" world, I hope you have seen glimpses of a life attempted to be well-lived by a faithful man with an extraordinary woman at his side, surrounded by good friends. Thank you all.

Here is the last sentence I shall write at the end of this journey of a near-century: My father was born on January 20, 1904. My sister Mary Ann passed away 8:30 p.m. this evening, Sunday, January 20, 2019, in the company of her devoted family, leaving me the last surviving member of the family of Carmen and Duke Walsh.

> Thoughts, like a loud and sudden rush of wings,
> Regrets and recollections of things past,
> With hints and prophecies of things to be,
> And inspirations, which, could they be things,
> And stay with us, and we could hold them fast,
> Were our good angels—these I owe to thee.

Henry Wadsworth Longfellow from *The Two Rivers*